PSYCHOANALYSIS AND ETHICS

ERNEST WALLWORK

Psycho-analysis and Ethics

YALE UNIVERSITY PRESS

NEW HAVEN & LONDON

Designed by Nancy Ovedovitz. Set in Galliard type by
The Composing Room of Michigan, Inc., Grand
Rapids, Michigan. Printed in the United States of
America by BookCrafters, Chelsea, Michigan.

Library of Congress Cataloging-in-Publication Data
Wallwork, Ernest.
Psychoanalysis and ethics / Ernest Wallwork.
p.   cm.
Includes bibliographical references and index.
ISBN 0-300-04878-5 (cloth)
       0-300-06167-6 (pbk.)
1. Ethics—Psychological aspects.   2. Freud, Sigmund,
1856–1939—Ethics.   3. Psychoanalysis—Moral and
ethical aspects.   4. Ethics, Modern—20th
century.   I. Title.
BJ45.W35   1991
171—dc20   91–15276
                                                   CIP

The paper in this book meets the guidelines for
permanence and durability of the Committee on
Production Guidelines for Book Longevity of the
Council on Library Resources.

10   9   8   7   6   5   4   3   2

TO ANNE

*The greatest change since 1893 in our attitude
towards the great problems of ethics has been due
to the new facts and the new approach provided
by modern psychology; and that in its turn owes
its rise to the genius of Freud.*

—Julian Huxley

*We need a moral philosophy which can speak
significantly of Freud. . . . We need a moral
philosophy in which the concept of love, so rarely
mentioned now by philosophers, can once again
be made central.*

—Iris Murdoch

Contents

Preface   ix

Acknowledgments   xi

List of Abbreviations   xiii

1 Introduction   1

PART ONE
Foundational Issues

2 The Hermeneutical Problem of
Reading Freud   19

3 The Determinism–Free Will
Problem   49

4 Reconciling the Paradox: Psychic
Determinism and Moral
Responsibility   75

PART TWO
Psychological Egoism

5 Overview of Psychological Egoism   103

6 The Pleasure Principle and
Psychological Hedonism   108

7 Narcissism   137

8 Object Love   160

PART THREE
Normative Implications

 9 On Modifying Normative
Standards: The Case of the Love
Commandment   193

10 Normative Aspects of
Psychoanalytic Practice   208

PART FOUR
Foundations of Ethics in Freudian Theory

11 Toward a Psychoanalytically
Informed Ethic   221

12 How Is Practical Reason Guided?
Happiness and the Basic Goods of
Life   244

13 Normative Principles and Social
Theory   260

14 Conclusion   288

Appendix A Why Take Psychoanalytic
Findings Seriously? The Credibility of
Freudian Theory   293

Bibliography   299

Index   327

Preface

Freud makes interesting company for an ethicist. He is subversive, of course, with his psychoanalytically derived observations regarding the developmental foundations and limitations of moral judgment and action. But he is also suggestive, surprisingly careful, often profoundly complex, and extraordinarily engaged with what turns out to be a broad range of moral issues.

This book attempts to provide an accurate, detailed, and sympathetic reading of Freud's moral psychology and to explore its chief implications for ethics. Examining the interrelated aspects of this moral psychology leads to a radical new interpretation of much in the Freudian corpus. Freud is generally regarded as deterministic and egoistic—as an anti-moralist. His revolutionary insights into the role of the superego in the development and functioning of conscience, his emphasis on aggression, narcissism, and the pursuit of pleasure, his critique of cultural repression and his insistence on the importance of unconscious determinants of thought and action are usually taken as the whole of his contribution to the psychology of morals and are seen as tending to undermine the very enterprise of morality. But close textual analysis of Freud's work, organized around and clarified by reference to perennial themes in moral philosophy, shows that Freud's view of determinism in fact allows for moral responsibility; his understanding of the pleasure principle and narcissism allows the possibility of acting out of concern for others; and his critique of the cultural superego is grounded in an ethic informed by ego rationality. This is because the attempt to make sense out of the tensions in Freud's thought regarding these issues requires that one strip away conventional interpretations of a number of central psychoanalytic tenets, including Freud's views on psychic determinism, narcissism, the pleasure principle, Eros, the death instinct, aggression, and the nature of the individual's ties to groups and to the wider society. A fresh look at these doctrines that seeks to reconcile apparent inconsistencies at a deeper level of philosophical analysis than Freud himself provides not only offers a new and different understanding of Freud as a moralist but also affords valuable clarification of some of the ongoing confusions and controversies in psychoanalytic theory and practice.

My concern to set forth an accurate reading of Freud for both philosophical and psychoanalytic readers accounts for the extensive exegesis given in the text. The divergence of this reading from conventional interpretations of Freud, and from the influential interpretations of Ricoeur, Habermas, Rieff, and Hartmann is made plain in the main body of the book; but detailed discussions of particular intellectual controversies, both philosophical and psychoanalytic, are, as much as possible, confined to the footnotes in an effort to make the central thrust of the argument more accessible to the different disciplines to which it is addressed.

The beginnings of the ethical theory that are teased out of the trajectory of Freud's psychoanalytic work in this book resonate with a number of currents in classical and contemporary philosophical ethics. The theory is naturalistic, grounded in a concept of human flourishing and regard for others, critical of exclusively Kantian-based ethics, yet respectful of certain Kantian emphases (such as the centrality of respect for autonomy), and concerned with the common good and special relations, as well as with individual rights. Significantly, this new understanding of Freud's ethic challenges post-modernist readings of Freud that find in him a model of the radically pluralistic self. Although it recognizes the decentering implications of the workings of the unconscious it allows for a self with sufficient cohesiveness and structure to counter the ethical relativism of much post-modernist thought. At the same time Freud's ethic acknowledges tensions between the private self and public responsibilities, impersonal moral reasoning and personal concerns and commitments. This book does not claim to offer a definitive way of resolving these tensions, but instead follows closely what psychoanalysis has to contribute to ongoing discussions of how we can be moral after psychoanalysis has brought to light the morally dubious springs of human behavior.

Acknowledgments

I owe a singular debt to my wife, Anne, who encouraged me to write this book, helped me work out many of the specific substantive issues in it, formulated and reformulated arguments, and substantially edited the manuscript in its entirety. I could not have written the book without her determination to help me clarify what I was trying to say.

I am also deeply indebted to my colleagues at the Washington Psychoanalytic Institute, where I am currently an advanced candidate in full psychoanalytic training. This book was already under way at the time I began my training; but my understanding of Freudian theory and practice have benefited enormously from course work and discussions at the institute. The experience of seeing patients that my work as a Clinical Associate of the Washington Psychoanalytic Clinic has made possible has underscored for me the importance of psychoanalytic practice for interpreting Freudian theory and has afforded an invaluable perspective from which to understand the role of morality in the lives of individuals. Particularly important to me have been the interest, support, and intellectual stimulation provided by Drs E. James Anthony, Judith Chused, Richard Gerber, John Kafka, Tom McGlashan, Arnold Meyersberg, Harvey Rich, and Joseph H. Smith. I am also grateful to a number of academic colleagues in the departments of religion and philosophy at Syracuse University and elsewhere who have read parts of this book at various stages and have offered encouragement and suggestions. They include Jonathan Bennett, Don Browning, Robert W. Daly, Arthur Dyck, Peter Homans, the late Lawrence Kohlberg, William F. May, David Miller, Michael Stocker, and James Wiggins. I also want to thank my students, graduate and undergraduate, at Yale and Syracuse for their many helpful suggestions and criticisms. As a fellow at the Kennedy Institute of Ethics at Georgetown University, I have benefited from profitable discussions of some of the ethical ideas formulated in this book. Colleagues Alison Wichman, Michele Carter, Jan Vinicky, and Evan DeRenzo in the Bioethics Office at the Clinical Center of the National Institutes of Health have provided a valuable sounding board for the usefulness in the context of clinical bioethics of some of the psychodynamic views developed here.

Syracuse University supported two semesters of writing; for that help, too, I am grateful.

My Yale editor, Charles Grench, was a source of quiet encouragement during the long gestation of this book. He and I know how much we owe to the canine sponsors of our collaboration.

Adam and Rachel who were born during the writing process, have provided with Anne a happy background of spontaneous love and joy. They have also taught me much about the springs of morality treated in these pages.

Abbreviations

Works by Sigmund Freud:

CP Sigmund Freud, *Collected Papers,* 5 vols (New York, 1959)

GW ——, *Gesammelte Werke,* ed. Anna Freud et al., 18 vols (London, 1940–[1952])

SE ——, *Standard Edition of the Complete Psychological Works,* trans. and ed. James Strachey et al., 24 vols (London, 1953–74)

Other abbreviations:

APQ *American Philosophical Quarterly*

IJP *International Journal of Psychoanalysis*

IRP *International Review of Psychoanalysis*

JAPA *Journal of the American Psychoanalytic Association*

JP *Journal of Philosophy*

PQ *Psychoanalytic Quarterly*

PR *Psychoanalytic Review*

PSC *Psychoanalytic Study of the Child*

Chapter 1
Introduction

> Philosophy, in so far as it is built on
> psychology, will be unable to avoid taking
> the psycho-analytic contributions to
> psychology fully into account and reacting
> to this new enrichment of our knowledge
> just as it has to every considerable advance
> in the specialized sciences.
>
> —Freud

No movement has had a more profound impact on popular morals in the twentieth century than psychoanalysis. Thanks to Freud's epoch-making discoveries, we are now aware of unconscious motivations that frequently seem to subvert moral conduct or at least to raise serious questions about the subterranean psychic costs to ourselves and others of attempting to do the "right thing." Even those who oppose Freud's views on human nature generally acknowledge the existence of hidden desires and on occasion are willing to entertain the possibility that a moral judgment may be a mere rationalization of self-interest or a convoluted expression of hostility. Indeed, Freud is a principal founder of the "hermeneutics of suspicion" (Ricoeur 1970) that pervades modern attitudes toward morality and that is often used to justify the unabashed selfishness and privatism commonly cited as distinguishing characteristics of our era (Rieff 1961, 1968; Lasch 1979; Bellah et al. 1985). The much-discussed contemporary culture of narcissism and egoistic individualism is inconceivable apart from Freud's criticism of the cultural superego (see Wallwork 1986).

And yet there has been surprisingly little serious scholarly attention paid to the twin questions: Do we correctly understand Freud on the various *psychological issues* that are relevant to morality? What are the *ethical implications* to be drawn from Freud's discoveries and those of his closest disciples?

Most of the literature on psychoanalysis and morality comes from psychoanalysts and sociologists whose primary concern has been to draw normative implications out of psychoanalysis for evaluating modern culture and personality formation (see Fromm 1941, 1947, 1955, 1956; Marcuse 1955; Rieff 1961, 1968; Erikson 1963, 1964; Lasch 1979), not with understanding how psychoanalytic findings relate to the deepest questions of philosophical ethics. In the writings of such once-popular writers as Erich Fromm, Philip Rieff, Herbert Marcuse, and Erik Erikson, one looks in vain for clarity as to the precise issues in ethics that psychoanalysis is capable of illuminating.

On the other hand, philosophical ethicists have not been particularly interested in psychoanalysis by and large. Those few philosophers who have studied psychoanalysis sympathetically and in depth (e.g., Ricoeur 1970; Habermas 1971; Wollheim 1971, 1984) have been concerned only incidentally with its *ethical* import. To be sure, Richard Rorty (1980, 1986) has recently drawn out what he takes to be the ethical implications of psychoanalysis, but his views are based more on an impressionistic reading of how Freud supports his own post-modernist, moral pragmatism than on a careful study of what Freud actually holds. In the writings of most ethicists, Freud, if he is mentioned at all, is treated as the chief modern enemy of morality, whose work is best ignored or flatly condemned in the process of getting on with the task of doing traditional moral philosophy, unimpeded by the sorts of depth-psychological considerations that have transformed everyday morality outside the academy.

This book takes up anew the matter of the relevance of psychoanalysis to ethics. It does so by addressing the question of whether Freudian theory and practice are completely antithetical to morality and, assuming that at least some of it is not, by drawing out the exact relevance of particular psychoanalytic findings for certain central issues in ethics. My approach— in contrast to that of psychoanalytic moralists like Fromm, Marcuse, Erikson, and Rieff—is philosophical, not psychological or sociological. I intend to examine psychoanalytic findings and claims about such matters as psychic determinism, the pleasure principle, narcissism, object love, and the defense mechanisms in order to explore their implications for such time-honored issues in ethics as moral responsibility, psychological hedonism, egoism (both psychological and normative), the normative principles of nonmaleficence, benevolence, and autonomy, and social ethics.

Psychoanalysts since Freud have imagined—erroneously—that ethics necessarily involves constructing evaluative *Weltanschauungen* about which rational persons will inevitably disagree, as in matters of taste,[1] and preach-

---

1. This emotivist construal of ethics as nothing more than an evaluative world view is presented by Freud in "The Question of a Weltanschauung" (*SE* 22 [1933]:158–82) and by Hartmann in *Psychoanalysis and Moral Values*. What Freud apparently had in mind was the now archaic unitary discipline of *moral philosophy*, which throughout the nineteenth century encompassed, in addition to ethics properly so-called, psychology, sociology, jurisprudence,

ing or telling others in some direct, casuistic way how to act.[2] But as practiced in contemporary philosophy, ethics involves neither a world view nor specific moral instruction. Rather, at its core, ethics is concerned with searching for and defending rationally our most basic general moral principles and virtues. In pursuing this task, ethicists not only defend a small set of highly general abstract normative prescriptions and ideals, they also analyze the language of moral discourse and the logic of ethical justification.[3] In this, they engage in exacting scholarly work and logically compelling argumentation. The failure of psychoanalysts to appreciate the rigorous analytic and logical work of contemporary ethicists has meant that they have not availed themselves of important intellectual resources for assessing the adequacy of their own highly controversial assumptions about the nature and grounding of morality.

A distinguishing feature of this book, in response to the avoidance of ethics by psychoanalysts, is its use of philosophical distinctions about moral issues in order to clarify some of the persistent conceptual confusions in psychoanalysis. For example, the understanding of the technical psychoanalytic concept of *psychic determinism* can be illumined by considering its meaning in relation to the full range of alternative philosophical positions on determinism and freedom of choice. Similarly, the psychoanalytic concept of narcissism overlaps to some extent (though not completely) the ethical categories of psychological egoism and self-regard; hence philosophical distinctions regarding the meaning of egoism are useful in identifying the multiple meanings of the term *narcissism* as used by psychoanalysts.

Freudian theory lends itself to illumination by way of philosophy be-

---

theology, and political theory. Today it is inaccurate to define the field of ethics this broadly, and doing so reinforces the false belief of many nonphilosophers that ethicists typically deal in large-scale imaginative visions that are impervious to appeals to evidence and logic and, hence, about which rational agents are free to engage in unrestrained speculation (see Hartman 1960). The fact is that ethicists—especially in the Anglo-American tradition—typically make use of careful conceptual, logical analysis of a sort that is susceptible to rigorous proof and disproof.

2. See Hartmann's (1960) criticism of the so-called "hidden preachers" among his psychoanalyst colleagues (presumably Fromm and Erikson).

3. Such analysis is usually assigned today to the field of *metaethics*. Metaethical study is nonnormative, because it seeks to establish what conceptually or logically is the case rather than what ought to be the case. Although metaethical study is often assumed to aid the core ethical task of defending a set of fundamental normative principles and values (see, e.g., Hare 1963), a small but influential group of contemporary philosophers holds that it does not in fact lend support to normative ethics (see, e.g., Ayer 1952; Williams 1985; and Rorty 1986).

cause psychoanalysis and ethics are concerned with many of the same phenomena, such as egoism, determinism, psychological and ethical hedonism, moral conscientiousness, and self-deception. Both philosophy and psychoanalysis share a concern with understanding precisely—"analyzing"—ordinary human conduct. Just as technical philosophical distinctions are meant to clarify ordinary discourse about moral action, so psychoanalytic concepts (e.g., the superego and narcissism) are meant to guide the psychotherapist in formulating clinical interpretations and theoretical generalizations about everyday behavior.

What makes philosophy potentially helpful to psychoanalysts is its specialized expertise in elucidating the subtle meanings of the ordinary terms we use in speaking of human action.[4] Psychoanalysts need to pay this kind of careful attention to the possibilities for precise distinctions as they deal with both the highly technical language of Freud's metapsychology and their own use of ordinary language in clinical work, because some important continuing theoretical conflicts among psychoanalysts stem from sloppiness in discourse—that is, analysts often assume that they mean the same thing when they use the same terms although the various and disparate meanings encapsulated in their technical discourse make it highly probable that this is not the case. Analyzing psychoanalytic language philosophically is helpful in arriving at new ways of interpreting psychoanalytic theory that can be useful in resolving some of these conceptually based conflicts. Ethical distinctions are in this way of heuristic value for psychoanalytic theory, quite apart from their necessary contribution to clarifying our understanding of how psychoanalytic findings are relevant to moral conduct, which is our main concern here.

In using ethics to translate psychoanalytic theory into ordinary language, I do not intend to ignore or understate the multiple ways in which psychoanalytic discourse forces us to rethink familiar moral concepts. Freud discovered aspects of human behavior concealed from his predecessors in part because he invented a new language, including new metaphors, for looking at ordinary experience. As Derrida (1984), Ricoeur (1970, 1981), and Rorty (1986) emphasize, it is precisely in not fitting received usages that Freudian concepts help us to see ourselves and others in new ways. To do justice to this jolting, deconstructing dimension of psychoanalysis, it is necessary to be willing to revise familiar ways of thinking morally. But this cannot be done until psychoanalysis and ethics are

---

4. Freud underscores the value of careful analysis of ordinary language, such as Ango-American philosophers pursue, when he writes that "linguistic usage . . . is no chance thing, but the precipitate of old discoveries" (*SE* 15 [1916–17]:98).

brought into closer conceptual contact along the lines being suggested here.

The principal aim of this book is to work out precisely some of the ways in which psychoanalysis is ethically relevant. That it has any relevance whatsoever will be questioned by some, on the grounds that there is a logical gulf between the descriptive and explanatory goals of psychoanalysis on the one hand and the normative and justificatory aims of ethics on the other. But one need not ignore the logical distinctions that separate the descriptive from the normative tasks to recognize that there are several specific ways in which psychological findings are relevant for ethics.

A psychological theory is obviously relevant ethically if it brings into question the very possibility of being moral—for example, by undermining moral responsibility with a doctrine of determinism or moral conduct with egoistic psychological claims. Or even if morality as such is not undermined, psychological findings may indicate the impossibility—or extreme difficulty—of following some specific moral requirement, thereby negating its reasonableness as a guide to action on "ought implies can" grounds. Psychological discoveries are also important ethically when they reveal hidden unconscious consequences of attempting to follow traditional principles or rules. For example, it may be shown that trying to act on the basis of a generally accepted rule or principle is ultimately self-defeating or exceptionally costly in terms of other moral principles, like non-injury to self or others. In addition, a psychological theory like psychoanalysis can help to expand our understanding of the nature of moral decision-making and, correlatively, of how such decisions may go wrong as a consequence of irrational distortions of perception and thinking processes. Psychoanalysis may thus be helpful in devising practical strategies for avoiding these irrational distortions and the disjunctions that sometimes occur between intentions and action.

Psychological views are also indispensable in fleshing out the meaning of abstract normative principles like beneficence, autonomy, and nonmaleficence (non-injury). For example, psychoanalysis expands our common-sense understanding of the duty to avoid harming others by demonstrating that injuries to self-esteem (which commonly occur in response to moral criticism) are more serious harms than our forefathers supposed, in part because they tend to trigger aggressive responses or a collapse of confidence that reverberate through everything else a person does. At the same time, psychoanalysis points out that many of the supposed injuries to the self once attributed to masturbation and sexual fantasies are seldom damaging in any significant sense at all. Psychological views are also essential for

identifying and aptly characterizing those virtues—for example, unflinching self-honesty—that are most helpful in disposing persons to actually act
morally, as opposed to hypocritically supposing that good intentions are
sufficient.

Finally, because a view of human nature is an essential part of every fully
developed normative theory, such a theory stands or falls in part on the
basis of the plausibility of its psychological assumptions (see R. B. Brandt
1959, pp. 114–49). One illustration of this foundational role that psychological theories play in ethics is Kant's argument that the basis of the moral
law is to be found in the subject, not the object of practical reason, a subject
capable of autonomous will. Much contemporary criticism of Kantian-
based ethics rests on psychological arguments to the effect that some aspects of the Kantian conception of persons is empirically wrong (see, e.g.,
MacIntyre 1981; Sandel 1982). Thus Sandel (1982) faults Rawls's Kan-
tian-inspired, duty-based ethical theory by focusing on its allegedly impoverished conception of persons as radically autonomous individuals. In
responding to his critics, Rawls has found it necessary to concede the
relevance of psychology to ethical theory even as he attempts to limit as far
as possible controversial claims about the essential nature of persons in
political philosophy.[5] Contemporary ethicists who favor virtues over normative principles assume a certain psychological predisposition for moral
behavior, although virtue theorists seldom explicitly defend clinically the
psychological beliefs they presuppose.

For most of this century, Anglo-American ethicists have shown little
interest in the above issues of "moral psychology," largely because until the
early 1970s the field of ethics was narrowly restricted to what is called
"metaethics"—namely, to questions about the *meaning* of general moral
terms like "good" and "ought" and the *kind of reasoning* that constitutes a
valid defense of normative claims. As long as the discipline of ethics was so
defined, there was no point in a philosopher turning to psychoanalysis (or
any of the other human sciences) for assistance. Freud, after all, has nothing
to contribute to the ordinary language understanding of prescriptive terms
like "ought" and "good" or to various uses of logic in justifying normative
standards.

During the past several decades, however, ethics has been recovering
many of the concerns of classical moral philosophy and expanding beyond

5. See, e.g., Rawls, 1980, 1982, 1985. For a critique of Sandel's interpretation of Rawls's
conception of the person, see Doppelt 1989.

the narrow confines of metaethics, partly as a consequence of the realization that multiple considerations (including psychological beliefs) go into the elaboration and defense of a complete ethical theory.[6] This, together with the revival of normative ethics (marked by the appearance in 1971 of Rawls's *A Theory of Justice*) and virtue ethics (fueled by the writings of Elizabeth Anscombe, Philippa Foot, and Alasdair MacIntyre), has generated a modest renewal of interest in psychology by ethicists during the last several decades.[7] But so far, this renewed interest has failed to bring forth any serious engagement by ethicists with psychoanalysis, which is attributable, I believe, to the fact that philosophers tend to presuppose very different *psychological* beliefs from those of psychoanalysts.

The moral psychology that prevails implicitly among most ethicists is a cognitivist one, and according to it, there is no problem—or at least no problem deemed worthy of investigation by ethicists—of rational agents being insufficiently motivated to attend to or be moved by a piece of ethical reasoning. Similarly, cognitivist psychology does not allow for any difficulty in achieving by reason alone the empathic identification necessary for some moral judgments, any need for strategies to protect against self-serving rationalizations, or any reason to worry about not really wanting to do what one sincerely believes to be the morally correct action or wanting to be moral for harmful reasons.[8] This cognitivist psychological bias that keeps ethicists from grappling seriously with psychoanalysis also diverts attention away from problems like rule-bound rigidity and moral hypocrisy, which have led psychotherapeutically informed persons outside philos-

---

6. For the purposes of this book, an "ethical theory" is a comprehensive, systematic set of moral guidelines. At the lowest level of abstraction and generalization, moral guidelines consist of "rules" regarding certain kinds of actions that ought or ought not to be done. Moral rules are, in turn, justified by more abstract principles. Because principles as well as rules may conflict, ethical theories consist of second-order principles and procedures that establish priorities among principles and otherwise provide for the adjudication of moral conflicts. For a handy delineation of these elements of moral theory, see Beauchamp and Childress 1989, pp. 3–24.

7. Examples of this renewal of interest in psychology among ethicists include R. B. Brandt 1979; Harman 1977; Richards 1971; Thomas 1989. Interest in psychology by philosophers is also evident in the growing number of articles on the cognitive developmental theories of moral development of Piaget, Kohlberg, and Gilligan. See, e.g., Kittay and Meyers 1987; Munsey 1980; and R. L. Simon 1982.

8. There are exceptions to these generalizations, however. See, e.g., Stocker 1970, 1976, 1979a, 1979b, 1981, 1987.

ophy departments to use depth-psychological insights to be moral in new ways.

Even those philosophers who have attempted to supplant the cognitivist orientation of much recent moral philosophy with an ethics of character or virtue have ignored psychoanalysis, mostly because it challenges the focus on conscious dispositions that has been the hallmark of virtue ethics since Aristotle. One looks in vain in the writings of contemporary exponents of moral virtues like Philippa Foot (1978), Peter Geach (1977), Alasdair MacIntyre (1981, 1988), and James Wallace (1978) for psychodynamically informed discussions of mixed motivations and strategies for avoiding self-deception, although it is hard to see how one can be morally virtuous without taking account of such phenomena.

The avoidance techniques of philosophers notwithstanding, issues like unconscious egoism and aggression, emotionally induced blind spots and errors in moral deliberation, and misfirings of good intentions do not go away simply as a result of choosing one psychology, more compatible with the existing biases of one's field, over another. They are perennial issues in moral philosophy, broadly conceived. Partly empirical, partly conceptual, they require that the ethicist take depth psychology seriously without sacrificing the logical precision that has been the pride and standard of modern ethics.

The interdisciplinary approach to the relation of psychoanalysis and ethics advocated here does not subsume ethics under psychoanalysis, as did the earlier efforts of Fromm, Marcuse, Erikson, Brown, and Rieff. Nor does it try to make psychoanalysis function as a full-blown moral philosophy. Rather, it preserves the integrity of both disciplines even as they are made to enrich one another. The *scientific and interpretive* integrity of psychoanalysis is protected against radical revisions designed to promote some particular normative philosophy by demanding no more ethical work of it than its procedures and findings are capable of delivering. At the same time, the *analytic and normative* integrity of ethics is protected from the reduction of ethics to psychology by using philosophical distinctions to frame the main questions posed and the arguments considered in examining psychoanalytic materials.

This approach permits identification and defense of the implicit moves made by psychoanalysts when they succeed in applying clinical insights to normative issues. But it also shows how some major topics in ethics are deeply affected by taking psychoanalytic findings seriously. Moreover, this helps us to understand why persons with psychodynamic knowledge tend to approach moral problems, say, in a medical setting differently from those who do not.[9]

It is essential to this interdisciplinary approach that psychoanalysis be understood accurately, particularly its core doctrines of the self in conflict and multi-motivated (overdetermined) behavior. Mental behavior is not ordinarily the outcome of a single all-pervasive motive, Freud discovered early in his career. It is rather the outcome of intrapsychic conflict between unconscious sexual and aggressive impulses, as modified by child–parent interactions during the first years of development, on the one hand and the ego's (and superego's) conscious and unconscious defensive reactions on the other.[10] Multiple unconscious drives, images, fantasies, and emotions are forever pressing toward primitive goals. Yet these drives are seldom experienced in their pristine forms. For the surface of the mind reacts against the disruptive forces emanating from the unconscious "cauldron of seething excitement" by driving them below the threshold of consciousness and impeding their expression. The motives that are driven out of consciousness in this manner do not lose their dynamic force, however. From their home in the unconscious workshop of the psyche, they continue to demand some form of expression, manifesting themselves in compromise formations such as hysterical and obsessional symptoms, dreams, sexual malfunctions, work inhibitions, moralistic condemnations, and slips of the tongue and pen (*SE* 15 [1915–16]:13–79; 18[1920]:150; 18[1923]: 235–54).[11]

For Freudians the self is in conflict precisely because incompatible men-

9. Psychoanalyst Jay Katz's (1984) distinctive contributions to the discussion of informed consent in medicine nicely illustrate the ethical significance of psychodynamic understanding.

10. Freud's biographer, Ernest Jones, rightly views the conflictual view of the self as Freud's most radical innovation: "Freud's revolutionary contribution to psychology was not so much his demonstrating the existence of an unconscious, and perhaps not even his explorations of its content, as his proposition that there are two fundamentally different kinds of mental processes, which he termed primary and secondary respectively, together with his description of them" (1957, p. 436). See also *SE* 14 (1915):173 and Brenner 1982.

11. The prevalence of compromise formations in mental life is one reason why it is too simple to claim, as Peters (1960, p. 55) does, that psychoanalytic explanations apply only to bizarre or decidedly odd behavior. It is true that psychoanalysis specializes in interpreting behavior that is ego-alien; but this does not mean that only odd or unintentional behavior is subject to psychoanalytic interpretation, for ego-syntonic actions may gradually become ego-alien in the course of psychoanalytic treatment and hence analyzable. See Greenson 1967, p. 96. Brenner's (1982) insistence on the ubiquity of compromise formations leads him to distinguish normal from pathological compromise formations.

tal purposes war against one another. For example, the president of an organization who says in his opening address "I declare this session closed" is expressing at least two aims at once. He obviously intends to open the meeting, but unconsciously he wants to get it over with for reasons he disavows. As Freud (1952, p. 63) points out in discussing this example, "errors are mental acts arising from the mutual interference of two intentions."

Freud made it a fundamental proposition of psychoanalytic theory that human motivations are always and everywhere "mixed" or "overdetermined," by which he meant that human behavior is usually the result of a plurality of different motives working simultaneously. This proposition is central to the psychoanalytic perspective on moral behavior: "It is very rarely that an action is the work of a single . . . impulse . . . In order to make an action possible there must be as a rule a *combination* of such compounded motives. . . So . . . human beings . . . may have whole numbers of motives for assenting [to an action]—some noble and some base, some of which they speak openly and others on which they are silent" (*CP* 5 [1932]:281–2). The psychoanalytic view of moral conduct thus differs from most other views in seeing conduct as ordinarily the result not of one all-pervasive motive but of many, usually conflicting motives (see Waelder 1936). The exact implications of this conflictual view of the self for morality and ethics remain to be seen; but it is apparent that Freudian theory accords an important place to the so-called higher mental functions, including morality, in explaining the disavowal of sexual and aggressive wishes and fantasies that parallel, interfere with, and conflate with ordinary practical rationality in determining human behavior.[12]

A point about psychoanalysis that is not often appreciated is that its domain of inquiry and expertise is limited by what is ceded to other academic disciplines. Contrary to the popular impression of psychoanalysis as an aggressively imperialistic discipline, most psychoanalysts follow Freud's lead in emphasizing that psychoanalytic theory needs to be filled out by

12. Commonly psychoanalysts simply assume the existence of what philosophers describe as practical rationality—i.e., the capacity of agents to act consciously in terms of both desires (goals, objectives, purposes, aims, wants, etc.) and beliefs about a situation and to achieve by action the goals desired (see M. Moore 1984). Freud assumes the presence of this capacity in the mature ego when he writes: "Actions and consciously expressed opinions are as a rule enough for practical purposes in judging men's characters" (*SE* 5 [1900]: 621; see also *SE* 13 [1913]:185–6). Yet Freud is intensely suspicious of ordinary consciousness, even if he acknowledges that "the criterion of being conscious" is "all we have" to base our actions on (*SE* 22 [1933]:70).

research in such allied disciplines as neurophysiology, biology, normal psychiatry, academic psychology, sociology, and anthropology.[13] Freud underscored the need for these complementary disciplines by his example of drawing judiciously on research in all these fields. As if to leave no doubt about such gleanings, he stated unambiguously that psychoanalysis "has never dreamt of trying to explain 'everything'" (*SE* 18 [1923]:252). He also wrote that "psycho-analysis has never claimed to provide a complete theory of human mentality in general, but only expected that what it offered should be applied to supplement and correct the knowledge acquired by other means" (*SE* 14 [1914]:50). In fact, Freud goes beyond even the sciences in his appreciation of the "knowledge acquired by other means," drawing heavily on the insights of poets, dramatists, novelists, and philosophers, whose writings he utilizes in formulating such key concepts as the oedipal complex, narcissism, Eros, and the death instinct.[14]

A similarly circumscribed attitude to the domain of psychoanalytic inquiry is evident in Freud's treatment of philosophy, with regard to which he is careful to note that while psychobiography might be useful in identifying weak spots in a theory that springs from its author's psychopathology, as contrasted with his or her "impartial logical work," nonetheless, "the fact that a theory is psychologically determined does not in the least invalidate its . . . truth" (*SE* 13 [1913]:179). Freud knew all too well how gratuitous criticisms based on alleged unconscious motives could boomerang on their users. And he had the perspicacity to ask in connection with the genetic fallacy of which he was accused unfairly by Allport (1950, pp. 103–10): "Who bells the cat?" once this kind of allegedly Freudian criticism gets out of hand.[15]

Despite its limited domain, psychoanalysis, like many other theories of human behavior, offers an *inclusive* vision, model, or paradigm of human

13. See *SE* 13 (1913):100; 18 (1923): 251–4. Marshall Edelson (1988) is a strong contemporary advocate of the limited domain of psychoanalytic inquiry and expertise but goes too far in restricting psychoanalysis to the study of unconscious fantasies.

14. That Freud did not always treat humanistic disciplines in the reductive way he treated religion is evident from his statement: "Before the problem of the creative artist analysis must, alas, lay down its arms" (*SE* 21 [1928]:177). Nor did he ever depart from the position that "psycho-analysis throws a satisfactory light upon some of the problems concerning art and artists; but others escape it entirely" (*SE* 13 [1913]:187). Freud's modesty vis-à-vis aesthetics is brought out by Ricoeur (1970) and Wright (1984).

15. Freud writes: "Analysis is not suited . . . for polemical purposes. . . . Anyone . . . who undertakes . . . [to use] analysis for polemical purposes must expect the person analyzed to use analysis against him in turn, so that the discussion will reach a state which entirely excludes the possibility of convincing any impartial third person" (*SE* 14 [1914]:49).

nature.[16] One advantage of this model is that it acknowledges the importance of the mind's connections both with the body (as do neurophysiology
and biology) and with specific social milieus (as do the social sciences). As
Freud first pointed out, a person's behavior is influenced not only by his or
her psychosexual development tracked through its various vicissitudes by
psychoanalysts, but also by the individual's unique genetic inheritance and
by the various chemical-hormonal happenings occurring within his or her
body.[17] Behavior is also influenced significantly by the social institutions
within which the individual develops from early childhood to adulthood
and to which he remains vulnerable at every stage of life.[18] Psychoanalysis's
portrait of human nature thus encourages interdisciplinary bridge building
among the several disciplines concerned with the study of human nature
and behavior, including several of the humanities that deal with unconscious meanings, like literary criticism and aesthetics, at the same time that
it challenges most traditional views of human nature with its findings
regarding unavowed impulses and processes, the persistence of infantile
patterns in adult life, and unacknowledged defensive strategies.[19]

Insofar as psychoanalysis sketches a global view of human nature, it
obviously goes considerably beyond the narrow confines of empirical science and impinges on age-old concerns of moral philosophy. There is an
inevitably evaluative aspect to all such attempts to delineate the most prominent characteristics of human nature, its forms of flourishing and pathological deviation in various environments. This is the truth of the argument

16. Don Browning draws attention to the metaempirical visions of putatively scientific
psychologies in *Religious Thought and Modern Psychologies* (1987). For a critique of Browning's
book, see Wallwork 1989.

17. See *SE* 13 (1913):174–5, 182.

18. Although Freud is famous for holding that the general configuration of the adult
personality is laid during the first five years of life, he also stresses the many ways in which the
ego and superego continue to evolve in interaction with the social environment over the
course of a person's lifetime (see, e.g., *SE* 18 [1921]:105–43). The vulnerability of the self to
the quality of social life is brought out especially in "Thoughts for the Times on War and
Death" (*SE* 14 [1915]:275–88), in which Freud stresses the contribution society makes to the
formation of moral character as well as to the dissolution of those very same virtues (as, e.g.,
when the nation-state violates traditional moral rules). The importance of the social factor in a
full explanation of behavior is also a central theme in such works as " 'Civilized' Sexual
Morality and Modern Nervous Illness," *Totem and Taboo, Group Psychology and the Analysis of
the Ego, Future of an Illusion, Civilization and its Discontents,* "Why War?", and *Moses and
Monotheism.*

19. For Freud's views on the special contributions that psychoanalysis can make to the
social services and the humanities, see SE 13 [1913]:165–90.

of those interpreters, friendly and hostile, who contend that Freudian theory is really a philosophy of life or a religio-ethical system of values that cannot be validated entirely by the kind of value-neutral empirical research that some take to be the litmus test of science. But this trespassing on territory beyond the realm of science, narrowly construed, certainly does not warrant dismissing as pseudo-scientific the many psychoanalytic hypotheses that are empirically or clinically verifiable. Nor does the mere fact that psychoanalysis overreaches the limits of what can be verified empirically mean that its broad portrait of human nature is intellectually unrespectable. (See Appendix A for a discussion of the credibility of psychoanalysis as an investigative technique in light of recent criticism.) All the human sciences find it necessary to postulate evaluatively imbued paradigms that go beyond what can be verified empirically. The issue is not whether psychoanalysis should be faulted for allowing evaluative elements to creep into its basic view of human nature, but whether those who use it, professionals and laity alike, are sufficiently aware of these implicit evaluative assumptions to engage in the kind of philosophical assessment that is required to defend them.

We need to know the values implicit in the psychoanalytic view of human nature, for the same reason that it is generally desirable to be aware of unconscious determinants of thought and action. It is only by making conscious unconscious evaluations that we are able to decide rationally whether they are warranted and whether, therefore, it is desirable to continue acting on them.

It is one of the merits of the interdisciplinary method being advanced here that it reveals, rather than conceals, the value judgments that are deeply embedded in psychoanalytic theory and practice. By making conscious the latent evaluative assumptions that underlie such concepts as narcissism and object love, the psychoanalyst is reminded that these evaluative assumptions are controversial and that evaluation of these assumptions requires not just consideration of argument and empirical evidence, but philosophical reflection on the grounding of evaluative claims.

This book is divided into four main sections. Part I explores two interrelated introductory issues: the hermeneutical problem of reading Freud and the foundational question of whether the psychoanalytic doctrine of psychic determinism undermines moral responsibility. Part II examines the issue of psychological egoism and the possibilities of moral conduct, with separate chapters on the pleasure principle, narcissism, and object love. Part III explores the normative implications of psychoanalytic findings and practice. And Part IV sets forth the general ethical theory that seems most compatible with psychoanalysis, using Freud's ethics and the morality implicit in psychoanalytic practice as base points.

Psychoanalytic theory is approached throughout this book primarily through a careful exegesis of Freud's writings. Several considerations justify this concentration on Freud. First, by comparison with other psychoanalytic texts, Freud's writings have the advantage of virtual canonical status in the discipline. Indeed, Freud's work is the starting point for virtually all subsequent clinically based psychotherapeutic theory. The foundational psychoanalytic paradigm is definitively set forth there, as are most of the essential concepts and propositions of psychoanalysis. Thus, even where clear improvements on the original formulations have been made, it is essential to start with Freud's seminal ideas in order to understand fully the nature of these changes and why they are for the better.

Second, Freud anticipates all the main movements in the recent history of psychoanalysis: ego psychology, object-relations theory, and self-psychology.[20] It is not surprising that these movements have developed within the Freudian tradition; they are present in germinal form in the founder's writings. Hence careful exegesis of Freud's writings leads easily to incorporation of the valid insights of these currently important contributions to psychoanalytic theory. At the same time, Freud's work underscores the bedrock psychoanalytic findings that tend to be obscured in the theories propounded by post-Freudian revisionists.

Third, Freud's original theory reflects his insights as a superb and subtle clinician who derived his theoretical views from personal engagement at close quarters. Freud's subtlety as a theorist is commonly missed by beginning students and some academic interpreters who are easily distracted by his penchant for dogmatic overstatements and what are by now archaic metaphors drawn from nineteenth-century physics and biology. But Freud's theoretical subtlety is apparent in his theorizing as a whole when viewed in light of the full range of qualifications and additional nuances that he adds virtually every time he returns to a familiar theme. In an important sense, Freud is the most contemporary of psychoanalytic writers, because his writings are so complexly textured that it is always possible to

20. Psychoanalytic ego psychology evolved out of the work of the second generation of psychoanalysts who were associated with Freud in Vienna during the 1920s and 1930s, such as Anna Freud, Heinz Hartmann, Erik Erikson, and Ernst Kris. The object-relations school of Fairbairn and Winnicott grew out of Melanie Klein's work in Britain. Self-psychology grew up around Heinz Kohut's recent work on narcissistic personality disorders.

find new meaning in them, even in those one has read many times.[21] Few subsequent psychoanalysts come close to matching Freud's clinical perspicacity, and this in itself is sufficient to warrant our starting with his writings in undertaking to work out the significance of psychoanalysis for ethics.

Finally, Freud is philosophically more interesting on ethical issues than most of his disciples, who typically either dismiss all concern with ethics as a sign of psychic ill health or, with a kind of conceptual imperialism, substitute medical notions of health and illness for the moral concepts of goodness and badness, rightness and wrongness (M. Moore 1984, p. 122). Freud, thanks to the classical Gymnasium education he received, is steeped in the great literary classics of Western civilization dealing with morality, as seen in his liberal use of quotations—in their original languages—from classical texts in all the major European languages, ancient and modern.[22] Freud also had moral-philosophical ambitions stemming from his youth, when his curiosity was directed more toward "human concerns" than medical problems (*SE* 20 [1925]:8). Although most interpreters, including Peter Gay (1988), follow Ernest Jones in underestimating the importance of philosophy in the development of Freud's work, his letters to Silberstein during his university years reveal his deep immersion in most of the philosophical problems of modern thought, as well as sophisticated knowledge of Kant, Schiller, Feuerbach, Hume, Carlyle, Darwin, Mill, and Brentano.[23] The relevance of this background to Freud's later psychological

21. Roy Schafer rightly observes that "Freud already knew much that we now pride ourselves on having only just come to know, even though he did not know it, and could not have known it, in quite the way that we do today" (1983, p. 16). Similarly, Erikson says somewhere of his own revisions of psychoanalytic theory that they can all be found in Freud's own texts.

22. Among the numerous classical quotations in Freud's writings, let me cite the motto of *The Interpretation of Dreams: Flectere si nequeo superos, Acheronta movebo* (Virgil, *Aeneid* VII. 312). Freud simply assumes that his quotations from classical literature are immediately recognizable by his readers. For discussion of Freud's classical education and humanistic beliefs, see Sterba 1969.

23. For an excellent discussion of Freud's philosophical background, including his letters to Silberstein, see McGrath 1986, esp. ch. 3. The following passages from Freud's letters to Silberstein highlight his philosophical interests: "About the first year at University I can tell you that I shall spend it entirely in studying humanistic subjects which have nothing at all to do with my future profession but which will not be useless to me" (letter dated 11 July 1873, trans. McGrath 1986, p. 96; see *ibid.*, p. 100). "We stand on the threshold of the second semester—for me a new life, in which I can for the first time pass as philosopher and zoologist, since I will be attending psychology, logic, and zoology courses" (letter dated 11 Apr. 1875,

work is hinted at in one of his letters to Fliess in 1896: "When I was young, the only thing I longed for was philosophical knowledge, and now that I am going over from medicine to psychology I am in the process of attaining it" (letter 44, in Freud 1954, p. 162). Freud's deep philosophical knowledge is most apparent, however, in the care and subtlety with which he deals with the deep issues that are the focus of this book.

Perhaps equally important for the ethical perspicacity of Freud's writings is the fact that he wrote during an era in which morality could still be taken for granted. Unlike his successors, who live in a culture that is still reeling from the shock of vulgar Freudianism, which Trilling (1955) aptly describes as "the slang of our culture," Freud was not embarrassed to employ moral language or to make clear moral pronouncements—for example, about the moral worthiness of potential patients for psychoanalysis (see, e.g., *SE* 7 [1905]:263).

Of course, philosophy was not Freud's chosen field, and he was not adverse to papering over some of the philosophical issues he could not avoid; but his excellent grasp of ancient Greek and post-Enlightenment British philosophy, as well as his efforts at combining the sciences with the humanities within the resources available in the German cultural orbit, make his works always thought-provoking, even when he is in error. His writings remain an untapped treasure chest of insights of great relevance to the perennial problems of moral philosophy, as he himself hoped they would when he stated that psychoanalysis "should find a place among the methods whose aim is to bring about the highest ethical and intellectual development" (letter to James Jackson Putnam dated 30 Mar. 1914, in Hale 1971, p. 170). "The application of [psychoanalysis to moral philosophy] . . . enables us both to raise fresh problems and to see old ones in a fresh light and contribute towards their solution" (*SE* 13 [1913]:185).

---

trans. McGrath 1986, p. 122). After critiquing Kant's concept of synthetic a priori judgments and expressing a preference for the English empirical philosophers in several letters of March and April 1875, Freud wrote in the summer of that year that his studies made it possible "always to hold to the side of the English who now enjoy a highly favorable prejudice with me: Tyndall, Huxley, Lyell, Darwin, Thomson, Lockyer, as well as others" (trans. McGrath 1986, p. 130).

PART I
Foundational Issues

Chapter 2
The Hermeneutical Problem of Reading Freud

Interpret! A nasty word! I dislike the sound
of it; it robs me of all security. If everything depends on my interpretation who can
guarantee that I interpret right? So after
all everything *is* left to my caprice. Just a
moment! Things are not quite as bad as that.
—Freud

Every psychological theory, apart from
what it achieves from the point of view of
natural science, must fulfil yet another major
requirement. It should explain to us
what we are aware of, in the most puzzling
fashion, through our "consciousness."
—Freud

No issue is more fundamental to the study of psychoanalysis than the
hermeneutical question: How should we go about reading Freud? Of
course, the problem of interpretation arises with any discourse, even in the
physical sciences, but it is particularly acute with respect to Freud. This is in
large part due to tensions and crosscurrents set in motion by the distinctive
enterprises of the metapsychology and the clinical theory.

In the metapsychology, Freud aims at the kind of causal explanation
characteristic of the natural sciences (*Naturwissenschaften*). In his clinical
writings and applied psychoanalysis, on the other hand, the emphasis is on
the interpretation (*Deutung*) and understanding *(Verstehen)* of the meaning
of human discourse and behavior, as it is in the humanities (*Geisteswissenschaften*). These two approaches differ radically in tone and intention, and it
is not clear how they are to be related to one another. What is evident,
however, is that the hermeneutical issue must be self-consciously addressed; for how one deals with it is decisive for one's understanding of such

central issues in psychoanalytic theory and practice as determinism, psychological hedonism, and object love.[1]

Indeed, so significant is this issue that Freud's interpreters can be categorized (and do in fact divide themselves) in terms of whether they see Freud's metapsychological or clinical writings as constituting the essence of psychoanalytic thought. Those who emphasize the metapsychology (and thus psychoanalysis's affinity with the natural sciences and with such doctrines as determinism and homeostasis) include Hartmann (1958, 1964), Grunbaum (1984), and Yankelovich and Barrett (1970); whereas those who see Freud's clinical writings as central and put the accent on his humanism, include, among others, Erikson (1963, 1964, 1968), Gedo (1984), Habermas (1971), Home (1966), Klein (1976), Ricoeur (1970, 1981),[2] and Schafer (1976, 1983).

THE METAPSYCHOLOGY

Freud himself often gives the impression that the natural-scientific model of the human psyche represented by the metapsychology is *the* basic

1. The importance of resolving this interpretive problem is illustrated by the sort of arbitrariness and confusion that mars the writings of Fromm and Rieff on Freud. Thus Fromm, on the basis of a metapsychological reading, claims that "love, according to . . . [Freud], is by its very nature egotistical and antisocial" (1955, p. 75), yet, on the basis of Freud's nonmetapsychological writings, asserts that "Freud holds that the aim of human development is the achievement of these ideals: . . . brotherly love, reduction of suffering, . . . and [moral] responsibility" (Fromm 1950, p. 18).

Similarly, Rieff draws exclusively on the metapsychology when trying to explain what Freud means by psychological hedonism (Rieff 1961, pp. 171–2) but ignores it entirely when discussing Freud's views on determinism and moral responsibility (ibid., pp. 11–12, 18). If he had approached the issue of moral responsibility through the apparent determinism of the metapsychology and, conversely, had sought the meaning of psychological hedonism in Freud's clinical writings, a very different portrait of Freud might have emerged from the one presented in *Freud: The Mind of the Moralist*.

2. Ricoeur (1970, 1981) belongs on the side of those who emphasize Freud's clinical writings, despite his insistence on the indispensability of the metapsychology. This is because Ricoeur puts the accent on what he calls the semantics of desire, maintaining that we can only deal with the unconscious and hence the metapsychology by means of "the representable and the sayable" (Ricoeur 1970, p. 150). Ricoeur succeeds more than most interpreters in relating the two sides of Freud's thought, primarily because he realizes that many of Freud's clinical observations regarding dreams, symptoms, parapraxes, and so forth make sense only in relation to and within the framework of the metapsychology. The metapsychology provides the theoretical framework that makes clinical psychoanalytic discourse possible, even though, in Ricoeur's view, that discourse is not entirely reducible to the mechanistic language of the metapsychology.

psychoanalytic theory.[3] Thus, in the famous last chapter of *The Interpretation of Dreams* (1900), the book in which Freud presented psychoanalysis to the world, he clearly implies that he is shifting to a more respectable level of explanation in moving from interpreting the meaning of dreams to presenting his foundational theory in terms of a "mental apparatus" that operates as a thermodynamic energic system.[4] Freud seems to believe here, as in the later metapsychological papers of 1915, that a truly *scientific* psychology must necessarily employ concepts and propositions exactly like those found in the natural sciences; and he seems to conceive of science in narrow, Helmholtzian terms derived from the reductionistic materialism of his medical school teachers (see Bernfeld 1944, 1951).

In the metapsychology, at least as it existed from 1900 to 1919, human behavior is viewed as a consequence of quasi-physical psychic energies and forces operating in accordance with lawlike generalizations that do not differ in their functional essence from those applicable to natural phenomena. To explain human conduct at this abstract theoretical level is to show how it works without employing the language of purpose, which

3. The *metapsychology* encompasses an ensemble of "basic concepts" (*Grundbegriffe*), "postulates" (*Voraussetzungen*), "hypotheses" (*Annahmen*), and "speculations" that are somewhat removed from interpretive clinical work and empirical verification (see Laplanche and Pontalis 1973, pp. 249–50). Examples include the theory of instincts, the fiction of the psychic apparatus, and the division of the psyche into topographical and structural agencies. By midcareer, Freud's metapsychology was sufficiently complex and developed to allow him to propose that a "metapsychological" account describes a psychical process in its dynamic, topographical, and economic aspects (*SE* 14 [1915]:181). Later, in *The Ego and the Id*, Freud (*SE* 19 [1923]) added the "structural" point of view without explicitly identifying it as a metapsychological perspective.

Freud attended to the metapsychology throughout his career. In the posthumously published "Project for a Scientific Psychology" (*SE* 1 [1895]: 295–387), written in 1895 but not published, Freud attempted to reduce psychology to neurology. Freud's first extended published account of the metapsychology, ch. 7 of *The Interpretation of Dreams*, translated much of the unpublished "Project" from physicalistic, neurological language into psychological terms. Except for occasional short discussions, such as that in ch. 6 of his volume on jokes (*SE* 8 [1905]: 159–81), it was ten years before Freud again delved deeply into theoretical problems (see *SE* 12 [1911]:213–26, 59–79).

A more complete exposition of the metapsychology was attempted in the papers on metapsychology (*SE* 14 [1915]: 105–260). The views presented there were substantively modified subsequently, notably in *Beyond the Pleasure Principle, Inhibitions, Symptoms and Anxiety*, and *An Outline of Psycho-Analysis*.

4. At the outset of this chapter, Freud describes the preceding interpretive part of the book as "the easy and agreeable portion of our journey . . ." and contrasts it with the difficult endeavor at hand—"to penetrate more deeply into the mental process involved in dreaming" (*SE* 5[1900]:511).

must be avoided, since purposes are the very phenomena to be explained (see Klein 1976, pp. 43–6). Explanation thus appears to be a highly reductionistic enterprise. A person's emotions are described as "drive discharges," reasons for action as "forces," and an individual's struggle with conflicting motives as the "regulation of the psychic apparatus by the pleasure principle," or homeostasis. Indeed, in the metapsychology, Freud often writes as if he has discovered not only unconscious fantasies and wishes, but, beyond and through them, another world of mechanistic forces at work in a thinglike mental apparatus.

Freud's investment in his metapsychology cannot be gainsaid. It represented a significant aspect of the scientific stature he wished to claim for psychoanalysis, and he returned to it throughout his career, tinkering, revising, and adjusting. Clearly, he never abandoned his commitment to empirical science, his belief in the organic substrata of mental behavior, or his fondness for applying neurophysiological categories and metaphors to psychological phenomena.[5]

But it must also be noted that Freud expressed great caution with respect to his entire metapsychological enterprise. He repeatedly described the metapsychology as "tentative," "speculative," and "hypothetical" (SE 14 [1914]:77; 14 [1917]:234; 18 [1920]:59; 20 [1925]:32–3, 59; 23 [1937]:225)[6] and even went so far as to call it a "phantasy," a "myth," a product of wish fulfillment on the part of its creator.[7] Although Freud is often regarded as having clung to a rigidly Helmholtzian view of science, it would appear that he reluctantly accepted the notion that even "scientific" theory makes some use of the speculative and imaginative qualities that go

5. Even after 1919, when Freud altered his dominant metapsychological paradigm, the mechanistic language of the 1900–19 period still makes an occasional appearance.

6. Thus, in *Interpretation* he writes: "We must always be prepared to drop our conceptual scaffolding if we feel that we are in a position to replace it by something that approximates more closely to the unknown reality" (SE 5 [1900]:610). See also SE 7 (1905): 216, n. 1.

Likewise, in "Instincts and their Vicissitudes," he cautions: "[T]his [metatheoretical] supposition [regarding the instincts] . . . is merely a working hypothesis, to be retained only so long as it proves useful" (SE 14 [1915]:124).

Again in 1917, he stated that: "We are not, of course, intending to disguise or gloss over the uncertain and tentative character of these metapsychological discussions" (SE 14 [1917]: 234, n. 2).

Ironically, Freud gives particularly strong voice to his doubts about the metapsychology's abstractions in his most speculative work, *Pleasure Principle* (see SE 18 [1920]: 59; 19 [1923]: 12).

7. See SE 22 (1933): 95, 212, where Freud refers to the metapsychology's instinct theory as his mythology.

into the creation of myths. Citing a line from Goethe's *Faust*, Part I, scene 6, he once referred to the metapsychology as "the Witch." "We must call the Witch to our help after all!" he stated and then continued: "Without metapsychological speculation and theorizing—I . . . almost said phantasying—we shall not get another step forward. Unfortunately, here as elsewhere, what our Witch reveals is neither very clear nor very detailed" (*SE* 23 [1937]:225).

In speaking this way about his own metatheoretical efforts, Freud was intent on keeping psychoanalytic theory open to revision where the clinical data required it. Words such as "tentative" and "speculative" were intended to remind the reader that psychoanalysis was still a young science, one that might have to revise substantially many of its initial concepts and hypotheses. With the metapsychology, Freud was not trying to formulate a closed system from which to make ironclad deductions.[8] Rather, he was attempting to provide a theoretical framework for ordering the clinical data. The goal was not dogma but scientific validity.

But Freud's disclaimers regarding the metapsychology go beyond its inadequacy with respect to particular points of clinical theory. It was not simply that Freud was aware of details that the metapsychology left out or could not yet explain (*SE* 22 [1933]:6). He believed that the entire metapsychological effort might be seriously defective and misleading because, like any other general theory, it required the a priori adoption of certain basic postulates (in the case of psychoanalysis, about the nature and functioning of instincts and the psychic apparatus, for example) that combine factual material with the purely speculative and are by their nature unproved and incomplete.[9]

The indefiniteness of all our discussions on what we describe as "metapsychology" is of course due to the fact that we know nothing of the nature

8. Indeed, Freud strongly rejected the notion that extrapolations could be made from his general theory to aspects of mental life that he had not yet studied carefully (see Waelder 1964, pp. 55–6; Hartmann and Lowenstein 1962, p. 144).

9. See *SE* 14 (1914):117–22, where Freud declares that scientific activity requires certain "basic concepts" and "postulates" (*Grundbegriffe*), which are at first necessarily tentative and indefinite but are progressively modified, reformulated, and made more precise as empirical work proceeds (see also *SE* 14 [1914]:77). And in *Pleasure Principle* Freud states that "In any case it is impossible to pursue an idea of this [metatheoretical] kind except by repeatedly combining factual material with what is purely speculative and thus diverging widely from empirical observation. The more frequently this is done in the course of constructing a theory, the more untrustworthy, as we know, must be the final result. But the degree of uncertainty is not assignable. One may have made a lucky hit or one may have gone shamefully astray" (SE 18 [1920]:59).

of the excitatory process that takes place in the elements of the psychic systems, and that we do not feel justified in framing any hypothesis on the subject. We are consequently operating all the time with a large unknown factor, which we are obliged to carry over into every new formula" (*SE* 18 [1920]:30–1; see also *SE* 18 [1920]:59). Freud keenly recognized the danger of overlooking some essential premises altogether or of doggedly pursuing inadequate initial hypotheses to erroneous conclusions[10] in formulating a basic, high-level, theoretical orientation for psychoanalysis, for the metapsychology purports to explain what is going on in the depths of the unconscious, where the mind and brain interact in ways that cannot be studied empirically. Thus Freud observed: "We know [only] two kinds of things about . . . our psyche (or mental life): firstly, its bodily organ and scene of action, the brain (or nervous system) and . . . [secondly], [what is revealed by] our acts of consciousness, which are immediate data and cannot be further explained by any sort of description. Everything that lies between is unknown to us, and the data do not include any direct relation between these two terminal points of our knowledge" (*SE* 23 [1940]: 144).

   To read the metapsychology as if it were the most definitive aspect of Freudian theory or as if it purported to formulate clear causal connections between these two different kinds of data is thus to go considerably beyond what Freud proposed. However forcefully and concretely Freud may have presented his metapsychological views at any one time, he remained essentially leery of abstractions too far removed from the phenomena they were intended to explain.

THE CLINICAL THEORY

   While the aim of psychoanalysis—and of the metapsychology—is always to render mental phenomena *intelligible*,[11] Freud did not ineluctably tie that process to the application of the metapsychology. Whatever the status of the metapsychological superstructure, for Freud, the work of intelligibility could go on because *"there is still plenty to be described that lies closer to actual experience"* (*SE* 20 [1925]:33, emphasis added).[12]

   10. See *SE* 5 (1900):511, also *SE* 18 (1920): 30–1, 59.
   11. The term "intelligible" (*verständnis*) is frequently employed by Freud in identifying the aim of narrative coherence in clinical work (see, e.g., *SE* 2 [1893–5]:8 [*GW* 1 (1892–9):87]; 10 [1909]:156, 204 [*GW* 7 (1906–9):382]).
   12. Freud was too sure of the veracity of his clinical insights to give them up for the sake of

It is the side of Freud that works "closer to actual experience" that contrasts and often seems to conflict with Freud the metapsychologist. Here, where Freud is relatively free of the mechanistic and scientistic viewpoint of the metapsychology, what is important to him is a process of *interpretation* (*Deutung*), defined as ascertaining the meaning (*Bedeutung*) of human behavior. The interpretive aspect of the psychoanalytic enterprise received its due right from the start of psychoanalysis. The case reports and discussion of the cathartic method of psychotherapy that Freud wrote for *Studies on Hysteria* (*SE* 2 [1893–5]) are primarily in an interpretive mode. Likewise, in an early programmatic statement in *The Interpretation of Dreams* Freud explained: "The aim which I have set before myself is to show that dreams are capable of being interpreted . . . '[I]nterpreting' [*Deutung*] a dream implies assigning a meaning [*Bedeutung*] to it—that is, replacing it by something which fits into the chain of our mental acts as a link having a validity and importance equal to the rest" (*SE* 4 [1900]:96).

Freud's concern with interpretation continued to be central in his case histories and writings on analytic technique and applied psychoanalysis. In these works, he strives to milk each patient's verbal productions, fantasies, and dreams for their nuances of meaning by working nonreductively with the subject's own (conscious and unconscious) meanings and motivations, which are taken as sufficient to explain the behavior under review. The emphasis is on fitting mental phenomena not into the categories of Freud's high-level scientific theory but into the subject's own narrative history. As Freud admits somewhat sheepishly, his case histories read like "short stories . . . that . . . lack the serious stamp of science" not because this is how he prefers to present his clinical material but because "the nature of the subject" demands the same kind of "detailed description of mental processes such as we are accustomed to find in the works of imaginative writers" (*SE* 2 [1893–5]:160).

In this interpretive, quasi-literary mode, Freud is deeply steeped in and inspired by the whole of the Western humanistic tradition. It is worth remembering, over against the fashionable emphasis put on the influence of the Helmholtz school, that Freud presented his choice of a career in medicine as having been partly inspired by hearing "Goethe's beautiful essay on

---

a tidy metatheory, however much he had invested in his metapsychological explanations (see Balint 1960, p. 17; also Holt 1965, p. 117). He specifically advised that the topographical approach of the metapsychology is "part of a *speculative superstructure* of psycho-analysis, any portion of which can be abandoned or changed without loss or regret the moment its inadequacy has been proved" (*SE* 20 [1925]: 32–3, emphasis added). See also *SE* 14 (1914):77.

Nature";[13] that humanistic philosophy was one of his passions and the humanist philosopher Brentano one of his favorite teachers; and that he frequently cited the great literary works of Western civilization and acknowledged the Greek dramatists and Shakespeare as his masters (Lenormand cited in Ellenberger 1970; p. 460; E. Jones, 1957, p. 422). The Freud of materialistic reductionism and physicalistic explanations thus exists side by side with the Freud who peppered his writings with quotations from Sophocles, Aeschylus and Homer, Euripedes and Virgil, the Bible, Shakespeare, Cervantes, Molière, Goethe, Ibsen, and Dostoevsky in the belief that these literary giants captured both the essence of human experience and its depth-psychological explanation far better than most academic psychologists.[14] In the tradition of the humanities, Freud found nourishment for the moral philosopher in him that dared to break with the normal reaches of science and declare the uniqueness of specifically human experiences.[15]

The interpretive side of Freud's thought, together with his numerous

13. In his *Autobiographical Study* Freud stated that, having been attracted by the doctrines of Darwin because they "promised an extraordinary advancement in our understanding of the world," he decided to "inscribe" himself in medicine as a career upon hearing a prominent professor recite Goethe's beautiful essay "On Nature" during a popular lecture (*SE* 20 [1925]: 8). Gay (1988, p. 24) contends that this "story bears the mark of mythmaking or, at least, of excessive compression," that Freud would have been moving in this direction for some time. Moreover, the fragment on which Freud bestowed such great significance was not even by Goethe, but only in Goethe's style. However, McGrath's (1986, pp. 90–1) analysis of Freud's probable mental state at the time—early February 1873—suggests that the essay had an emotional impact, glossed over by Gay, that helps to explain the essay's relevance to Freud's decision to become a scientist, which he announced to Silberstein on 17 Mar. 1873.

14. The Greek dramatists, of course, provided the inspiration for the *Oedipus complex* and the concept of *narcissism*. Of the Bible's influence, Freud said: "My deep engrossment in the Bible story (almost as soon as I had learnt the art of reading) had, as I recognized much later, an enduring effect upon the direction of my interest [towards human concerns, as contrasted with natural objects]" (*SE* 20 [1925]: 8). Freud began his lifelong reading of Shakespeare when he was eight years old. Cervantes' *Don Quixote* was an especially important influence during his adolescence, when he and Silberstein learned Spanish and developed their own mythology and vocabulary out of Cervantes (Gay 1988, pp. 22–3). How deeply Goethe left his mark on Freud is indicated not only by his attributing his choice of a career in medicine in part to an essay he believed to be by Goethe, but also by his frequent quotations from Goethe. Freud's other favorite writers included Heine, Milton, Flaubert, Kipling, Mark Twain, Gomperz, Zola, and Anatole France. He was also deeply influenced by Kant, Lamarck, Schiller, Hegel, Schelling, J. S. Mill, Darwin, and Fechner (see, e.g., Holt 1973).

15. In 1925, Freud recalled how as a youth he had felt "an overpowering [philosophical] need to understand something of the riddles of the world [and of human nature] . . . and perhaps even to contribute something to their solution" (*SE* 20 [1925]: 253).

disclaimers regarding the accuracy of the metapsychology, has led some students of Freud to locate the heart of psychoanalysis in what George Klein (1976) calls "the clinical theory."[16] The hallmark of the clinical theory is the notion that psychoanalytic generalizations are properly about the meanings and motivations of human subjects and that embedded in the body of Freud's own work is a set of general interpretations of ordinary emotions or purposive actions, such as the oedipal complex, penis envy, and the defense mechanisms of resistance, repression, projection, displacement, dissociation, and so forth, that comprise a rival theory to the metapsychology.

In the clinical theory, the "causes" of human behavior are not, as they are in the metapsychology, impersonal forces and mechanisms entirely distinct from the motivations they are used to explain. Rather, from the perspective of the clinical theory, the "causes" of behavior are to be found in what Freud calls "unconscious purposes"— that is, latent hopes, fears, jealousies, loves, hates, and ambitions—that are not all that different in kind from ordinary conscious reasons for action. Advocates of the clinical theory believe that Freud's major contribution to psychology lies in his general interpretations, which constitute a language of self-recognition of practical use to analyst and patient in uncovering and understanding the disavowed aims of the self.[17]

Clinical theorists are willing to recognize the importance of the metapsychology for Freud's personal understanding of himself as a scientist, but they dismiss it as marginal to his clinical findings and thus as of minimal importance for the *real* substance of his work. Moreover, the clinical theorists attack the scientific validity of the metapsychology on the grounds that it was not clinically derived but was instead artificially constructed in conformity with certain outdated notions in late nineteenth-century philosophy of science and then superimposed on the clinical data. To the clinical theorists, the metapsychology's natural-science mode of discourse is neither appropriate to the unique human subject matter of clinical investigation nor testable by the specific methods of psychoanalysis.[18] At best, champions of the clinical theory argue, the metapsychology consists of a set

16. Among the leading advocates of interpreting Freud primarily through his clinical work are Gill (1976), Habermas (1971), Home (1966), Klein (1976), and Schafer (1976, 1983).

17. Freud himself recognized that because of the unique nature of the psychoanalytic enterprise, whose subject-matter "is the mental processes of human beings," which can be studied only in human beings (*SE* 20 [1926]:254), it is essential that "our theories . . . be understood by our patients" (*SE* 20 [1926]:195).

18. As I shall point out in Appendix A and later, this is not actually the case.

of clumsy metaphors (such as Freud's energetics and topography and structuralism) that masquerade as scientific generalizations and attempt, but
fail, to get at the dynamic, powerful, and subterranean nature of unconscious beliefs and desires.

A DIALECTICAL ALTERNATIVE

Although recent interpreters of Freud divide over whether the metapsychology or the clinical theory most adequately captures the essence of
psychoanalysis, it seems obvious that Freud's work defies any such di-
chotomous attempt at containment. Those who adopt the natural-scientific
model as definitive fail to do justice to the numerous ways in which Freud
deviates from the metapsychology on issues of central importance to
psychoanalysis.

For example, as George Klein (1976) brings out, Freud radically rein-
terprets "sexuality" to include not only a wide variety of distinctive bodily
sensations but also the *meanings* associated with them. Framed in terms
close to actual experience, Freud's revolutionary discoveries regarding sexuality are largely outside the metapsychology's drive-discharge theory,
which takes orgasmic tension reduction as paradigmatic. Likewise, Freud's
thoughts on various issues of moral psychology involving object relations,
such as narcissism, object love, and conscience formation, and his views
pertaining to the psychology of religion and aesthetics are not expressed in
terms that fit the ideal type of the metapsychology.

On the other hand, certain aspects of human mental functioning simply
cannot be subsumed within the confines of the clinical theory. Some mental
phenomena, such as the workings of primary process and of primal sexual
and aggressive urges and the intrapsychic functioning of the defense mechanisms, are in fact more usefully conceptualized in terms of drives and
"forces," displaceable "energies," repressions, "blocks," and hidden causal
connections than in terms of "meanings." To dismiss the metapsychology,
as do advocates of the clinical theory, is to run the danger of disregarding
many of the essential truths about human behavior that Freud discovered
and couched in the admittedly archaic language of his abstract general
theory.

Ricoeur is thus right in insisting, over against those hermeneuticists and
clinical theorists who scorn the metapsychology (e.g., Habermas, Klein,
and Schafer), that though imperfect, Freud's metatheory nevertheless "preserves something essential" (Ricoeur 1981, p. 261) and that its economic,
structuralist (id, ego, superego), and topographic (conscious, precon-

scious, unconscious) metaphors, while admittedly flawed, embody notions of the psyche that must be included in any adequate representation of psychoanalytic facts.

In contrast to those clinically oriented theorists who wish to restrict psychoanalysis to the interpretation of meanings and motivations and who consequently regard the task of theory as "limited to restoring the integral, unmutilated and unfalsified text" (ibid., p. 260)—a task with respect to which they view the metapsychology as wholly irrelevant—Ricoeur correctly argues that the reality of analytic praxis calls for a theory in which the psyche is represented not only "as a text to be interpreted" but also as a "system of forces" (ibid., p. 258). Ricoeur perceives that what the metapsychology necessarily attempts is a theoretical model that accounts for the power of indestructible primal desires and of the "mechanisms" of primary process and defense "that distort the text"—that is, resistance, repression, compromise, displacement, and so forth (ibid., p. 260). What the metapsychology provides is a systematic way of thinking about unconscious processes that dispossess the immediate certitude of consciousness: "The Freudian metapsychology [is] . . . an adventure of reflection; the dispossession of consciousness is its path . . . It is a wounded Cogito that results from this adventure . . . a Cogito that sees its original truth only in and through the avowal of the inadequacy, illusion, and lying of actual consciousness" (Ricoeur 1970; p. 439). From the standpoint of the metapsychology, I am forced to acknowledge the possibility that I am deceived in every statement I make about myself.

For Ricoeur, the flaw in Freud's metapsychology lies not so much in the attempt to go beyond clinical narrative or even in its content as in the fact that its economic and mechanistic metaphors are not adequate to the phenomenology or to the symbolic communication that takes place in analytic practice as well as in human communication and interaction generally. The metatheory does not succeed in "codifying and integrating into a single unified structure meaning and force, textual interpretation, and the handling of resistances" (Ricoeur 1981, p. 259). Ricoeur realizes that this is no easy task and that the integrating philosophical perspective needed for such work, if there is one, is not yet within our reach (1970, p. 341); but he is critical of Freud's metapsychology because its relentless archaeological vision does not allow for a sufficiently teleological account of human behavior (see Ricoeur 1970, bk 3).[19]

19. Ricoeur is much more critical of the metapsychology in his 1981 article "The Question of Proof in Freud's Writings" (1981, pp. 247–73) than in his 1970 book. In the latter he argues that what the metapsychology offers is a text, or "language," which permits talk about

It certainly is the case that Freud did not manage to provide an integrated theory that does justice to the two poles of his thought. On the most substantive level, the two modes of thought represented by the metapsychology and the clinical theory often seem to be ineluctably at odds with each other and to demonstrate a fundamental inconsistency in Freud's work. The metapsychology's deterministic view of the psyche as a thinglike apparatus that virtually "runs by itself" (Freud 1954, p. 129) contrasts with the clinical theory's emphasis on the patient taking increased responsibility for his or her unconscious wishes and actions based on the ability to change and control those subterranean impulses (*SE* 19 [1925]:133–4). The metapsychology's concept of the pleasure principle as a kind of thermostat that constantly regulates every mental act in terms of its probable pleasurable or unpleasurable effects (*SE* 14 [1915]:120) stands in opposition to the clinical theory's understanding of the ego's capacity to "suspend" or "renounce" the quest for pleasure in disinterested pursuit of the truth (*SE* 11 [1910]:165). The apparent egoism of a psychic organism motivated exclusively by drives that ultimately aim only at their own satisfaction through discharge (*SE* 14 [1915]:122–3) clashes with Freud's clinical description of "mature" object love as other-regarding (*SE* 11 [1912]:180; 16 [1916–17]: 345).

Moreover, Freud's method of presenting his ideas exacerbates the sense of inherent confusion and contradiction. On most fundamental issues in his theory of personality, Freud moves back and forth between the metapsychological and clinical points of view and between various versions of the metapsychology (economics, dynamics, topography, structuralism) without much cross-reference or attempt at reconciliation.[20] Mechanistic and interpretive explanations appear to vie with each other in ways that seem to produce inconsistencies and ignore philosophical distinctions, to the frustration of many contemporary readers.[21]

---

an economics of force from within the framework of a semantics of desire. Ricoeur here finds a way of bringing together dialectically analytic theory and therapy. By contrast, his 1981 article seems far less profound, in part because it embraces Habermas's view that the metapsychology is "superimposed upon analytic experience" (p. 159).

20. Paradoxically, this confusion is in part what makes Freud's discoveries so brilliant, as Derrida, Ricoeur, Lacan, Kristeva, and Rorty repeatedly remind us. By formulating a theoretical framework that never settles on one description of psychic processes, psychoanalysis offers a way of thinking or, rather, several ways of thinking that invite continuous reinterpretation of the products of human behavior. What I am objecting to in the text is not Freud's contribution to the deconstructive movement, with its radically pluralistic conception of the self, but to the fact that the two poles of Freud's thought seem to land him at times in logical contradictions.

21. Sherwood (1969) correctly notes that Freud does not make a sharp distinction be-

Further, Freud tends to state his metapsychological points as flat, un-qualified assertions that are modified only obliquely by the partial contra-diction of clinical material. Typically, Freud lets his bald metapsychological pronouncements stand until clinical anomalies accumulate to the point of requiring a theoretical adjustment. Then, when he proposes a new general formulation, he usually makes no attempt to reconcile it with prior state-ments. Thus, in later editions of books like *The Interpretation of Dreams*, *The Psychopathology of Everyday Life*, and *Three Essays on the Theory of Sexuality*, new formulations are superimposed on older ones, which are left largely unchanged even when the new and the old clash directly (see Holt 1972 p. 4; 1973, pp. 36–7). Even in his late writings, after he had introduced a new metapsychological paradigm, Freud unselfconsciously reverts here and there to seemingly discarded claims couched in his early mechanistic meta-psychological rhetoric. This makes it very easy to misconstrue Freud and to see him as a dogmatist; for the bald statements of the metapsychology, when isolated, as Freud tends to present them, from the clinical referents and qualifications that modify them, have their own appearance of coher-ence.

In trying to make sense of the Freudian corpus, it has become com-monplace in recent years to locate the reason for the contradictions in the tension between psychoanalytic theory and praxis (see Habermas 1971; Klein 1976; Ricoeur 1981). According to this reading, the reality of clinical analysis forced Freud to produce explanations in terms of intentions or reasons for action that deviated from the mechanistic, causal explanations of the metatheory; yet Freud was too wedded to mechanistic notions to be able to revamp the metapsychology in a way that would bring the clinical material and the organizing ideas of the metatheory closer together.[22]

---

tween causes and motives or reasons for action or between explanations in the physical sciences and explanations of human behavior. This is not because Freud sought to reduce meanings and motivations to neurophysiological events, but because he was aware that the mind is inseparable from the brain and the psyche from the soma and that, consequently, a full explanation of human behavior requires some attention to the influences emanating from these sources. For a defense of the legitimacy of this approach over against that of the separate domain thesis, see Eagle 1980.

22. Freud's difficulty in relating the metapsychology to clinical interpretation was exacer-bated by the intellectual climate in which he worked. Rather than attend to the interrelation between mind and body or the complementarity of mechanistic and interpretive explanations of human behavior, leading philosophers of the era set themselves against any such bridge building. The efforts of Dilthey, Wildebrand, and Rickert, e.g., were devoted to developing a separate methodology for human studies, the intent of which was to make the human sciences exclusively interpretive by divorcing them completely from the type of causal explanation utilized in the natural sciences.

In fact, however, it is a mistake to try to explain the inconsistencies in Freudian theory in terms of a split between theory and practice that views theory as consistently mechanistic and reductionistic, with the only deviation to be found in isolated clinical observations. Freud's metatheory itself mixes mechanistic and teleological explanations, because Freud started off following his esteemed teacher, Franz Brentano, in adopting a dualistic theoretical approach to mental phenomena which involved working back and forth between the evidence of the inner subjective world and the objective world studied by the natural sciences.[23]

The metapsychology thus is far from a pure type. Many of its key concepts, such as "instinct" (*Trieb*) and "dynamic conflict," are hybrids whose elements are derived from both discourse appropriate to the physical sciences and discourse belonging to the humanities. For example, viewed biologically, instinct is defined as a physical-chemical force or energy—that is, as "the demand made upon the mind for work in consequence of the connection with the body" (*SE* 14 [1915]:122). Here the emphasis is on a *drive* mechanistically issuing from a particular somatic *source*.

But instinct also has a teleological dimension for Freud, in which it

23. Brentano's influence on Freud has been seriously underestimated. Freud not only took at least five (unrequired) courses from Brentano, he greatly admired him as a philosopher. In a letter to his friend Silberstein dated 8 Nov. 1874, he wrote that Professor Brentano "is a magnificent man, scholar, and philosopher" (cited and trans. McGrath 1986, pp. 101–2). By 7 Mar. 1875, Freud reported to Silberstein that he and his friend Paneth were beginning to discuss philosophy directly with Brentano (ibid., p. 112). Freud's admiration for Brentano's dialectical skill is evident in his letter to Silberstein of 27 Mar. 1875: "Brentano cannot possibly be disproved before one has heard, studied, and plundered him. So sharp a dialectician demands that one sharpen one's strength on his before measuring oneself against it" (ibid., p. 118).

Under Brentano's influence, Freud even considered doing a double Ph.D. in philosophy and zoology.

Although Gay (1988, pp. 29, 31) dismisses Freud's philosophical explorations with Brentano as a passing phase with little lasting impact, McGrath's (1986, pp. 113–20) illuminating account of Freud's relation to Brentano indicates that it was Brentano's philosophical outlook that led Freud to abandon what he himself later referred to as his "one-sided" materialism and to adopt, in its stead, Brentano's philosophical dualism, with its dual objective and subjective (or phenomenological) approach to understanding reality. By April 1875 Brentano's influence had sufficiently loosened Freud's earlier infatuation with Helmholtzian materialism for him to refer to himself as a "former materialist" (McGrath 1986, p. 98). This suggests that Freud's apparent return to monistic materialism at the outset of the "Project" may have been a short-lived intellectual regression (see ch. 3 below), as he himself may be implying in the well-known letter to Fliess in which he wonders about the state of mind in which he composed the "Project" (1954, p. 134). See Barclay 1964 for some additional ways in which Brentano's psychology appears to have influenced Freud.

stands for a motive[24] directed toward certain "aims" that are knowable only insofar as they are "represented" [*repräsentiert*] by "ideas in the mind," as they are in the clinical setting.[25] According to Freud, "if the instinct did not attach itself to an idea" and thus present itself as a reason for action, "we could know nothing about it" (*SE* 14 [1915]:177).[26] This aspect of the metapsychology's instinct theory is interpretive and teleological rather than mechanistic. Where instincts constitute reasons for action, the *aims* of the instincts are more important than their sources.

When Freud addresses the metapsychology's "dynamic point of view," he also mixes mechanistic with interpretive perspectives. Read mechanistically, the dynamic point of view refers to clashing psychic "forces" or "energies" (*SE* 15 [1916]:67). But it has an interpretive side as well, which refers to "purposeful intentions working concurrently or in mutual opposition" (ibid.).

What Habermas, Klein, and, to some extent, Ricoeur miss is the extent to which Freud integrates clinical insights into his metatheory.[27] They also

24. See Rapaport 1960. Rapaport was the first prominent psychoanalyst to articulate expressly the view that drives in psychoanalytic theory are "motives."

25. It should be noted that Freud's divergent views of instinct as physical-chemical forces and as teleological reasons for action were contemporaneous. His concept of instinct is genuinely a hybrid; the discrepancies are not simply the result of changes in his theory over time.

26. In "The Unconscious" Freud declares that the physical-biological characteristics of the instincts are totally inaccessible to us: "No physiological concept or chemical process can give us any notion of their nature. On the other hand, we know for certain that they have abundant points of contact with conscious mental processes; with the help of a certain amount of work they can be transformed into, or replaced by, conscious mental processes, and all the categories which we employ to describe conscious mental acts, such as ideas, purposes, resolutions and so on, can be applied to them" (*SE* 14 [1915]:168).

27. Ricoeur realizes that psychoanalysis is inevitably a mixed *discourse* and goes to some lengths in his 1970 book to explain how the metapsychology purports to account for motives and thus for the directionality of human psychic behavior. But he is sufficiently impressed by the archaeological aspects of the metatheory to argue that the antithetical movement of "progression" is "unthematized" in psychoanalytic *theory*, even though psychoanalytic practice constantly presupposes it (see Ricoeur 1970, pp. 491–2). Going even further in his 1981 article "The Question of Proof in Freud's Psychoanalytic Writings" he claims that the points in Freud's theory at which human purposefulness appears are inconsistent with the reigning paradigm and that "to be thematized, would require a conceptual framework different from that of its topography and economics" (Ricoeur 1981, p. 259). That "Freud's theoretical model (or models) is (are) inadequate to analytic experience and practice" (ibid.) does not disturb Ricoeur because he supplements Freud's view of human nature with a teleological vision that brings together the "archaeology" of Freud with the "teleology" of Hegel in what he calls a philosophical anthropology that takes seriously a hermeneutics of suspicion and of restoration, both of which are seen as aspects of symbolic communication.

overlook how, as Freud's work gradually evolved, he substantially modified the metapsychology at critical junctures in order to do greater justice to what we know about ourselves and others through ordinary self-reflection and folk psychology.

ON READING FREUD DIALECTICALLY

In interpreting Freud, it is essential to do justice—contra Habermas and Klein—to both sides of his thought, at the level of theory no less than of practice. Ricoeur comes as close as anyone to such a dialectical reading in his 1970 book, but ultimately he fails to appreciate the full extent to which Freud qualifies the metapsychology to make room for what he knows to be true at the level of ordinary experience and clinical practice. For the fact is that the metapsychology makes liberal use of bridge concepts such as "instinct" and "the dynamic point of view" that have clinically interpretable referents that must be appreciated on the level of ordinary folk psychology in order for the metapsychology itself to be properly understood. With these bridge concepts, Freud was struggling to do justice to both non-teleological and teleological explanations of human mental life that we have yet to reach consensus about how to combine theoretically.

Freud himself realized that a dialectical reading from the different points of view he utilized is the best approach to understanding psychoanalytic theory. Noting the complexity of the psychic phenomena under investigation in his metatheory, he suggested that the reader, like the investigator, must juggle multiple points of view that have yet to be pulled together into a coherent theory:

> The extraordinary intricacy of all the factors to be taken into consideration leaves only one way of presenting them open to us. We must select first one and then another point of view, and follow it up through the material as long as the application of it seems to yield results. Each separate treatment of the subject will be incomplete in itself, and there cannot fail to be obscurities where it touches upon material that has not yet been treated; but we may hope that a final synthesis will lead to a proper understanding. (*SE* 14 [1915]:157–8)

The clear implication of this passage is that the metapsychology should be taken not as a tightly organized general psychological theory but as a set of perspectives and loosely organized propositions that together form the rough contours of a paradigm of human mental life within which mechanistic and interpretive explanations both find a place.[28] Freud realized that

28. The metapsychology is nowhere presented by Freud as a complete general psychology. This is in part because Freud disliked sweeping generalizations and distrusted theoretical

his metapsychological theory was highly metaphorical and warned against taking literally the physicalistic metaphors with which he started out framing mental life. He wanted his readers to remember that he himself was "in no danger of over-estimating" the value of heuristic metaphors (*SE* 2 [1895]:291). His self-conscious purpose in using metaphors and similes drawn from a wide variety of fields—such as electrical engineering, physics, biology, economics, geology, chemistry, drama, and archeology—was "to throw light from different directions on a highly complicated topic . . . never [before] . . . represented" (ibid.), the elusive and complex dynamics of the unconscious.

In a sense, Freud played with these diverse representations in his metapsychology so as to approximate stereoscopic vision of the invisible and complex phenomena he was trying to describe.[29] Thus, he writes of his notion of the psyche as a microscope or photographic apparatus: "Analogies of this kind are only intended to assist us in our attempt to make the complications of mental functioning intelligible by dissecting the function and assigning its different constituents to different component parts of the

---

systems in psychology. On one occasion toward the end of 1926, he responded to a complex systematization of one part of psychoanalytic theory by observing that "he felt like someone who had hugged the coast all his life and who now watched others sailing out into the open ocean. He wished them well but could not take part in their ventures: 'I am an old hand in the coastal run and I will keep faith with my blue inlets'" (Waelder 1964, p. 56, n. 8). Again, contrasting his own approach with that of "system builders" like Jung and Adler, he observed in a 1917 letter to Lou Andreas-Salome: "You have observed how I work, step by step, without the inner need for completion, continually under the pressure of the problems immediately on hand and taking infinite pains not to be diverted from the path" (in E. Freud 1975, p. 319. See also *ibid.*, p. 10).

Freud was also acutely aware of what he repeatedly refers to as the "gaps and uncertainties" of his general theoretical perspective (*SE* 22 [1933]:6). In 1909, he wrote to Putnam: "You are quite right in finding that our explanations are unsystematic and full of gaps. Actually our body of knowledge still is incomplete and as a whole is only in the process of becoming" (letter 12, in Hale 1971, p. 90). In 1919, he (*SE* 17 [1919]:159) reminded his audience: "As you know, we have never prided ourselves on the completeness and finality of our knowledge and capacity." His general attitude toward the incompleteness of theory and the necessity for a plurality of unsynthesized points of view within theory is part of the epistemological orientation expressed in the case history of "Little Hans": "All knowledge is patchwork, and . . . each step forward leaves an unsolved residue behind" (*SE* 10 [1909]:100).

29. Freud wrote: "In psychology we can only describe things by the help of analogies [*Vergleichungen*]. There is nothing peculiar in this; it is the case elsewhere as well. But we have constantly to keep changing these analogies, for none of them lasts us long enough" (*SE* 20 [1926]:195). In one of his late observations about theory, Freud wrote that "if we wish to do justice" to the "elusive domain of the psychic, we must not seek to render it through linear contours, as in drawing or in primitive painting, but rather through blurred fields of color, as in modern painting" (*GW* 15 [1933]:85–6).

apparatus . . . *We are justified, in my view, in giving free reign to our specula-tions so long as we retain the coolness of our judgement and do not mistake the scaffolding for the building*" (*SE* 5 [1900]:536, emphasis added).

Because Freud recognized clearly that his metapsychological poetics bore "only a very limited resemblance to [his] . . . subject [matter]," he was not afraid to subvert his own physicalistic metaphors by introducing compet-ing imagery, such as his frequent depiction of the mind as a set of political groupings and as a city built on ancient foundations (see, e.g., *SE* 2 [1893–5]:139; 17 [1917]:143; 21 [1930]:69–71; 22 [1932]:221; 23 [1940]: 173; 23 [1937]: 259–60). Even in the metapsychology itself, he mixed his metaphors: topography clashes with energetics, the biology of instincts with the physics of a closed system of forces. Indeed, Freud brazenly admit-ted that his descriptive devices were "incompatible with one another" (*SE* 2 [1893–5]:291). What interested him was the heuristic usefulness of various metaphorical trappings in illuminating previously unknown and, in some respects, unknowable properties of the mind;[30] and what he requires his readers to do is to look beneath these metaphorical trappings to his reliably dialectical and dynamic conception of mental activity.[31]

As for the important question of what these metaphors are trying to get at, the answer cannot be given either globally or in the abstract. Because the metapsychology is more a set of perspectives than a systematic theory, its propositions refer to three completely different kinds of phenomena: in part to *noninterpretable mental processes* like condensation and displacement in dream work, but also to *interpretable mental states* like ego-alien uncon-

30. Freud points to the unknowability of the unconscious in a well-known footnote in *Interpretation:* "There is at least one spot in every dream at which it is unplumbable—a navel, as it were, that is its point of contact with the unknown" (*SE* 4 [1900]:111). See also *SE* 4 (1900):525.

31. Freud always situated theory in relation to the clinical experience from which it derived and to which it refers. Thus he says of one of his earliest metapsychological propositions that it "is provisionally justified by its utility in co-ordinating and explaining a great variety of psychical states" (*SE* 3 [1894]:61; see also *SE* 7 [1905]:27; 19 [1924]:149). His well-known definition of psychoanalysis similarly situates theory in relation to clinical procedures and therapy: "Psycho-Analysis is the name (1) of a procedure for the investigation of mental processes which are almost inaccessible in any other way, (2) of a method (based upon that investigation) for the treatment of neurotic disorders and (3) of a collection of psychological information obtained along those lines, which is gradually being accumulated into a new scientific discipline" (*SE* 18 [1922]:235). Accordingly, the metatheory's adequacy is to be tested against its clinical usefulness—that is, whether it "enables us to see from another angle what we already know, to group it differently and to describe it more convincingly" (*CP* 2 [1914]:250). Freud then goes on to contrast "the greyness of theory" with "the ever-green realm of observation" (ibid.).

scious wishes and occasionally to *neurophysiological and biological phenomena* (i.e., to brain anatomy and biological instincts). What the metapsychology does primarily is to provide a language for thinking about the noninterpretable workings of the mind—for example, the primal unconscious urges that underlie meaning, the ego's defense mechanisms and the nature of intrapsychic conflict, the psychic function of dreams and neurotic symptoms, the sources of ego defects, and the laws that the unconscious follows in dream work and symptom formation (e.g., in the phenomena of displacement, condensation, and secondary elaboration). The metapsychology also provides a metaphorical way of conceptualizing interpretable unconscious motives that are commonly experienced subjectively as similar to alien forces and energies (although they may not continue to be experienced in this way once they are acknowledged by the conscious mind). Less frequently, the metapsychology links the psyche to the soma, on the basis of either neurophysiological or biological assumptions that attempt to deal with the ineluctable fact that the human mind is influenced in some way by neurobiological conditions.[32] Because these three different metapsychological referents must be identified and coordinated by the reader, the meaning of the propositions that Freud couches in the language of the metapsychology can be interpreted only in their complex textual contexts.[33]

The chief function of the metapsychology is to help us to understand psychic phenomena that become available to consciousness in the clinical context.[34] Consciousness is both the starting point and the end point of

32. For a discussion of Freud's ambiguous stand on the mind–body problem, see Rubinstein 1965. A new solution to this centuries-old problem appears to be emerging from the kind of multidisciplinary work that Eric Kandel is pursuing, which involves cognitive psychology, psychoanalysis, and neurobiology. On the basis of empirical research with the sea snail *Aplysia*, Kandel (1983, p. 1277) argues that mentation is necessary to account for behavior not only in humans but also in much simpler forms of life. His work in cell and molecular biology thus expands our vision by allowing us to perceive previously unanticipated interrelations between biological and psychological phenomena in which the irreducibility of internal mental processes is acknowledged alongside study of the cellular and molecular mechanisms that in various combinations underlie them.

33. Freud considered it one of the advantages of psychoanalytic theory that it attempts to be comprehensive in its treatment of the various factors that affect human behavior. He writes: "We have thus been able to find a place in our structure for the most various and contradictory findings of earlier writers, thanks to the novelty of our theory . . ., which combines them, as it were, into a higher unity. Some of those findings we have put to other uses, but we have wholly rejected only a few. Nevertheless our edifice is still uncompleted" (*SE* 5 [1900]:592). With this, neurobiologist Kandel agrees (1983, p. 1282).

34. A common problem with books on Freud by intellectual historians stems from the

metapsychological inquiry. Hence, the question of how we arrive at knowledge of the unconscious is answered by Freud thus: "It is of course only as something conscious that we know it"; but then he adds "after it has undergone transformation [*Umsetzung*] or translation [*Übersetzung*] into something conscious" (*SE* 14 [1915]:166; *GW* 10:264; see also Ricoeur 1970). The aim of the metapsychology to account for the transformation or translation of the unconscious into the conscious cannot but dislocate our ordinary sense of the trustworthiness or truthfulness of consciousness. As Freud puts it, "The more we seek to win our way to a metapsychological view of mental life, the more we . . . learn to emancipate ourselves from the importance of the symptom of 'being conscious' [*Bewusstheit*]" (*SE* 14 [1915]:193; *GW* 10:291). The net effect of viewing the attribute of being conscious as a symptom is that consciousness (upon which so much traditional philosophy rests) ceases to be self-evident, and yet "the attribute of being conscious, which is the only characteristic of psychic processes that is directly present to us," must in some sense still be relied on.[35]

The coherence of Freud's thought, such as it is, is to be found, then, neither in the metapsychology nor in the clinical theory alone, but in the dynamic, conflictual theory of personality that Freud constructs by qualifying these perspectives, one with the other. This is why interpretations of psychoanalysis that are based on one or the other polar theory tend to go seriously astray and distort essential Freudian doctrines. However, if one avoids the quite natural tendency to approach all Freud's work with preconceptions derived from a preference for one or the other of these seemingly clear-cut interpretive schemes, it is possible to discover in Freud's writings a dynamic, comprehensive view of human nature that leaves neither the clinical nor the metapsychological perspectives out of account.

The trick to reading Freud is to find that formulation of an issue that is in greatest harmony with everything Freud says about it from all the various points of view he adopts, giving due attention to the evolution of his theory

---

historian's tendency to place him primarily in the context of the cultural development of ideas rather than in the clinical context. Frank Sulloway's thesis (1979) that Freud's development is better understood in the context of Darwinian evolutionary biology than on the basis of his need to order clinical data is a case in point. For discussion, see Gedo's (1986; pp. 246–7) criticism of Sulloway.

35. Ricoeur (1970, pp. 137–42) uses Freud's distinction between primal repression (*Urverdrängung*) and secondary repression, or repression proper (*eigentliche*), to make the important point that by virtue of our inability to go behind primal repression, we are always in the epistemological condition of not knowing. "Primary repression means that we are always in the mediate, in the already expressed, the already said," Ricoeur writes (ibid., pp. 140–1).

over time. Focusing on Freud's moral thought is particularly helpful in this hermeneutical endeavor, because the logical interdependence of the various elements that constitute his moral theory makes it possible to test the accuracy of a particular interpretation not only against the details of the relevant texts but also for its coherence with logically related doctrines. Thus, for example, what Freud appears to hold about object love can be tested for its consistency with what he maintains about the related issues of hedonism and narcissism. This is congruent with Rawls's notion of reflective equilibrium. The idea is to find the closest fit between an emerging interpretation of Freud's views on a particular topic and the evolving structure of his thought as a whole by working back and forth between the two. Fortunately, as we shall see in exploring Freud's writings on determinism, hedonism, narcissism, object love, moral sentiment, conscience, and practical rationality, the various aspects of his moral psychology, taken together, constitute an internally coherent view of human nature (albeit one that stresses the plurality, multiplicity, incoherence, and conflict of the self) that makes sense of much in his writings that is otherwise baffling.

THE DEVELOPMENT OF FREUD'S THEORY

Although no interpretation of Freud that does not relate the metapsychology to his clinical work is apt to be successful (since it is within this conceptual scheme that Freud first began to order and relate the clinically based phenomena with which psychoanalysis is principally concerned), it is no less important to recognize the chronological changes in his metatheory over time and the way in which these modifications relate to our ordinary self-understanding. These modifications in the original metatheory begin to appear in Freud's earliest metapsychological writings and become increasingly important as his thought matures.

There are three major stages in the evolution of Freud's theory, each marked by a distinct paradigm (Loevinger 1976, pp. 314–95) or model of the mind (Greenberg and Mitchell 1983, pp. 14–20). At each stage Freud moved further away from the mechanistic materialism of his Helmholtzian teachers that found expression in his most abstract early metapsychological speculations.[36]

36. Although Freud was undoubtedly influenced by his Helmholtzian medical school teachers, the importance of this heritage in the evolution of his ideas has been much overplayed, at the expense of his humanistic side, ever since it was elaborated in Bernfeld's work (Bernfeld 1944, pp. 341–2; 1951). As Holt (1967) points out, many of Freud's intellectual heroes (e.g., Goethe and Fechner) were deeply involved in the mechanism–vitalism contro-

The writings of the first stage, from approximately 1883 to 1899, cohere around a passive reflex model of the mind, in which excitations arising endogenously or exogenously are conveyed to the central nervous system, which tries to rid itself of stimulation. The psychoneuroses are thought to be brought about by environmentally induced emotional traumas; hence, this first model is sometimes described as Freud's "trauma paradigm" (see Loevinger 1976, p. 341). There is no explicit drive theory at this stage. Rather, Freud posits various affects that develop in response to sexual toxins and a wide range of environmental stimuli. When a strong emotional reaction is blocked and the mind cannot rid itself of the accumulated tension, the affect remains in a "strangulated state" and operates continuously to fuel neurotic symptoms until it is expressed appropriately. Consequently, the aim of therapy is to bring to consciousness the original experience, along with its affect. When this is done and the affect is discharged, or "abreacted," the symptom is supposed to disappear because the force that has maintained it is extinguished.

The trauma theory collapsed with Freud's discovery that in many cases the alleged traumatic sexual seductions never took place (see Freud 1954, pp. 215–18);[37] but before it did so, Freud toyed with a neurophysiological and neuroanatomical metatheory in the untitled manuscript he sent to his friend Wilhelm Fliess in 1895, later entitled "Project for a Scientific Psychology" by Ernst Kris when it was published posthumously in 1950.

The premise of the "Project" is that mental states have no reality independent of physical causes and are fully reducible to them. The first sentence of the "Project" states that the author's "intention is to furnish a psychology that shall be a natural science: that is, to represent psychical

---

versy, so that he was thoroughly exposed to both sides of the humanist versus materialist debate.

Historian McGrath (1986, p. 98) concludes from the Silberstein correspondence and other evidence regarding his university years that Freud's materialist phase was confined to his first year and a half at the University of Vienna. He notes, for example, that Freud's plan to spend the winter semester of 1875–76 in Berlin taking courses from Emil du Bois-Reymond, Helmholtz and Rudolf Virchow was abandoned after he came under the countervailing influence of Brentano (ibid., p. 102).

37. Jeffrey Masson (1984), of course, has fueled controversy over whether Freud really "discovered" that the seductions had not taken place. But his evidence that Freud abandoned the seduction hypothesis to assuage criticisms of his earlier theory is shaky. The textual evidence upon which Masson relies shows, rather, as one reviewer of Masson's book puts it, "that Freud continued to believe in the importance at times of actual childhood seduction and abuse, as ongoing clinical experience led him to a new thesis about the importance of fantasy" (Allison 1987, p. 365). See also Malcolm 1984; Masson 1984.

processes as quantitatively determinate states of specifiable material parti-cles" (*SE* 1 [1950]:295).

However, even in the "Project" itself, Freud acknowledges that he is unable to achieve this goal because he cannot explain conscious perception in mechanistic terms of antecedent physical conditions and causal laws (Freud 1954, p. 417) or "give a mechanistic explanation of primary de-fence" (ibid., p. 428). Indeed, it can be argued that Freud actually breaks with the materialism of his Helmholtzian teachers in the "Project" by positing a decidedly nonmechanistic "I," capable of noticing signals of displeasure, judging qualitative differences (such as that between reality and fantasy), and taking remedial action.[38]

As early as 1898, Freud declared that of necessity he intended to focus his work solely on psychological rather than neurophysiological explana-tions of behavior[39]—that is, on mental-state explanations couched in terms of desires and beliefs, conscious and unconscious, of human agents.[40]

38. Holt argues similarly that the "Project" posits an observing ego as "a prime mover, the willer and ultimate knower, and thus a vitalistic homunculus with some degree of autonomy" (1965, pp. 99–100).

39. In a letter to Fliess dated 22 Sept. 1898, Freud writes: "I . . . have no desire at all to leave the psychology hanging in the air with no organic basis. But, beyond a feeling of conviction [that there must be such a basis], I have nothing, either theoretical or therapeutic, to work on, and so I must behave as if I were confronted by psychological factors only" (1954, p. 264).

In later writings, Freud also periodically renounced any claims about the neurophysi-ological substructure of psychoanalysis. For example, in the Preface to the third edition of *Three Essays* (1914) he declared: "I must . . . emphasize that the present work is characterized not only by being completely based upon psychoanalytic research, but also by being deliber-ately independent of the findings of biology" (*SE* 7 [1914]:131). See also *SE* 1(1893):170; 5 (1900):536; 14 (1915):168, 174–5.

40. It should be noted that in these passages about the predominantly psychological focus of psychoanalytic theory, Freud indicates only that mental-state explanations are to be consid-ered as *provisionally* independent of neurophysiological happenings. The psychoanalyst is justi-fied in treating mental-state explanations as sufficiently explanatory for the purposes of psy-choanalysis, while neurologists continue to investigate how far chemical-physical factors are capable of explaining psychological phenomena. (See also *SE* 11 [1910]:217.)

But if Freud's case for the provisional independence of psychological explanations does not preempt the neurophysiological sciences, neither does it anticipate their eventual complete success in explaining all mental life. In a number of places, Freud indicates that it is an open question as to how far neurophysiology will be able to go in explaining mental states (see, e.g., *SE* 14 [1915]:174). Moreover, his own neurological and anatomical statements generally refer to broad antecedent conditions that underlie or parallel, but do not necessarily control, the specific reasons and motives involved in an agent's doing what he or she does. Thus they do not imply materialism.

After the "Project," the absence of unambiguous textual support for Freud's putative

Freud's mental-state explanation of the psychoneuroses at this time is that symptoms like Miss Lucy's olfactory sensation of smelling burned pudding are due to an incompatibility of ideas, especially an incompatibility of unconscious ideas with "the dominant mass of ideas constituting the [patient's] ego" (*SE* 2 [1893–5]:116).

The fact that Freud did not consistently live up to this avowed intention of avoiding neurophysiological explanations—that he continued to speak of a vague "dependence" of psychological phenomena on neurophysiological happenings and to lapse sporadically into discourse about the chemical nature of psychic properties[41]—has been taken as lending support to the supposition that he never abandoned the apparently monistic materialism of the "Project."[42] However, Freud generally takes pains in his mature work not to commit himself on the mind–body problem and to insist only that mental life is in some *currently indeterminable* way dependent on neurophysiology. For example, he writes in "The Unconscious":

> This question [of how an idea is influenced by its neurophysiological substrata] . . . is a difficult one because it goes beyond pure psychology and touches on the relations of the mental apparatus to anatomy. We know that in the very roughest sense such relations exist. Research has given irrefutable proof that mental activity is bound up with the function of the brain as it is with no other

commitment to monistic materialism is itself suggestive, for it implies that somewhere along the line Freud abandoned physiological reductionism or came to see that his private speculations on the matter were unsupportable on psychoanalytic grounds and thus irrelevant to *psychoanalytic* theory.

41. See, e.g., *SE* 5 (1900):537–8; 14 (1915):120; 18 (1920):24, 60; 20 (1925):25–6; 23 (1940):195–7.

42. Holt, while acknowledging that Freud's turn from the anatomical-physiological orientation of the "Project" to the more psychological model of *Interpretation* represented a "major turn" in Freud's lifework, has nevertheless argued on the basis of Freud's continued use of physicalistic language that "when Freud replaced the explicitly physicalistic model of the Project with a psychological one, he did so only partially and inconsistently" (1965, p. 94). Others who have noted that Freud repeatedly lapsed into discourse about the chemical nature of psychic energy and the anatomical location of various psychical properties include Kanzer (1973) and Rubinstein (1965).

But, despite these lapses, Freud continued to maintain that psychoanalysis "must keep free of any alien preconceptions of an anatomical, chemical or physiological nature, and work throughout with purely psychological auxiliary hypotheses" (*GW* 11 [1917]:14; trans. Jones 1953, p. 395). It should also be emphasized that Freud's interest in the relationship between the body and the mind is quite different from that of materialism, which assumes that the body and its laws completely determine mental states.

organ. We are taken a step further—we do not know how much—by the discovery of the unequal importance of the different parts of the brain and their special relations to particular parts of the body and to particular mental activities. But every attempt to go on from there . . . has miscarried completely. (*SE*, 14 [1915]:174)[43]

Insofar as Freud hints at a position on the mind–body problem in his mature writings, the general drift of his comments is toward a form of interactionism, in which physiological processes are acknowledged to influence psychological events and vice versa.[44] Freud puts this position succinctly when he states that "the relation between the body and mind (in animals no less than in human beings) is a reciprocal one" (*SE* 7 [1905]:284).[45]

Freud's second period, from approximately 1900 to 1919, was launched by his realization—following the discovery that many allegedly traumatic childhood seductions had not occurred—that fantasies are realities, too—

43. Freud sometimes seems to go further, however, and register a belief that neurophysiology will eventually succeed in fully explaining psychological phenomena. For example, in a passage that is sometimes cited in support of his alleged continued commitment to the materialism of his youth, he writes that "all our provisional ideas in psychology will *presumably* some day be based on an organic substructure" (*SE* 14 [1914]: 78, emphasis added). However, the wording of the passage indicates that it is an open question what the relationship between the mind and the brain will turn out to be and leaves open the possibility that the phenomena of the mind may turn out to have physiological *substrates* or *correlates* without being fully determined by them.

Several recent philosophers of science (e.g., M. Moore 1984, pp. 32–6) argue that Freud's position here on the provisional independence of mental-state explanations is the most reasonable contemporary option, since the issue of whether neurophysiological events can explain mental states fully is not a conceptual issue, as hermeneuticists and clinical theorists usually suppose, but an empirical matter. However, contemporary biologists are now contending that their work is unlikely to diminish interest in mentation or to trivialize it by reduction. Rather, cell and molecular biology appear to offer an alternative to reductionism that allows us to perceive previously unanticipated interrelations between biological and psychological phenomena. See n. 32 above.

44. Although Freud was not systematically reductionistic in the materialistic senses sometimes attributed to him, he did hold that the body and brain influence the mind, including conscious thought and action. This is why he continues to refer to neurophysiological and biological explanations of behavior—rightly so, for the *logical* nonreducibility of explanations in terms of reasons (conscious and unconscious) does not mean that physiological factors, such as body chemistry, may not influence the way people behave.

45. For arguments in defense of Freud's interactional perspective, see Rubinstein 1965 and Holt 1967.

namely, psychic realities.[46] This gave rise to a new interest in the intrapsychic sources of motivation and eventually to the "drive model" that first begins to take shape in the "wish model" presented in chapter 7 of *The Interpretation of Dreams*. With the drive model there is an attempt to be more specific about the most basic human motivations. By contrast with the trauma theory, in which environmental circumstances are determinative, drives and their derivatives are now determinative, and environmental factors contingent (Greenberg and Mitchell 1983; p. 29). *Drive* denotes "the psychical representative [*Repräsentant*] of the stimuli originating from within the organism and reaching the mind, as a measure of the demand made upon the mind for work in consequence of its connection with the body" (*SE* 14 [1915]:122). We do not know drives or instincts as biological entities but only via the ideas or representational aims toward which they are directed ("Every instinct tries to make itself effective by activating ideas that are in keeping with its aims" [*SE* 11 (1910):213]). The mind is still viewed as seeking to rid itself of noxious motivations via action; but there is now a more complex understanding of what prevents this from happening. There are two independent, irreducible groups of drives or motives, identifiable by their representable aims: the sexual instincts and the ego or self-preservative instincts. Although Freud focuses his attention during this middle period primarily on the sexual instincts, their development through the psychosexual stages, and pathological fixation, the concept of independent ego instincts is essential to his account of the forces that oppose sexuality. It is the resistance and repression emanating from the ego that account for the fundamental psychoanalytic portrait of the self-in-conflict that is first clearly articulated during this period.

At its most abstract, the drive metatheory often appears mechanistic in its mode of causal explanation and, as such, incompatible with the clinical theory's method of explaining action in terms of the teleological intelligibility of the agent's own wishes, aims, purposes, and reasons. However, this mechanistic model is philosophically distinct from the materialistic model of the "Project." It does not depend on neurobiological explanations, since the mechanistic forces are conceptualized almost entirely within the mental rather than the physical realm. (Consider, e.g., Freud's treat-

---

46. Freud later confessed: "When . . . I was at last obliged to recognize that these scenes of seduction had never taken place, and that they were only phantasies which my patients had made up . . . , I was for some time completely at a loss." But finally: "I was able to draw the right conclusions from my discovery: namely, that the neurotic symptoms were not related directly to actual events but to wishful phantasies, and that as far as the neurosis was concerned psychical reality was of more importance than material reality" (*SE* 20 [1925]:34).

ment of the defense mechanisms, in which mechanistic explanation is not tied to brain physiology.) Whereas materialism makes the mind a passive reflex apparatus, the mechanistic model envisions a mind that can be active, with forces and processes of its own, and not just something that responds to outside forces. (For example, within the mechanistic mode of thought, an unconscious wish can automatically trigger such dream work as displacement and condensation to produce a pleasurable dream.) Nonetheless, the mind still appears to behave like "a thing" that responds to the push and pull of psychic forces, rather than an actor whose inner desires and goals help to explain the individual's behavior.

However, during this middle period, Freud did not pursue consistently the mechanistic model of mind and the mode of scientific explanation that it presupposes. Even as early as chapter 7 of *The Interpretation of Dreams,* the scope of Freud's mechanistic claims is somewhat ambiguous. At some points, Freud seems to have wanted to limit himself to developing only a *provisional* and *partial* mechanistic theory, one that would be capable of explaining the production of dreams and neurotic symptoms by invoking the most primitive forms of mentation; but elsewhere in this metapsychological chapter he seems to be trying to explain all psychic processes in this way. The fact remains, however, that the metapsychological exploration in *The Interpretation of Dreams* does go primarily to the question of how the mind works when it spontaneously creates dreams and similarly unintended phenomena, as contrasted with motivations for conscious behavior.

After *The Interpretation of Dreams* (e.g., by 1905, when Freud wrote *The Three Essays on the Theory of Sexuality*), Freud's early metapsychological imagery, while still predominantly mechanistic, was not consistently or exclusively so. In the *Three Essays* and in such subsequent early metapsychological works as "Formulations on the Two Principles of Mental Functioning" (*SE* 12 [1911]) Freud appends such biological notions as drive, organism, development, and evolution to his mechanistic metatheory, even when these Darwinian inheritances are clearly at odds with the dominant Newtonian flavor of most of the language and metaphors of his early metapsychological formulations.[47]

In the metapsychological papers of 1915, Freud once again made a stab at working out a complete mechanistic metapsychological theory of the mind; but again the effort floundered, as it had in the "Project," on the

47. For discussion of these competing images, see Yankelovich and Barrett 1970; Rieff 1961, p. 21; and Loewald 1980.

shoals of the phenomena of ordinary consciousness to which he sought to do justice (*SE* 1 [1895]:307), and he ended up publishing only five of the twelve metapsychological papers written at this time.[48] The published papers all dealt primarily with aspects of unconscious mental activity, with the exception of "Mourning and Melancholia" (*SE* 14 [1917]:237).[49] The seven papers that he destroyed or did not complete pertained to consciousness, obsessional neurosis, transference neurosis, conversion hysteria, anxiety, sublimation, and projection. Although it is a matter of speculation why Freud chose not to disseminate these, it may well be that he found the mechanistic model unequal to the task of explaining self-consciousness and self-directed actions.

In this regard, it is worth noting that Freud seems to have remained ambivalent throughout his second period as to the scope of his mechanistic ambitions, in a way that echoes chapter 7 of *The Interpretation of Dreams*. For even while he was trying to work out an overarching mechanistic metatheory in his metapsychological papers, which he originally intended as a book entitled "Preliminaries to a Metapsychology," he declared that psychoanalysis did not "provide a complete theory of human mentality in general," but only of the unconscious (*SE* 14 [1914]:50). And he wrote to Putnam in 1914 that psychoanalysis "as a science itself is not even half complete" (letter 80, in Hale 1971, p. 171).[50] Throughout the period from 1900 to 1919, when Freud freely employed mechanistic images in his metapsychology, ego instincts, separate from the libido, were postulated *precisely in order to safeguard what we know about ourselves by means of ordinary self-consciousness*. By the time Freud attempted a truly general psychology, in the post-1919 period, he had abandoned his earlier mechanistic paradigm in favor of predominantly biological metaphors of development.

In Freud's late, post-1919 writings, the psyche is pictured much more

48. The published papers were "Instincts" (*SE* 14 [1915]:117–40); "Repression" (*SE* 14 [1915]:146–58); "Unconscious," (*SE* 14 [1915]:166–204); "Metapsychological Supplement" (*SE* 14 [1917]:222–35); and "Mourning and Melancholia" (*SE* 14 [1917]:243–58).

49. This exception is closer to clinical experience than the other papers that were published, in that it focuses primarily on self–object relations. In it, Freud began to break with the mechanistic model and shift to a more descriptive, object-relations orientation.

50. Freud does not even claim to possess a complete theory of sexuality (*SE* 7 [1905]:130), much less a complete theory of the mind (see *SE* 14 [1914]:50 and n. 32). Although Freud moves toward a general psychology in his late writings in his efforts to account for the ego and superego, he continues to indicate that his efforts in this direction fall short of a complete theory. At the outset of *New Introductory Lectures*, e.g., he declares that "it has been my chief aim to make no sacrifice to an appearance of being simple, complete or rounded-off, not to disguise problems and not to deny the existence of gaps and uncertainties" (*SE* 22 [1933]: 6).

consistently as an organism and as a developing self in interaction with its environment (see Loewald 1980; Bibring 1941).[51] This new paradigm reflects radically different assumptions in Freud's view of human nature from those pertaining in the original, heavily mechanistic metapsychology. Whereas in the 1900–19 period, *drive* denotes the intrusion of varying quantities of psychic energy derived from somatic sources into the mind, which in turn is conceived as functioning mechanically to reduce tension by ridding itself of noxious input via action, the new paradigm begins with the introduction of a novel theory of the instincts that identifies them chiefly in terms of their long-range aims. The ego and superego are now defined by their structural-functional properties (such as perception, reasoning, control over motility, self-observation, self-criticism, and intentionality) that cannot be explained as drive derivatives. Anxiety, which in the earlier mechanistic model had been attributed to repression and the buildup of instinctual drives, is now seen as originating in the ego's or self's awareness of danger.

As Freud gradually articulated an alternative, nonmechanistic metatheory in his late writings, he came to accept the facts of ordinary consciousness and intentionality as irreducible aspects of human nature which he did not attempt to explain away. As he put it in *An Outline of Psycho-Analysis,* psychoanalysis starts from the *"fact without parallel, which defies all explanation or description—the fact of consciousness"* (*SE* 23 [1940]:157, emphasis added).[52] This makes the metatheory dependent on clinically interpretable meanings, which now have a rock-bottom, incorrigible status. Of course, psychoanalysis moves beyond what is available through ordinary introspection, but not without first postulating a conscious "I" with uniquely human capacities for self-reflection as a necessary epistemological condition of the possibility of psychoanalytic knowledge. "[T]he property of being conscious" is "in the last resort our one beacon-light in the darkness of depth-psychology" (*SE* 19 [1923]:18). Yet, what we think is self-reflective is always already a disguise, so it becomes necessary to move beyond consciousness into the obscure depths of the psyche. This is why the metatheory is essential.

The unity and coherence of Freud's thought is to be found, then, by

51. A number of secondary interpreters have noted the radical change in the model employed by Freud in the post-1919 period. See, e.g., Guntrip 1973; Loevinger 1976; Greenberg and Mitchell 1983.

52. Elsewhere, Freud maintains that "the attribute of being conscious . . . forms the point of departure for all our investigations" (*SE* 14 [1915]:172)—but does not emphasize the given, inexplicable nature of this fact. See also *SE* 14 (1915):166; 19 (1923):19.

relating the metapsychology to clinical findings *in the context of Freud's ever changing theoretical views*. How this interpretive approach works in practice and its implications for moral psychology are illustrated in the chapters that follow. Fortunately, as we shall see, the various elements of Freud's moral psychology—that is, his views on determinism, responsibility, hedonism, narcissism, object love, altruism, and moral obligation—dovetail with an evolving, internally coherent view of human nature that undergirds what he holds about the issues in normative ethics, which will be examined in the final sections of the book.

Chapter 3
The Determinism–Free Will Problem

Nothing in the mind is arbitrary or
undetermined.

—Freud

Analysis . . . set[s] out . . . to give the
patient's ego *freedom* to decide one way or
the other.

—Freud

Everyone with a passing familiarity with the subject is aware of the
"deterministic" Freud—the Freud who speaks of "the strict determination
of mental events" (*SE* 18 [1923]:238) and of "the illusion of Free Will" (*SE*
17 [1919]:236; see also *SE* 15 [1916–17]:106). Freud is famous for saying
that "psycho-analysts are marked by a particularly strict belief in the determination of mental life" (*SE* 11 [1910]:38) and that the "belief in psychic
freedom and arbitrariness . . . is unscientific . . . and . . . must give
ground before the claims of a determinism which governs even mental life"
(*GW* 11 [1916–17]:104).[1] According to this Freud, to "breach . . . the
determinism of natural events at . . . [any] single point" is to throw "overboard the whole *Weltanschauung* of science" (*SE* 15 [1916–17]:28).

Such statements, along with Freud's thoroughgoing explorations of the
extent to which conscious behavior is unconsciously controlled, lend *prima
facie* support to the widespread belief that psychoanalysis is committed to
the doctrine of universal or complete determinism. This metaphysical doctrine holds that all human action is causally necessitated by antecedent
conditions and universal, invariant laws of nature that govern all things
nonpurposively. Since determinism in this sense, when applied to human
actions, seems to imply that an agent could not have acted other than as he
did, it is commonly thought to rule out any freedom of choice or moral

1. This last quotation has been retranslated to reflect the fact that *Willkürlichkeit* here
means "arbitrariness," not "free will," as the *SE* supposes (see *GW* 11 [1916–17]:104 and
compare *SE* 15 [1916–17]:106).

responsibility. Freud's critics almost invariably attribute universal determinism in this sense, along with its concomitant anti-freedom and anti-responsibility, to him (see, e.g., Kohut 1977, p. 244; Morse 1982, p. 987; Sulloway 1979, pp. 94–7; Yankelovich and Barrett 1970, pp. 63, 217, 282; Allport 1961, pp. 561–2). But even many of his devotees and defenders agree that Freud postulated a "psychic determinism . . . as strict as physical determinism" (Arlow and Brenner 1964, p. 7; see also E. Jones 1953, pp. 365–6).[2]

Indeed, in both psychological and philosophical circles, it is now commonplace to cite psychoanalysis as providing important empirical evidence for determinism that was unavailable to earlier proponents of the doctrine such as Hobbes and Hume. Before Freud, the natural sciences had searched for invariant laws governing the events of the external world, but the mind had been exempt. With Freud, the quest for causes and determinants was turned on the human psyche itself, with impressive results. Thus, for example, in several articles that are standard fare in introductory philosophy anthologies, Hospers has argued that the developments in the science of the mind brought about by psychoanalysis virtually prove "psychic determinism"—by which he means that there is *no* freedom of choice (see Hospers, 1950 and 1961b; repr. in Sellars and Hospers 1952, pp. 560–75; Feinberg 1965, pp. 272–82; P. Taylor 1967). Similarly, Brenner's standard introduction to psychoanalysis asserts that determinism is one of the "fundamental hypotheses" of psychoanalysis and that it has been "abundantly confirmed" (1957, p. 2).[3]

Most discussions of Freud's psychic determinism tend to overlook the fact that there are a variety of different determinist positions, some of which allow for a type or degree of freedom and responsibility denied by forms of universal or complete determinism modeled after the physical sciences, though they also hold that everything that happens is causally determined.[4]

2. Other interpreters who attribute complete or universal determinism to Freud include Browning (1987); Hospers (1950, 1961b); Jahoda (1977, p. 15); McAllister (1956, p. 314); Sulloway (1979); Vergote (1958, p. 254); and Weiss (1968, p. 59).

3. It should be noted that in fact there is no way of empirically or logically *proving* the universality of causation. All that can be done *empirically* is to show single instances of causation. Likewise, determinism cannot be established *logically*, because change might reasonably be thought to be caused by random events rather than the operation of generalized rules.

4. A range of philosophical positions go under the rubric of "determinism." Sometimes the term is used to express the view that no change ever occurs without some cause (see B. Blanshard 1961, in Hook 1961, p. 19). This view allows for different kinds of causes and somewhat flexible explanatory principles, since "cause" can include "motives" and "final causes," as well as "natural causes" or conditions that are everywhere accompanied by some invariable change. "Determinism" is also used more narrowly, however, to mean that "for

Because of this lack of precision, many treatments of Freud leave unclear whether, in a particular instance, what is being attributed to him is the extreme, or "hard," determinist doctrine that human beings are not "free" in any of the senses essential for moral responsibility or some "softer" version of determinism that at least attempts to save some place for moral action.[5]

Nevertheless, quite a few prominent interpreters of Freud—among them Sulloway (1979, pp. 94–7), Yankelovich and Barrett (1970, pp. 63, 217, 282), Allport (1961, pp. 561–2), Hospers (1950, 1961b), and Browning (1987, pp. 40–1)—make it obvious that they see him as a hard determinist. They specifically contend that if the psychoanalytic theory of determinism is true, none of us is ultimately responsible for our conduct, and that therefore moral judgments cannot be passed appropriately on anyone. In this view, Freudian determinism would make "any moral characterization of . . . behavior . . . meaningless" (Daley 1971, p. 179). Indeed, some who take this perspective believe that Freud has so demonstrated the extent to which our actions are unconsciously determined that his work bears important responsibility for "undermining . . . will and decision in our whole age" (May 1969, p. 194). Since hard determinism, if true, would undermine the very possibility of our being moral, and since much of the secondary literature assumes that Freud's psychic determinism is precisely of this kind and so incompatible with morality, it is essential to ascertain what Freud really does claim regarding determinism and free will.

---

everything that ever happens, there are conditions such that given them, nothing else could happen" (R. Taylor 1967, 2:359). Further confusion occurs because there are varying definitions of "event" and "caused" and also several ways of conceiving of the alleged connections and interdependencies between events and causes. (For a short comparison of the various types of determinism, see R. Taylor 1967.)

Even universal, or metaphysical, determinism, which holds that everything that happens is determined by antecedent causes, can be broken down into "hard determinism" and "soft determinism" (see James 1969).

5. For ambiguous attributions of determinism to Freud, see the Editor's Introduction to *The Psychopathology of Everyday Life* (*SE* 6 [1901]:xiii–xiv). The theory of hard determinism holds that *everything that happens is determined by antecedent causes*. It also holds some specific theory, T, about the causation of human action—a theory which, if true, rules out there being any moral responsibility. Soft determinism also holds that *everything that happens is determined by antecedent causes* but denies that this rules out moral responsibility. One form of soft determinism identifies a kind of determinism governing mental states that it sees as compatible with freedom and responsibility, while the other form proposes a restrictive definition of "freedom" that preserves a semblance of its ordinary meaning, while holding that everything that happens is strictly determined by antecedent causes such that it could not be other than it is.

THE AMBIGUITY OF FREUD'S TREATMENT

Given the *Sturm und Drang* that has arisen around the determinism issue, it is surprising to find how little Freud actually discusses the matter and how ambiguous he is in what he does say. In the entire twenty-three volumes of the *Standard Edition,* there are only eight references to "determinism," and most of these are only very brief (see Freud 1980, 2:117). Freud's most extended discussion appears early on, in *The Psychopathology of Everyday Life* (1901). After 1919, he appears to drop the issue from active consideration.[6] Despite the forcefulness of some of his determinist-sounding statements about "psychic determinism" (*psychischer Determinismus*) and "free will" (*freier Wille*) and the determinist implications of the mechanistic aspects of his metapsychology, Freud never makes as clear a commitment to determinism in the hard sense that rules out there being any responsibility as most secondary interpreters seem to think.

The parts of Freud's writings that suggest some level of causal determination[7] in fact coexist with his explicit view that one of the chief goals of psychoanalysis is to increase the patient's "freedom" (*Freiheit*), "autonomy" (*Selbständigkeit*), and "initiative" (*Initiative*) (see *GW* 13 [1922]: 279–280, n. 1; 8 [1912]: 372; 13 [1921]:126). Thus, the aim of psychoanalysis is to "free" (*befreien*) the patient from intrapsychic "chains" (*die Fesseln*) (*GW* 13 [1922]:228; *CP* 5 [1922]: 128), which normally increases the patient's "self-control" (*Selbstbeherrschung*) (*GW* 8 [1912]:385; *CP* 2 [1912]:329) and gives "the patient's ego *freedom* (FREIHEIT) to decide one way or the other" between conflicting motives (*GW* 13 [1923]; *SE* 19 [1923]: 50, n. 1). For Freud, it is the mark of a relatively healthy ego to be able to deliberate and exercise self-control and willpower in choosing and pursuing goals.

At the very least, then, there is a paradox that deserves further consideration: for, while the drift of Freud's determinist-sounding statements appears to be that *all* behavior is causally determined in a sense that rules out there being any freedom or moral responsibility, the goal of therapy is to augment the patient's decision-making and action-taking freedom.

Part of the difficulty in pinning down Freud's position stems from the

---

6. Most of Freud's post-1919 references to psychic determinism appear in autobiographical statements pertaining to his earlier views (see, e.g., *SE* 18 [1923]:238). The only exception is the following, ambiguous statement that "the behaviour of human beings shows differences, which ethics, disregarding the fact that such differences are determined, classifies as 'good' and 'bad'" (*SE* 21 [1930]:111).

7. See, e.g., *SE* 6 (1901):253–4; 15 (1916–17):28; and Weiss 1968, p. 59.

fact that he nowhere clearly defines what he means by the terms "psychic determinism" (*psychischer Determinismus*), "psychic freedom" (*psychische Freiheit*), and "free will" (*freier Wille*).[8] As will be discussed at length below, the language that Freud uses can as easily be read to mean that mental events are not totally arbitrary or capricious as to claim that they are governed so strictly by antecedent conditions and mental laws that the human subject is, like an inanimate object, passively at the mercy of forces acting within and upon him. The English translation in the *Standard Edition* conceals much of this ambiguity by selecting English words that seem to firmly buttress the presentation of Freud as a scientistic determinist. But examination of the terms used in the original German text, as well as of the context in which the statements are made, makes the matter much less certain.

Perhaps because there is a lack of conclusiveness on determinism in Freud's occasional comments regarding the issue, those seeking to attribute to him the extreme doctrine of hard, universal determinism and its denial of all moral responsibility have often resorted to constructing their argument primarily on inferences drawn from their reading of Freud's general theory (Hospers 1952; Yankelovich and Barrett 1970). This approach is sometimes supplemented by an examination of Freud's cultural milieu, based largely on Bernfeld's intellectual-historical investigations (1944; 1949; 1951), which emphasize the acknowledged Helmholtzian materialistic determinism of Freud's medical school teachers (Iturrate 1977, p. 36; MacIntyre 1958, p. 90; Yankelovich and Barrett 1970, p. 65; E. Jones 1953, pp. 365–6). The strong assertions of the deterministic bent of psychoanalysis that were made by some of Freud's first and closest disciples are also called on to impute strict universal determinism and the denial of freedom of choice to the master (see, e.g., Yankelovich and Barrett 1970, p. 63).

Ernest Jones, for one, is often quoted for his confident declaration that:

> *Freud came from his early training deeply imbued with the belief in the universality of natural law* and with a disbelief in the occurrence of miracles or spontaneous or uncaused acts . . . *He would certainly have subscribed to the . . . words of his [Helmholtzian] teacher Meynert* . . . : "Everything in the world is only appearance and the appearance is not identical with the essence of things; . . . *even the freedom we feel in ourselves is only apparent."* . . . *The apparent freedom is really based on law, therefore on necessity.* (E. Jones 1953, pp. 365–6, emphasis added)

But Jones's statement itself appears to confuse a disbelief in arbitrariness with the belief that things caused by laws could not have been otherwise. Moreover, insofar as it makes the latter view Freud's on the ground that it

8. For Freud's usage of some of these terms, see *GW* 4 (1901):282–3.

was clearly Meynert's, it ascribes the hard version of universal determinism to Freud by hearsay and association. Automatic reliance on this kind of sleight of hand is unconvincing and unwarranted.[9] There is nothing nearly so unequivocal in Freud himself. And significantly, Freud's cultural milieu was not as predominantly Helmholtzian or as rigidly determinist as some interpreters would have us believe.

The original Helmholtzian manifesto, which asserted that all the phenomena of life could be explained materialistically, was issued in 1847 by a small group of physiologists—among them Helmholtz, du Bois-Reymond, Brücke, and Ludwig. By the 1870s, when Freud became associated with Brücke and others originally of this persuasion, there was some question as to the doctrine's continuing vitality even among its original adherents. For example, Cranefield (1966, p. 38) cites evidence from Ludwig's *Lehrbuch* of 1852 showing that this particular Helmholtzian, at least, viewed the mind as retaining "its ability to create thought and to influence the muscles" independently of physiological changes in the nervous system[10]—that is, that the mind was not entirely mechanistically and materialistically determined.[11]

The emphasis on Helmholtzian thought is also faulty in that it misses other, equally important influences on Freud. For example, Freud was an

9. Yankelovich and Barrett, e.g., in arguing that a "cardinal characteristic of Freud's [mental] apparatus . . . is that [it is . . . a] . . . closed system [that] operates in completely deterministic patterns" (1970, p. 63) quote not Freud but Jones: *"Freud never wavered in this attitude [belief in determinism]* . . . He would have endorsed the view of the great anthropologist, Tylor, that the history of mankind is part and parcel of the history of nature; our thoughts, wills and actions accord with laws as definite as those which govern the motion of the waves. Freud believed in the thoroughgoing meaningfulness and determinism of even the apparently most obscure and arbitrary mental phenomena" (1953, p. 366, emphasis added).

Yankelovich and Barrett then go on to assert that, as used by Jones—and as attributed by them, via Jones, to Freud—" 'meaningfulness' and 'determinism' . . . are virtually equivalent terms. A mental phenomenon is meaningful only if it occurs as a result of conditions, is clearly predictable, and would always result from those conditions and objects" (1970, p. 63).

Having thus transitively applied Jones's views of psychic determinism to Freud and psychoanalysis as a whole, thereby making Freud a hard determinist, they then righteously ask: "Why should this be so? Why should it be 'meaningless' for such an event to occur outside such a chain? To assert that determinism is the only 'meaningful' way to grasp human history is pure metaphysics, and not at all a generalization drawn from empirical observation" (ibid.).

10. For further discussion, see Cranefield 1957, 1966; Shakow and Rapaport 1964.

11. Moreover, some of those who, like Freud's teacher Meynert, agreed with Helmholtzians that German medicine should be based on solid, material facts adhered to the German idealist tradition stemming from Kant through Schopenhauer. For a discussion of Meynert's philosophical idealism, see McGrath 1986, pp. 141–8.

avid pupil of Brentano,[12] who was also Husserl's teacher from 1884 to 1886 and thus a progenitor of phenomenology. Brentano stressed the role of intentionality in psychic life.[13] Freud agreed with him that all psychic activity is meaningful—that is, intentional in the sense of being self-involved and object-oriented—and known cognitively only through consciousness.[14] This in itself does not commit Freud (or Brentano, for that matter) one way or the other on the actual determinism issue. But Brentano also held that human beings have "freedom of the will"—that they are able to deliberate and to bring about some of the things they decide and that the

12. For Freud's relationship to Brentano, see ch. 2, n. 23 above. It was with Brentano, a devotee of the English empiricist philosophical tradition, that Freud studied the English philosophers and psychologists, including J. S. Mill, one of whose volumes of collected papers he translated, on Brentano's recommendation. In addition, Brentano and Josef Breuer were close friends, and Breuer was the Brentanos' family physician; so it is likely that Freud was in touch with Brentano through Breuer, with whom he was then working on *Studies on Hysteria* (1893–5). For further discussion of Brentano and Freud, see Rapaport 1960, p. 13; Barclay 1964; and McGrath 1986, pp. 114–15, 118–19, 126–7).

13. What Brentano meant by "descriptive psychology" is very close to what Husserl called phenomenology. Moreover, Husserl himself observed that without Brentano's doctrine of intentionality, "phenomenology could not have come into being at all" (cited in Chisholm 1967, p. 366). The influence of Brentano on both Husserl and Freud may help explain why so many hermeneuticists in the Husserlian tradition (e.g., Ricoeur, Habermas, and Samuel Weber) have been attracted to the writings of Freud. One of the principal claims of hermeneuticist readers of Freud is that psychoanalysis is not unequivocally antithetical to freedom of the will (see esp. Habermas 1971, pp. 214–73; Ricoeur 1966, 1970).

14. The influence of Brentano appears most discernible where Freud discusses the intentionality of psychic acts, psychic representations, and internal object relations (see *SE* 2 [1893–5]:77, 97, 121–4, 157, 271; *SE* 15 [1916–17]:23, 28, 40). In keeping with Brentano's contention that all psychic acts are intentional, he contends that even unconscious mental processes as purposeful.

Summarizing his comparison of the two men, Barclay observes that "both taught that the focal point of psychic activity was the intentional image. Brentano saw the intentional image as the production of perception impressed and guided by not only the external or primary consciousness, but by what he termed secondary consciousness or self-involvement. Freud, utilizing the concept of energy, also distinguished such an object relationship, calling it the cathexis. The cathexis is the result of an object relationship from without the mind and also the focus of a specific quantity of energy producing the particular motivational attraction of the object-image" (1964, p. 32). As Holt puts the last point, "Freud's doctrine . . . [that] psychic energy . . . is directional" (in the sense that it is differentiated in accordance with the object toward which it is directed) makes "psychic energy . . . a teleological concept" (1967, p. 23). On the ego as a teleological concept, see Waelder 1967; Compton 1972, p. 32.

Rapaport further observes that Freud's treatment of the problem of reality testing leads to "an analysis of the 'belief in reality' (*CP* 4 [1917]:146) . . . along Brentano-like lines. . . . This influence pervades the *Papers on Metapsychology*" (1960, p. 13).

incompletely determined character of psychology does not keep it from being a natural science.[15]

The point here is not that these latter views of Brentano's should be imputed to Freud, but rather that Freud was certainly exposed to views on the freedom versus determinism issue that would have counterbalanced the Helmholtzian doctrine that often seems to be presumed to have dominated his theorizing.

Without falsely minimizing the strands of Freud's thought that are mechanistic and that place him partly in the positivist camp, it can be said that Freud's view of human nature also undeniably bears a strong humanistic stamp that derives not only from Brentano but also from the influence of the Bible, the Greek dramatists, and Shakespeare, as well as more immediately from the great German philosophical and Romantic tradition of Kant, Lamarck, Goethe, Hegel, and Schelling.[16] In summarizing this side of Freud's thought, psychologist Robert Holt observes that Freud regarded the person as "both the active master of his own fate and the plaything of his passions . . . , capable of choosing among alternatives . . . [and] of resisting temptations and of governing his own urges, even though at times he is a passive pawn of external pressures and inner impulses" (1973, p. 18).

CHANGES AND TENSIONS IN FREUD'S VIEWS

In trying to come to grips with how Freud applies the determinist thesis (i.e., that everything that happens is determined by causes) to human actions, it is helpful to keep in mind certain orienting points. First, Freud's ideas on the matter were not static. He did not set out to formulate a consistent "doctrine of human nature" or theory about the causation of human action as a philosopher might. To the contrary, he self-consciously sought to keep his theoretical speculations about human nature and action open to continuing revision in light of new clinical evidence.[17] As a conse-

15. See Chisholm 1967.

16. See Rapaport 1960, pp. 11–15, and Sterba 1969 for material on the impact of Freud's humanistic heritage on psychoanalysis.

17. Freud appreciates the role of theory in orienting scientific research but insists that even the most seemingly basic scientific postulates are really hypotheses (*SE* 14 [1914]:77). Psychoanalysis is a "science" for Freud largely because it refuses to solve "the problems of our existence uniformly on the basis of one overriding hypothesis, which, accordingly, leaves no question unanswered" (*SE* 22 [1933]:158). He contrasts this open-ended approach with that of philosophy thus: "Psycho-Analysis is not, like philosophies, a system starting out from a few sharply defined basic concepts, seeking to grasp the whole universe with the help of these. . . . On the contrary, it keeps close to the facts in its field of study, seeks to solve the immediate

quence, Freud developed *several* models of the mind during the course of his long career, and these divergent models suggest changing perspectives on the determinism issue.

During Freud's early neurophysiological period, exemplified by the "Project for a Scientific Psychology" (1895), mechanistic and determinist elements are very much in the ascendant in his thought. The psychological model that replaced Freud's early neurophysiological speculations,[18] the outlines of which were first sketched in chapter 7 of *The Interpretation of Dreams,* is also sometimes seen to imply hard determinism because of its heavy use of mechanistic metaphors—though Freud's enunciation of the freedom-enhancing goal of psychoanalysis during the 1900–19 period indicates that his commitment to determinism at this time is, at the very least, ambiguous. Finally, in the post-1919 period, the evidence strongly suggests that to the extent that Freud's earlier models of the mind might be interpreted in ways that seem to imply hard determinism, his later theory of the ego clearly acknowledges that although the character of the mature or healthy ego is established by causal roots running all the way back to the infantile past, the ego is nevertheless an active entity that has some capacity for freedom of choice within the limits set by innate desires, unconscious defense mechanisms, primary and secondary processes, and the regulatory principles that govern psychic activities.

Second, it should be observed that Freud uses the language of moral freedom and responsibility in his clinical writings throughout his career, so that from the outset there is always some tension in his thought on the determinism issue. For example, in the case of "Miss Lucy," discussed in *Studies on Hysteria* at a time when Freud's faith in the stricter form of determinism was presumably at its height, Freud speaks of his patient's *deliberate* and *intentional act of volition* in suppressing the memory that precipitated her hysterical symptoms and declares that she is morally responsible for this "act of moral cowardice" (*SE* 2 [1893–5]:123).

Likewise, in the papers on psychoanalytic technique written during his middle period, Freud advises psychoanalysts to respect "the *patient's personal freedom* [*der persönlichen Freiheit des Analysierten*] as [much as] is compati-

---

problems of observation, gropes its way forward by the help of experience, is always incomplete and always ready to correct or modify its theories. There is no incongruity (any more than in the case of physics or chemistry) if its most general concepts lack clarity and if its postulates are provisional; it leaves their more precise definition to the results of future work" (*SE* 18 [1923]:253–4).

18. Freud abandoned neurophysiology for psychology in 1898. See his letter to Fliess dated 22 Sept. 1898, in Freud 1954, p. 264.

ble with the . . . restrictions" of psychoanalytic work (*GW* 10 [1912]: 133) and commends the new psychoanalytic therapy to fellow physicians for its success in helping patients regain "self-control" (*Selbstbeherrschung*) (*GW* 8 [1912]:385).[19] In the post-1919 period, when he began to work significantly with ego psychology, Freud expanded on these clinical remarks and went to great lengths to make a place, as a *theoretical* matter, for the ego's freedom of action.

THE ARGUMENT FOR FREUD'S DETERMINISM

The Scientific Postulate Argument

Of the various attempts to make Freud into a hard determinist who would rule out any freedom or responsibility, three emerge as plausible and merit closer consideration, though they all depend primarily on Freud's early writings and fail to account for the numerous statements sounding notes of freedom and responsibility that appear both in Freud's clinical writings and in his late theorizing.

What can be called "the scientific postulate argument" claims that Freud took his doctrine of determinism from the natural sciences, in which the general determinist postulate that everything that happens is determined by antecedent causes is joined with a world view that regards the human subject as the passive instrument of inner and outer forces. The chief textual support for this interpretation is Freud's passing remark, made in the context of an imaginary dialogue with a critic of the psychoanalytic explanation of parapraxes, that "[i]f anyone makes a breach . . . in the determinism of natural events at a single point, it means that he has thrown overboard the whole *Weltanschauung* of science" (*SE* 15 [1916–17]:28).

On the face of it, this statement certainly seems to commit psychoanalysis to a form of metaphysical determinism in which the subject is viewed as a mere object. But such an interpretation becomes less clear on a close reading. Freud is not here addressing the question of whether whatever happens is the only possible outcome of conditions given prior to the event, but the much narrower issue of whether apparently chance occurrences, whether in nature or in the mind, are "worth explaining" (ibid.). This suggests that what Freud may have had in mind here is not metaphysical determinism at all, but "methodological determinism," which

19. As interpreters of Freud have long appreciated (e.g., Kris 1951; Gray 1982), his clinical writings and technical papers often anticipate later changes in or clarifications of theoretical formulations.

holds only that the scientist act "as if" the methodological "postulate" or "working hypothesis" of causal determination is true.[20] Insofar as science establishes definite causes, it restricts the domain of freedom. But science by itself is incapable of proving the truth or falsity of metaphysical determinism.

This alternative reading of the passage, which does not see Freud as here espousing metaphysical determinism, becomes even more persuasive when it is remembered that Freud generally sought to avoid metaphysical statements (Mannoni 1971, p. 82) and that insofar as he did commit himself metaphysically, he tried to avoid dogmatic pronouncement on complex philosophical issues that, as he put it, "solve . . . all the problems . . . and leave . . . no question unanswered" (SE 22 [1933]:158).

Also, Freud frequently underscored the hypothetical nature of the scientist's methodological premises by referring to them as "beliefs" or "presuppositions" (see, e.g., SE 14 [1915]:117; 18 [1923]:238). And it is noteworthy that in summary statements about the implications of psychoanalytic discoveries for the determinism issue, Freud was generally careful to confine himself to saying only that they "*restrict* . . . [the role that can be assigned] the arbitrary factor in psychology" (SE 9 [1906]:105, emphasis added) and that psychoanalytic findings have helped people "appreciate the *extent* of determination in mental life" (SE 6 [1901]:240, emphasis added). He does not claim that his work confirms or proves the truth of universal or metaphysical determinism.

Finally, when Freud discusses what "science" presupposes about determinism, the German word he employs, *Wissenschaft*, has broader connotations than the English word "science." The German word includes the interpretive disciplines in the humanities, such as law and history, alongside the natural sciences that are strictly regulated by invariable natural laws. Thus, when Freud writes that "the universal concatenation of events" is an essential presupposition of the scientific method (SE 15 [1916–17]:28), what he appears chiefly to have in mind is that these events can be made *intelligible*—not that everything is rigidly determined. His is the proclivity not to let chance count as chance but to interpret it. This "hermeneutic compulsion," as Derrida (1984, p. 25) calls it, is grounded in the

20. Freud writes that as long as a hypothesis is useful practically, it may be treated "as if" it were true. Thus he writes: "The . . . earliest . . . [hypotheses] have always been rather rough. 'Open to revision' we can say in such cases. It seems to me unnecessary for me to appeal here to the 'as if' which has become so popular. The value of a 'fiction' of this kind (as the philosopher Vaihinger would call it) depends on how much one can achieve with its help" (SE 20 [1926]:194).

supposition that everything is intelligible. But an event may be rendered intelligible without its being determined beforehand by forces and laws beyond human influence. Freud's somewhat disconcerting tendency to mix hermeneutical interpretations that are compatible with some freedom of choice with the natural-scientific mode of explanation would seem to imply that he understands "science" as that which presupposes the intelligibility of the world, without the additional metaphysical requirement that everything be set and ordered by laws entirely outside human agency.

The Genetic Argument

Another argument for Freud's determinism, "the genetic argument," is chiefly propounded by philosopher John Hospers[21] and is built on the notion that personality is destiny. Here the central claim is that psycho-analysis sees a person's allegedly free choices and voluntary actions as in fact completely controlled by his personality (comprised in Freudian terms, of id, ego, and superego), which in turn has been molded by influences from early infancy and cannot be changed subsequently, even if the individual wishes to change (Hospers 1952, pp. 563–64). This is strong medicine. It seeks to place Freud squarely in the hard-determinist camp, among those who see metaphysical determinism as undermining moral responsibility.

Thus, Hospers writes that for Freud "our very acts of volition, and the entire train of deliberation leading up to them, are but facades for the expression of unconscious wishes, . . . compromises and defenses" (1952, p. 564). In this view, attributed by Hospers to Freud, free will is a complete illusion which the psychoanalyst, by dint of special experience and training, learns to pierce. According to Hospers, the psychoanalytic specialist knows what the ordinary person does not know. Thus, "[In ordinary parlance,] we talk about free will, and we say, for example, the person is free to do so-and-so . . . *if* he wants . . . [But] we forget [what the analyst remembers] that his wanting to is itself caught up in the stream of determinism, that uncon-scious forces drive him into the wanting or not wanting to do the thing in question" (1952, p. 568, emphasis original). What Freud teaches, in Hospers's view, is that every "choice" is fixed beforehand. "[T]he glaring fact is that it all started so early, before we knew what was happening. The personality-structure is inelastic after the age of five, and comparatively so in most cases after the age of three . . . To speak of human beings as

---

21. The discussion that follows draws on Hospers's frequently reprinted article "Free Will and Psychoanalysis" (1952). For a later discussion of his views, see Hospers 1961a, pp. 493–524.

'puppets' [whose motives are manipulated from beyond by invisible wires or by inside springs] . . . is no idle metaphor, but a stark rendering of a literal fact" (ibid.).

Hospers finds a perfect example of the mockery that psychoanalysis makes of our ordinary notions of free will in the spectacle of an anal personality whose childhood dynamics have issued in a hand-washing compulsion. The individual

> "freely decides" every time; he feels that he must wash . . . [his hands], he deliberates for a moment perhaps, but always ends by washing them. What he does not see, of course, are the invisible wires inside him pulling him inevitably to do the thing he does: the infantile id-wish concerns preoccupation with dirt, the super-ego charges him with this, and the terrified ego must respond, "No, I don't like dirt, see how clean I like to be, look how I wash my hands!" (Ibid., p. 566)

So too, in Hospers's lexicon of psychoanalytic determinism, a frequently divorced woman of masochistic personality type "*must* choose" yet another unsuitable, abusive mate over a kind and generous suitor. Her apparent "deliberations" are but "irrelevant chaff in the wind"—irrelevant to the deterministic workings of her unconscious (ibid., p. 565).

But a convincing case can be made that Hospers seriously misreads Freud on the determinism issue. Freud, whose approach to human behavior is finely nuanced, nowhere says anything approaching Hospers's full-blown genetic thesis, that all behavior is controlled by infantile unconscious dynamics ossified into ineluctable character traits. Freud does, of course, relentlessly explore the infantile origins of various character traits, obsessions, compulsions, sexual proclivities and dysfunctions, and hysterical symptoms. But he does not say that the general configuration of the normal adult personality, which is admittedly laid down in outline in infancy, is "determined" by these infantile causes in such a way that freedom and responsibility are precluded. And he certainly does not hold that the system unconscious (*Ucs*), or the id, completely determines all a mature adult's decisions and actions.

Indeed, such a notion would preclude the contrast that Freud's own theory and therapy presuppose, between the rational decision making of the comparatively free ego and the compulsive behavior of the emotionally ill and of the normal individual when he or she is in the grips of parapraxes or neurotic conflicts.[22] The most that Freud claims regarding the determin-

---

22. For examples of this contrast, see *SE* 5 (1900):591, 621; 7 (1905):263–4; 23 (1940):172–3.

istic implications of his discoveries about the infantile and unconscious determinants of behavior is that they have "contributed towards restricting the arbitrary factor in psychology" (*SE* 9 [1906]:105), which is not at all the same thing as saying that behavior is rigidly determined by unconscious processes.

These points find their clearest support in Freud's clinical discussions. Even when he is dealing with the obsessive-compulsive personality disorders that Hospers takes as paradigmatic of a thoroughgoing determinism, Freud never suggests that *all* a person's acts are determined in the way that Hospers indicates.[23] Thus, in his famous study of the "Rat Man" (*SE* 10 [1909]:155–318), Freud makes clear that the kind of compulsive behavior on which Hospers relies belongs to the realm of mental "disease" (*SE* 10 [1909]:223) and "disorder" (*SE* 10 [1909]:229), not to normal conduct. He expressly contrasts the obsessional wishes and impulses of his patient that required him to do or to refrain from particular acts upon pain of magically causing dire injury to his loved ones with the "normal personality" that the illness was in danger of "swallow[ing] up" (*SE* 10 [1909]:249).[24]

Certainly, for Freud, the relatively normal personality has its own etiology, such that it is limited to choices consistent with developed preferences and desires.[25] But Freud also assumes that a person is free (in the senses discussed below) within these limitations to choose consciously what to do and is thus reasonably regarded as a responsible moral agent. What the ego wants is not inexplicable: its choices have grounds that can be causally

23. Freud is careful to circumscribe the role of unconscious motives. In the course of explaining his claims about such motives in the explanation of parapraxes, e.g., he states: "You will notice that we do not deny these [more accessible, conscious] factors. Indeed, in general it doesn't often happen that psychoanalysis contests anything which is maintained in other quarters; as a rule, psychoanalysis only adds something new to what has been said" (1952, p. 49).

24. Freud argues that the statistically normal ego is somewhat neurotic, even on occasion psychotic (*SE* 23 [1937]:235); but he does not use this insight to eliminate the distinction between persons who suffer from debilitating mental illnesses and those who do not. The former are predominantly under the control of mental disorders, while normal persons experience only temporary psychopathologies or limited characterological problems in certain spheres of action. The normal person is always to some extent influenced by motivations beyond his or her knowledge and ability to control, but there are also areas in which the ego has some capacity for evaluation and choice.

25. Freud's comment in *Civilization and its Discontents* to the effect that certain personality differences are "determined" (*SE* 21 [1930]:111) applies to these interpersonal differences in motivation but not to the issue of whether the choices based on these differences are themselves determined in the sense that they could not be other than what they are.

elucidated. But given a variety of desires, the relatively healthy ego is capable of rationally evaluating competing wants and deciding which among several wants is the one(s) most desired, and by this choice guiding subsequent actions. Such behavior differs significantly from the "partial paralysis of the will and [the] . . . incapacity . . . [to come] to a decision" that characterize the obsessional neurotic (*SE* 10 [1909]:241).

Freud brings out vividly just how the normal state of affairs contrasts with the inner tyranny of irrational compulsions when he describes what it is like to suffer from an obsessional neurosis:

> The ego [or the I] feels uneasy; it comes up against limits to its power in its own house, the mind. Thoughts emerge suddenly without one's knowing where they come from, nor can one do anything to drive them away. These alien guests even seem to be more powerful than those which are at the ego's [or the I's] command. They resist all the well-proved measures of enforcement used by the will, remain unmoved by logical refutation, and are unaffected by the contradictory assertions of reality. Or else impulses appear which seem like those of a stranger, so that the ego [or the I] disowns them; yet it has to fear them and take precautions against them. The ego [or I] says to itself: "This is an illness, a foreign invasion." It increases its vigilance, but cannot understand why it feels so strangely paralysed.[26] (*SE* 17 [1917]:141–2)

Freud similarly distinguishes the determined aspects of obsessional conduct from normal behavior in the case history of the "Rat Man":

> He [the patient] . . . said that, though he considered himself a moral person, he could quite definitely remember having done things in his childhood which came from his other self. I remarked that here he had incidentally hit upon one of the chief characteristics of the unconscious, namely, its relation to the infantile. The unconscious, I explained, was the infantile; it was that part of the self which had become separated off from it in infancy, which had not shared the later stages of its development, and which had in consequence become *repressed*. It was the

26. Warrant for translating the ego as "the I" is provided not only by Freud's original use of the pronoun *ich* (literally, "I") as a noun (*das Ich*) but also by explicit statements like the following, in which he states his preference for terms rich in the connotations of spoken language and criticizes the substitution of contrived technical terms like "the ego" that arouse no personal associations for the reader: "We base ourselves on common knowledge and recognize in man an organization of the soul which . . . we call . . . his I" (cited and trans. by Bettelheim 1983, p. 61). Freud continues: "Beside this 'I,' we recognize another mental region, more extensive, more imposing, and more obscure than the 'I,' and this we call the '*Es*' ['id'; literally, 'it']. . . . You will probably protest at our having chosen simple pronouns to describe our two agencies or provinces instead of giving them orotund Greek names. In psychoanalysis, however, we like to keep in contact with the popular mode of thinking" (*SE* 20 [1926]:195).

derivatives of this repressed unconscious that were responsible for the *involuntary thoughts which constituted his illness. (SE* 10, 177–8; emphasis added in part, deleted in part)[27]

However much Freud recognized that the neurotic cannot behave otherwise in the areas in which he is in the throes of unconscious infantile wishes and defenses, and therefore is not morally responsible for the product of his obsessions, it is nevertheless the case that he believed that in the normal course of events, the individual grows up "by a process of development . . . out of the sum of his infantile predispositions" into an adult whose behavior is not predominantly compelled and who does have "moral responsibility" (*SE* 10 [1909]:185). For Freud, the mature ego's decision-making capacities constitute what is ordinarily called the "will," pursuant to which the reasonably healthy person can make use of realistic knowledge to come to a decision and exercise some degree of control in his or her own house—even if the relatively free ego can be understood from another point of view in terms of its multitudinous historical roots, current inputs, and given structures.

Freud's therapeutic goals in treating obsessional neuroses, as in treating other personality disorders, also starkly contradict Hospers's view of Freud as a hard determinist whose views about the causation of human action rule out moral responsibility. Freud's therapeutic goal was to make the unconscious, hidden meanings "articulate" in order to force the obsession to release its grasp (*SE* 10 [1909]:242, 186–7). According to Freud,

> the wildest and most eccentric obsessional ideas can be cleared up if they are investigated deeply enough . . . When, as so often happens, an obsessional idea has not succeeded in establishing itself permanently, the task of cleaning it up is correspondingly simplified. . . . Once the interconnections between an obsessional idea and the patient's experiences have been discovered, there will be no difficulty in obtaining access to whatever else may be puzzling or worth knowing in the pathological structure. (*SE* 10 [1909]:86–7)

Freud is not talking simply of enlightenment when he uses the terms "cleared up" and "cleaned up," but of change—*increased freedom* (in the senses discussed below and in ch. 4)—built on understanding. Indeed,

---

27. Freud goes on to indicate that he accepts the possibility of ordinary reasons for action that are not compelled or determined when he explains that the defensive thoughts forged to combat obsessional ideas exist as "hybrids" between obsessional thought and "purely reasonable considerations" (*SE* 10 [1909]:222). Defensive thoughts "accept certain of the premises of the obsession they are combating" and thus "are established upon a basis of pathological thought" and yet "use the weapons of reason" (ibid.).

when Ernst Lanzer, the "Rat Man," himself expressed doubt as to whether it was possible for him to get free of the "*involuntary* thoughts which constituted his illness" (*SE* 10 [1909]:177–8, emphasis added), Freud leapt to counter his passive acceptance of the continuing hold of the "derivatives of [the] repressed unconscious" and vigorously held out the hope of liberating success as the desired result of their therapeutic enterprise.[28] In several places in that case report, Freud noted with satisfaction that the patient was "freed of his obsessions" and restored to normal mental functioning as the unconscious *meaning* of his behavior became known to him (*SE* 10 [1909]:173, 207–8, n. 1, 249, n. 1).

Another version of the genetic argument for determinism has been propounded recently by psychiatrist and historian of medicine Edwin Wallace (1986a), who points out that genetic determinism need not entail the kind of predestination, fatalism, and inevitability implied by Hospers's account or deny the distinction between compelled and uncompelled behavior. By contrast with Hospers, Wallace observes that psychoanalysts do not normally trace all the determinants of an individual's behavior to the inception of personality in early childhood—as if the individual were like a clock with the course of its life a function of the recoil of the springs (ibid., p. 938). Rather, the individual is viewed as a complex, open system, capable of interacting with the environment on the basis of subjective judgments involving the weighing of considerations and even the active formulation of novel solutions; yet the psychoanalyst can still assert that the individual's behavior is always the inevitable consequence of all the antecedent internal and external conditions at the moment of decision making.[29] The necessary and sufficient conditions for all human behavior are to be found in the interaction between the antecedent state of the actor, with his particular constitutionally and historically determined desires, perceptions, anxieties, and inhibitions, and the immediately preceding (or current) environmental situation. "To hold that for a different decision to have been made something would have had to be different in the antecedent conditions does not negate that deliberation occurred and that it affected the outcome," Wallace

28. For critical discussion of Freud's technique in the "Rat Man" case, see Kanzer 1952; Zetzel 1966; Lipton 1977, 1979.

29. E. R. Wallace distinguishes the "intersectional" concept of causation, which holds that behavior is "the effect of the intersection between the historically-constitutionally determined personality structure of the individual and the actual current situation" (1986a, p. 937), from the "transeunt" concept of causation, which locates the proximate causes of behavior outside the acting individual. It is the former that is said to be the implicit psychoanalytic concept of determinism.

writes (ibid., p. 939). The psychoanalytic determinist need only believe that the individual's deliberation is itself determined in the sense that the individual's history and constitution determine the range and intensity of desires, particular conscious and unconscious fantasies, the pattern of defenses and compromise formulations, and the degree to which the individual can restrain or divert his impulses. Thus, Wallace claims that insofar as behavior is not externally compelled, it is free; although as a function of the individual's history and personality structure, it is strictly determined (ibid., p. 942).

One of the advantages of Wallace's version of the genetic determinist thesis over Hospers's is that it makes it possible to distinguish between compulsive behavior and behavior that is experienced as free (because it is ego-syntonic—i.e., the will is integrated and is the will one wants). But Wallace acknowledges that Freud failed to envision this variant of genetic determinism and its apparent compatibility with psychoanalytic practice. Rather, Freud vacillated between a version of the universality of causation doctrine that does not entail the possibility of "free will" (defined as unnecessitated choosing) and ordinary lay assumptions about the normal person's capacity for freedom of choice and action and "was in no way a thoroughgoing determinist" (ibid., p. 962). Although Wallace sees Freud's vacillation as a chink in the armor of psychoanalytic determinism, it is possible to see it as raising doubts about the compatibility of Wallace's own hard-determinist thesis[30] with classical psychoanalysis, and thus as a goad to pursuing further the question of whether there may be a form of determinism that does less violence than the hard form to the psychoanalytic and ordinary view of persons as responsible moral agents. Such a view would

---

30. Wallace (1986a, p. 968) attempts to make room for some traditional moral concepts and to redefine "responsibility" in terms of "causal efficacy"; but his efforts at reconciling responsibility with universal determinism remain a form of "hard determinism" because they leave no place for accountability in the sense that praise- or blame-related responses are ever really appropriate (see Bennett 1980, p. 15; also Strawson 1974). Wallace summarizes his position thus: "The psychoanalyst's demeanor in the analytic situation is probably the closest approximation to activity totally consistent with a conviction in universal determinism—. . . *thus, by my argument, the nonjudgmentalness of the analytic hour would be not merely a technical maneuver, but the logical consequence of the thesis of universal determinism*" (1986a, p. 960, emphasis original). Wallace appreciates the difficulty his position poses for ordinary beliefs, however (see ibid., p. 962). "Universal determinism appears to disentail praise and blame . . ., and yet persons seem universally to engage in them. If determinism is correct, it seems that we are necessitated to act as if we believed a patent falsehood! *I suggest, however, that determinism is no less valid for all this* and that, consequently, we face yet another of those mighty ironies with which life is replete (ibid., p. 962, emphasis original).

have the advantage over the genetic interpretations of Hospers and Wallace of capturing more of the paradox that permeates the full psychoanalytic view of the freedom and psychic determinism matter.

The Metapsychological Argument

Freud's use of mechanistic metaphors gives rise to the third principal way of attributing to psychoanalysis the doctrine of hard determinism with its disentailment of moral responsibility. The contention of "the metapsychological argument" is that Freud's likening of the human psyche to a mechanical device implies that it operates in strict accordance with invariant causal laws.[31] The adherents of this argument cannot imagine that the Freud who formulated the mechanistic theory presented in the "Project" (1895) and at the end of *The Interpretation of Dreams* (1900) and reiterated in the metapsychological papers (e.g., *SE* 14 [1915]:104–215) and elsewhere could have believed that psychic states occurring within the "mental apparatus" could have been other than they are and thus compatible with freedom of choice and responsibility.

Yankelovich and Barrett make "the metapsychological argument" in one of its purest and strongest forms. In *Ego and Instinct* they argue that "Freud conceived the psychic apparatus primarily as a *closed system* . . . [that] operate[s] within its own intrapsychic territory according to its own *autonomous laws* . . . in *completely deterministic patterns*" (1970, pp. 62–3, emphasis added in part). Thus regulated, "the psychic apparatus [has] . . . no room in it for choice or freedom" (ibid., p. 66). The "iron laws" of nature, "rather than the individual's own free choice determine man's behavior" (ibid., p. 217).

There are several problems with relying exclusively on the metapsychology in support of Freud's alleged determinism. One is Freud's own warning against taking the metaphors and hypotheses of his metapsychology too seriously (see ch. 2 above). More important, this argument, like the genetic argument, runs afoul of the stark fact that Freud himself never lost sight of, that a principal aim of therapy is—within the limits set by both psyche and environment—to increase the patient's freedom of choice and independence (see *SE* 12 [1912]:106; 23 [1940]:175). The contention that Freud unequivocally believed in hard determinism is significantly undermined by statements such as that in *The Ego and the Id* in which he declares that

31. See Yankelovich and Barrett 1970, pp. 63, 217, 282. Among others who characterize Freud as a complete determinist in reliance on the metapsychological argument are Weiss (1968, p. 59); Ricoeur (1966); Habermas (1971, pp. 246–7); Abramson (1984, p. 114).

analysis, in making a person aware of unconscious as well as conscious reasons for action, "does not set out to make pathological reactions impossible, but to give the patient's ego *freedom* [FREIHEIT] to decide one way or the other" (*SE* 19 [1923]:50, n. 1, emphasis original; see also *GW* 13: 237ff.).[32]

Moreover, as previously noted, even during the heyday of his mechanistic metapsychology (1885–1915), the language of moral choice is not entirely absent from Freud's writings. Its unselfconscious usage, as well as the implications of the substance of his remarks, contradict the claim that Freud's brand of determinism undercuts the very possibility of morality. For example, in one early lecture, Freud writes forcefully and directly about the reality of "*conscious will-power*" (*SE* 7 [1905]:266, emphasis added). He explains that because willpower "governs only conscious mental processes, . . . [while] every mental compulsion is rooted in the unconscious," the transformation of unconscious material into conscious material expands the individual's control over his impulses (ibid.). To the extent that the ego is aware of the full compass of the self's impulses and wishes—that is, to the extent that they have become conscious, "the *will . . . carries out what the ego orders* and modifies anything that seeks to accomplish itself spontaneously," so that the individual's impulses and actions can be harmonized with the ego's demands (*SE* 17 [1917]:141, emphasis added). Conversely, when a part of the mind's activity is withdrawn from conscious knowledge, it is also withdrawn "from the *command of* . . . [the individual's] *will*," which then becomes powerless to exert its influence (*SE* 17 [1917]:142).

Freud makes clear, however, that his recognition of the impotence of the will vis-à-vis unconscious impulses does *not* mean, even during his peak mechanistic period, that he believed that no will—and no choices—meaningfully exist in the labyrinth of the mind. Indeed, Freud expressly heralds a genuine ability on the part of the patient to choose actions with respect to desires as a major achievement of psychoanalysis.[33] From analysis, the individual is to learn to delay and *direct* the quest for satisfaction. Thus, the successful patient can

---

32. Similarly, in discussing the rare cases of psychotherapy with homosexuals that results in rekindling interest in the opposite sex, Freud remarked that psychoanalytic treatment leaves the homosexual patient "to *choose* whether . . . to abandon the path that is banned by society" (*SE* 18 [1920]:151, emphasis added).

33. During the peak period of the mechanistic metapsychology (1895–1915), Freud also speaks of the analyst's own necessary "increase in self-control . . . acquired" through training analysis (*SE* 12 [1912]:117).

give up a gratification which lies to hand but is not sanctioned by the world she lives in, in favour of a distant and perhaps altogether doubtful one, which is, however, socially and psychologically unimpeachable. To achieve *this mastery of herself* she must be taken through the primordial era of her mental development and in this way reach that *greater freedom within the mind* [*jenes Mehr von seelischer Freiheit*] *which distinguishes conscious mental activity*—in the systematic sense—from unconscious. (*CP* 2 [1915]:390; *GW* 10. 319–20)

After 1919, when Freud abandons the mechanistic model for an organic metatheory that does not rely on intrapsychic "forces" and "causes" as definite as those governing physical things (see Loewald 1980, pp. 102–37), this same sort of moral-choice language becomes markedly more prevalent in his work. He again speaks of analysis as an aid to self-mastery and freedom: "The making conscious of repressed sexual desires in analysis makes it possible . . . to obtain a mastery over them which the previous repression had been unable to achieve . . . Analysis *sets the neurotic free from the chains of his sexuality*" (*SE* 18 [1923]:252, emphasis added).

But whereas in his earlier writing, when psychoanalysis was defined primarily as the study of the unconscious, Freud had not sought to account for the *ego*'s behavior, in his later writings there is a systematic effort to find a theoretical place for autonomous ego capacities which would support the claim that in psychoanalysis the "ego develops from perceiving instincts to controlling them" and that "psychoanalysis is an instrument to enable the ego to achieve a progressive conquest of the id" (*SE* 19 [1923]:55–6, emphasis added).[34]

THE PARADOX OF DETERMINISM AND THERAPEUTIC FREEDOM

In the preceding discussion, it has been argued that Freud is not what philosophers call a "hard" determinist. But how *are* we to understand Freud's views on freedom and responsibility in light of what he says about psychic determinism? Several different ways of interpreting Freud's apparently paradoxical stance emerge from a review of the literature. One tack, which leaves open the possibility that, despite his clinical pronouncements, Freud might still be, on one level, a hard determinist, is to say that there is simply an irreconcilable conflict between Freudian practice and theory; that ultimately, the therapeutic goal is inconsistent with Freud's general theory of human nature—that, in short, the left hand does not know what

34. See also *SE* 18 (1923):251; 23 (1940):173.

the right hand is doing.[35] MacIntyre makes the point—which is advanced also by Ricoeur (1970), Habermas (1971, pp. 246–73), and Abramson (1984, pp. 114–15)—that "the psychoanalyst as therapist contrasts compulsive and unfree neurotic behavior with normal free choice; but as theorist his conception of unconscious causation leads him to deny this contrast by seeing both as unfree" (1958, p. 91). And Ricoeur (1970) has impressed many interpreters with the argument that Freud was more or less forced by the hermeneutical aim of his clinical practice to subscribe to a doctrine of human freedom in that realm, but that this practical belief in freedom and responsibility was not incorporated or "thematized" in his general theory.

The problem with this interpretation, besides the fact that it inelegantly assigns fundamental inconsistency where it is not demonstrably necessary, is its failure to attend either to the specific ways in which Freud speaks about determinism or to how in his mature writings Freud tries to make room in his theory for freedom of choice.

Another interpretation of Freud's views on freedom and responsibility holds that there is no paradox at all, because the apparently contradictory sides of his thought are reconciled by means of a "thin" conception of freedom. This thin theory of freedom, which is advanced by a number of eminently respectable philosophers, including Hobbes, Locke, and Hume, claims that universal determinism is true and yet compatible with freedom because what is essential for conduct to be free is that it not be compelled or coerced—not that it not be caused.[36] For the thin theory of freedom, freedom is not opposed to causation. The opposite of a free act is not an act that is caused but one that is coerced or compelled. One acts freely when one acts in accordance with one's own preferences; but this is perfectly consistent with those preferences themselves being determined. From this perspective, a kleptomaniac's stealing is not free because the individual is compelled to commit the theft. But an act like walking along a beach can be

---

35. Curiously, some interpreters claim that Freud is both a determinist and a believer in human freedom of choice, without bothering to address the apparent conflict. Thus Bruner argues that Freud, as a "child of his century's materialism, . . . was wedded to the determinism and the classical physicalism of nineteenth-century physiology so boldly represented by Helmholtz," yet, in the very next paragraph, declares that Freud holds that "the patient who is cured is the one who is now free enough of neurosis to decide intelligently about his own destiny" (1957, p. 280).

36. What I am calling "the thin theory of freedom" is sometimes viewed as a form of "soft determinism" (see n. 1 above). But it deserves to be differentiated from it, since it is not really a version of determinism, but rather a way of showing how the single thesis of universal determinism is compatible with moral responsibility when freedom is understood in a certain very specific sense.

free if it is in keeping with one's desires or preferences. The universal determinist's claim that conscious desires and preferences have their own causal history and explanation, such that the person could not act otherwise, does not make the actions performed in accordance with them less free, according to the thin theorist's definition of freedom. Acts are free for the thin theorist as long as we are doing what we want to do, even if we have no real choice.

Since Freud often seems to understand freedom as entailing a lack of compulsion, as in his description of psychoanalysis as freeing or liberating the neurotic from compulsions, it is tempting to see him as implicitly subscribing to the thin theory of freedom. This position would enable him to maintain, without contradiction, that all actions are causally determined and yet some actions are free (in the sense of not being compelled). If this were Freud's position, there would be no problem about free will, because he would hold, with Hume, that the whole dispute derives from a confusion in the meanings of words. Once certain crucial terms such as *free* and *voluntary* were used correctly, the whole problem of free will would dissolve, and the apparent opposition between determinism and freedom in the history of moral psychology would be resolved.

But the problem of freedom of choice does not really disappear when the thin theorist wields his semantic wand, for the conception of freedom employed by adherents of this doctrine is so circumscribed that it fails to do justice to the concept of free choice that is essential for the ascription of moral responsibility. A genuinely free action is not merely one that is in keeping with our desires and preferences; it is one that is *avoidable* or *could have been different in some way*. To say that an action is free means at the very least that the agent could have done otherwise, given the very same conditions—not just that the person felt that he was free because he approved of what he found himself doing anyway. If the thin theory of freedom were valid, it is hard to see how anyone could be held morally responsible. The excuse generally afforded only the insane would seem to be available to everyone—that "I could not help what I did"—and the distinction, for all practical moral purposes, between hard and soft determinism would come to naught.

In any event, it is highly doubtful that Freud intended to take the thin theory option as a way out of the determinism versus freedom dilemma. He nowhere indicates that he subscribes to this particular philosophical understanding of how these two commitments—to causality and to freedom—can be reconciled. Instead, he simply sets forth apparently mutually contradictory views, one deriving from the mechanistic model of the human psyche that he proposed initially, the other from the freedom-enhancing goal of his therapeutic work. Thus it would seem more reasonable to assume that Freud simply meant what he said about the tentative and restricted nature of his theoretical model-building and never took the mechanistic model as literally as those who seek to derive a determinist metapsychology from it, rather than to impute this sophisticated philosophical move to him. After all, he does say that the mechanistic model is designed primarily as a preliminary scaffolding to assist in understanding the obscure functioning of *unconscious* processes. As for *conscious* processes, Freud maintained throughout the heyday of the mechanistic model that this was not the province of depth psychology and that knowledge of it was to be derived mainly from sources other than psychoanalysis, which is not to deny a place for will and freedom in the conscious realm.

An additional difficulty with attributing to Freud the thin theory of freedom is that he does not consistently adhere to this theory's restricted conception of freedom as uncoerced behavior. Particularly in his late writings Freud uses freedom (*Freiheit*) in a more robust sense than merely the absence of coercion or compulsion. In these writings the ego or self has the "power" both to deliberate about and to decide among competing motives for action, and thus to make a difference in what the agent does. Of course, the ego is itself caused. But the crucial point is that, under appropriate conditions, the ego becomes itself a cause (see ch. 4 below).

A third—and ultimately the most persuasive—perspective on Freud's views on determinism,[37] which will be pursued in chapter 4, claims that freedom and responsibility are not problematic for Freud because he is groping toward a new understanding of determinism, appropriate to the psychological sciences, that accounts for the development of relatively free decisions and choices by comparatively mature, healthy adults. Freud nowhere abandons the postulate that everything is determined by causes, but he moves increasingly further away from notions of determinism derived from the physical sciences, which are suggestive of a psychology of passivity, and develops the implicit notion that causes and laws take on a

---

37. A fourth possible interpretation of Freud's simultaneous commitment to determinism and freedom scarcely merits mention. According to this, Freud saw the masses of persons who have not been analyzed as strictly determined by unconscious forces and successful analysands as having some limited control over the unconscious causes that determine the behavior of the unanalyzed (see Kaplan 1957, p. 219). On this view, freedom is not something antecedently given to the normal ego but something achieved only through psychoanalysis. But this notion is both absurd and offensive, and there is absolutely no textual support for it in Freud's own writings.

different character when they govern not physical things but mental activities, especially the higher functioning of the ego.

Whatever Freud thought about the thesis of metaphysical determinism—and he nowhere even hints at what it might mean—the essential thing about the psychoanalytic view of determinism is that it is *psychic* determinism. Psychic determinism holds only that all psychological behavior is *motivated* and guided in a general way by the regulatory principles that govern psychic behavior, not that it could not be other than it is.

Freud holds on to the paradox that freedom of choice is compatible with determinism not by narrowly restricting freedom to a contrived definition but by seeing that the emergence of the capacity for relatively free decision making and action occurs within a context of psychological determinism. As Rapaport (1951) puts it, the human capacity for autonomy is an achievement in part made possible by the very drives that yield to autonomous control. It occurs by means of the development of psychic structures and hierarchies that permit feedback loops from higher to lower. In this process, the self comes into being as itself a center of motivation that can, by utilizing mature ego functions, self-reflectively examine its own motivations and choose among those with which it wishes to identify itself. Such choices are always limited by the determined aspects of every action. But once a certain level of maturity and psychic health has been attained, the ego has it within its power to introduce novelty and affect the future.

It may be that for much of his career Freud's personal world view was deterministic in a way that challenged his ethical and clinical commitment to freedom and responsibility. But the point is that he was not ineluctably tied to a deterministic world view that precluded moral responsibility, or at least that he did not wish to saddle psychoanalysis with it, and that, accordingly, he developed an understanding of "psychic determinism" that was sufficiently flexible to permit his theory to grow over time to the point where, in his late writings, he found a way of doing theoretical justice to his earlier, commonsense clinical assumptions about freedom and moral responsibility.[38]

38. This third reading has the not incidental consequence that it lends support to those contemporary psychoanalysts who, like Gray (1982) and Rangell (1981), identify the aim of psychoanalysis as to augment the patient's freedom or autonomy. Gray, e.g., argues that the chief therapeutic aim of psychoanalysis—viz. "greater autonomy"—is lasting to the extent to which "the relatively autonomous aspects of the patient's psyche" are *"involved in a consciously and increasingly voluntary co-partnership with the analyst"* (1982, pp. 623–4, 645, emphasis original). Rangell argues similarly that the ego that achieves insight into a previously unconscious compromise formation "is now confronted with the possibility of action which presents an opportunity but also a responsibility" (1981, p. 120). For both authors, the psycho-

Throughout, he accepted, entered into, and struggled with the determinism–freedom paradox.[39]

---

logical activities that go by the name of choice, decision, and free will (ibid., p. 127) are simply "empirical" facts about human beings with which the psychoanalyst is allied. In supposing this, Gray and Rangell appear to represent the mainstream of contemporary American psychoanalysts. They are opposed by psychoanalysts like Brenner, who, starting from the metaphysical determinist doctrine, identify not increased autonomy but self-knowledge and reduced suffering as the therapeutic aims of psychoanalysis. It would not make sense for a determinist like Brenner to include increased autonomy among the aims of therapy, since autonomy obviously cannot be augmented if it does not exist.

39. Philosophically, this third approach is more satisfying than either hard determinism or indeterminism, because moral responsibility requires not only a certain degree of freedom but also a certain form of determinability, for indeterminism is as much of a threat to moral responsibility as determinism, as Freud recognized.

Chapter 4
Reconciling the Paradox: Psychic Determinism and Moral Responsibility

> Obviously one must hold oneself
> responsible.
>
> —Freud

THE IDIOSYNCRATIC MEANING OF PSYCHIC DETERMINISM

The case can be convincingly made that what seems to be a contradiction between freedom of choice and psychic determinism is in part a semantic misunderstanding between Freud and his readers. To Freud, *psychic determinism* means only that all mental events are *caused*. The adjective *psychic* specifies that the *kinds* of causes relevant for psychoanalysis are primarily mental causes or motives, by contrast with the nonpurposeful forces that are causative in the natural sciences.[1]

One of the main reasons for the misunderstanding surrounding Freud's use of *psychic determinism* derives from the ambiguity of the key word *cause*. To speak in terms of causes is not necessarily to speak in terms of *determining* causes. A cause may be any phenomenon that affects the occurrence of an outcome, even if its existence does not *require* that outcome.

It is often assumed that a causal explanation of an event always involves showing how it is related to antecedent events by an invariable law. But a

1. Others who have seen that psychic determinism refers to "having motives" include Waelder (1963), Loewald (1980, pp. 91–3), J. H. Smith (1978, p. 92), Basch (1978), and Fingarette (1972). Although none of these writers except Basch specifically addresses Freud's use of the concept, what they say about its meaning in contemporary psychoanalysis applies equally to the founder's use of the term. Thus, Loewald notes that "the main impact of psychic determinism resides in its being *psychic* determinism: the causes are conceived not as purely external or physical and biological, but as potentially personal, unconscious processes having a psychological effect on overt behavior. And secondly, these causes thus are susceptible to being influenced and modified in their turn by psychological processes. If this were not so, the whole idea that the reactivation of unconscious conflicts and their re-creation and working through in analysis could lead to change in present behavior would fall to the ground" (1980, p. 92).

causal explanation need not take this form. A cause is simply an appropriate answer, in certain contexts, to the question Why? Different types of causal explanations count as answers to this question. When the phenomenon to be explained is a human action, motives, in the sense of reasons for action, may be the causes or determinants of behavior without it being assumed that no other result is possible.

Thus, in seeking to explain why Mr Smith drove to the supermarket, say, it is usually sufficient to cite the individual's "reason," by making reference to both his desire (for some milk to drink) and his belief about how that desire might be fulfilled (that the supermarket has milk for sale). Here, a reason is the *psychological* cause of the event (the trip to the store), because it can be deduced retrospectively that the combination of desire and belief pertaining to the fulfillment of the desire moved the person to the act.

But the mere existence of a desire and beliefs regarding its satisfaction do not necessarily constitute a determining cause of action. The individual may have other, competing desires and beliefs on which he prefers to act, and in a normal psychological state, when the alternatives are available at some level of consciousness, he is free to deliberate and to choose which desire–belief set he will act on.

Freud, of course, parses "reasons" into conscious and unconscious motives and is primarily interested in repressed unconscious reasons that, unlike most conscious reasons, often compel persons to act against their overt intentions. The patient who is regularly late for his therapy appointments may have little ability to control his behavior until he realizes that he is resisting deeper probing into the repressed sources of his emotional difficulties. But the fact that repressed unconscious reasons may sometimes compel behavior in this way and become determining causes of action, far from showing that human behavior is always determined, actually reveals that persons are free within limits to make choices, since eventual awareness by the ego of the initially hidden motives that exist side by side with conscious ones provides the individual with the capacity to choose which reasons to act on. Thus, when the habitually late patient grasps the unconscious reasons for his tardiness (e.g., anger at the analyst for not being continuously available, heightened by sexual longings for the analyst, anxiety over guilt and feared punishments for these feelings, and resistance to the surfacing of these painful wishes, which conflict with habitual submissive attitudes toward idealized authorities), other, competing desires, such as a wish to get on with the therapy and to enjoy the self-esteem that comes from taking charge of one's own life, may come to the fore and become the basis of behavior that is partially chosen.

In being brought to consciousness or, more accurately, within the domain of the ego's secondary process, both the determinants of the patient's decision and the mode of determination change. It is not that causes cease to operate but that they are now reasons, rather than forces, that can be evaluated cognitively. A conflict of reasons for action is quite different from a conflict of opposing unconscious forces, one of which overcomes another by its superior "strength." The conflict is then more like the conflicting arguments of contending attorneys. One argument is "stronger" or has more "force" or "weight" than the other in the sense that it is more reasonable or persuasive.[2] As Stephen Toulmin notes regarding this difference: "A man who can give in detail his reasons for acting as he does is (roughly speaking) the one whose conduct we should regard as least 'determined.' The success of psycho-analysis, so far from destroying the last grounds . . . for belief in free-will, should re-emphasize the importance of 'reasons for action,' as opposed to 'causes of action,' and so the possibility of free choice" (1954, pp. 138–9). Although Toulmin confines freedom of choice to *consciousness*, Freud realized that much of our rational decision making takes place unconsciously, in the preconscious, so that, in a way, he extends voluntary decision making to the secondary-process mentation of the unconscious ego, when it is not adversely affected by neurosis. As Rangell puts it, "Just as man 'knows' more than he knows he knows, i.e., from memories and thoughts not permitted into consciousness, so does he decide more than he allows himself to know he decided" (1986, p. 18).

In the main, then, Freud uses the term "psychic determinism" to signal that some particular kind of behavior (e.g. dreams, symptoms, parapraxes, and free associations[3]) do not occur accidentally or fortuitously, as his predecessors had thought, but are governed by repressed unconscious

2. In several articles on the decision-making function of the ego, Rangell (1969, 1971, 1981, 1986) draws a similar distinction between reason-based decisions and unconscious intrapsychic conflicts. He writes: "What is important here is that another type of conflict is being recognized and introduced at this point from the usual type envisaged in the conventional use of the term 'intrapsychic conflict.' . . . To the traditional meaning of psychoanalytic conflict as an opposition between forces, as exemplified in the classical oppositional ego–id conflict, is added a second meaning of conflict as a 'choice', a 'decision–dilemma' type of intrapsychic conflict, a crucial type of intrasystemic conflict within the ego. This is now a competition between alternatives, a dilemma over which a decision must be made or, as given by Webster, conflict involving 'competition or opposing action of incompatibles—antagonism, as of divergent interests'" (1969, p. 600).

3. Psychic determinism is linked with explaining dreams in *SE* 15 (1916–17):106; with symptoms in *SE* 18 (1923):237–8; with parapraxes in *SE* 6 (1901):240–54; and with free association in *SE* 18 (1923):238.

motives. This claim, in which causes are seen as motives, is far different from the assertion that an individual's behavior could not be other than what it is. Thus, when Freud states that "psychoanalysts are marked by a particularly strict belief in the determination of mental life," he goes on to explain that: "For them there is nothing trivial, *nothing arbitrary or haphazard.* They expect in every case to find sufficient *motives* where, as a rule, no such expectation is raised" (*SE* 11 [1910]:38, emphasis added). In like vein, he observes that: "If we give way to the view that a part of our psychical functioning cannot be explained by *purposive ideas,* we are failing to appreciate the extent of determination in mental life" (*SE* 6 [1901]:240, emphasis added).

That this is Freud's meaning can be further buttressed by tracing the chronology of his use of the term *psychic determinism.* The phrase makes its first appearance in *The Psychopathology of Everyday Life,* where it is used repeatedly to carry the thesis that seemingly trivial behavior—like slips of the tongue and pen, repeated accidental self-injuries, and "thoughtlessly" hummed tunes—do not happen purely by chance but have unconscious motives or "determinants." This, and not the advocacy of a specific metaphysical doctrine of universal determinism, was what was at stake for Freud, as he himself later made clear when, discussing *The Psychopathology,* he stated:

> In 1901 I published a work in which I demonstrated that a whole number of actions which were held to be unmotivated are on the contrary *strictly determined,* and to that extent I contributed towards restricting the *arbitrary* factor in psychology . . . I showed that when someone makes a slip of the tongue it is *not chance,* nor simply difficulty in articulation or similarity in sound, that is responsible, but that in every case a disturbing ideational content—a complex—can be brought to light which has altered the sense of the intended speech under the apparent form of a slip of the tongue . . . Once one has accustomed oneself to this view of determinism in psychical life, one is justified in inferring from the findings in the psychopathology of everyday life that [other apparently meaningless ideas and actions] . . . may not be arbitrary either, but *determined by an ideational content* that is operative in him. *SE* 9 [1906]:104–5, emphasis added; see also *SE* 15 [1916–17]:107.

Freud's use of psychic determinism in contexts such as these is meant primarily to justify the psychoanalyst's interest in the seemingly inexplicable details of psychic life, no matter how seemingly trivial, and his readiness to take them as indicative of unconscious tendencies. Since a great deal of conscious intentional conduct is left unaffected by such claims as to the unconscious motives that explain ego-alien behavior, nothing earth-shattering is necessarily implied with respect to freedom of choice (in the sense of the ego's siding with one alternative on rational grounds) by Freud's principal use of psychic determination, although, of course, there are circumstances in which unconscious motives subvert conscious intentions and do determine behavior (see discussion of the "Rat Man" above).

Freud also sometimes employs the concept of psychic determinism to make the more general point that there is causal continuity in the *whole* mental life of the individual (see *SE* 11 [1910]:52). On these occasions, he asserts obliquely that "nothing in the mind is arbitrary or undetermined" (*SE* 6 [1901]:242). Many interpreters take these comments to imply an extension of the strict assumptions about causal determinism found in the natural sciences to all mental activities, including deliberations, choices, and apparently voluntary actions. But this is not the point that Freud himself makes in these passages. Complete psychic determinism for Freud is the thesis that *all* mental activities are "meaningful"—that is to say, "purposeful"—as in consciously intended conduct. He states:

> According to our analyses it is not necessary to dispute the right to the feeling of conviction of having a free will. If the distinction between conscious and unconscious motivation is taken into account, our feeling of conviction informs us that conscious motivation does not extend to all our motor decisions. . . . But what is thus left free by the one side receives its motivation from the other side, from the unconscious; and in this way determinism in the psychical sphere is still carried out without any gap. (*SE* 6 [1901]:254)

The point of this passage is that the whole of psychic life is motivated by goals and purposes akin to conscious intentions, for Freud is here extending the model of ordinary intentionality to the unconscious.[4] Far from suggesting that conscious intentions (*Absicht*) are to be explained by nonpurposeful causes, the concept of complete psychic determinism is actually

---

4. Freud makes much the same point about complete psychic determinism when, in discussing his original discoveries concerning the psychopathologies of everyday life, he observes that: "All of these [unintended actions] . . . were shown to be strictly determined and were revealed as an expression of the subject's suppressed *intentions* or as a result of a clash between *two intentions* one of which was permanently or temporarily unconscious. The importance of this contribution to psychology was of many kinds. The *range of mental determinism* was extended by it in an unforeseen manner; . . . and . . . a class of material was brought to light which is calculated better than any other to stimulate belief in the existence of *unconscious mental acts* even in people to whom the hypothesis of something at once mental and unconscious seems strange and even absurd" (*SE* 18 [1923]:240, emphasis added). Here too, the concept of complete psychic determinism extends the model of purposive or intentional behavior from ordinary conscious experience to behavior that had formerly seemed purposeless.

used by Freud to make quite the reverse point: that seemingly random, unintended behavior is meaningful[5] and so can be brought within the domain of conscious deliberation and purposeful action (see *SE* 6 [1901]:28, 40).

In speaking of complete psychic determinism, Freud presupposes that the concept of conscious "intentionality" is understood in its ordinary sense, as entailing deliberation and voluntary direction of one's efforts in pursuit of some goal. Thus, he states that "the starting point" of psychoanalysis is provided by our ordinary awareness of "our acts of consciousness, which are immediate data and cannot be further explained" (*SE* 23 [1940]:144, 157).[6]

For Freud, what the thesis of complete psychic determinism denies is that our actions might take place "for no motive . . . for no psychological reason" (*SE* 2 [1883–95]:294), because if this were the case, it would be impossible to subject unconscious impulses to the control of the ego, as psychoanalytic therapy seeks to do. The doctrine of psychic determinism does insist on the *universality* of causation. But this by no means entails a belief in the *uniformity* of causation, which holds that the same causal relations always pertain because they follow invariable laws of nature. Though commonly confused, the two concepts, universality of causation and uniformity of causation, are very different, and the failure to understand this is another major reason why Freud is often misread on the determinism issue.

To assert, as Freud does, that every mental event is caused is not at all the same as to claim that every mental event is inevitable by virtue of the operation of general laws of nature.[7] As we have seen, Freud thinks of

---

5. Freud makes it plain that by "meaning" (*Bedeutung*) he understands "sense" (*Sinn*), "significance" (*Sinn*), "intention" (*Absicht*), "purpose" (*Absicht*), and "tendency" (*Tendenz*). See *SE* 15 (1916–17): 36, 40; *GW* 11. 29, 33; Freud 1952, p. 64.

6. In a footnote, Freud criticizes "the American doctrine of behaviourism . . . [for] think[ing] it possible to construct a psychology which disregards this fundamental fact [of consciousness]!" (*SE* 23 [1940]: 157, n. 1).

7. Freud thinks in terms of broad antecedent conditions of behavior in the form of instinctually based desires and their repression as underlying, without determining, more specific reasons and motives. Elucidation of these conditions is necessary for understanding certain broad dispositional tendencies, but these relatively plastic motives may be shaped and molded in more specific directions by the ego in its commerce with the environment. How this can be done is nowhere spelled out by Freud, but one compatible contemporary theory rests the case for the ego's freedom of choice on its capacity for redescription. For example, an individual can redirect her behavior by redescribing her world as one in which there is something good to eat in the icebox instead of one in which she is hungry. This process appears

purposes and intentions directed toward "idea[s] in . . . [the] mind" (*CP* 2 [1906]:16) as the "causes" of human conduct; and such teleological or final causes are not the sorts of determinants that necessitate the actions that follow from them.[8] To the contrary, they are the stuff of voluntary choices.

Of course, the ego is itself caused. Freud is not an indeterminist for whom freedom of choice requires some kind of magical, capricious, free-floating, uncaused cause existing outside the empirical world. The ego is anchored in a body, a history, and a surrounding milieu, and it functions in terms of its own governing principles; but given appropriate opportunities, the ego, nonetheless, normally develops some capacity and power to deliberate and to choose.

It is sometimes alleged that Freud viewed psychotherapy as providing the patient with nothing more than a "feeling of freedom" that is ultimately illusory,[9] the claim here being that the successfully analyzed patient behaves differently from before not because he or she is truly freer but only because analysis has effected changes in the cause–effect sequence that determines his or her behavior.[10] Unconscious compulsions have been replaced by the decisions of an ego that is itself completely determined in its preferences by motives and forces that are the product of the developmental interaction of organism and environment. The successfully treated patient may think that he or she does what he or she wants, but the wanting and deciding among wants are themselves completely determined independently of anything done by the agent.

If this interpretation of therapeutic agency were correct, then the feeling of greater freedom that accompanies a successful analysis would indeed be meaningless, and Freud would be simply confused and inconsistent—or highly cynical—when he speaks otherwise of the ego's increased mastery and self-control and the ego's freedom to choose. The outcome of successful psychoanalysis would be nothing more than a delusion, since the patient would be convinced by a mere "feeling" of freedom that he has obtained

---

to be implied by Freud in *SE* 5 (1900):617. In Freud's view, whether or not a particular ego has the capacity for self-guidance is established by clinical-empirical study, not dictated a priori by the doctrine of psychic determinism.

8. Freud's writings are replete with reasons of this kind. His implicit position seems to be that every decision a person makes is both determined by antecedent motives and free insofar as the act of committing the self adds a genuine element of novelty to choice (for discussion, see Ricoeur 1966).

9. For the view that the subjective experience of freedom is always an illusion, see Menninger 1942; Knight 1946; Alexander and Staub 1956.

10. See, e.g., E. R. Wallace 1986a, p. 943.

freedom of action, whereas in fact his conduct is still determined by forces beyond his control (see Mazer 1960; Basch 1978, p. 258).

Freud emphasizes, however, that the patient not only *feels* freer but actually *is* freer. Through analysis, the patient is said to "acquire the *extra piece of mental freedom [jenes Mehr von seelischer Freiheit]* which distinguishes conscious mental activity . . . from unconscious" (*SE* 12 [1915]:170, emphasis added; *GW* 10. 319–20). The subjective sense of freedom is pretty much beside the point; after all, consciousness can be deceived. The goal of psychoanalytic therapy is to expand the range of "conscious will-power" to unconscious motives (*SE* 7 [1905]:266). "It is only by the application of our highest mental functions, which are bound up with consciousness, that we can *control* all our impulses" (ibid., emphasis added).

But if Freud means what he says here about willpower, what then are we to make of his other statements that seem to say that free will is an illusion? What at first appears to be an irresolvable conundrum turns out to hinge on a mistaken impression that in these other observations Freud is refuting the doctrine of free will, an error that derives primarily from a mistranslation of a key passage by the editors of the *Standard Edition*, as well as from a general failure to attend to the specific contexts in which Freud pits psychic determinism against "psychic freedom."

The passage most frequently cited in support of Freud's alleged commitment to universal determinism in the hard sense that precludes moral responsibility is translated in the *Standard Edition* as "Faith in undetermined psychic events and in *free will* . . . is quite unscientific" (*SE* 15 [1916–17]:106).[11] Recourse to the original German text discloses that this translation is wrong, however. Freud's own words are "Glaube an psychische Freiheit und Willkürlichkeit . . . ganz unwissenschaftlich ist" (*GW* 11 [1916–17]:104). *Willkürlichkeit* here means "arbitrariness" or arbitrary act, not "free will" in the sense of a rational "choice," and *Freiheit* refers to completely unconditioned happenings, not to a rational choice among alternative courses of action—as Freud makes clear three sentences later when he reiterates his claim that "the idea produced by the man was *not arbitrary nor indeterminable*" [*nicht willkürlich, nicht unbestimmbar*] (*SE* 15 [1916–17]:106; *GW* 11. 104, emphasis added). If Freud had wished to declare free will illusory, he would presumably have made this clear by using *freier Wille* or *die Willensfreiheit* or *die Selbstbestimmung* rather than the ambiguous term *Freiheit*. But he nowhere uses these other terms in connec-

11. Those who cite this passage in support of attributing universal determinism to Freud include Weiss (1968, p. 59), Spero (1978, p. 7), and Iturrate (1977, p. 36).

tion with what psychic determinism precludes. Correctly translated, the passage reads: "Faith in [unconditioned] psychic freedom and in arbitrary choices . . . is quite unscientific." In context, it speaks to the validity of the psychoanalytic notion that dreams have meaning; and when Freud's statement is seen in this light, it is clear that he is here primarily concerned with countering a belief in the complete randomness or arbitrariness of dream images. What Freud meant here by psychic freedom (*psychische Freiheit*) was the capriciousness or randomness of dreams, not freedom of rational choice within the limits set by the general principles governing psychic processes. Freud does not deny us that latter freedom. His contention is that dreams are not arbitrary but are determined or caused by hidden motives. Otherwise, "what occurs to . . . [the dreamer] might be anything in the world" (*SE* 15 [1916–17]:106), and dream interpretation would be impossible.

The corollary of Freud's contention that dreams are not "free," or totally capricious, is *not* that all human conduct is inevitable, but that dreams "make sense" and are explicable in the sense of "interpretable."[12] There is absolutely no reason to read this section as if it were interrupted by a totally gratuitous, one-phrase assertion that all allegedly free choices are illusory, since nothing is said in context about such choices at all—which is not surprising, inasmuch as they do not occur in dreams.

THE COMPATIBILITY OF PSYCHIC DETERMINISM AND FREEDOM OF CHOICE

By what he says about the unpredictability of human conduct,[13] Freud implies that "psychic determinism" is meant to be compatible with some freedom of choice even after one has understood psychodynamically the causes that are at work within a person. He writes:

12. The other three passages in which Freud is thought by many to deny freedom of choice are no more concerned with the "hard" form of universal determinism than the one discussed in the text above. In one, on parapraxes (*SE* 15 [1916–17]:49), Freud is concerned with defending the "determination" of seemingly meaningless slips of the tongue by hidden motives against belief in "psychical freedom," which he defines as the complete *arbitrariness* of such behavioral events. The second, the only one in which Freud actually employs the expression "the illusion of free will," is concerned with the unreasonableness of the narcissist's belief in the realizability of grandiose fantasies (*SE* 17 [1919]:236) and may be read as supporting Freud's belief in some capacity for free choice, rather than denying it. In the third, and most troubling potentially, about the subjective conviction of free will (*SE* 6 [1901]:253–4), Freud's point is only that decisions, important and unimportant, conscious and unconscious, are *motivated*, and that this being the case, "determinism [meaning purposefulness] in the physical sphere is still carried out without any gap" and is thus "complete."

13. For a succinct contemporary discussion of why the human sciences cannot predict conduct, see MacIntyre 1981, pp. 84–102.

At this point we become aware of a state of things which also confronts us in many other instances in which light has been thrown by psychoanalysis on a mental process. So long as we trace the development from its final outcome backwards, the chain of events appears continuous, and we feel we have gained an insight which is completely satisfactory or even exhaustive. But if we proceed the reverse way, if we start from the premises inferred from the analysis and try to follow these up to the final result, then we no longer get the impression of an inevitable sequence of events which could not have been otherwise determined. We notice at once that there might have been another result, and that we might have been just as well able to understand and explain the latter. (*SE* 18 [1920]:167)

Although this passage can be read as pointing only to the epistemological problem of knowing all the determining causes of behavior,[14] the way in which Freud goes out of his way to state that the patient's conduct could have been otherwise seems intended to deny complete determinism in the sense that the result is automatic or inevitable, especially when it is coupled with what he says elsewhere about how the mature ego is able to decide one way or the other among competing motives (*SE* 19 [1923]: 50, n. 1).[15] What Freud appears to be after is a broader concept of determinism that makes room for the ego's relatively autonomous self-steering capacities (see Rapaport 1951, 1958; Rangell 1969, 1971, 1986).

14. One reason why prediction is difficult is that psychoanalysts believe behavior to be "overdetermined" (*überdeterminiert*) in the sense that there are usually several motives for any mental occurrence. Because it is difficult to ascertain which of the various and usually conflicting tendencies is strongest, it is hard to predict precisely what sort of subtle reconciliations will be achieved. (See Waelder 1936.)

15. The analyst's predictions may be better than the lay person's as a result of knowing the magnitude and nature of unconscious motivations and ego strengths, but they are not dissimilar in kind from those of anyone who makes an educated guess about what someone will do on the basis of knowing the sorts of motives and considerations that typically weigh most heavily with him or her. Of course, the psychoanalyst places less trust than the lay person in an individual's own statement of his motives, for he or she is generally in a better position than the lay person to understand the unconscious reasons that also motivate a person. But the kind of causation involved is not qualitatively different, for a person's unconscious motives are not alien forces but part of himself, and thus can be made conscious and used in guiding future behavior.

Waelder recalls a discussion during which Freud was asked whether it would have been possible to predict Jung's repudiation of psychoanalysis on the basis of a dream that revealed his latent hostility to Freud. Freud's answer was that "it could not have been foreseen because one did not know the strength of the intrapsychic . . . tendencies" (Waelder 1963, p. 36). Waelder argues convincingly that because psychoanalysis examines only behavioral "tendencies," not the necessary and sufficient conditions of the natural sciences, its determinants do not "have the stringency of the classical concept of determinism."

Except in cases of serious personality disturbances, Freud believes that people have some leeway, thanks to the various factors that determine mature ego functioning, in what they do with the various motives at work within them. Most individuals are able to monitor their potentially dangerous motives sufficiently to veto criminal acts, even when internal desires have some tendency in that direction.[16] The "I," or ego, is like "a constitutional monarch," in that it is normally capable of "imposing [its] . . . veto on any measure put forward by Parliament" (*SE* 19 [1923]:55).[17] Hence, no radical realignment of our ordinary view of the legal or moral person as normally responsible for avoiding criminal conduct and grossly immoral behavior is envisioned by Freud, although he recognized that psychoanalysis is in a position to identify numerous new excusing conditions as a result of its unique method of investigating irresistible unconscious compulsions.

Freud's 1920 testimony as an expert witness before an Austrian governmental commission charged with investigating the handling of psychiatric casualties during World War I illuminates this view. In it, Freud draws a careful distinction between soldiers suffering from war neuroses and malingerers feigning mental illness in order to avoid the dangers at the front. Since the former could not control their anxieties, Freud argues, it would be an "injustice" to treat them as responsible for their conduct. The assumption supporting this conclusion is similar to that of Aristotle: that we cannot be held responsible for actions due to ignorance or irresistible compulsion. Malingerers, on the other hand, should be deemed responsible for their actions, and thus deserving of blame and punishment, because

16. Although Freud is impressed by the extent to which the ego is habitually guided by compromises among mixed motives made below the level of consciousness, he assigns to the normal ego the power to intervene when behavior is about to get completely out of line. "Actions and consciously expressed opinions are as a rule enough for practical purposes in judging men's characters . . . Many impulses which force their way through to consciousness are even then brought to nothing by the real forces of mental life before they can mature into deeds. In fact, such impulses often meet with no psychic obstacles to their progress, for the very reason that the unconscious is certain that they will be stopped at some other stage" (*SE* 5 [1900]:621).

17. If this imagery seems to divorce the ego too much from the process of decision making, Freud corrects this impression with stronger claims on behalf of the ego indicating clearly that it may be actively engaged in decision making and in guiding actions involving competing motives (see text below). Waelder (1963) does justice to these claims of Freud when he compares the ego's power to that of a bloc of swing voters in a close election who are able to shift the balance of power decisively in one direction or another. In this analogy, the ego is the deciding factor when the alignment of motives for and against a decision is close.

they act with comparative freedom on the basis of rational calculations of self-interest.[18]

Freud's case histories also contain statements that clearly address the issue of moral responsibility. For example, Freud tells the " Rat Man" that "moral responsibility" is a developmental achievement of the mature ego and does not apply to the behavior of children or to uncontrollable compulsions that derive from infantile unconscious motivations. In his case history, Freud reports:

> I pointed out to him that he ought logically to consider himself as in no way responsible for any of these traits in his character; for all of these reprehensible impulses originated from his infancy, and were only derivatives of his infantile character surviving in his unconscious; and he must know that *moral responsibility* could not be applied to children. It was only by a process of development, I added, that a man, with his moral responsibility, grew up. (*CP* 3 [1909]:323, emphasis added)

Once again, this distinction between mature and immature behavior implies that adults *are* ordinarily responsible, in the sense of *deserving* praise, blame, or punishment, for those actions or part-actions that are due to motives they know about and can influence through rational deliberation and choice.[19] Indeed, having such leverage over one's conduct is a precondition of successful psychoanalysis. The patient must take "responsibility" for repressed motives in order for psychoanalytic therapy to work. This is one reason why Freud argues that analysis is best done with those

18. Returning to the malingerer–neurotic distinction in 1926, Freud underscores the complexity of ascertaining the responsibility of the neurotic, who is defined as a person whose "ego has lost its unity": "All our social institutions are framed for people with a united and normal ego, which one can classify as good or bad. . . . Hence the juridical alternatives: responsible or irresponsible. None of these distinctions apply to neurotics. It must be admitted that there is difficulty in adapting social demands to their psychological condition. This was experienced on a large scale during the last war. Were the neurotics who evaded service malingerers or not? They were both" (*SE* 20 [1926]:221). Although Freud holds that neurotics are to some indeterminate degree responsible for some aspects of their behavior, he also observes sagely that there is "no sense in reproaching them" (ibid., p. 222).

19. The legal theorist Michael Moore (1984) is essentially correct in concluding, on the basis of a philosophical examination of psychoanalysis, that there is nothing in "the psychiatric view of persons" that contradicts the presupposition in law and morality that a person is an autonomous, rational agent. But Moore's attribution of determinism to Freud and Freudians prevents him from seeing that Freud would have agreed. Where the two would presumably part company is primarily with regard to specific excusing conditions, with Moore less lenient on this point than Freud.

who are, except in certain areas of their lives, "otherwise masters" of themselves (*CP* 2 [1920]:205).

THE EGO'S CAPACITY FOR CHOICE

The strongest evidence for Freud's belief in freedom of choice is contained in his theoretical pronouncements about the mature ego. In his early writings, Freud commonly presupposes freedom of choice when he speaks of "consciousness" and the "ego." But this tacit belief in the ego's capacity for choice is difficult to square theoretically with the original metapsychological portrait of the mind as a passive reflex apparatus, even when account is taken of Freud's point that this model is woefully incomplete and designed primarily to help elucidate the functioning of the unconscious mind (see ch. 2 above).

In his later writings, however, Freud goes to considerable effort to explain *how* the ego gains some degree of autonomy from the id, despite psychoanalysis's emphasis on the extent to which the ego acquiesces in the id's dictates. Freud explains that in its transactions with reality, the activities of the ego are not programmed entirely by the id, because the ego normally has at its disposal desexualized or neutral energy that makes it possible for the ego to deviate from the id's desires (*SE* 19 [1923]:44–6; 20 [1926]:95–6, 98). Thus, the ego may act independently of the id: "by *deciding whether* . . . [the id's unsublimated desires] are to be allowed satisfaction, by *postponing* that satisfaction to times and circumstances favourable in the external world or by *suppressing* their excitations entirely" (*SE* 23 [1940]:145–6, emphasis added).

Further, because instinctual desires are plastic and not fixed, the mature ego possesses the ability to choose, mostly preconsciously, among various ways of *sublimating* the id's commands and therefore to redirect unacceptable desires toward goals that are syntonic with the ego's developed interests. In making these choices, the ego employs its capacity for "judgement," which Freud defines as "the intellectual action which *decides* [*entscheidet*] the choice of motor action" (*SE* 19 [1925]:238, emphasis added; *GW* 14. 14). After this kind of second-order sorting has been accomplished, judgment "puts an end to the postponement due to thought and . . . leads over from thinking to acting" (ibid.). Acts of judgment relating to formerly unconscious desires may result "*either* in . . . accepting *or* in . . . condemning . . . what had formerly been repudiated" (*SE* 20 [1925]:30, emphasis added), for in executing such judgments, "the ego has voluntary movement at its command" (*SE* 23 [1940]:145).

Freud here expresses a critical tenet of free-will theory—namely, that persons have the *power*, after second-order reflection, to choose from among their several wants and select the particular desire or combination of desires that will lead them all the way to action.[20] Freud differs from libertarians in part in holding that subjective feelings of freedom are deceptive, in part in contending that the ego is itself caused, thought not in such a way as to preclude all freedom to deliberate and to choose. And so Freud embraces the paradox that freedom arises within a context of a certain form of complete *psychic* determinism (see J. H. Smith 1978).

The ego's capacity to choose goals and to carry out its decisions, while an important principle, is never absolute. Choices are limited by the ego's own preferences, by powerful a priori motivations, and by defensive patterns that can be shaped and guided but not eliminated entirely. If only through sublimation, the ego must find some way of satisfying the strongest instinctual desires. Otherwise its best intentions are apt to be subverted by contrary motivations that become more compelling the more they are disowned. Unlike emotions and desires that *remain* unconscious, the ego's preferences are directly modifiable by second-order reflection and evaluation. For example, the ego is in a position to evaluate the authenticity of its various desires, their relative worth in comparison with other ego and non-ego desires, and the consequences of following the ego's preferences for the self as a whole (i.e., the self that is constituted by the interplay of ego, id, and superego).

Here we have the paradox of the importance to free choice itself of acknowledging unchosen instinctual and developmental determinants of behavior. As Freud puts it:

> People usually overlook the . . . essential point . . . that the pathogenic conflict in neurotics is not to be confused with a normal struggle between mental impulses both of which are on the same psychological footing. In the former case the dissension is between two powers, one of which . . . is preconscious or conscious while the other has been held back at the stage of the unconscious. For that reason the conflict cannot be brought to an issue; the disputants can no more come to grips than, in the familiar simile, a polar bear and a whale. *A true decision can only be reached when they both meet on the same ground. To make this possible is, I think, the sole task of our therapy.* (SE 16 [1916–17]:433, emphasis added)

This brings us to the philosophical significance of Freud's unique treatment of the freedom versus determinism issue: psychoanalysis's middle way

20. For discussion of this point, see Frankfurt 1971.

between the British empiricist-utilitarian view that freedom is the absence of external coercion in the realization of desires and the contrasting Kantian conception of freedom as absolute moral autonomy.[21]

Like Locke and Mill, Freud appreciates that a person is not genuinely free if he or she is coerced or constrained by others from acting on the basis of inner preferences. The excessively repressive nature of civilization is one of Freud's dominant themes. But unlike the mainstream of the British tradition that runs from Hobbes to contemporary utilitarians, Freud does not believe that the self is free merely because it is not prevented by *external* restraints from pursuing the objects of its desires. With Kant, he sees that the self's passions can themselves enslave. One is not the author of one's acts if one can do nothing more than passively acquiesce in whatever desires one happens to have, even if they are an essential part of human nature.

Likewise, Freud rejects the British tradition's psychological assumptions about the ease with which the self can identify its own desires or preferences. In contrast to Hobbes, Locke, and Bentham, Freud points out that there are considerable psychological obstacles to knowing our innermost desires, so that we may be constrained *internally* from acting out our deepest wishes, even though from an external perspective we appear to be free. For Freud, in order to account for freedom of action, it is necessary to articulate expressly the ego's ability to step back with some degree of detachment from the desires one happens to have, because these are not necessarily the desires that the self wants at a deeper level to guide its actions.

But if Freud disagrees with the psychological naiveté of the British tradition's environmentalist approach to freedom, he is no less critical of Kant's alternative approach. For Kant, freedom lies in the ego's self-determination through conformity to universalizable moral principles that have

21. Rapaport (1958) makes a similar point when he argues that the psychoanalytic understanding of "autonomy" falls between the view that the individual must be somewhat independent of the environment and the view that the agent must be somewhat independent of inner forces. Abramson argues similarly that the psychoanalytic understanding of the "liberation" achieved by therapy falls between the Hobbesian and the Kantian accounts of freedom (1984, pp. 131–8). But because he believes, wrongly, that Freudian theory is completely deterministic, he grounds the freedom-oriented side of psychoanalysis solely in Freud's therapeutic work, believing it to be wholly unarticulated at the level of theory. It is not surprising, however, that Freud himself should seek a reconciliation of these traditions on the level of theory, since he was well trained intellectually in both. He studied the British empiricist-utilitarian tradition, as well as Kant, in depth with Brentano and stood within the Kantian-Schopenhauerian tradition insofar as he built on Meynert's work. See McGrath 1986, pp. 126–7, 142–4.

their ground in reason alone, completely independently of any prior conditioning by desire.[22] In Freud's view, Kant's concept of a noumenal moral self that rules itself in sovereign independence of any and all desires is not only illusory but also a prescription for the loss of psychological freedom. As Freud's clinical writings on obsessional neuroses and superego morality make clear, any attempt to tyrannically subdue the emotions from on high in practice means that the ego's actions are increasingly determined by unconscious desires that cannot be monitored and guided, precisely because they are not allowed entry into the morally "good" person's self-concept.

Freud addresses the Kantian misconstrual of inner freedom when he declares to an imaginary ego: "'You over-estimated your strength when you thought you could treat your . . . instincts as you liked and could utterly ignore their intentions. The result is that they have rebelled and have taken their own obscure paths to escape this suppression'" (*SE* 17 [1917]:142). Thus Freud does not regard freedom as the radical independence of practical reason from the passions but instead, in his post-1919 work, invites us to redefine freedom primarily as a matter of choosing among and guiding actions arising out of preexisting motives that are nevertheless somewhat plastic as to their goals and modes of gratification. This requires, as a first step, that the individual recognize that without some special effort, he does not necessarily understand his own motivations very well. There is "a great deal more . . . going on in [the] . . . mind than [is] . . . known to . . . consciousness," Freud points out (*SE* 17 [1917]:143). "The news that [does] reach . . . consciousness is incomplete and often not to be relied on" (ibid.). Therefore, to increase moral freedom, Freud instructs that it is necessary to "turn your eyes inward, look into your own depths, learn first to know yourself" (ibid.) in order to make unconscious motives "accessible to all the influences of the other trends in the ego" (*SE* 23 [1937]:225).

For this to be efficacious, however, something more is required than mere intellectual understanding. To acknowledge a disavowed desire in the psychoanalytic sense is not the same as to recognize it cognitively in the abstract. Mere intellectual understanding has "as much influence . . . [on decision-making] as a distribution of menu-cards in a time of famine has upon hunger," Freud declares (*SE* 11 [1910]:225). Becoming conscious of

---

22. Kant was aware that in reality human beings are ruled by emotions as well as by reason; but he insisted that rational beings should seek to be wholly free of the emotions. For a brief discussion, see Katz 1984, pp. 108–10.

an unpalatable unconscious wish involves, first, acknowledging the defenses that have led to its disavowal and, then, *experiencing that wish as one's own,* as proceeding from oneself, in a way that brings it within the sway of the ego's guidance.[23]

Psychoanalysis is well known for shrinking the realm of moral responsibility, by bringing to light new excusing circumstances. The presence of a deep psychopathology like a psychosis or a severe obsessional disorder, for example, means that individuals who would once have been deemed morally accountable for their actions are now seen to lack the capacity either to understand certain actions or to control their behavior, so that attribution of moral responsibility to them is unwarranted. Psychoanalysis also enables us to understand a variety of compromise formations in relatively mature personalities that indicate either that in a particular situation an individual was not capable of deliberation or voluntary choice or, at least, that what he or she did, did not issue from the relatively autonomous sectors of the personality.[24] In such situations praise- and blame-related feelings and attitudes are inappropriate.[25]

It is less often appreciated that psychoanalysis also expands the realm of moral responsibility. For Freud would have us take responsibility not only for our overt acts and the conscious intentions that motivate them but also for those inner inclinations and defenses of which we are not yet conscious.[26]

23. When the relatively normal individual becomes conscious of previously unconscious wishes or processes, the ego's freedom to bring about something new is dramatically increased. As Loewald observes: "Psychoanalysis has always maintained that the life of the individual is determined by . . . early experiences . . .; but everything depends on *how* these early experiences are repeated in the course of life, to what extent they are repeated passively—suffered again even if 'arranged' by the individual that undergoes them . . . —*and to what extent they can be taken over in the ego's organizing activity and made over into something new—a re-creation of something old as against a duplication of it*" (1980, pp. 89–90, emphasis added).

24. See Strawson 1974, pp. 7–9 for a discussion of how the terms on which we hold other persons morally accountable are altered when the agent is considered psychologically abnormal or undeveloped. Strawson contrasts agent-based excusing conditions with excuses that focus on circumstances that coerce or compel.

25. For discussion of reactive attitudes and feelings, see Strawson 1974 and Bennett 1980.

26. Moore observes that psychoanalysis is "perhaps unique in its claim that its insights compel a reassessment of responsibility that both generally diminishes and generally increases the items for which each person is responsible" (1984, p. 381). But because he attributes hard determinism to psychoanalysis on the basis of its original mechanistic metatheory, he concludes that these implications for responsibility are "symptomatic of a kind of conceptual schizophrenia" (ibid.). This contrasts with my attempt to explain why these divergent implications for responsibility are compatible.

In his 1925 essay on "Moral Responsibility for the Content of Dreams," Freud argues that we must take responsibility, in the sense of owning as ours, the content of unconscious or repressed wishes that, while hidden, may still motivate behavior and are a definite part of the self. He states:

> Obviously one must hold oneself responsible for the evil impulses of one's dreams. What else is one to do with them? . . . [They are] a part of my own being. If I seek to classify the impulses that are present in me according to social standards into good and bad, I must assume responsibility for both sorts; and if, in defence, I say that what is unknown, unconscious and repressed in me is not my 'ego', then I shall not be basing my position upon psycho-analysis, I shall not have accepted its conclusions—and I shall perhaps be taught better by the criticisms of my fellow-men, by the disturbances in my actions and the confusion of my feelings. I shall perhaps learn that what I am disavowing not only 'is' in me but sometimes 'acts' from out of me as well.[27] (*SE* 19 [1925]:133)

If we take the implications of psychoanalysis seriously, we are responsible in several different ways for our multiply motivated conduct. We are responsible *retrospectively,* in the sense of deserving modest praise, reward, or punishment for what we have *consciously intended,* unless we have been impeded in our decision making or action by a mental aberration, such as an irresistible compulsion, neurotic conflict, or serious mental illness. There is nothing in psychoanalysis that refutes this ordinary, everyday meaning of moral responsibility for past actions.[28]

What Freud teaches is that because our actions are multiply motivated, their voluntary aspects tend to be mixed with behavior that is involuntary. Thus a professional performance may be executed with the skill intended but with an unintended melancholy overtone due to unconscious anger displaced from a parental substitute onto the self. The ratio of the voluntary component of an action to its involuntary elements varies both among persons (in accordance with differences in basic personality configuration)

27. Freud argues similarly in *Introductory Lectures* that "if a man has repressed his evil impulses into the unconscious and would like to tell himself afterwards that he is not responsible for them, he is nevertheless bound to be aware of this responsibility" (*SE* 16 [1916–17]:331). In this connection Freud interprets Sophocles as saying in effect: "'You are struggling in vain against your responsibility and are protesting in vain of what you have done in opposition to these criminal intentions. You are guilty, for you have not been able to destroy them; they still persist in you unconsciously'" (ibid.). As Rangell puts it, in psychoanalysis "man . . . becomes responsible not for less but for more than he knows" (1986, p. 19).

28. Indeed, while it is true that psychoanalysis helps us to understand that not all conduct is controlled by conscious intention, there is much on the clinical side, such as a patient taking responsibility for previously disavowed motivations, to confirm the psychoanalytic acceptance of this form of moral responsibility.

and in the same person from moment to moment. Even in the relatively healthy individual, the fact that so much in the mind remains unconscious makes it exceedingly difficult to be confident that we know enough about an individual's inner mental life to be sure about the degree to which an act is voluntary or involuntary. Nonetheless, Freud felt that in the absence of evidence of mental aberration, ordinary judgments of intentional actions normally suffice. "Actions and consciously expressed opinions are as a rule enough for practical purposes in judging men's character," he wrote (*SE* 5 [1900]:621).

Psychoanalytic understanding would also have us be *prospectively* responsible for increasing our self-knowledge and gaining control over those unconscious motives that contribute, perhaps decisively, to our conduct. This is similar to the time-honored notion that a person must take responsibility for his own character, though psychoanalysis expands the realm with which one is morally charged to include typical unconscious motives, spontaneous reactions, and settled behavioral patterns that were previously considered beyond conscious control.[29]

In therapy, the analyst often has to convince the patient that his own motives have played a part in some occurrence to get him to accept the task of self-improvement in the future. An example is Freud's insistence that Dora take responsibility for the motives underlying her cough:

> I now return to the reproach of malingering which Dora brought against her father. . . . I was obliged to point out to the patient that her present ill-health was just as much actuated by motives and was just as tendentious as had been Frau K.'s illness, which she had understood so well. [Frau K. was Dora's father's mistress who faked illness to be with him at a resort.] There could be no doubt, I said, that she had an aim in view which she hoped to gain by her illness. That aim could be none other than to detach her father from Frau K. She had been unable to achieve this by prayers or arguments; perhaps she hoped to succeed by frightening her father (there was her farewell letter), or by awakening his pity (there were her fainting-fits), or if all this was in vain, at least she would be taking her revenge on him. (*SE* 7 [1905]:42)

29. This prospective responsibility for our character is one reason why we hold persons retrospectively responsible for specific acts they were powerless to change at the moment of acting. We think they had something to do with the development of the characteristic style of behavior out of which they acted. Even if they did not directly choose it, we consider it possible that they may have had a part in choosing to be unconscious of both it and its behavioral consequences. As Evans notes, "the inability to change is perhaps, then, grounded in a choice for which the person *is* responsible" (1984, p. 359) in that in the past the person did not take sufficient prospective responsibility for his or her own character.

Freud admits that Dora could not simply "will" her symptoms away, but because "illnesses of this kind *are* the result of intention," they do yield to therapeutic efforts aimed at the unconscious mental states involved (*SE 7* [1905]:45). "An attempt must first be made by the roundabout methods of analysis to convince the patient herself of the existence in her of an intention to be ill" and of her "responsibility" for it (ibid.).[30] Psychoanalysis as a therapy is in the service of taking prospective responsibility for one's character in this sense (see *SE* 16 [1916–17]:433).

Finally, psychoanalysis expands our ordinary understanding of responsibility by implicitly teaching that we are morally responsible *retrospectively*, not just prospectively, for *actions* (as contrasted with dispositions and character traits) that we did not consciously intend. If, in acting as I consciously intend, I also do something harmful that I unconsciously wished to bring about without being aware of it, I am *responsible*—that is, I deserve some degree of disapprobation—for the desire to injure and for any actual deleterious consequences that my conduct may have inflicted, once the causal consequences of my unconscious mental states become clear, even if, before I acted, I did not know that I wanted to do anything injurious and therefore did not form a conscious intention to do it. Responsibility for unconsciously guided actions that do harm is justified because the *behavior* is in fact my own (it proceeded "out of me," not from some alien force). The action was *self*-determining in the broader meaning that depth psychology confers on the term "self."[31] Freud even holds that I have no real choice about accepting responsibility for past unconsciously motivated behavior. "I am somehow compelled to do so" (*SE* 19 [1925]:133) as soon as I am aware that the actions proceeded out of me.[32] I own the action retro-

30. Another example is Freud's discussion of assuming responsibility for the motives involved in forgetting appointments. See *SE* 6 (1901):153.

31. M. Moore argues against what he calls this "radical extension of responsibility" to unconsciously motivated past actions on the grounds that we can only be responsible for acts we consciously intend. He writes: "We need to know if events such as dreams, forgotten appointments, or neurotic symptoms are truly intentional actions . . . [in order to claim that someone] can fairly be held responsible" (1984, p. 345). This may be the case in criminal law (Moore is a law professor), but in morality we do sometimes rightly feel responsible for past actions that we did not consciously intend but that nonetheless issued from us. Thus we do not misspeak when we apologize for such behavior.

32. Indeed, Freud contends that most people assume responsibility unconsciously for socially unacceptable behavior, regardless of whether they intended what they did or imagined doing. Because this spontaneous assumption of responsibility so commonly results in excessive self-punishment, we are better off psychologically if we acknowledge our responsibility than if we do not; for this allows us to assume a more realistic self-evaluative stance toward our own behavior.

spectively by sincerely acknowledging that I caused it to happen and by sincerely regretting that I did not know myself well enough to succeed in monitoring my motivations so as to prevent the injury from occurring. Such sincere regret normally entails prospective responsibility in that in the act of acknowledging my responsibility for the regretted behavior I commit myself to do what is necessary not to act out of such motives in the same way in the future.

Psychoanalysis more fully supports assigning moral responsibility in such instances than does the Western moral tradition generally, because it reveals that the person who acts thoughtlessly or without any conscious intention to do harm unconsciously "intends"—in the sense of "aims at"— these consequences. The harmful behavior, though thoughtless, was not a random compulsion that must remain forever outside the agent's ability to control. Rather, it was motivated by unconscious reasons for action that should be understood as aspects of the "self" that acts. If these motives have not been subjected to conscious guidance, they should have been or should be, and the agent should assume responsibility for what he or she has failed to accomplish in this regard, even though that failure may be perfectly understandable.

In using the term *moral responsibility* in several senses, and broadening its usual limitations, Freud generally avoids such terms as *guilt, guilty,* and *morally blameworthy.* This is not because he denies the appropriateness of what might be referred to as realistic *remorse* for actual misdeeds. To the contrary, Freud clearly differentiates the ego-based sentiment of remorse from irrational guilt.[33] He is leery of the term *guilt* and its variants because it connotes an indiscriminate self-punishment that is often irrational either because it is excessively harsh in light of the actual deed or because it is triggered by mere fantasies.[34] Terms like *guilt* and *blame* are also avoided by

33. At the end of *The Interpretation of Dreams,* for example, Freud recommends that "for practical [moral] purposes" we need to distinguish between "actions" and mere "impulses . . . [that] are brought to nothing by the real forces of mental life before they can mature into deeds" (*SE* 5 [1900]:621). There is a real difference, he argues, between taking responsibility for an actual misdeed and for a mere wish. "The Roman emperor was in the wrong when he had one of his subjects executed because he had dreamt of murdering the emperor," he writes (*SE* 5 [1900]:620). It is needful and "right to bear in mind Plato's dictum that the virtuous man is content to *dream* what a wicked man really *does*" (ibid., emphasis original). In fact, this distinction is crucial to our very willingness to accept "responsibility for the immorality of [our] . . . dreams," since we can do so only if we can avoid condemning ourselves for the mere fact of having such "ethically objectionable" impulses.

34. According to Freud, guilt as a phenomenon of conscience originates in fear of external authority figures and then evolves with the establishment of the superego, or conscience, into

Freud because they tend to be used intrapsychically against the self in ways that end up being morally self-defeating. This is likely to happen because the belittling, disparaging, and condemning connotations of these terms in combination with the superego's proclivity for applying them indiscriminately to the entire self tend to trigger self-defensiveness. And self-defensiveness functions intrapsychically as an obstacle to the very self-understanding that is essential to responsibility. The accused ego feels like a terribly naughty or totally bad child, and these feelings in turn fuel motives of denial, repression, and revenge, rather than honest self-scrutiny and efforts at self-improvement.

Neurotic guilt such as this differs in its underlying dynamics from *remorse*, which is the term Freud prefers for the feelings of self-reproach that come with recognition that one has committed an actual misdeed (*SE* 21 [1930]:131). Freud stresses that remorse "relates only to a deed that has been done" and not to mere intentions or wishes. It is realistic and appropriate for a person to feel remorse "because he really has done something which cannot be justified" (ibid.).

The term *responsibility* rather than *remorse* is preferred by Freud in contexts calling for prospective accountability for guiding previously unconscious motivations in the future. *Responsibility* in these contexts connotes an orientation toward the self of gentle caretaking or stewardship rather than punitive self-condemnation and correction. This gentler attitude permits the substitution of self-honesty for denial and repression. And this in turn allows continuous active engagement of the self with itself to replace the passivity with which the ordinary neurotic submits to ego-alien motives. As Loewald observes about this use of the concept of responsibility in Freud's work, it implies a movement from passivity to activity:

> To acknowledge, recognize, understand one's unconscious as one's own means to move from a position of passivity in relation to it to a position where active care

---

fear of the harsh superego itself (see, e.g., *SE* 21 [1930]: 124–5, 127–8). At the first stage, external moral prohibitions call for renunciation of instinctual satisfactions upon pain of external punishment and loss of love. When the renunciation is carried out, ordinarily no sense of guilt remains. At the second stage, after prohibitions are internalized, "instinctual renunciation is not enough" (*SE* 21 [1930]: 127). The newly created conscience presses for punishment (in the form of a sense of guilt or of self-injuring behavior) simply because desires or wishes persist, whether or not they are actually acted on (ibid.). To the ever vigilant superego, transgression can be found in mere thoughts and desires. At this point, "[a] threatened external unhappiness—loss of love and punishment on the part of the external authority—has been exchanged for a permanent internal unhappiness, for the tension of the sense of guilt" (*SE* 21 [1930]:128). Guilt becomes a more or less permanent mental fixture.

of it becomes possible, where it becomes a task worthy of pursuit to make one's business and concern those needs and wishes, fantasies, conflicts and traumatic events and defenses that have been passively experienced and reproduced. . . . Psychoanalysis as a method of treatment . . . [involves] assuming responsibility for oneself.[35] (1980, pp. 95–6)

Again, the point of assuming responsibility for unseemly unconscious motivations is not to induce irrational guilt or self-hatred but to acknowledge the presence of motives as parts of the self that should have been—and should now be—guided by the ego.

These applications of moral responsibility assume that it makes sense to speak of "self-determination" as an alternative to both indeterminism and hard determinism. The problem with indeterminism is that it seems to imply that a "free" act, being causally undetermined, is capricious or random. But if our actions are really capricious, it is difficult to see in what sense they can be viewed as being within the control of an agent or ascribable to that agent.[36] The problem with hard determinism is that it seems to render every action ultimately unavoidable and thus to undercut our ordinary sense of being responsible for our actions. By contrast, the concept of self-determination offers a mediating position by holding that persons can become the sources or causes of their own action, even though they are themselves the products of a complex network of various types of causes extended over time and now hierarchically organized. The strength as well as the functional capacities of the self that determines an action can be explained developmentally, so that we cannot say that everyone has the

35. Loewald points out elsewhere that the capacity to assume active responsibility of this sort depends on the presence of psychic structures that arise developmentally from the oedipal child's acceptance of guilt for incestuous and murderous desires. Thus, despite the emphasis in the text on Freud's avoidance of irrational guilt, there remains a place for acknowledgment of guilt that is grounded in phantasy rather than reality. Loewald writes: "Responsibility to oneself, in the sense of being responsive to one's urgings . . . involves facing and bearing the guilt for those acts we consider criminal. Prototypical, in oedipal context, are parricide and incest. From the standpoint of psychic reality it matters little if these acts are, from the viewpoint of objective reality, merely fantasies or symbolic acts . . . Self-responsibility, involving parricide in psychic reality and in symbolic form . . . , is, from the viewpoint of received morality, a crime. But it is not only a crime of which humans inevitably become guilty in the process of emancipating individuation . . . ; self-responsibility at the same time is the restitutive atonement for that crime. Without the guilty deed of parricide there is no autonomous self. . . . Guilt and atonement are crucial motivational elements of the self. Guilt then is not a troublesome affect that we might hope to eliminate in some fashion, but one of the driving forces in the organization of the self" (1980, pp. 393–4).

36. For discussion of how indeterminism threatens moral responsibility, see Hobart 1934; Strawson 1974; and Bennett 1980.

same capacity to guide his or her own behavior or to assume responsibility for what he or she has done.[37] The various preferences that guide a person, their strengths and weaknesses, can be explained. But for the relatively normal, mature personality, there remains some leeway within the constraints set by the principles that govern mental functioning and by the inevitability of multiple causes of behavior to rationally assess the desirability of preferences and to choose among alternative courses of action in a way that makes a difference to the outcome. Persons thus have some, albeit limited (and varying) capacity to determine and guide their own actions rather than allowing them to be caused by something other than themselves.

The psychoanalytic concept of responsibility encourages acknowledgment of the unconscious motives that are at work within us, not for purposes of feeding self-condemnation or fueling nihilistic abandon ("If it is, so be it"), but in order to gain some degree of mastery or leverage over such motives in the future. "Where id was, ego shall be," Freud declares (*SE* 22 [1933]:80). Growth in psychoanalytic freedom lies in the slow, gradual process of self-understanding and reinterpretation that alone provides an opportunity to gain access to and some degree of control over elemental motives that will otherwise erupt and disrupt our best intentions.[38] Psy-

37. Freud recognized that our having the capacity to choose and to carry our choices into action is itself a by-product of favorable childhood experiences and environmental circumstances that not everyone enjoys to the same degree (see *SE* 21 [1930]:111). We are therefore warned against applying to everyone the same standards. But Freud also assumes that once capacities for deliberation and choice exist, we are not totally determined with respect to what we do with these abilities. For a recent contribution to our understanding of why some people have difficulty taking responsibility for their behavior, see Coen 1989.

38. One of the distinguishing characteristics of the psychoanalytic view of human autonomy is that it depends not only on the structural ego being able to function without undue disturbance from the depths but also on the ego's predominantly preconscious access to and ability to roam freely over archaic memories, deep emotions, and spontaneous fantasies. Archaic elements must become available to the higher mental functions assigned in theory to the ego so that their power can be employed in accordance with the purposes of the self as a whole (see Kohut 1973, pp. 365–6; 393, n. 13; Rangell 1986, p. 18). The ego functions most autonomously, then, when it is acknowledged that completely irrational desires and forces exist within the self that can only be yielded to, not controlled. This suggests that a receptive moment enters into every voluntary act (Ricoeur 1966). As J. H. Smith notes, acknowledgment of such "a receptive moment at the heart of every psychic act does not reduce activity to passivity. The person in the act of decision has the power to actively consider the variety of motives and the valency of their objects and to choose in the light of memory and anticipation" (1978, p. 100). Psychological autonomy here implies acceptance of limitations plus an awareness that the limitations provide room for the continued exercise of the self.

choanalytic freedom thus combines acceptance of those deep parts of oneself that cannot be eliminated or overly shaped with efforts at active self-guidance. Where for Plato the psyche is a charioteer that guides, controls, reigns in the passions and appetites (see the *Phaedrus*), for Freud the ego is like a "rider guiding the horse where it wants to go" (*SE* 19 [1923]:25).

Freud's famous retake of Plato's equestrian metaphor of the psyche has been taken by some as yet another expression of his deterministic bent. But determinism is certainly not what Freud intended. First, he subsequently took pains to correct the erroneous impression that he regarded the structural ego as completely helpless in the face of overwhelming unconscious drives that made the ego's freedom illusory. Writing in 1926, in *Inhibitions, Symptoms and Anxiety,* to support the view that "the ego controls the path to action," Freud stated:

> At this point it is relevant to ask how I can reconcile this acknowledgement of the might of the ego with the description of its position which I gave in *The Ego and the Id*. In that book I drew a picture of its dependent relationship to the id and to the superego and revealed how powerless and apprehensive it was in regard to both and with what an effort it maintained its show of superiority over them. This view has been widely echoed in psycho-analytic literature. Many writers have laid much stress on the weakness of the ego in relation to the id and of our rational elements in the face of the daemonic forces within us . . . Yet surely the psycho-analyst, with his knowledge . . . should, of all people, be restrained from adopting such an extreme and one-sided view. (*SE* 20 [1926]:95)

Second, a closer examination of Freud's original horse-and-rider statement in *The Ego and the Id* shows that Freud was not saying that unconscious desires wholly determine behavior by overpowering or subverting rational choice. Freud leads up to his use of the Platonic metaphor by first disagreeing with the notion that "the ego behaves essentially passively in life, and that . . . we are 'lived' by unknown and uncontrollable forces" (*SE* 19 [1923]:23). This is too one-sided, he says. The ego is like a man on horseback who checks and guides the superior strength of the horse. In this Freud agrees with Plato and the mainstream of the Western philosophical and religious tradition that there is a genuine role for the ego and for reason. But, Freud says, Plato goes too far, as do many other moralists, in making the rider radically independent of the horse and urging him to exert control by aggressive domination. In Freud's alternative account, the rider and the horse are symbiotic—parts of the same self. The rider (the ego) must to some degree respect where the horse wants to go, yet normally he also has available borrowed forces that can be used to help transform the raw elemental strength of animal impulses into socially acceptable, ego-syntonic action. In a still later use of the horse-and-rider analogy in *New Introductory Lectures* (1933), Freud writes: "The horse [id] supplies the locomotive energy, while the rider has the privilege of *deciding on the goal* and of *guiding* the powerful animal's movement" (*SE* 22 [1933]:77, emphasis added). Freud emphasizes the rider's "guidance" as opposed to the "control" stressed by Plato, who gave the charioteer a whip. The Freudian lesson is that to fulfill its own functions well, the ego must be responsive to the psyche's "animal" or id impulses even as it directs and guides them toward goals that are satisfactory to the self as a whole.

Freud's reconstituted metaphor does away with the classical Western concept of the self as a transcendental or supra-empirical subject that exists prior to its ends as a pure subject of agency. Instead, the rational part of the self is reunited with the passions, from which it is deemed to derive much of its power for self-guidance. In this account, the self is envisioned as vulnerable to inner and outer contingencies, such that certain favorable conditions, like favorable genetic endowment plus the love and esteem of others, are essential for the distinctly human capacity for self-guidance to emerge and to continue to function in ordinary daily life. And yet, reason is not in Freud's view "powerless in comparison with . . . instinctual life . . . The voice of the intellect is a soft one, but it does not rest till it has gained a hearing" (*SE* 21 [1927]:53).

PART II
Psychological Egoism

Chapter 5
Overview of Psychological Egoism

Man has always known he was a spiritual
[*geistige*] being; it remained for me to show
him that he was instinctual.

—Freud, in conversation with
Ludwig Binswanger

Psychoanalytic findings are unquestionably relevant to the much-discussed doctrine of psychological egoism. This doctrine holds that as a matter of empirical fact, human beings are constituted so that each seeks—and can only seek—his or her own welfare or self-interest. As a thesis about what people actually desire, psychological egoism is not a normative doctrine, for it does not purport to state what is *desirable,* only what is *desired.* But it has long been recognized as having considerable ethical significance by virtue of the restrictions it places on our capacity to be moral. Indeed, if psychological egoism in its most restrictive sense is a true description of human nature, we lack the capacity to be either impartial or other-regarding—that is, to be moral at all.

To many readers, it may appear self-evident that Freud, like Hobbes, with whom he is frequently compared, was a psychological egoist. Solomon Asch expresses this common viewpoint when he contends, about Freud, that "he failed to find a place for the growth of interest in other human beings and concern for them which is not based on the gratification of needs having reference only to the self" (1952, p. 19). And Fromm answers the rhetorical question "Did Freud recognize the moral factor as a fundamental part in his model of man?" thus: "The answer to this question is in the negative. Man develops exclusively under the influence of his self-interest, which demands optimal satisfaction of his libidinal impulses, always on the condition that they do not endanger his interest in self-preservation" (in Roazen 1973, p. 52).

Apparent support for this interpretation is not hard to find in Freud's work. His most widely read books, *The Future of an Illusion* and *Civilization and its Discontents,* aggressively seek to compel the reader to confront the real motives behind human behavior, particularly egoistic and competitive motives. In terms of specific doctrine, Freud's claim that the pleasure principle regulates all mental activity seems to imply that we always act only with a view to obtaining the most pleasurable—or the least unpleasurable—subjective states of ourselves. Likewise, his doctrine of narcissism is usually read as indicating that we value others primarily for satisfying our personal needs, especially our need for self-aggrandizement. And the "orthodox" psychoanalytic explanation of many so-called higher social motivations, such as altruism, invokes doctrines of aim inhibition and reaction formation that suggest that these manifestations of our "better selves" are mere facades for selfishness.[1] It is for these reasons that psychoanalysis is popularly viewed as the chief theoretical prop for psychological egoism.

Among Freudian scholars, however, there is hardly unanimity as to whether psychoanalysis implies psychological egoism.[2] Even among those who do attribute this doctrine to Freud, there is considerable disagreement over whether his particular version of it is compatible with being moral, as were the hedonist psychologies of the classical Greeks and the early utilitarians.[3] On this last issue, psychoanalysts are far more likely than academicians to view Freudian theory as only limiting, not undermining or negating, our moral capacities. The usual psychoanalytic assumption is that Freud recognized that there are ways of being moral that are not at odds with self-interest. For example, the fully mature person is generally pictured by psychoanalysts as obtaining satisfaction through other-regarding

1. Martin Hoffman, e.g., states that "the doctrinaire view . . . in . . . psychoanalysis . . . has been that altruistic behavior can always be explained ultimately in terms of instrumental self-serving motives in the actor" (1976, p. 124).

2. Some interpreters of Freud are not even consistent in what they say about his position on psychological egoism. Fromm, e.g., argues both that the Freudian self is guided exclusively by self-interest (1973, p. 52) and that "Freud holds that the aim of human development is the achievement of these ideals: . . . brotherly love, reduction of suffering, independence, and responsibility" (1950, p. 18).

3. To Plato and Aristotle, the pursuit of the self-interested end of happiness, or *eudaimonia*, necessarily coincides with the pursuit of moral values. Even Aquinas supposes that the injunction to self-preservation, which is the first precept of the natural law, leads to no special problems about what one owes to others. The classical utilitarian moralists, such as Bentham and J. S. Mill, suppose that we are moved to action only by pleasure and the absence of pain; but this does not prevent them from praising "those who can abnegate for themselves the personal enjoyment of life when by such renunciation they contribute worthily to increase the amount of happiness in the world" (Mill 1962a, ch. 2; see also Bentham 1834). Sidgwick ([1907] 1962) highlights the problems in making the transition from the desire for one's own pleasure to that for the general happiness. For a brief discussion, see MacIntyre 1967.

conduct. Thus "there is fairly general agreement [among psychoanalysts] on one point: the ego must not side with egotism. Narcissism is very definitely *mauvais goût,* a strong and healthy ego does not love the ego" (Nielsen 1960, p. 428).

By contrast, academic psychologists and philosophers portray Freud's doctrine of psychological egoism as effectively undermining morality as such. Ian Gregory speaks for this position when he declares that Freud sees human beings as "wholly subject to the dictates of the pleasure principle. Man may achieve a certain guile in pursuing his satisfaction, *i.e.,* he becomes subject to the reality principle, but his end is always the same, his own gratification. He is in short, wholly self-absorbed, utterly selfish, not capable of forswearing instinctual satisfaction" (1975, p. 102).

If this familiar interpretation is correct, we cannot be moral. Even the most minimal moral requirements—that one should do no active harm, for example—would be undermined whenever the egoist's own interests would be better served by acting to the contrary and the opportunity presented itself.[4] An egoist might use moral language, of course, urging adherence to this or that ethical constraint, but only with the manipulative aim of getting others to act in ways believed to best advance his or her wholly selfish interests. What passes for the "morality" of psychological egoists is thus no more than scheming.

But what of the passages in which Freud unambiguously suggests the possibility of genuinely non-egoistic behavior. For instance, Freud writes of loving others "for their sake" (*ihnen zu Liebe*) (*SE* 18 [1921]:92), using precisely the language traditionally employed by moralists to signal genuine benevolence. Moreover, he insists that his debunking of civilized morality is not intended to undermine "moral" meanings and pursuits entirely, but only to unmask the unrealistic assessments of human nature that moralists have embraced. He writes:

> It is not our intention to dispute the noble endeavours of human nature, nor have we ever done anything to detract from their value . . . We lay a stronger empha-

4. The advocate of universal normative egoism, which holds that "everyone ought to look out for or maximize his or her own interests," is committed to holding that if Mary acts to further her interests, her action is acceptable to the normative egoist's own best interest. But the doctrine of psychological egoism holds that a person cannot be *motivated* to act on this principle. The thesis of psychological egoism is that "human beings are so constituted that each seeks, and can only seek, his own welfare" (Glasgow 1976, p. 75), though, of course, it is always possible for a person to make a mistake and act in a manner that is not in fact in his or her best interests.

sis on what is evil in men only because other people disavow it and thereby make the human mind, not better, but incomprehensible. If now we give up this one-sided ethical valuation, we shall undoubtedly find a more correct formula for the relation between good and evil in human nature. (*SE* 15 [1916–17]:146–7)

It is also difficult to square the assertion that Freud is a psychological egoist with his many statements of personal commitment to moral standards like "justice" and "consideration for one's fellow men" (letter 92, in Hale 1971, p. 189), as well as his aspiration that psychoanalysis might help patients become morally better persons (letter 36, ibid., p. 121)—more responsible, loving, and capable of carrying out their moral intentions.[5]

These and other strands in Freud's thought may not be sufficient by themselves to unequivocally establish his commitment to a non-egoistic psychology; but they do raise substantial doubts about the assumption that orthodox psychoanalysis permits only the *narrowest* egoistic conduct. The three chapters that follow, on the pleasure principle, narcissism, and object love, take up a neglected dimension of Freudian scholarship by addressing the questions: Do the central psychoanalytic doctrines entail psychological egoism and the rejection of the possibility of morality? If not, what restrictions, if any, does acceptance of these doctrines place on our capacities for moral conduct—that is, on our compliance with certain normative standards like the core Judeo-Christian commandment to love one's neighbor as oneself.

In these chapters, by contrast with most accounts of Freudian theory, the technical meanings of psychoanalytic terms—especially the *pleasure principle, libido, narcissism, object cathexis, aim inhibition,* and *sublimation*—will be coordinated with ordinary moral language. More precisely, the *pleasure principle* will be examined in terms of *hedonism* in chapter 6, *narcissism* in terms of *egoism* in chapter 7, and *object love* in terms of genuine *benevolence* and *altruism* in chapter 8. This approach obviously requires careful conceptual analysis, not only of the technical vocabulary of psycho-

5. Freud vacillated on whether psychoanalysis could help people morally (see letter 75, dated 13 Nov. 1913, in Hale 1971, pp. 163–4). This vacillation appears to derive from his beliefs about the limitations of psychoanalytic treatment, which he felt could help basically moral people act more consistently with their moral opinions but not make up for developmental shortcomings. These limitations explain Freud's statement to Putnam that "Analysis makes for integration but does not of itself make for goodness" (letter 91, dated 7 July 1915, ibid., p. 188). But this leaves open the possibility that psychoanalysis may, by replacing repression with sublimation, serve "every form of higher development" (letter 36, ibid., p. 121).

analysis but also of the ordinary moral terms to which these technical concepts are tied on the clinical side of psychoanalytic discourse.[6]

By attending carefully to the rival conceptual possibilities of these moral terms as unearthed by philosophers, nuances of meaning become apparent within the technical concepts of psychoanalysis itself that open up ways of resolving some of the apparent contradictions in Freudian theory. Here, as elsewhere in this study, philosophical ethics becomes an invaluable hermeneutic tool in understanding psychoanalysis on its own terms. At the same time that philosophical ethics deepens one's reading of Freud, it also highlights the significance of his empirical findings for the field of ethics.

After the deep psychological foundations of Freudian theory are worked out in connection with the topics of hedonism, narcissism, and object love and it is seen how psychoanalysis handles the central question of this section of the book—namely, whether we are psychologically able to be moral—it will be possible to address the further significance of psychoanalysis for ethics, including its normative implications and its contribution to understanding typical problematic issues in moral theory.

6. Clinical psychologists and psychoanalysts often grow impatient with the conceptual analyses of philosophers, preferring to concentrate, instead, on empirical questions. But it is rather obviously the case that the empirical answers one comes up with depend to a large extent on the conceptual schema by means of which one analyzes the facts about human behavior. It follows that philosophical elucidation of the meaning of such terms as *hedonism, egoism,* and *altruism* can be of enormous assistance to the empirically oriented behavioral scientist.

Chapter 6
The Pleasure Principle and Psychological Hedonism

> Psychology is still groping in the dark when it concerns matters of pleasure and pain.
> —Freud

> It is of no concern to us in this connection to enquire how far, with this hypothesis of the pleasure principle, we have approached or adopted any particular, historically established, philosophical system. We have arrived at these speculative assumptions in an attempt to describe and to account for the facts of daily observation in our field of study . . . We would readily express our gratitude to any philosophical or psychological theory which was able to inform us of the meaning of the feelings of pleasure and unpleasure which act so imperatively upon us.
> —Freud

The psychoanalytic concept of the *pleasure principle (Lustprinzip)* is most frequently cited as evidence of Freud's commitment to psychological egoism (see, e.g., Allport 1961, pp. 144–8; Gregory 1975, p. 102; Thomas 1989, p. 76). The implicit assumption here is that regulation of mental processes by the pleasure principle entails psychological *hedonism,* which, in turn, entails psychological *egoism.* However, those who take this position seldom probe very deeply the multiple ways in which Freud uses the concept of the pleasure principle: first, as the regulatory principle of the *entire mental apparatus;* second, as the regulatory principle of the *primary process* of the unconscious, or id, where it is defined in part by contradistinction to the reality principle; and third, as the ultimate goal served by the reality principle's regulation of *the ego's secondary processes.* When these various uses of the term *pleasure principle* are attended to with an eye to the behavioral implications of the concept, it is possible to see that the psychoanalytic perspective on hedonism might be compatible with finding satisfaction in the pursuit of non-egoistic goals, such as the good of a loved one or the common good of a group.

Psychological *hedonism* simply holds, to use J. S. Mill's felicitous definition, that "human nature is so constituted as to desire nothing which is not either a part of happiness or a means to happiness" (Mill 1962b, p. 292). There is nothing in this definition or in Sidgwick's somewhat more precise alternative—that desire and "volition [are] always determined by pleasures or pains actual or prospective" (1962, p. 40)—which necessarily limits happiness or its means to the pursuit of self-interest.[1] Thus, it is consistent with psychological hedonism for people to desire the good of others and to obtain satisfaction from benevolent conduct, even when it is at considerable cost to themselves. For if we desire another's good, satisfaction of this desire, with its accompanying yield of pleasure, is achieved precisely by being non-egoistic.[2]

Not all psychological hedonists acknowledge the possibility of non-egoistic conduct, but some do. The question that needs to be addressed, then, is whether the psychoanalytic doctrine of the pleasure principle permits non-egoistic conduct, as classical hedonistic theories do; and, if so, how?

1. Psychological hedonism is sometimes defined more broadly as "the assertion that actions or desires are determined by pleasures or displeasures, whether prospective, actual, or past" (R. B. Brandt 1967, p. 433). Brandt's addition of past pleasures to the present and prospective pleasures mentioned in Sidgwick's definition is intended to pick up modern psychological theories of conditioning, which hold that our present interests and values are conditioned by pleasant past experiences. This broader definition could be misleading in the present context, where the focus is on whether the psychoanalytic perspective on hedonism implies egoistic hedonism, because the truth of the conditioning theory does not establish that people want only pleasure. As Brandt observes: "All the theory claims is that *whatever* values one has have been acquired because of past enjoyments or punishments of one sort or another" (ibid., p. 434). The narrower definitions of Mill and Sidgwick are employed throughout this chapter, because they are useful in distinguishing Freud's conditioning hypotheses from his beliefs about present- and future-oriented pleasure seeking and pain avoidance and their implications for the main issue of psychological egoism—viz., whether people are motivated to act only for their own interests.

2. Adam Smith argued along these lines for non-egoistic hedonism thus: "How selfish soever man may be supposed, there are evidently some principles in his nature, which interest him in the fortune of others, and render their happiness necessary to him, though he derives nothing from it, *except the pleasure of seeing it*" (1964, p. 257, emphasis added). Butler took this approach to hedonism even further and held that the individual who inhibits the universal human desire to help others will not be happy. By refusing to be benevolent, Butler believed, a person damages his or her own self-interest (1964, pp. 225–40).

CONCEPTUAL AND THEORETICAL COMPLEXITIES

Untangling Freud's views on psychological hedonism is complicated by the incredible complexity of the workings of the pleasure principle, the details of which are often difficult to ascertain because of the convoluted development of the concept occasioned by Freud's use of it with different paradigms of the mind over time. The pleasure principle, which Freud first calls the "unpleasure principle" (*SE* 5 [1900]:600), undergoes a metamorphosis with the shift in Freud's work from the more mechanistic model of the psychic *apparatus* employed between 1895 and 1919 to the more biologically based model of the psychic *organism* developed after 1919. The pre-1920 version of the pleasure principle holds that the entire psychic apparatus is regulated by the desire to avoid or discharge unpleasurable tension.[3] (An increase in tension may be triggered by an instinctual increase in excitation, an external trauma, or an intrapsychic conflict.) In its broad metapsychological contours, this version appears to be predominantly a present-oriented, rather than a future-oriented psychological hedonism.[4] However, as discussed in Freud's nascent ego psychology of this time, the conscious mind, which is triggered by a present discomfort that moves it to act, nevertheless seems able to plan for prospective states of affairs, as in classical hedonist theories.[5]

With the publication of *Beyond the Pleasure Principle* in 1920, the metapsychological model of the pleasure principle caught up with the developing ego psychology and took on a more teleological form. At this point, the pleasure principle provides the end-states toward which the life and the death instincts are directed. This aligns the psychoanalytic theory of hedonism even more fully with classical theory.

Freud's understanding of the pleasure principle and its implications for

---

3. The discharge version of the pleasure principle owes much to Freud's early interest in neurophysiology and to the belief he shared with many of his contemporaries that the most general principles of physics apply to psychological phenomena (see Laplanche and Pontalis 1973, p. 342). It seemed to be justified by Fechner's principle of constancy, which, in turn, was warranted by the principle of the conservation of energy. But it was also influenced by clinical considerations and tied "to Breuer's 'talking cure,' to catharsis as the therapeutic method, and abreaction as the curative process" (Apfelbaum 1965, p. 176).

4. Fechner, from whose "principle of the pleasure of action" Freud borrowed the idea of the pleasure principle, held that "our acts are determined by the pleasure or unpleasure procured *in the immediate* by the idea of the action to be accomplished or of its consequences" (Laplanche and Pontalis 1973, p. 322).

5. For discussion of the distinction between the "psychological hedonism of the present" and the classical "pleasure theory of goals," see R. B. Brandt 1959, pp. 307–18; 1967.

his views on psychological hedonism are often misunderstood. This is not only because people fail to attend to the great differences between pre-1920 and post-1919 pleasure-principle theory, but also because Freud's highly general definition of the pleasure principle as aiming at the reduction of tension leaves room for very different operations in the specific contexts in which he discusses it—as applied to a fictive primitive psychic apparatus, the unconscious, or id, the ego, and the whole mind.[6] Too often, what Freud says about the pleasure principle in one of these contexts is taken by the unsuspecting reader as the whole of Freud's explanation of it. But one cannot really understand how the pleasure principle manifests itself or the limitations it imposes on human behavior without attending to how the details of these context-specific discussions qualify, in surprising ways sometimes, what Freud is often taken to say about the human being's pursuit of pleasure.

THE PLEASURE PRINCIPLE IN FREUD'S EARLY DRIVE THEORY (1900–1911)

In his early theoretical work on psychological hedonism in *The Interpretation of Dreams* (1900) and in "Formulations on the Two Principles of Mental Functioning" (1911), Freud describes the pleasure principle in terms of its operation in a "primary" primitive psychic apparatus and then in the more complicated "secondary" mental apparatus derived from it.[7] The pleasure principle regulates the primitive mental apparatus by directing its efforts "towards keeping itself so far as possible free from stimuli" (*SE* 5 [1900]:565). Under it, the apparatus seeks "to avoid an accumulation of excitation and to maintain itself . . . without excitation" (*SE* 5 [1900]:598). The primitive psychic apparatus is "built upon the plan of a reflex . . . [arc]" (*SE* 5 [1900]:565, 598). As Freud explicates it up in an

---

6. The concept of the pleasure principle has generated a great deal of confusion both within psychoanalysis and without, largely because it is more a "family of terms" in Wittgenstein's sense than a single concept. Freud himself comes close to realizing this on those repeated occasions when he explicitly refuses to assign the concept a single meaning (see, e.g., *SE* 18 [1920]:62). Instead, he tends to shape the term's meaning to the context in which he employs it or the strategy for which it is being employed—e.g., to make his model conform more to the natural-scientific model or to lay bare what people really want beneath their self-deception. However, as J. H. Smith (1977, p. 1) points out, the concept is not endlessly protean and hence meaningless. Certain limits to its valid usage are imposed by historical precedent and logical consistency.

7. The "Project" begins similarly with a primitive neurological system that provides a base point for understanding the more complex workings of the developed brain (*SE* 1 [1950]:296–7).

initial, highly schematic version, a momentary sensory excitation impinges on the apparatus from without and is promptly discharged along a motor path (*SE* 5 [190]:565). But this description is a self-conscious "theoretical fiction," a heuristic device intended to establish a beginning point as a basis for further elaboration, and Freud immediately postulates that "the exigencies of life interfere with this simple function" and furnish the impetus for the development of the primitive psychic apparatus (ibid.).[8]

The "exigencies of life" come "first in the form of the major somatic needs" and complicate the initial picture because the excitations produced are continuous, rather than momentary, and internal, rather than external (ibid.). What this means is that the discharge of tension sought by the pleasure principle is no longer simple, immediate, or complete. Freud assumes that this change of affairs is enough to require a new way of dealing with experience, but he does not fully explain why this should be so.[9] Instead, he moves directly to a description of the new, more complicated way in which the primary processes of the primitive mental apparatus—which is now closer to a model of the mind—seek satisfaction. What happens is that the excitation arising from an internal need is temporarily

8. It has frequently been noted that Freud equivocates about whether the pleasure principle regulates psychic activities by eliminating tension, by lowering the level of excitation, or by maintaining a stable state of psychic equilibrium within certain limits. In one place, he even states that the pleasure principle's function "is to free the mental apparatus entirely from excitation *or* to keep the amount of excitation in it constant *or* to keep it as low as possible" (*SE* 18 [1920]:62, emphasis added; see also *SE* 14 [1915]:120; 18 [1920]:55–6).

The reason for this becomes clear once one recognizes that each of these three descriptions belongs to a different context. Roughly stated, in the fictive primitive apparatus, the pleasure principle is said to function to completely eliminate tension. But this goal cannot be achieved in more developed systems in which internal stimuli are stored; thus Freud postulates that the pleasure principle either lowers tension or maintains a relatively stable equilibrium. Although he does not proceed further and make this explicit, it seems to be the case that the primary process of the unconscious functions to lower excitation as far as possible, while the secondary processes of the ego seek to maintain psychic equilibrium. Because Freud believed that archaic functions continue to exist alongside the more developed functions that arise from them, he assumes that the pleasure principle's archaic aim of completely eliminating tension is still operative somewhere in the developed psychic organism. The idea of reducing tension to zero reappears in Freud's later thought as the "Nirvana principle," which expresses the trend of the death instinct toward the stimulus-free condition of inorganic life.

9. In Freud's neurological speculations in the "Project," the primitive neurological apparatus is said to be modified in higher animals by the presence of resistance, as a result of which the threshold of tension is increased before discharge occurs, and by the greater complexity of the structure, which provides alternative pathways along which excitation can pass. Thus higher organisms enjoy a flexibility of response not present in the simple reflex arc model and a correspondingly more complex mode of functioning.

discharged by some means or other, as when a hungry infant is fed. A mnemic (memory) image of his "experience of satisfaction" is laid down and is linked in memory with the excitation produced by the need. Thus an image of "nourishment" is linked with the excitation of hunger. Thereafter, the reoccurrence of the particular excitation will cause a psychical impulse, called a "wish," to seek to recathect the memory image of satisfaction and to reevoke the original experience of satisfaction, ending in hallucination. Although Freud states that "no psychical apparatus exists which possesses a primary process only" (*SE* 5 [1900]:603), nevertheless, this kind of mental functioning persists piecemeal, in dreams and in psychosis, and developmentally, as a transitional stage in the mental processes of the neonate.[10]

The primitive thought-activity that ends in hallucination does not succeed in bringing about actual satisfaction, however, and the need persists. There is disappointment and frustration. A further, major transformation of the mental apparatus beyond the hallucinatory mode is therefore necessary for satisfaction and survival (see *SE* 5 [1900]:566; 12 [1911]:219). The result, spurred by the experience of frustration, is the second type of mental apparatus that Freud postulates, and it is this, which is analogous to the part of the adult mind known as the ego, that makes it possible for the pleasure principle sometimes to turn on itself in a move that is key to understanding how one can get away from the purely egoistic.

In the second mental apparatus, or ego, the attempt at satisfaction by means of hallucination must be abandoned. For this to happen, it is necessary to halt the regression of the wish impulse before it goes beyond the mnemic image all the way to reevoking the hallucinatory perception of satisfaction itself (*SE* 5 [1900]:566, 599; 12 [1911]:219). "This inhibition of the regression and the subsequent diversion of the excitation" along paths that connect with the external world and its sources of actual satisfaction is "the business of [the] second system," a business which goes by the name of the "secondary processes" (*SE* 5 [1900]:566; *SE* 12 [1911]:219).

Although not "entirely free from the pleasure principle" (*SE* 5

---

10. Freud writes: "Dreams, which fulfil their wishes along the short path of regression, have merely preserved for us in that respect a sample of the psychical apparatus's primary method of working, a method which was abandoned as being inefficient. What once dominated waking life, while the mind was still young and incompetent, seems now to have been banished into the night—just as the primitive weapons, the bows and arrows, that have been abandoned by adult men, turn up once more in the nursery. *Dreaming is a piece of infantile mental life that has been superseded.* These methods of working on the part of the psychical apparatus, which are normally suppressed in waking hours, become current once more in psychosis and then reveal their incapacity for satisfying our needs in relation to the external world" (*SE* 5 [1900]:567).

[1900]:600),[11] the secondary processes involve very different conditions of drive discharge associated with the pursuit of real, rather than hallucinatory, pleasure. Freud postulates that in the secondary system, energy is bound at first in a state of relative quiescence while the psyche proceeds with thought, which he conceives of as "essentially an experimental kind of acting" (*SE* 12 [1911]:221) that tests out various possibilities for obtaining real satisfaction in the external world. The inhibition of discharge while thought takes place is a crucial development, for it represents a significant modification of the role of the pleasure principle, which allows the secondary mental apparatus to work with disagreeable memories or ideas. In the primitive mental apparatus, where there is no such inhibition, the unmitigated rule of the pleasure principle means that "a distressing mnemic image" will be dropped immediately if anything happens to revive it, because otherwise immediate discharge would begin to produce displeasure (*SE* 5 [1900]:600). But in the secondary processes, the psyche can bring in disagreeable thoughts because the inhibition of discharge allows the secondary system to block the development of the unpleasure that would otherwise proceed from them (*SE* 5 [1900]:600–1).

Indeed, it is essential that the secondary system have a way of working with unpleasurable memories and ideas, independently of the intensity of their affect, because it is only in this way that it can assess suitable and unsuitable means of obtaining genuine satisfaction. As Freud puts it in an early variation on his famous dictum "Where id was, there ego shall be [or is in the process of becoming]": "Thinking must aim at freeing itself more and more from *exclusive regulation* by the unpleasure principle and at restricting the development of affect in thought-activity to the minimum required for acting as a signal" (*SE* 5 [1900]:602, emphasis added).

When this happens, the secondary processes of the ego are governed by the reality principle, as opposed to "the pure pleasure principle" which continues to rule the unconscious. Under this new principle, "what . . . [is] presented in the mind . . . [is] no longer what . . . [is] agreeable but what . . . [is] real, even if it happen[s] . . . to be disagreeable" (*SE* 12 [1911]:219). Freud rightly declares that "this setting-up of the *reality principle* prove[s] . . . to be a momentous step" (ibid.). With further development along this line,

> the ego learns that it must inevitably go without immediate satisfaction, postpone gratification, learn to endure a degree of pain, and altogether renounce certain sources of pleasure. Thus trained, the ego becomes 'reasonable,' is no

11. See n. 8 above.

longer controlled by the pleasure-principle, but follows the REALITY-PRINCIPLE, which at bottom also seeks pleasure—although a delayed and diminished pleasure, one which is assured by its realization of fact, its relation to reality. (1952, p. 365)

Up to this point, Freud's psychological hedonism still seems thoroughly egoistic. The reality principle "modifies" mental functioning by substituting empirical perception and logical reasoning for the blind, immediate pleasure seeking of the unconscious, but it continues to serve—even to "safeguard"—the pleasure principle's ultimate goal of reducing tension and maintaining equilibrium. "A momentary pleasure, uncertain in its results, is given up," Freud states, "but only in order to gain along a new path an assured pleasure at a later time" (*SE* 12 [1911]:223).

If this, in gross outline,[12] were all Freud had to say about how the ego handles the pleasure principle, the reality principle would merely substitute a psychological egoistic hedonism of the long run for a hedonism of the present moment, which would not be to move significantly beyond egoistic hedonism. In fact, the reality principle would then conclusively confirm his supposed psychological egoism, since the ego, unlike the unconscious, is capable of self-consciously embracing the self's interests and thereby pursuing the organism's interests "selfishly."

However, as Freud unpacks what happens when the "dominance" of the pure pleasure principle of the unconscious is "transformed" by the ego,[13] it

12. Freud's discussion of some of the changes in psychic function that come with the emergence of the reality principle is, of course, much more extensive than is indicated in the text above. Thus he notes that with the advent of the reality principle and the heightening of the *conscious* apprehension of the external world, the organism is able to appreciate different "sensory *qualities*" of pleasure "in addition to" the gross categories "of pleasure and unpleasure which hitherto had alone been of interest to it" (*SE* 12 [1911]:220). This is the basis of his emphasis on the qualitative differences that reside in the sensorily distinct erogenous zones (see *SE* 7 [1905]:183–93 and Klein 1976, pp. 72–120, 210–38).

13. In *The Interpretation of Dreams* Freud speaks of the second system's "transforming" the workings of the primitive mental apparatus (see e.g., *SE* 5 [1900]:599, 604). Once this transformation has occurred, normally by the prime of life, the secondary process "come[s] to inhibit and overlay" the primary process, thereby achieving a certain "domination" over it, although some unconscious wishes will always remain inaccessible to the understanding and voluntary control of the secondary processes and may always exert "compelling force upon all later mental trends" (*SE* 5 [1900]:603). There is thus some tension in Freud's thought regarding the extent to which the reality principle comes to dominate and even "dethrone" the pleasure principle. On the one hand, it *serves* the pleasure principle by providing "an assured pleasure coming later"—indeed, he explicitly states that "the substitution of the reality-principle for the pleasure-principle denotes *no dethronement* of the pleasure-principle, but only a safeguarding of it" (*CP* 4 [1911]:18, emphasis added). On the other hand, he declares that insofar as the

becomes apparent that even within the early drive theory there is a good deal more at stake than merely delaying instinctual gratification for a more "certain and greater success" at securing *the same ultimate goal* at a later time.[14] The very nature of pleasure becomes bifurcated, as the self-conscious agent (ego, or I) begins to experience, remember, and search for pleasure in opposition to the primitive pleasure seeking of the unconscious.

One of the earliest statements of this possibility appears in *The Interpretation of Dreams*, where Freud is just beginning to sketch some aspects of ego function, still within an overall drive-discharge framework. He writes: "Among these *wishful impulses* derived from infancy, which can neither be destroyed nor inhibited, there are some *whose fulfilment would be a contradiction of the purposive ideas of secondary thinking*. The fulfilment of these wishes would no longer generate an affect of pleasure but of unpleasure" (*SE* 5 [1900]:604, emphasis added). Here, Freud is suggesting that under the impact of the ego's secondary processes and the momentous changes in the nature of consciousness, thought, and action that accompany the emergence of the reality principle (see *SE* 12 [1911]:219–21), what would have been pleasure for the primitive apparatus registers for the conscious ego as displeasure.[15] Freud calls this process by which the ego turns a possibility of pleasure into a source of displeasure a "*transformation of affect*" (*SE* 5 [1900]:604).[16]

---

reality principle makes use of thought processes, realistic perceptions, efficacious actions, and the like, instead of the hallucinatory behavior of the id, the mature ego "*dethrone[s]* . . . the pleasure principle which dominates the course of events in the id . . . and replace[s] . . . it by the reality principle" (*SE* 22 [1933]:76, emphasis added).

14. To put it another way, Freud's ambiguity regarding the precise goal of the pleasure principle—i.e., whether it aims at the reduction of tension to zero, the lowering of excitation, the maintenance of equilibrium, or more robust pleasurable sensations—permits a good deal of latitude vis-à-vis the "modifications" that the ego is capable of introducing.

15. Freud has been criticized for using the pleasure principle in this way, on the grounds that the concept is made to embrace its own negation (Yankelovich and Barrett, 1970, p. 86). And in fact Freud opens himself to charges of this sort when he apologizes for the pleasure principle's being so "indefinite" (*SE* 14 [1915]:121) and "obscure" (*SE* 18 [1920]:7) that "the most various things might be understood by it" (1954, p. 137). But Freud's use of the pleasure principle to point to both desire and its repression entails no error of logic, no manifestation of fuzzy thinking, if the distinct operations of the ego and the unconscious primary processes mean that pleasure can turn around on itself.

16. The problem of explaining this "transformation of affect" plagued Freud for years. The issue is first raised in a letter to Fliess of 6 Dec. 1896 (Freud 1954, pp. 173–81), is touched on in the "Dora" case history (*SE* 7 [1905]:28–9), and taken up again at the outset of his paper on "Repression" (*SE* 14 [1915]:146–8) and at the end of the first chapter of *Beyond the Pleasure Principle* (*SE* 18 [1920]:10–11). A fresh solution is proposed in the opening paragraphs of ch. 2 of *Inhibitions, Symptoms and Anxiety* (*SE* 20 [1926]:91ff.).

Several aspects of Freud's emerging view of the ego in the period 1900–11 are at work in the notion that the ego's "purposive ideas" can come into conflict with the pleasure seeking of the unconscious. First, the ego has its own instincts, separate and distinct from the sexual drives of the unconscious.[17] These are completely under the sway of the reality principle, and their satisfaction yields its own pleasure, which the ego experiences as it goes about the business of self-preservation through successful interaction with the external environment.[18] Whereas the unconscious sexual instincts are oriented primarily toward the experience of immediate pleasure *qua* pleasure, the reality-ego, still ultimately at the service of pleasure seeking, is capable of orienting itself toward what is useful and can derive pleasure from purposeful activity, even when it does not afford what would be pleasure calculated in primary-process terms (see *SE* 12 [1911]:223).

Although Freud never adequately clarifies the nature of the ego instincts during the period (1900–19) in which he employs this concept and their workings remain highly ambiguous,[19] it appears even in the early writings of this period that the ego's instincts are capable of supporting or growing into interests in persons and objects outside the self. This would mean that the motives for which the ego instincts are ultimately responsible would not all be directed exclusively at instinct gratification and so would allow for more complicated human interactions. In the formal language of the metapsychology, a desire that arises out of an ego instinct's somatic "source(s)" may be directed at "objects" in the outside world that gratify it without necessarily being directed toward the "aim" of the instinct, which is always satisfaction in the sense of a need reduction.[20] For example, Freud's prototypical ego instinct, hunger, creates the desire to eat, and out of this comes the hungry infant's interest in the mother as an object of

17. Freud first brings all the nonsexual "great needs" together under the heading of the "ego instincts" (*SE* 11 [1900]:214–15). As Bibring (1941, pp. 103, 108) points out, the ego instincts stand for the ego, which remains a relatively unknown quantity in Freud's early work and are a noncommittal way of dealing with the self's "interests."

18. Freud comes close to implying that the ego is capable of enjoying its own competence in *"mastering stimuli"* (*SE* 14 [1915]:120), an idea that R. White develops in his well-known discussion of the sense of efficacy that comes with the experience of competence. See White 1959, 1960, and 1963.

19. Laplanche and Pontalis (1973, p. 147) draw attention to the confusing duality in Freud's early concept of the ego instincts. On the one hand they are viewed as tendencies *emanating* from the organism (or from the ego insofar as it is the agency responsible for the organism's preservation) and directed toward relatively specific external objects (e.g., food); on the other, as attached to the ego as if to their *object*.

20. As Bibring puts it, "the general aim of libido appears to be pleasure, but its particular aims are derived from the particular objects to which it is directed" (1941, p. 109).

desire as well as a source of satisfaction of hunger drives. Satisfaction of the "aim" may be an unanticipated by-product of an action relating the ego to its object.

A second aspect of Freud's emerging ego theory that is important for understanding how the ego's "purposive ideas" are capable of opposing unconscious pleasure seeking concerns the ego's transformation of libidinal drives through such processes as displacement and sublimation and the threat to the ego's consolidation of itself around these more refined sentiments posed by the outbreak of raw instinctual desires. The ego transforms the primitive unconscious sexual drives in such a way[21] that if the original repressed sexual instincts do succeed in breaking through to direct or substitute satisfaction, what is experienced is disgust, shame, guilt, or some other form of ego displeasure.[22] The ego's negative reaction to raw instinctual drives itself becomes a source of unpleasurable tension that results in suppression or repression of ideas, wishes, and so forth. The ego's opposition to raw libidinal drive satisfaction is ultimately in the service of the pleasure principle, because, taken at its highest level of generalization, where it regulates the whole psyche, the pleasure principle is directed very broadly toward the reduction of displeasure wherever it occurs. Thus, the ego's displeasure resulting from its sublimated or displaced sentiments or goals being threatened by an outbreak of raw libidinal desire may outweigh

21. Stewart (1967, pp. 121, 126–7) points out that even Freud's earliest economic formulations distinguish between two vicissitudes of tension reduction: in the first, the apparatus is unburdened by the discharge of energy; in the second, energies are not discharged, but "displaced" from one drive schema to another *inside* the mental apparatus. This second, cathexis hypothesis makes it possible for energy to be "bound" in such a way that it loses its pressure for discharge, which, from the drive-discharge perspective, is tantamount to its disappearance from the system. (See *SE* 3 [1894]:48.)

22. In his seminal discussion of the pleasure principle in *Interpretation,* Freud makes clear the displeasure with which the ego reacts to the satisfaction of some unconscious desires. He observes that "the way in which *disgust* emerges in childhood . . . is related to the activity of the secondary system" and its encounters with primary-process wishes (*SE* 5 [1900]:604, emphasis added). This point is further elaborated in *Pleasure Principle,* where Freud declares that "if . . . repressed sexual instincts [succeed] in struggling through, by roundabout paths, to a direct or to a substitute satisfaction, that event, which would in other cases have been an opportunity for pleasure, *is felt by the ego as unpleasure.* As a consequence of the old conflict which ended in repression, a new breach has occurred in the pleasure principle at the very time when certain instincts were endeavouring, in accordance with the principle, to obtain fresh pleasure. The details of the process by which repression [by the ego] *turns a possibility of pleasure into a source of unpleasure* are not yet clearly understood or cannot be clearly represented; but there is no doubt that all neurotic unpleasure is of that kind—*pleasure that cannot be felt as such*" (*SE* 18 [1920]:11, emphasis added).

whatever discontent results from the strangulation or diversion of more primitive drives.

MODIFICATIONS OF THE PLEASURE PRINCIPLE IN THE PERIOD 1911-19

Freud himself gradually came to realize that he must move beyond his initial presentation of the reality principle's simple replacement of the pure pleasure principle in terms of mere postponement and temporary tolerance of displeasure and reality testing in order to account more fully for the conflict between the ego and the instinctual drives and the resulting senses of pleasure and displeasure.[23] Between 1911 and 1919, he attempted to explain why instinctual discharge, which by definition is directed to the attainment of pleasure, can be perceived as displeasure by the ego. He explained that the ego passes through its own stages of development.[24] As this happens, it forms a unity out of refined sentiments and sublimated goals that exclude incompatible instinctual impulses.[25] The ego seeks to defend its coherence against the reassertion of the excluded and repressed raw instinctual drives.[26] The importance of the resulting ego organization is such that the ego's displeasure when it is threatened with the return of the repressed material can far outweigh the discontent produced by the strangulation or diversion of the repressed primitive drives.[27] Conversely, the

23. This section presupposes Freud's reworking of the theory of the instincts during the period 1911–19 and the emergence of new ideas about the libidinized ego and primary and secondary narcissism. This reworking will be discussed extensively in ch. 7 and 8 below.

24. Freud first introduces the hypothesis that the ego has its own developmental line paralleling (yet perhaps partly independent of) the psychosexual stages in 1913 (*SE* 12 [1913]:324–5). Similarly, he declares that "a unity comparable to the ego cannot exist in the individual from the start; the ego has to be developed" (*SE* 14 [1914]:77).

25. Freud's metapsychological papers of 1915 paved the way for the later structural theory of the ego presented in *The Ego and the Id* (1923) by introducing such basic postulates as the libidinal cathexis of the ego (*SE* 14 [1914]:76–80), the growth of the ego through internalization of object relations (*SE* 14 [1915]:243–58), and the vicissitudes undergone by the sexual instincts in the process of development, especially the "reversal" of the instinct's aim into its opposite and the "turning round of an instinct upon the subject" (*SE* 14 [1915]:126ff.).

26. The notion that the ego's defenses are triggered by displeasure dates back to the beginnings of psychoanalysis. The "Project" seeks the origin of defenses in an "experience of pain." In *Studies on Hysteria* the ego is said to react defensively against the unpleasurable affect that results when unconscious ideas turn out to be incompatible with socially acceptable beliefs.

27. By 1920, he was writing: "Another occasion of the release of unpleasure, which occurs with no less regularity [than that due to opposition from the reality principle], is to be found

ego gets its own pleasure and is recompensed for its mastery of unconscious drives by the opportunities afforded for substitute gratification of its sublimated drives.[28] The pleasure yield from activities directed toward sublimated goals differs from the direct instinctual satisfaction sought by the unconscious, in part because of the nonlocalized character of the ego's enjoyment. Whereas satisfaction of libidinal drives is focused on particular erogenous zones, such pleasures as the "intellectual pleasure" offered by science and the love and approval of parents have no such specific sites (*SE* 12 [1911]:224).

Third, the ego's capacity for self-reflection makes a considerable difference to the way it handles pleasure seeking. Unlike the unconscious, which acts automatically, the ego does not seek to gratify each and every desire that comes along. It is capable of taking a *long-term* view of the individual's interests, with pleasure the ultimate, but not necessarily the immediate, goal. The ego's capacity for life-long planning carries with it notions of a self (as the German term for "the ego" or "I," *das Ich*, connotes)—an entity capable of making determinations with reference to how they fit with the self's view of itself and of the good.[29] This permits much

---

in the conflicts and dissensions that take place in the mental apparatus while the ego is passing through its development into more highly composite organizations . . . In the course of things it happens again and again that individual instincts or parts of instincts turn out to be incompatible in their aims or demands with the remaining ones, which are able to combine into the inclusive unity of the ego. The former are then split off from this unity by the process of repression, held back at lower levels of psychical development and cut off, to begin with, from the possibility of satisfaction. If they succeed subsequently, as can so easily happen with repressed sexual instincts, in . . . [achieving] satisfaction, . . . the ego [experiences] . . . unpleasure" (*SE* 18 [1920]:10–11).

28. Freud's first published use of the concept of sublimation occurs in the *Three Essays on the Theory of Sexuality* (*SE* 7 [1905]:156), though the word *sublimation* had been used earlier in the Fliess correspondence (letter 61, *SE* 1 [1897]:247) and in the "Dora" case history (*SE* 7 [1905]:50, 116). The term evokes the sense of "sublime" in the arts and the meaning "sublimation" has in chemistry where it refers to the process of directly causing a solid to become a gas. The significance of sublimation for the ego's goals is referred to frequently throughout both his early and his mature work. See, e.g., *SE* 7 [1905]:178, n.2, 238–9; 9 [1908]:187–90.

Hartmann draws attention to the fact that "the activities of the functions that constitute the reality principle" include sublimated activities that "can be pleasurable in themselves" (1964, p. 244). He goes on to argue that Freud "did not mean to negate the pleasure we derive from the world outside; [to the contrary], . . . he repeatedly commented on the advantages the ego provides for instinctual gratifications" (ibid., p. 245).

29. From the outset, Freud uses the term *das Ich* to designate both the personality as a whole (the self) and one of its principal psychical agencies. There is thus a danger in using the term exclusively in the second sense, as Hartmann (1964, p. 114) proposes. See Laplanche and Pontalis 1973, pp. 131–2.

greater latitude of behavior under the pleasure principle than the mere summing up of discrete pleasurable sensations.

The extent to which Freud, even in his pre-1920 period, develops a highly complex and encompassing view of psychological hedonism that goes considerably beyond simple drive discharge or tension reduction is best seen in his discussion of the case of the ascetic religious believer. In Freud's portrait, the religious believer is guided in his earthly behavior by a belief in reward in the afterlife,[30] much as Pascal commends in his famous Wager Argument for the religious life.[31] Thus it is consistent with the pleasure principle for a believer to renounce absolutely "pleasure in this life" by focusing on the idea of "compensation in a future existence" (*SE* 12 [1911]:223; see also *SE* 14 [1916]:311). Although absolute renunciation of pleasure is scarcely the popular idea of hedonism, Freud points out that no departure from the rule of the pleasure principle is entailed. "Even religion is obliged to support its demand that earthly pleasure shall be set aside by promising that it will provide instead an incomparably greater amount of superior pleasure in another world" (*SE* 14 [1915]:311).

With this example, Freud seems to recognize that in its pleasure seeking, the ego looks at what will give it satisfaction in life as a whole, taking a broad range of considerations into account. This would seem to allow the individual, whether religious or not, to embrace a non-egoistic act if it is part of a life plan adopted as the self's way to ultimate happiness. For example, someone might discipline his baser tendencies and sacrifice his more immediate interests in order to obey the rules of moral and professional conduct laid down by his chosen profession, all because he thinks that life as a doctor, lawyer, teacher, accountant, or scientist will make him happy, even taking into account the burdens of arduous training and the occasional need for "selflessness" and "dedication" required to care adequately for patient or client or to achieve sought-after results.

There remains the question of whether such calculated behavior really qualifies as "non-egoistic." For Kantians who emphasize the purity of moral intentionality ("holiness of the will"),[32] the person who acts for

30. It appears that Freud thought that morality ultimately had to be justified in part by long-run calculations of personal happiness (see ch. 12 below).

31. Pascal argues that since we cannot know for certain whether God exists and since, if he does, the rewards for observance of religious precepts are infinite, the prudent person will believe and observe, because he has an infinity of pleasure to gain and little in this world to lose (1958, pp. 233–4).

32. Kant writes: "Nothing in the world—indeed nothing even beyond the world—can possibly be conceived which could be called good without qualification except a *good will* . . . The good will is not good because of what it effects or accomplishes or because of its

ulterior motives, such as happiness, is never truly moral, because he or she ultimately acts not for others or out of a sense of categorical duty but for a reward. Such action is not disinterested and thus, by Kant's definition, is not moral. It seems unnecessarily pinched, however, to preclude an act from being viewed as "moral" or even as "non-egoistic" simply because one factor entering into its motivation has to do with the long-term interests of the self. Seen in more immediate focus, a particular act can indeed be undertaken out of duty or concern for others, even if there is also present in its background the agent's sense of how the particular act fits into his conception of himself and his life plan.

When Freud talks about the ego's transformation of the pleasure principle,[33] he is obviously being drawn away from his drive-discharge theory of hedonism by his nascent ego theory. In place of a present-oriented psychic apparatus regulated solely by the immediate aim of lowering tension through discharge, there is an "I" capable of acting *teleologically* in terms of beliefs about satisfactions over the whole of a lifetime, including satisfactions experienced by substituting more refined pleasures for raw drive gratification. But in his pre-1920 writings, Freud has difficulty accounting for *how* the ego manages to conform to the pleasure principle while so substantially modifying it. This is in part because he does not yet have a well-delineated ego theory in place, but mostly because he is pulled in two different theoretical directions. He is by no means ready to abandon entirely his original drive-discharge theory. Yet, at this very point, he is also beginning to formulate a developmental, biologically based theory of personality in which qualitatively new modes of functioning emerge as the organism progresses along its developmental line from the more simple to the more complex.

BEYOND THE PLEASURE PRINCIPLE (1920–1938)

In the post-1919 period, the "new turn" in Freudian theory that takes off with the appropriately named *Beyond the Pleasure Principle* opens the way

---

adequacy to achieve some proposed end; it is good only because of its willing, i.e., it is good of itself . . . An action performed from duty does not have its moral worth in the purpose which is to be achieved through it but in the maxim by which it is determined. Its moral value, therefore, does not depend on the realization of the object of the action but merely on the principle of volition by which the action is done, without any regard to the objects of the faculty of desire" (1959, pp. 9, 10, 16).

33. Marcuse underscores the extent of this transformation by describing it as "a change not only in the form and timing of pleasure but in its very substance. The adjustment of pleasure to the reality principle . . . implies the transubstantiation of pleasure itself" (1955, p. 13).

for the triumph of the biologically oriented paradigm of personality forma-tion, although Freud never explicitly repudiates the drive-discharge model and occasionally, in his later writings, refers back to it as if it were largely unimpaired. Taken together, several major changes in Freud's mature theo-ry decisively alter his earlier views on psychological hedonism.

First, in an effort to account for why people act self-destructively, Freud introduces the notion of a death instinct.[34] This concept, which "is held to represent the fundamental tendency of every living being to return to the inorganic state" (Laplanche and Pontalis 1973, p. 97), represents an out-right repudiation of psychological hedonism, since with it, Freud acknowl-edges foursquare that people are not always motivated by pleasure and the avoidance of pain. The pleasure principle is not necessarily supreme. Some-times it is pain rather than pleasure that attracts, as in sadomasochistic behavior and self-destructive repetition compulsions.

Freud was moved to this point in part by the need to confront the traumatic war neuroses generated by World War I, in which "shell-shocked" soldiers suffered recurring dreams that recapitulated their worst combat experiences. Similarly, the tenacity with which patients clung to self-de-structive patterns of behavior, even after cognitively understanding them, impressed him as potent evidence contradicting his original formulations of the pleasure principle. This material illuminated for Freud persuasive examples of unpleasurable repetition from everyday life:

> the benefactor who is abandoned in anger after a time by each of his *protégés*, however much they may otherwise differ from one another, and who thus seems doomed to taste all the bitterness of ingratitude; . . . the man whose friendships all end in betrayal by his friend; . . . the man who time after time in the course of his life raises someone else into a position of great private or public authority and then, after a certain interval, himself upsets that authority and replaces him by a new one; . . . , again, the lover each of whose love affairs with a woman passes through the same phases and reaches the same conclusion. (*SE* 18 [1920]:22)

Cumulatively, these observations, which reflect some of his own prob-lems with protégés and friends, led Freud to the breakthrough conclusion "that there really does exist in the mind a compulsion to repeat which overrides the pleasure principle" (ibid.). As he explained:

> It is incorrect to talk of the dominance of the pleasure principle over the course of mental processes. If such a dominance existed, the immense majority of our mental processes would have to be accompanied by pleasure or to lead to plea-sure, whereas universal experience completely contradicts any such conclusion. The most that can be said, therefore, is that there exists in the mind a strong

34. See *SE* 18 (1920):38–41, 44–57, 60.

tendency towards the pleasure principle, but that that tendency is opposed by certain other forces or circumstances, so that the final outcome cannot always be in harmony with the tendency towards pleasure. (*SE* 18 [1920]:9–10)

At this point, clearly, Freud no longer subscribes to the totalitarianism of psychological hedonism. Yet, despite the hypothesis of the death instinct, psychological hedonism continues to be recognized as a powerful motivational tendency; accordingly, it remains an important question from the psychoanalytic standpoint whether this qualified version of psychological hedonism entails as a necessary correlate psychological egoism. If hedonism, whenever and to the extent that it comes into play, necessarily orients the individual only toward his own self-interest, that leaves morality with only the death instinct to stand on. And that would be profoundly troubling, because it would link morality inexorably to self-destruction and self-abnegation. A morality that is unable to draw on the powerful and universal human desire for happiness would not only appear unappetizing and mean-spirited, like the worst of superego moralism, it would also be severely weakened both motivationally and through the kinds of ultimate justifications that could be given for it. Human beings, acting on their tendency to seek pleasure, would be unlikely very often *to be able* to genuinely take the interest of others into consideration, since at their instinctual core they would seek to act for the benefit of others only when the latter's interests coincided, or at least were not in active conflict, with their own. It being a time-honored precept of moral philosophy that "ought implies can," there would be precious little left that could be truthfully said to fall within the realm of what one "ought to do"—the moral realm. Moreover, the classical argument that the pursuit of the good and the right is a constituent part of human well-being would appear as counterfactual nonsense, knocking the props out from under much moral exhortation.

A second major change in Freud's mature theory, equally relevant to the issue of psychological hedonism, concerns his new view of the relation of instincts to the mind. This new perspective on how instincts motivate behavior, which begins to be developed in *Beyond the Pleasure Principle,* makes it easier to envision pleasure as a prospective goal that encompasses a *multiplicity* of *qualitatively distinct types of experiences.*

In the earlier drive-discharge model, the instincts impinge from the body—and from the external environment—on a machine-like psychic apparatus that is automatically regulated by the pleasure principle to either keep constant or reduce the quantity of excitation within the psychic system. In the new model, the instincts belong to the psyche itself. They are the instincts *of* the psyche, which is now clearly conceived as like a biological organism rather than a mechanism disturbed by intruding energy.

In this new model, which Freud never completely consolidated, the competing earlier meanings of pleasure are variously assigned to the life (Eros) and the death instincts. These instincts are discussed primarily in terms of their orientations toward distant end-states, although in addition they, like their predecessor, the pleasure principle, are also charged with the regulation of current tensions.

As a matter of ordinary language and expectations, it is surprising that Freud should allocate some aspects of the *pleasure* principle to something called a *death* instinct. But it is the original notion that the pleasure principle seeks a reduction of tension to zero that Freud reassigns to the death instinct. Along with this comes the "Nirvana principle," which "expresses the trend of the death instinct" (*SE* 19 [1924]:160).[35] According to Freud, the Nirvana principle is teleologically directed toward the breakdown of vital unities and the eventual return of the living entity to an inorganic state of complete repose.[36] Freud now bleakly says that "*the aim of all life is death*" (*SE* 18 [1920]:38, emphasis original).[37]

Most of the remaining early connotations of the pleasure principle, such as its tendency to seek psychic equilibrium and its modified functioning under the aegis of the reality principle, are reassigned to or subsumed by Eros, the name Freud employs in his final instinct theory to connote the whole of the life instincts, embracing both the sexual instincts proper and the instincts for self-preservation. According to Freud, Eros acts in opposi-

35. Although Freud compares the aim of the death instinct to the phenomena of inertia in the world of physics, in point of fact inertia in the physical realm is nothing more than opposition to change, whereas it becomes an active tendency in Freud's biologically based paradigm of the mind (see Bibring 1941, p. 119).

36. As Bibring points out, Freud's metatheoretical efforts to account for aggression end up by shifting the criterion of instinct from "source" to "aim," thereby subverting his whole earlier treatment of the instinctual bases of behavior. The quantitative view of the instincts gives way to a qualitative one (see Bibring 1941, p. 105). Bibring also makes the important point that the qualitative view of the instincts undercuts the earlier distinction between "instinct" and mental "principle" (as in the pleasure "principle" and the reality "principle") so that these concepts are now very much alike (1941, p. 128). This makes it possible to group the principles with the instincts, as Freud does when he writes that "the *Nirvana* principle expresses the trend of the death instinct; the *pleasure* principle represents the demands of the libido; and the modification of the latter principle, the *reality* principle, represents the influence of the external world" (*SE* 19 [1924]:160).

37. Freud subordinates the life instincts to the death instincts in *Pleasure Principle* but amends this view in the *New Introductory Lectures on Psycho-Analysis* where he treats the two instincts as synchronous (see *SE* 22 [1933]:107–8).

tion to the death instinct's promptings and seeks to create and maintain vital unities that presuppose high levels of tension. Thus, Eros embodies the will to live and is the force in the world that builds things up and combines them into ever larger and more complex unities.[38] The activity of the life instincts thus "coincide[s] with the Eros of the poets and philosophers . . . [to] hold . . . all living things together" (*SE* 18 [1920]:50) and represents a striking departure from the energy-based model of instincts as tending toward tension reduction.

As a consequence of these radical theoretical shifts, it now becomes possible for Freud to move beyond his former gloomy view of pleasure as sporadic, intermittent relief from continuously renewed tension. Positive pleasures are now considered among the end-states toward which the life instincts motivate behavior.[39] This new position enables Freud to declare, against his own former view of pleasure as the abrogation of displeasure, that human beings are not "content to aim at an avoidance of unpleasure— a goal, as we might call it, of weary resignation" (*SE* 21 [1930]:82). Rather, they hold "fast to the original, passionate striving for a positive fulfilment of happiness."[40] Freud thus responds to the rhetorical question "What do people show by their behavior to be the purpose and intention of their lives?" by declaring that

> [human beings] strive after happiness; they want to become happy and to remain so. This endeavour has two sides, a positive and a negative aim. It aims, on the one hand, at an absence of pain and unpleasure, and, on the other, at *the experiencing of strong feelings of pleasure* . . .In conformity with this dichotomy in his aims, man's activity develops in two directions, according as it seeks to realize— in the main, or even exclusively—the one or the other of these aims. (*SE* 21 [1930]:76, emphasis added)

Rieff is therefore in error when he characterizes Freud's psychology of pleasure as devoid of "any ecstatic implications" and unequivocally op-

---

38. Freud came to realize that the libido and the ego instincts are alike in being broadly life-embracing and life-preserving. Thus he could reassign much of what he had said earlier about the ego instincts and the libido to the new, broader concept of the life instincts, or Eros.

39. As Loewald points out, "the [new] idea of a life instinct bespeaks an orientation toward a view in which life is not altogether motivated by forces of the past but is *partially motivated by an attraction coming from something ahead of us*" (1980, p. 141, emphasis added).

40. There is now a large body of evidence indicating that human beings are as interested in seeking out pleasurable experiences as they are in tension reduction. For example, direct observation of infants reveals that from day one, they seek out stimuli rather than ward them off when in the state of alert activity (see Shapiro and Stern 1980).

posed to hedonism in the popular sense of enjoyment (1961, pp. 171, 357).[41]

Once positive pleasures are conceived as possible end-states of action, Freud begins to abandon his earlier *quantitative* hedonism, which holds that pleasures consist essentially in the same *kind* of experience and differ only in quantity and duration, in favor of *qualitative* hedonism, according to which behavior is directed toward a variety of qualitatively distinct pleasurable end-states.[42] Whereas Freud formerly believed (at least when writing at the metapsychological level) that pleasures were limited to the monolithic experience of tension reduction, or at least that surface phenomenological differences could be explained ultimately by tension reduction, in his mature writings he acknowledges that the pleasures people seek differ qualitatively—that is, that sensual bodily sensations differ from the enjoyment of intellectual activities which, in turn, differ from the delights of interpersonal love.[43]

These changes in the understanding of pleasurable experience rest not only on the new instinct theory but also on the structural theory presented in *The Ego and the Id* (1923).[44] Unlike Freud's early writings, in which psychic structures are conceptualized as static entities existing independently of the drives that disrupt them, the later theory envisions the ego and the superego as psychic structures that develop through the "organization" of the instinctual drives, as the innate capacities of human beings

41. Rieff correctly notes that Freud's pleasure principle is not exactly hedonism in the popular understanding of the term. But Freud is far from holding that psychoanalysis demonstrates "the futility of hedonism" or that pleasure is at best a kind of self-defense against the increment of tension, as Rieff claims (1961, pp. 171, 357).

42. For an excellent comparison of quantitative and qualitative hedonism, see Edwards 1979.

43. Freud recognized the possibility of qualitatively different pleasures from the outset (see the "Project") and attempted to explain them in two ways. He attributed the different sensual experiences of sucking, biting, eliminating, stroking, and touching to humankind's perceptual equipment—i.e., to "the *Pcpt.* [Perceptual] system" (*SE5* [1900]:616). Other qualitative differences among pleasurable and unpleasurable experiences he attributed broadly to "consciousness," or "the Cs. [Conscious] system," which permits a more finely tuned differentiation than is possible in more primitive organisms. But the mechanical model of the mind with which he was working at the time inclined him to quantitative hedonism.

44. Laplanche and Pontalis note that Freud tried to account for the qualitative differences among our pleasurable and painful experiences in terms of the ego's modification of the pleasure principle (1973, p. 242). They go on to observe that this doctrine "fit[s] badly into the energy-based model of the instinct as a tendency towards the reduction of tensions."

unfold and are shaped by interaction with the environment.[45] Hartmann underscores the significance of this "structuralization" process for the pleasure principle by contrasting it with the reality principle's functioning. Under the reality principle in Freud's early conceptualization, there is only postponement of gratification and temporary toleration of displeasure. But with structure formation, the "conditions themselves on which the pleasurable or unpleasurable characters of a situation rest have been changed" (Hartmann 1964, p. 248). This "reassessment of pleasure values" consequent on ego and superego development is described by Hartmann "as a partial domestication of the pleasure principle" (ibid.) in which it comes under the control of the ego and the superego. As a result, "the pleasure principle develops a bias in favor of the ego or superego" (ibid., p. 249). This is why, in Freud's later work "pleasure and unpleasure" are more frequently assigned to ego-mediated satisfactions of the self as a whole, even to "conscious feelings . . . attached to the ego" and, correlatively why it is the ego that is now assigned the principle role in turning "a possibility of pleasure into a source of unpleasure" (*SE* 18 [1920]:11; 22 [1933]:93).

The first clear evidence of Freud's gradual substitution of qualitative hedonism for quantitative hedonism appears in 1924, in "The Economic Problem of Masochism." In his earlier writings, Freud had attempted repeatedly to explain subjective feelings of pleasure and displeasure in quantitative terms, by holding that displeasure is caused by a quantitative increase in the amounts of stimulus prevailing in the mental apparatus, while pleasure is caused by the diminution of tension (see *SE* 1 [1950]:312; 5 [1900]:598; 14 [1915]:120–1; 16 [1916–17]:356).[46] But he acknowledges in his 1924 discussion of foreplay that the reverse of what is theoretically expected on the quantitative model occurs normally, when plea-

---

45. For further discussion of these contrasting models of the psyche, see Stewart 1967, pp. 119–20.

46. These quantitative generalizations strike most readers as highly implausible, because subjective experiences of pleasure involving an increase in tension and of displeasure involving its decrease come readily to mind. Moreover, the pleasure principle, taken at its highest level of generalization where it purports to govern all behavior, refers to the self-regulation of a biological system to fulfil the needs and interests of the organism. In organisms capable of affective experience, need-fulfilling objects and experiences can, but need not, evoke affective pleasure; conversely, detrimental experiences to an organism can, but need not, evoke the experience of pain. (For discussion of this point, see J. H. Smith 1977, pp. 1–10.) In Rapaport's (1957–59, I:74) extreme formulation, the pleasure principle at this metapsychological level "has not *per se* anything to do with pleasure or pain," because it refers to the regulation of a system, not to conscious, subjective experiences of pleasures and pain (1957–9, 1:74, cited in J. H. Smith 1977, p. 3).

sure, rather than pain, accompanies "the accumulation of tension" that results from kisses and bodily caresses.[47] This observation had been made earlier, in *The Three Essays on the Theory of Sexuality*,[48] but this time it leads to the significant theoretical concession that "pleasure and 'pain' cannot, therefore, be referred to a quantitative increase or decrease of something which we call stimulus-tension" (*CP* 2 [1924]:256).[49] Freud now emphasizes the qualitative aspects of pleasure: "It seems as though they [pleasurable and painful experiences] do not depend on this quantitative factor, but on some peculiarity in it which we can only describe as qualitative. We should be much farther on with psychology if we knew what this qualitative peculiarity was" (ibid.). The theoretical shift away from the quantitative approach to pleasure evident in this remarkable passage exactly parallels Freud's abandonment during the same period of his earlier quantitative theory of anxiety in favor of regarding anxiety as an ego function. Just as anxiety becomes an informative experience for the ego with regard to threats from various sources evoking defense, positive pleasures of various kinds signal possibilities of pleasure to the ego that stimulate appropriate action.[50]

47. Freud had earlier acknowledged some difficulties with the quantitative approach. In the "Project," he observes that the problem of accounting quantitatively for the qualitative differences in phenomenologically experienced pleasures and pains presents formidable theoretical difficulties that remain to be surmounted. Likewise, he acknowledges in *Three Essays* that he is working "in the dark in questions of pleasure and unpleasure" (*SE* 7 [1905]:183) and that his own metapsychological approach to the problem is highly speculative. In *Introductory Lectures on Psycho-Analysis* he acknowledges that his drive-discharge speculations have not borne fruit (*SE* 16 [1916–17]:356). And in *Pleasure Principle*, he admits that it might not be possible to correlate quantitative and qualitative phenomena regarding pleasure (*SE* 18 [1920]:30–1). He writes that psychoanalysis has not yet "succeed[ed], *if that is possible,* in discovering what sort of relation exists between pleasure and unpleasure, on the one hand, and fluctuations in the amounts of stimulus affecting mental life, on the other" (*SE* 14 [1915]:121, emphasis added).

48. But there he avoids the problem posed for the drive-discharge theory by viewing foreplay as part of a series of acts that culminate in discharge. The "forepleasure" is thus required to produce "the necessary motor energy for the conclusion of the sexual act," which brings about the highest intensity of pleasure by "discharge of the sexual substances" (*SE* 7 [1905]:210).

49. Psychoanalytic theorists follow Freud's distinction here when they warn their readers not to equate the metapsychological use of the term *pleasure* with any ordinary experience of it. See, e.g., Schur 1966; J. Smith 1977.

50. Klein (1976, pp. 210–38) and Rieff (1961, p. 171) question whether Freud understood pleasure as a stimulant of positive action, because they believe he was misled by the metapsychology's drive-discharge explanation of pleasure. Klein writes: "Although Freud put aside his model of the libido and discharge in shifting from a purely quantitative conception of

The primary text dealing with Freud's mature views on qualitative hedonism is chapter 2 of *Civilization and its Discontents*. Significantly, Freud signals his shift to qualitative hedonism linguistically by substituting "happiness" (*das Glück*) for "pleasure" (*die Lust*). The term *das Glück* in its colloquial German sense resonates with *eudaimonia* in Greek and *felicitas* and *beatitudo* in Latin. Like them, it carries rich connotations of the goal of life being fulfillment, excellence, well-being, and self-realization.[51] Choice of the term implicitly conveys the message that it takes more for a person to be pleased with life as a whole or with the self (conscious and unconscious, past, present, and anticipated) than a string of separate agreeable sensations of the same monotonous sort, differing from one another only in their intensity and duration.

In the wide-ranging discussion of the implications of the "programme of the pleasure principle" for "happiness" that is the focus of chapter 2, various "strategies," "life plans," and ways of finding happiness in life are explored, and the point is made that there is a variety of qualitatively distinct, unique pleasures that people "show by their behavior" are generally conducive to "real satisfaction."[52]

First, there is the exquisite pleasure that "comes from the (preferably sudden) satisfaction of needs which have been dammed up to a high de-

---

anxiety as an overflow of pent-up libido to the structural view, he did not give up that model where pleasure experience was concerned" (1976, p. 213). But Klein notwithstanding, there is an exceedingly close relationship between Freud's treatment of the two great feeling-states of anxiety and pleasure. Positive pleasure and anxiety both arise out of the ego's relations with others and the natural environment, and both elicit behavioral responses. Hence, when Freud shifts from a quantitative theory of anxiety, he also shifts from a quantitative theory of hedonism.

51. *Das Glück,* like the English word *happiness,* is sometimes differentiated from pleasure solely by virtue of being longer-lasting. In this narrow usage, happiness is not different in *kind* from pleasure in the sense of a unitary subjective sensation of some sort. But *das Glück,* as Freud uses it in *Civilization and its Discontents,* is closer to the ordinary meaning of happiness. It covers not only being pleased with various aspects of one's life but being pleased with one's life as a whole. See Rashdall 1924, repr. in Frankena and Granrose 1974, pp. 344–5, for a discussion of the distinction between happiness with life as a whole and particular pleasant and unpleasant experiences.

52. There is also considerable evidence in Freud's letters of his belief in qualitatively distinct pleasures. In a letter dated 29 Aug. 1883 to his fiancée, Freud distinguishes such pleasures as "an hour's chat nestling close to one's love, the reading of a book that lays before us in tangible clarity what we think and feel, the knowledge of having achieved something during the day, the relief of having solved a problem" from less refined "gratifications" that are "so different" in kind that the cultured person cannot be said to enjoy them (letter 18, in E. L. Freud 1975, p. 50). He goes on to hint at his later theory of sublimation by suggesting that "the quality of refinement" is due to the "habit of constant suppression of natural instincts."

gree" (*SE* 21 [1930]:76). But there are in addition several very different sources of happiness that psychoanalysts would describe today as ego-mediated pleasures.[53] One of these is the artist's or writer's "joy in creating, in giving his phantasies body" which are said to have a "special quality" that seems "'finer and higher'" than the "sating of crude and primary instinctual impulses" (*SE* 21 [1930]:79–80). Another of the qualitatively unique pleasures singled out in chapter 2 of *Civilization and its Discontents* is the special enjoyment that accompanies the pursuit of knowledge, such as a scientist experiences "in solving problems or discovering truths" (*SE* 21 [1930]:79). Intellectual satisfaction is milder than instinctual satisfaction, Freud observes. "It does not convulse our physical being" like a sexual orgasm, but it is not simply a less intense experience of the same kind. Successful intellectual work, like artistic creativity, produces "a special quality" of satisfaction (ibid.). "Freely chosen" activities, Freud continues in a footnote, provide yet another "source of special satisfaction" (*SE* 21 [1930]:80, n.1). For what we choose to do enables us to give expression to the unique inclinations and developed capacities that distinguish us from others.

Still another unique pleasure is said to be found in intimate love, in what Freud calls the "fulfillment" of a "passionate striving." That the joys of love are different in kind from genital sexuality is highlighted by Freud's observation that love involves a mutual mirroring of selves, a reciprocity of "satisfaction in loving and being loved" (*SE* 21 [1930]:82). Many years earlier, Freud had written more fully in a similar vein that love entails not only "bodily satisfaction," but a "union" of sensual enjoyment with "mental" satisfaction, consisting of emotional intimacy together with high "estimation" or valuation of one's partner (*SE* 12 [1915]:169).[54] Interpersonal love of this sort is one of life's "culminating peaks," writes Freud. "Apart

---

53. Freud's mature qualitative hedonism is reflected linguistically by the new ambiguity surrounding the word *pleasure* when used in connection with ego-mediated satisfactions. In the late writings, Freud's use of the term *pleasure* in connection with the ego turns out not to have a single referent; rather, the pleasure of the whole self that the ego negotiates has a variety of qualitatively different referents. This broadening of the concept of pleasures parallels Freud's broadening of the concept of sexuality as his work matures. Just as the meaning of *sexuality* is expanded first to include the sensual experiences associated with the mouth, anus, skin, and genitals and then to a wide range of aesthetic and intellectual activities, so, too, *pleasure* is broadened to include qualitatively different kinds of experiences, ranging from convulsive orgasms to the scarcely perceptible satisfaction that accompanies the reading of a good book or the exercise of developed skills.

54. Freud wrote to the Swiss pastor Oskar Pfister: "You are aware that for us the term 'sex' includes what you in your pastoral work call love, and is certainly not restricted to the crude pleasure of the senses" (letter dated 9 Feb. 1909, in Meng and Freud 1963, p. 16).

from a few queer fanatics, all the world knows this and conducts its life accordingly."[55]

The final qualitatively unique enjoyment that Freud identifies in *Civilization and its Discontents* is that of aesthetic appreciation. "The enjoyment of beauty," he writes, "has a peculiar, mildly intoxicating quality of feeling" (*SE* 21 [1930]:82).

Freud's reiteration to the point of monotony of the phrase "special quality" in reference to the foregoing ego-mediated enjoyments is rather striking evidence that eventually he subscribed to the qualitative psychological hedonism of J. S. Mill, one of whose works he translated into German as a young man (see E. Jones 1953, pp. 55–6).[56] However, unlike Mill, Freud holds that erotic gratifications are indispensable constituents of all so-called higher and finer pleasures.

The different pleasures enumerated are distinguishable as *qualities* of feeling. This means that none of these qualitatively distinct pleasures can be a mere means to some other kind of pleasure and none is replaceable, in the sense of providing precisely the same enjoyment, by one of the other ego-parlayed pleasures or by a sexual orgasm, even though it is a psychoanalytic commonplace that people generally seek to compensate for a pleasure that is currently unavailable to them by trying to obtain pleasure from another, sometimes perverse, source. An artist, for example, may compensate for feeling badly about his or her creative work by promiscuous sexual behavior; but that substitution is clearly not fully satisfactory, otherwise he or she would not feel distressed about such behavior.

Thus, by contrast with quantitative hedonists like Bentham, for whom such phenomenologically different pleasures as intellectual work and sexual intercourse involve greater or lesser amounts of the same basic agreeable feeling, Freud recognizes that developed ego pleasures and enjoyments are distinguishable phenomenologically, in terms of their depth, subtlety,

55. That Freud meant to include the joys of friendship along with those of mutual erotic love in his list of qualitatively distinct pleasures in ch. 2 of *Civilization* is obvious from what he says elsewhere about intimate personal relations involving shared work and common interests. In a letter to Pfister around this time, Freud states in reference to their long friendship that "there is a *special value* in personal relations" (letter dated 7 Feb. 1930, in Meng and Freud 1963, p. 132, emphasis added).

56. For discussion of Freud's knowledge of Mill, see Jones 1953, pp. 55–6; McGrath 1986, pp. 101, 123, 137–8; M. Sherwood 1969, p. 174, n.21. Like Mill, Freud tends to confuse the psychological doctrine that some pleasures are qualitatively unique with the moral evaluation that some pleasures are more desirable than others, but we are interested in this chapter only in the psychological side of Freud's theory. Freud's ethical hedonism is discussed in ch. 12 below.

breadth, and refinement. Clinically, of course, it is exceedingly important that these sorts of experiential discriminations be recognized, because psychotherapy requires very precise delineation of such diverse experiences as mourning, melancholia, elation, anxiety, guilt, shame, doubt, hope, and despair. In fact, this is probably one major reason why Freud felt compelled to move toward qualitative hedonism as he began to specify the etiology of these clinical conditions more carefully.

Nonetheless, he remained convinced that quantitative hedonism reigns in the unconscious, and so he contrasts ego-mediated appreciation of quality with the id's purely quantitative or "economic" calculations.[57] The point of this contrast is to bring out the bedrock depth-psychological discovery that our motivations are generally mixed. This means that people are more selfishly calculating in totting up arithmetically the probable satisfactions and dissatisfactions from complex situations than they consciously imagine. However, Freud also maintains that the person who has attained maturity and strength of character through the kind of "*qualitative* alteration" of personality that occurs with the aid of psychoanalysis is able to put "an end to the *dominance* of the quantitative factor" (my emphasis) over his or her behavior (*SE* 23 [1937]:227, 228).

Freud's claim that the developed ego is guided by qualitative hedonism helps to bring out just how in his late writings "the programme of the pleasure principle" is compatible with non-egoistic and, hence, moral behavior. This compatibility is largely a consequence of the fact that *happiness* as Freud uses the term for the goal of life is a different *kind* of end than the quantitative one of maximizing a single kind of agreeable feeling. "Happiness" in life is an "inclusive end" rather than a single "dominant end." That is to say, the activities through which it is sought are not means in an instrumental or neutral sense, but parts of a whole. To pursue happiness as an inclusive goal through such activities as artistic creativity, intellectual work, sensuality, love, and aesthetic appreciation is to enjoy each of these activities as contributing something qualitatively unique to a life plan. Insofar as these activities are "means," it is in the sense of being "constitutive of" the comprehensive end of happiness in life as a whole. It is only through such activities that genuine happiness in the sense of a "positive fulfilment" is possible.[58] Though happiness in this inclusive sense is considered our ultimate goal, it does not provide the determinate criterion for

57. See, e.g., *SE* 22 (1933):74.

58. E. Jones picks up on this "broad sense" of happiness in psychoanalytic theory when he observes that "by happiness we do not here mean simple pleasure, but a combination of enjoyment . . . with self-content" (1945, p. 59).

making contemporary choices that quantitative hedonism, with its one-dimensional scale against which arithmetic sums of satisfactions can be measured, does. There are too many different kinds of enjoyable activities and too many different modes in which happiness can be achieved for it to provide a clear criterion for practical action in the present. As Freud says regarding "the programme of becoming happy, which the pleasure principle imposes on us": "Very different paths may be taken in that direction. . . . Every man must find out for himself in what particular fashion he can [find happiness in life]. . . . All kinds of different factors will operate to direct his choice" (*SE* 21 [1930]:83). If happiness as an end-state is compatible with this degree of latitude, however, it would appear to be too indeterminate to dictate only egoistic behavior, at least if some of the penultimate activities through which it is sought are of a non-egoistic character.

That happiness can be sought through activities that are congruent with non-egoistic conduct is brought out by Freud's examples of the various paths that are conducive to this end. Many of the activities he mentions as sources of special enjoyment—for example, artistic creativity, the pursuit of truth, freely chosen professional work, and love—are such that the primary objective is often not predominantly one's own pleasure. In fact, two of Freud's examples—those of the creative painter and the original scientist—are illustrations *par excellence* of disinterested devotion to objective tasks and ideals.[59] As Freud says of his own involvement in the creative process in a letter written upon completing the analysis of happiness in *Civilization and its Discontents:* "All I know is that I worked terribly hard . . . I was aware only of the objective, not of myself" (letter 243, in E. L. Freud 1975, p. 390).[60] *The Future of an Illusion* (*SE* 21 [1927]:54) contains the observation that such disinterested devotion to the truth (as impersonal *Logos*) on the part of the agnostic or atheistic scientist may motivate some of the same altruistic acts as those embraced by the religious believer. But the secular scientist is less "self-seeking" than the believer because there is no thought

59. Freud appears to build disinterestedness into the object orientation of the reality principle of the ego. The "original reality ego" is so named because it "distinguishes internal and external by means of a sound objective criterion" (*GW* 10 [1915]:228; *SE* 14 [1915]:136), which is presumably independent of calculations of the pleasurableness of the task, work, or enterprise.

60. Eissler observes correctly that "mental achievements of the magnitude characteristic of Freud can arise . . . only when ambition is purified of narcissism and converted into object-directed strivings" (1964, p. 193).

of reward in a future state of bliss. Truth is pursued even though it offers "no compensation for . . . [those] who suffer grievously from life" now.[61]

Pleasure, of course, may accompany the exercise of developed artistic and intellectual skills, but this is not always the case, at least not at every step. And even when it is, the artist or the scientist is not apt to be solely or even predominantly motivated by thoughts of the agreeable feelings that are likely to be extracted from his or her daily labors. The enjoyment that is experienced often comes as an unanticipated by-product, the factor of surprise itself augmenting the enjoyment in a very special way. The pleasure is the creative person's own, but it is found in activities that are not motivated by self-interest alone, even if they would not be done were there no hope that some happiness could be obtained eventually from them.[62]

Freud does not construe narrowly, then, the happiness at which the ego aims as always involving a self-interested goal. To the contrary, persons are observed to find pleasure in a wide range of activities, including fulfilling the needs of others, and even in moral conscientiousness.[63] For there is

61. This represents the development of a point that Freud had made much earlier about the tension between intellectual activities and his early conception of the pleasure principle. In "Formulations on the Two Principles of Mental Functioning," he notes that "science is . . . the most complete renunciation of the pleasure principle of which our mental activity is capable" (*SE* 11 [1911]:165).

62. Psychoanalyst Edith Jacobson underlines the importance of disinterested creative work in a passage reminiscent of Bishop Butler's argument against psychological egoism: "As the author begins to write, he may 'fall in love' with his book. Since the book represents to him his own creation, his way of self expression, this 'love' may be rather of a narcissistic type. Moreover, the function as such—the acts of thinking and writing—may be a highly vested, preferred form of self satisfaction. After his work is published, its praise by the public, the splendid sale of the book, the gain of money from it, all these gratifications may be the writer's additional narcissistic rewards. But all these manifold narcissistic elements involved in such creative ego activity are bound to interfere with the function of thinking and writing if the major aim of the book does not remain the writer's true interest in the selected field, in the special material he deals with, in the discoveries he has made, or the ideas which he wants to develop: in short, an 'objective' interest. The object-directed nature of his interest will find expression in a quiet devotion to his work, to the point of self forgetfulness or even self sacrifice" (1964, pp. 81–2).

63. Because Freud imagines possibilities for individual happiness through the sublimation of unconscious desires, he does not feel compelled, as he would if he held only to a doctrine of sensual satisfaction as pleasurable, to search for happiness in utopian solutions, as do Marcuse and Brown, who fail to recognize Freud's alternative. The truth in the Marcuse–Brown position on the inevitability of conflict between the individual's desire for pleasure and the demands of civilized society is that Freud does hold that some satisfactions (e.g., perverse sexuality and aggression) are, indeed, asocial and antisocial. This means that some frustration

"satisfaction" to be obtained in acting benevolently in accordance with one's "ego ideal" and "a feeling of triumph when something in the ego coincides with the ego ideal" (*SE* 18 [1921]:110, 131). Such pleasure in benevolent conduct may occur even when the other's improved welfare has absolutely no subsequent effect on the agent. In other words, moral agents may find their long-term pleasure in the very traditional ways of doing good, just, kind deeds, though they are not apt to be truly happy in life unless these pleasures are complemented by others, including the once-devalued joys of sexual gratification and the free play of fantasy. Psychological hedonism of this sort is compatible with considerable altruism. It does not imply a narrow egoistic hedonism unless linked, via additional psychological assumptions, like those associated with the libido and narcissism, to a more subtle form of self-interest. Hence, it is to the question of whether narcissism and object cathexis are compatible with genuinely moral behavior that we now turn.

---

of desire is inevitable if we are to enjoy the benefits of social cooperation, which most people also desire.

But this does not mean that we can never be even moderately happy in civilized society. Mature adults, Freud says in effect, can live with some frustration, as long as they are compensated by sources of real enjoyment that grant a measure of satisfaction to instinctual desires in ways that are compatible with social life. To reform contemporary society in ways that increase the likelihood that individuals will find happiness within society through less repressive channels of sublimation, thereby reconciling the individual's quest for happiness with the constraints required for social cooperation, this is Freud's vision.

Chapter 7
Narcissism

> Sin of self-love possesseth all mine eye,
> And all my soul, and all my every part;
> And for this sin there is no remedy,
> It is so grounded inward in my heart.
>
> —Shakespeare

> Narcissism is the universal and original
> state of things, from which object-love is
> only later developed, without the narcissism
> necessarily disappearing on that account.
>
> —Freud

> Self-love, my liege, is not so vile a sin
> As self-neglecting.
>
> —Shakespeare

If the pleasure principle does not imply egoism, does narcissism? Some students of Freud believe that we are inevitably moved by self-love, even when we appear to be acting on moral principle or for the sake of others, and that such motivations are basically egoistic in a sense that makes all claims to a moral basis for conduct spurious. Rieff, for example, reads Freud as holding that all human relations are but devious means of self-love—the implication being that morality, insofar as it rests on non-egoistic concerns, is illusory.[1] Rieff's title, *Freud: The Mind of the Moralist,* is misleading. It would be a more accurate reflection of his views if it were changed to *Freud: The Mind of the Anti-Moralist.* In "loving" or caring about someone, Rieff contends, the Freudian self chases "love round an object back to itself

1. "Psychological man," a cultural type ostensibly shaped by the Freudian revolution, is presented by Rieff as a "trained egoist" (1961, p. 2), incapable of genuine commitment either to a community or to another individual. For Rieff, the Freudian self "cannot [even] conceive of an action that is not self-serving, however it may be disguised or transformed" (ibid., p. 61). This depiction of the psychoanalytic doctrine of human nature has been widely accepted by contemporary social critics such as Lasch (1979) and Bellah et al. (1985), who, following Rieff, charge psychoanalysis with culturally subverting all values other than satisfaction of the isolated individual's arbitrary preferences. For criticism of this thesis, see Wallwork 1986.

again" (1961, p. 174). Psychoanalytic scrutiny, he continues, unmasks "all loves . . . as self-satisfactions: from the love of the child for the parent-provider, to the love of spouses which reincarnates these parent-images, to the parent's 'narcissistic' love for his own children" (ibid.).[2]

But Rieff's influential interpretation of narcissism is seriously flawed by its superficiality. By uncritically assuming that narcissism is equivalent to self-love and that self-love is identical with egoism, Rieff fails to appreciate Freud's exceedingly broad understanding of what narcissism encompasses and the complex patterning of self–other motivations that the concept opens to understanding. In fact, Freud does not limit the term *narcissism* to self-absorption and egoism, although these are undoubtedly its principal popular connotations. True, withdrawal into the self and exclusive devotion to the self's interests, narrowly conceived, are encompassed by Freud's understanding of narcissism, as they are by the Greek myth. But for Freud, the term also encompasses self-love, self-regard, and self-affirmation as underlying motivations in behavior that is not manifestly self-interested. In the technical psychoanalytic lexicon, *narcissism* covers all forms of motivation in which there is unconscious emotional investment in the ego, self, or self-representation, even when the *manifest* behavior is other-regarding or even self-sacrificial. In fact it is only because Freud broadened the meaning of narcissism in this way that it is possible to speak, as we do today, of a philanthropist's benevolence or a parent's sacrifice for a child's education or career as narcissistically motivated.[3]

In discussing Freud's views on narcissism, it is important to note that the fundamental issue raised by psychoanalytic claims about the ubiquity of narcissistic motivations is not whether persons are *cognitively* capable of taking the interests of others into account. Freud does not deny that normal adults can cognitively recognize the needs and interests of others in deciding among alternative courses of action. The ego is as capable of gathering such information and using it in purportedly moral judgments as it is of examining its own interests in the context of making prudential judgments.

2. In a similar vein, Singer argues that "for Freud, loving another person comes down to self-love, and every beloved must be a mere substitute for that person who loved us when we were incapable of loving anyone but ourselves . . . [To the question]: 'What is it that the lover really desires in another person?' Freud thinks it must be access to primal narcissism" (1983, 1. 33–4; see also Wallace 1986, p. 94).

3. Freud's broad understanding of *narcissism* is evident when one contrasts his use of the term with its chief medical usage in the late nineteenth century, which referred primarily to a sexual perversion in which a person focuses exclusively on his or her own body as an erotic object (Ellis 1898; *SE* 7 [1905]:218 n.; 14 [1914]:73).

Indeed, psychoanalysis as a clinical technique in which the analyst must understand the analysand depends on this capacity, as Freud himself recognized. Using the term *empathy* (*Einfühlung*) for the intellectual process of reverse role-taking, he declares that it plays "the largest part in our understanding of what is inherently foreign to our ego in other people" (*SE* 18 [1921]:108).

Similarly, Freud does not dispute that our *conscious* intentions are frequently non-egoistic. In fact, he goes out of his way to distinguish *consciously* altruistic *conduct* from both egoistic and narcissistic *motivations* (*SE* 16 [1916–17]:417–18.)[4] The real question raised by the psychoanalytic theory of narcissism is whether our purportedly moral intentions are what they seem to be or mere facades hiding deeper, self-interested purposes of the self. In other words, what must be determined is whether we are *psychologically* capable of genuinely intending the good of others for their own sake. And on this issue Freud has bequeathed us continuing confusion that derives largely from the ambiguity of the technical meanings he conferred on the term *narcissism* as he wove it into the larger body of psychoanalytic theory.[5]

The concept of narcissism evolved at the height of Freud's metapsychological drive-discharge speculations in 1914 as an extension of the libido theory—indeed, as one of the two main directions taken by the libido (the other being object love). In "On Narcissism" Freud defined it as the "libidinal cathexis of the ego" (*Libidobesetzung des Ichs*) (*SE* 14 [1914]:75; *GW* 10 [1914]:141).[6] This certainly sounds "self-centered." Yet there is much play in the joints of this definition of narcissism, and Freud uses the term in several different ways that say different things about

4. In *Introductory Lectures on Psycho-Analysis* altruism (*Altruismus*) is said to be "the antithesis" of egoism and narcissism, because the latter are self-referential, whereas altruism is other-regarding. In altruism, as in object love, the object "draws to itself a portion of the ego's narcissism," but altruism "is distinct from the latter in its lack of the desire for sexual satisfaction in the object" (1952, pp. 424–5).

5. Few terms in the psychoanalytic lexicon are as enigmatic as *narcissism*. This is because Freud played with the concept theoretically, extending its meaning far beyond its connotations in everyday speech, thereby affording psychoanalysis a new way of comprehending a wide range of human motivations in a new light.

6. Freud had first introduced the concept of narcissism before 1914 (see *SE* 11 [1910]:100; 12 [1911]:60–61, 72; 13 [1913]:88–90, 93, 130, 159, 189). But it was not until the paper of 1914 that his views were first definitively crystallized. This occurred while he was still holding steadfastly to earlier ideas, even as he moved to new ground, the result being an admixture of the old and the new, with both conceptual and semantic confusion (see B. E. Moore 1975, p. 245).

self-involvement. He is able to do so because each of the terms in the definition—*libido, cathexis,* and *ego*—have several very different meanings, the multiple coalescing of which permit widely diverse psychic phenomena to be classified as narcissistic.[7] For instance, *libido* sometimes refers to *psychic energy* that can be transferred intrapsychically from the unconscious to the ego with the result that the ego is empowered for its tasks of perception, thought, judgment, and action. But it also refers to *sensual motives* of all kinds, ranging from autoerotic urges to "all that may be comprised under the word 'love'" (*SE* 18 [1921]:90). It even covers such nonsensual motives and valuations in which love is directed toward the self, such as vanity and self-affirmation.

The *ego* that is the object of narcissistic investment is no less ambiguous than the libido that is invested, since it refers interchangeably both to the "self," as contrasted with other persons, and to the intrapsychic structure responsible for consciousness, reasoning, and practical deliberation that psychoanalysts distinguish topographically from the unconscious and structurally from the id and the superego.[8]

Finally, *cathexis,* the term linking the libido to the ego, is just as ambiguous as the terms it connects.[9] From the metapsychology's economic point

7. As a consequence of all the vagaries built into its definition, narcissism has been used as a partial explanation for such diverse and obscurely related clinical phenomena as the regressive egoism of the physically ill and hypochondriasis, autoeroticism, sleep, homosexual object choice, most perversions, romantic love, parental love, compassion, resistance in psychotic disorders, exhibitionism, sadism, masochism, the evolution of the self in relation with others, the masculinity complex in women, the war neuroses, idealization, group formation, hypnosis, friendship, jealousy, the repetition compulsion, superego formation, secondary gain in symptoms, humor, and self-referential attitudes and dispositions (see B. E. Moore 1975, pp. 250–1). This makes it tempting to abandon the concept altogether as helplessly inexact (for discussion, see Pulver 1970, p. 324) or to limit its applicability severely, as Joffe and Sandler (1967) have attempted to do. But I agree with Moore (1975) that the term is invaluable in linking phenomena not ordinarily thought to be linked at all and that something essential is lost in narrowly restricting the term's meaning.

8. For discussion, see Hartmann 1964, pp. 126–7. The ambiguity of the term *ego* in Freudian theory allows Hartmann to define narcissism as "the libidinal cathexis . . . of the self" (ibid., p. 127).

9. *Cathexis* is the word of Greek derivation chosen by Freud's English translator for the German *Besetzung,* which has many connotations. In military usage *Besetzung* stands for occupation of a position or territory, but its most general meaning is for putting something into a place (L. Brandt 1961). *Cathexis* is defined technically, from the economic point of view, as a charge of "psychic energy." But that concept has been criticized by a number of leading psychoanalytic theorists, including Kubie (1947), Gill (1976), and Schafer (1976). Loevinger argues that when Freud's "drive paradigm is replaced [after 1923] by the ego paradigm, there is no question that cathexis theory . . . [becomes] obsolete. Energy, psychic energy if you will,

of view, it denotes an investment of psychic energy in the ego or in self-representations. But this energy may be manifested in highly diverse ways, such as social or intellectual competence ("ego strength"), passionate devotion to or mere interest in a hobby, professional field, or area of knowledge ("ego interests"), or valuation of an internal representation of oneself or something allied with oneself. The last, valuation of oneself or something allied with oneself, is crucial for understanding narcissism, but it is qualitatively different from the amount of energy one has available to invest in some aspect of oneself or one's activities.[10]

Freud claims that narcissistic motivations are ubiquitous because we are always concerned to some extent with maintaining a positive, somewhat grandiose self-image and in satisfying our egoistic needs and interests. He states that "we . . . postulat[e] . . . a primary narcissism in everyone" (*SE* 14 [1914]:88). "Narcissism is the universal and original state of things, from which object-love is only later developed, without the narcissism necessarily disappearing on that account" (*SE* 16 [1916–17]:416). Even "parental love, which is so moving [in its altruistic devotion], . . . is nothing but the parents' narcissism born again, which, transformed into object-love, unmistakably reveals its former nature" (*SE* 14 [1914]:91).

However, in order to understand what Freud means when he speaks about the ubiquity of narcissism in these terms and whether he intends to preclude the possibility of non-egoistic conduct, it is necessary to examine precisely what he says about narcissistic motives as he distinguishes among the principal subtypes of narcissism, as a developmental stage, a type of object choice, a mode of relating, and a self-referential attitude (see Pulver 1970 for a similar breakdown).[11] The discussion that follows shows that

---

becomes what it must have been originally, a description of human feelings without pretension of quantitative meaning or high-level explanatory power" (1976, pp. 370–1).

10. Freud himself was not entirely satisfied with his work on narcissism. After completing his pivotal essay of 1914, he wrote to Abraham: "The narcissism was a difficult labor (*schwere Geburt*) and bears all the marks of a corresponding deformation" (letter dated 18 Mar. 1914, cited in E. Jones 1955, p. 304). Nonetheless, Freud continued to expand the range of clinical phenomena attributed to narcissism, without bothering to formulate a more precise definition or to relate earlier propositions to the major theoretical modifications introduced in his final years. (See Hartmann 1964, p. 126.)

11. Freud's *structural* use of the concept of narcissism as the libidinal cathexis of the ego will not be discussed in this chapter, even though the "neutralization" of libidinal energy entailed by this process means that delibidinized motivational power is made available to the ego, which can use it in a wide range of actions, some of which are presumably non-egoistic in character. I will not take this tack in part because Freud does not explicitly state that this is the way in which non-egoistic actions arise.

these four principle types of narcissism have different behavioral consequences. While narcissistic motives are generally contrasted with object-regarding ones, some types of narcissistic motives turn out to be compatible with, even positively supportive of, genuine object love.

NARCISSISM AS A DEVELOPMENTAL STAGE

The first of Freud's four types of narcissism connotes an infantile stage of development characterized by the libidinal state known as "primary narcissism" (*SE* 23 [1940]:150). There are actually two candidates for the description of this stage in Freud's writings, depending on whether one puts the emphasis primarily on self-absorption or self-love.

Those psychoanalytic theorists, like Jacobson (1964, p. 15), Mahler (1968), and B. E. Moore (1975, p. 253), who characterize narcissism primarily in terms of complete self-absorption prior to the formation of object relations follow Freud's identification of the developmental stage of primary narcissism with the earliest infantile period.[12] The neonate during this period is as yet completely unaware of anything but its own experiences of bodily satisfactions and frustrations. Alternatively, those psychoanalysts, like Lacan (1977, pp. 1–7), Laplanche and Pontalis (1973, p. 256), and Kohut (1971), who emphasize the self-referential character of narcissism—in the sense that the infant is aware of himself or herself as a person among others—cite those passages in which Freud argues that the developmental stage of primary narcissism comes later, after an earlier stage of self-absorption during which there is not even a rudimentary awareness of the differentiation of self and object. For most of his career, Freud himself favored the second of these alternatives, although the standard interpretation for many years has been that primary narcissism describes the infant's most primitive relation with its environment, since it was in this connection that Freud referred to it ambiguously in his last writings (*SE* 23 [1940]:150).

12. Jacobson says that she finds the term *primary narcissism* "a very useful term for the earliest infantile period, preceding the development of self and object images, the stage during which the infant is as yet unaware of anything but his own experiences of tension and relief, of frustration and gratification" (1964, p. 15). Mahler draws on Freud's bird's-egg analogy in characterizing the first weeks of extra-uterine life as the substage of "normal autism" or "*absolute* primary narcissism, which is marked by the infant's lack of awareness of a mothering agent" (1968, p. 10). Mahler's next substage of primary narcissism, the symbiotic stage proper, which begins around the third month, is "not such an absolute primary narcissism, inasmuch as the infant begins dimly to perceive need satisfaction as coming from a need-satisfying part object—albeit still from within the orbit of his omnipotent symbiotic dual unity with a mothering agency, toward which he turns libidinally" (ibid.).

What is most important is not which usage is correct since both have some claim to legitimacy in Freud's writings and in traditional usage, but how the two substages of early infantile narcissism are described and their implications for behavior.

The developmentally earlier of the two stages is also referred to by Freud as autoeroticism (*SE* 7 [1905]:181–2; 12 [1911]:77; 14 [1914]:76–7).[13] The neonate's libido during this stage of its most primitive relation with the environment "is not directed towards other people, but obtains satisfaction from the subject's own body" (*SE* 7 [1905]:181).[14] The newborn is exclusively preoccupied with the sensual satisfactions gained in sucking, chewing, biting, and eliminating.[15]

The first stage is narcissistic, however, only in a very special sense. The newborn cannot be described as *self*-satisfied, *self*-absorbed, or as loving it-*self,* because the "self" and the "not self" have yet to be differentiated. At best, this stage of life is aptly described as narcissistic only in the sense that the infant's pleasures are experienced as occurring in parts of an undifferentiated self-world (Decarie 1965, p. 80, cited by Pulver 1970, p. 328). As Piaget correctly remarks regarding Freud's views on this first stage of life, "the primary narcissism of nursing is really a narcissism without Narcissus" (cited by Kegan 1982, pp. 78–9).[16]

Self-love clearly cannot be the primary motivation of early infancy if there is no self to love. Rather, it must develop alongside object differentia-

---

13. Freud anticipated his later views on autoeroticism in a letter to Fliess dated 9 Dec. 1899 (letter 125, in Freud 1954, p. 303), in which he writes that "the lowest of the sexual strata is auto-erotism, which renounces any psychosexual aim and seeks only local gratification." Freud also links the autoerotic stage with primary narcissism in passages like the following: "We have been driven to assume that at the beginning of the development of the individual all his libido (all his erotic tendencies, all his capacity for love) is tied to himself . . . The condition in which the ego retains the libido is called by us 'narcissism', in reference to the Greek legend of the youth Narcissus who was in love with his own reflection" (*SE* 17 [1917]:138–9).

14. "We call this state absolute, primary *narcissism*. It lasts till the ego begins to cathect the ideas of objects with libido, to transform narcissistic libido into object-libido" (*SE* 23 [1940]:150).

15. Although Mahler's work on "normal autism" seems to support Freud's hypotheses about this stage, recent research indicates that infants are pre-wired to be object-oriented from the first days of life and, hence, that there is no developmental stage during which the newborn is totally unaware of any relationship to caretakers. For a summary and discussion of relevant research, see Greenspan 1988, pp. 9–10, 20–4.

16. Psychoanalyst Van der Waals makes much the same point when he observes that "psychologically there is not yet a self, nor a nonself" (1965, p. 295), so that autoeroticism does not fit the original sense of narcissism as self-love.

tion. Realizing this, Freud acknowledges that "the ego [as a self] cannot exist in the individual from the start; the ego [or self] has to be developed" (*SE* 14 [1914]:77). In fact, "love" is also a developmental achievement, since it characterizes the relations of selves or part-selves, not instincts, to other selves (*SE* 14 [1915]:137–8).[17] It is thus wrong to conclude from what Freud says about the earliest stage of human life that we are eternally attempting to recapture the original condition of self-love by chasing love through others back to ourselves again. In the beginning, we did not so much love ourselves as we sought sensual gratification anarchically in the limited bodily ways open to us in an undifferentiated self-world.

Freud generally uses the term *primary narcissism* for the second developmental stage, which follows the stage of autoeroticism and precedes the next developmental stage of object love.[18] During this halfway phase, the child's motivational goals have developed beyond unconnected sensual satisfactions to gratifications of a "self" as a somewhat (or partially) distinguishable entity. "In this intermediate stage," Freud states, the sexual drives find an object, but "this object is not an external one, extraneous to the subject, but it is his own ego, which has been constituted at about this same time . . . [To] this new stage, . . . we have given . . . the name of 'narcissism'" (*SE* 13 [1913]:88–9).[19] Freud here anticipates the central notion of

17. Freud is quite explicit about the inability of "instincts" to "love." "[W]e are not in the habit of saying of a single sexual instinct that it loves its objects, but regard the relation of the ego [as a self] to its sexual object as the most appropriate case in which to employ the word 'love'" (*SE* 14 [1915]:137–8).

18. Freud first posits the existence of a developmental stage of narcissism between autoeroticism and object love in the "Schreber" case (1911). Of this stage, he writes: "There comes a time in the development of the individual at which he unifies his sexual instincts (which have hitherto been engaged in auto-erotic activities) in order to obtain a love-object; and he begins by taking himself, his own body, as his love-object, and only subsequently proceeds from this to the choice of some person other than himself as his object" (*SE* 12 [1911]:60–1).

19. Freud vacillates as to how the first stages of life should be described. In addition to the account, mentioned above, that states that the most primitive stage is autoeroticism, which is followed by the narcissistic stage out of which object relations develop, Freud also argues that the first stage is properly described as narcissistic, after all, as well as that there is a stage prior to autoeroticism when the infant takes "the mother's breast [as] the first object of the sexual instinct" (*SE* 16 [1916–17]:314; 18 [1923]:245). Part of the problem is that Freud keeps changing the meaning of the terms *autoeroticism* and *narcissism* as his thought evolves. But it is also the case that he simply cannot decide whether the libido is first invested in objects and then turned inward in narcissism or is first invested in the ego (or self) and then directed outward onto objects. In retrospect, we can say that Freud was right to vacillate, because the self concept and the object concept, self-love and object love, develop simultaneously with the gradual differentiation of the self from the primary caretaker(s). For a discussion of these inconsistencies, see Balint 1960.

contemporary psychoanalytic self-psychology, that the human being has two births (Mahler et al. 1975). The first is the parturition, the actual physical birth. The second, more gradual and more subtle, is the birth of the self that commences with the first differentiation of the child from its primary caretaker(s) between six and eighteen months.[20] It is Freud's considered opinion that the intermediary stage between autoeroticism and object love is properly narcissistic as the first stage of autoeroticism is not, because the child at this developmentally later stage, which will henceforth be identified as *primary narcissism,* "behaves as though he were in love with himself" (*SE* 13 [1913]:89).

Narcissism at this second stage manifests itself in two ways: as an exaggerated egoism and as grandiosity. Egoism is need-centered. Grandiosity or megalomania is "self"-centered; it manifests the human infant's peculiar overvaluation of itself. This overvaluation is apparent in such characteristics as the infant's "over-estimation of the power of . . . wishes and mental acts, the 'omnipotence of thoughts,' a belief in the magical force of words, and a technique for dealing with the external world—'magic'—which appears to be a logical application of these grandiose premises" (*SE* 14 [1914]:75). The infant, deeming itself the center of the universe—"His Majesty the Baby" (*SE* 14 [1914]:91)—tends to use other people selfishly for his or her own gratification or aggrandizement. The similar desires of others are not even acknowledged, much less valued.

The child at the stage of primary narcissism is "egoistic" as it could not be earlier, because there is now a self to be interested in.[21] But the young child does not choose egoism over alternatives, because the alternatives have not yet developed. Object relations exist in the sense that the child is now cognizant, as he or she was not earlier, of the existence of other individuals in the immediate environment, but not as persons with their own needs and interests, only as instruments of his or her own satisfaction. Caretakers are valued, but only insofar as they are of assistance in satisfying needs or reflecting the self's grandiosity. Freud does not make as much as some contemporary psychoanalysts (see Erikson 1963, pp. 247–74; Kohut 1971, pp. 123–4) of the child's need for adult "mirroring" of its grandiosity at this stage—for example, with applause following the infant's first falter-

20. Lacan supposes that the self—the I—is precipitated during the "mirror stage" at approximately six months by the subject's acquisition of an image of himself (1977, pp. 1–7).

21. Domash and Balter characterize the orthodox psychoanalytic description of the egoism of the child at the stage of primary narcissism in this way: "[The] 'egoistic' orientation [of] the child is so intensely and symbiotically related to the mother that he feels absolute dominion over her, wholly entitled to her care and concern, including nothing less than death if necessary" (1979, p. 378).

ing attempts to walk. But the importance of emphatic mirroring appears to be assumed in what Freud says about the child's need to be loved unconditionally by his primary caretaker (*SE* 5 [1900]:398n.; 10 [1912]:181; 14 [1914]:87–9; 17 [1917]:156).

The view is sometimes put forward that Freud envisions the complete abandonment of primary narcissism with the advent of object love that accompanies the onset of oedipal dynamics. But it is Freud's contention that we never completely outgrow the second developmental stage of primary narcissism. The "narcissistic organization is never wholly abandoned," Freud writes: "A human being remains to some extent narcissistic even after he has found external objects for his libido" (*SE* 13 [1913]:89). This recognition of the "residue of infantile narcissism" (*SE* 14 [1914]:100) is not meant to deny that significant developmental transformations occur after this stage. No one has ever accused Freud of slighting the importance for human development of the anal and oedipal stages that come later. But the claim that we remain narcissists for ever, at least "to some extent," underscores Freud's conservationist or archeological view of mental life, which leads him to insist that once motivations have been formed, they coexist side by side with those that develop later. As Freud puts this general observation: "Every earlier stage of development persists alongside the later stage which has arisen from it" (*SE* 14 [1915]:285).[22]

Freud handles the coexistence of narcissistic motivations traceable to the early years in two ways. The first and more familiar is that infantile narcissistic motives remain within the unconscious behavioral repertoire of the individual, where they remain available for use if triggered by a crisis that induces regression. For example, the compulsion to display oneself with narcissistic grandiosity may not be a regular part of an adult's character, but it may come to the fore in all its embarrassing infantile splendor during a period of unusual stress. A Caspar Milquetoast or Walter Mitty in the right circumstances—for example, after a demotion at work—may become a verbal or sexual exhibitionist, much to the surprise of everyone, including especially Caspar or Walter. Commenting on cases such as these, Freud writes: "The earlier mental state may not have manifested itself for years, but none the less it is so far present that it may at any time again become the mode of expression of the forces in the mind, and indeed the only one, as though all later developments had been annulled or undone" (*SE* 14 [1915]:285).

Second, some motives that first appear during the stage of primary narcissism continue to exist as ubiquitous elements in the personalities of

22. Ricoeur sees in the theory of narcissism the climax of Freud's archeological vision (1970, pp. 445–6).

normal adults. This is not the case with all the motivations attributed to this stage of development; otherwise there could be little subsequent development. Adults do not always seek self-aggrandizement in the same ways and with the same persistence that they did as infants. Though all people seek approval from others, the self-aggrandizing motive is substantially modified during the maturational process. But the egoism of primary narcissism does persist into adulthood in the sense that we continue to care deeply, as we did as children, about satisfying our basic needs and interests. We are always to some extent, if only in the back of our minds, Freud argues, trying to exploit the external environment, including other people, for selfish purposes. We also tend to make our own needs more important in the general scheme of things than they are.

Because Freud insists so emphatically on the ubiquity of narcissism in the form of egoism, he has been popularly accused of reductionism—that is, of explaining all "higher" forms of behavior, such as benevolence, in terms of unconscious, self-referential motives. But a careful reading of those texts in which Freud speaks of the persistence of egoistic motives shows him repudiating reductionism (see, e.g., *SE* 14 [1915]:285–6; 18 [1921]:138). His aim in making the case for egoism as strong as possible is to drive home to his readers, against entrenched psychic defenses to the contrary, that egoistic motives coexist alongside more developed motives, with which they form complex combinations.

Needless to say, whether genuinely non-egoistic behavior is possible depends on the stage of object love that normally succeeds primary narcissism. But one point is already clear from the transition from autoeroticism to primary narcissism: namely, that Freud's stage theory envisions the possibility of qualitative transformations in the self–other motivational capacities of the developing child. Piagetian psychologists commonly fault Freudian theory for its alleged failure to appreciate that new developmental stages are qualitatively different from their predecessors; but the transformation from autoeroticism to primary narcissism involves nothing less than the emergence of the distinctively human capacity for self-consciousness that appears with the utterance of "I." If Freud can envision such a momentous transformation within the first years of life, it is at least worth investigating whether he imagines an equally dramatic development from narcissism to genuine object love.

NARCISSISTIC OBJECT CHOICE

Freud's second main use of *narcissism* denotes a *type of object choice* that is not fully other-regarding, because the choice of the object is made on the basis of an identification with some aspect of the self.[23] The narcissistic lover is primarily in love with himself or herself. Narcissists, Freud writes, "are plainly seeking *themselves* as a love-object" (*SE* 14 [1914]:88). A person loves in the other according to his or her narcissistic type:

(a) what he himself is (i.e., himself),
(b) what he himself was,
(c) what he himself would like to be,
(d) someone who was once part of himself.

(SE 14 [1914]:90)

Unlike Narcissus in the Greek myth, who does not even hear the nymph Echo, the narcissistic lover is related to other people, but others are valued primarily for some similarity they possess in common with the lover—what he was, is, would like to be, or was identified with. Other people are little more than stand-ins for himself; or, if they are acknowledged to be different, they are appreciated for gratifying his or her persistent need "of being loved" (*SE* 14 [1914]:89).[24]

The narcissistic object choice is especially marked in certain personalities, those with what are now known as "narcissistic personality disorders."[25] The narcissist displays a grandiose sense of self-importance or

23. Freud introduced the term *object choice* in *Three Essays on the Theory of Sexuality* (1905). *Object* means "person" in this context, as in "love object." The term *choice* does not refer to a conscious or intellectual selection among alternatives, but rather to the irrevocable and determining character of finding a particular object or type of object (*Objecktfindung*) at a decisive moment in one's history (see Laplanche and Pontalis 1973, p. 277).

24. Freud provides a good portrait of the narcissistic character in an 1883 letter to his fiancée. Describing the personality traits of a mutual acquaintance, Nathan Weiss, who had recently committed suicide, Freud contends that "his death was by no means an accident" (E. L. Freud 1975, p. 59). His chief defect, Freud says, was "his main driving force—self-love; I might almost say self-adulation . . . He was incapable of any self-criticism, overlooked, forgot and forgave himself anything he had done badly or which showed him up in a bad light; on the other hand, anything that raised his self-importance he cultivated and exhibited in front of others . . . He took pleasure in his own speech, in his own thoughts, yes, even in insignificant, indifferent actions of everyday life, and was convinced that no one could perform them as well as he. Everything he said and thought . . . was meant to conceal the lack of deeper substance . . . Much of the high opinion in which people held his ability was inspired by himself . . . He was incapable of friendship and could talk to a man for years without once asking what he did . . . His life seemed to be an open book; only after his death did we discover that he concealed a lot" (ibid., pp. 60–2). Freud goes on to describe how even his attempts to "appear as a noble, unselfish human being" were feigned.

25. Narcissistic disorders, in contemporary psychoanalytic theory, occupy an intermediary position between the classic neuroses, with relatively intact ego functioning, and the psychotic disorders.

uniqueness; recurrent fantasies of unlimited success, power, beauty, brilliance, or ideal love; a craving for constant attention and admiration; and lack of empathy (*SE* 14 [1914]:88–91; 18 [1922]:257). A humorous illustration is offered in the fable by James Thurber about the seal who was so opinionated that whenever the Great Seal of the United States was mentioned he thought that he was meant (Gombrich 1984, p. 12). However, not all narcissists publicly exhibit the flamboyant grandiosity, obvious self-preoccupation, and boorish craving for adoration that the ideal type suggests.

A case of less exhibitionistic narcissism is offered by Freud in his analysis of the seemingly other-directed love of certain male homosexuals. In his essay on Leonardo da Vinci, whom he terms a perfectly sublimated homosexual, Freud argues that the young men whom the pederast loves are "substitute figures and revivals of himself in childhood—boys whom he loves in the way in which his mother loved *him* when he was a child" (*SE* 11 [1910]:100; cf. Kohut, 1978, 1:822; Wolf 1977, p. 210). The narcissistic character of such same-sex relations is revealed by the discovery in therapy that the fantasies now directed at young men were long ago directed by the older lover at himself or, more accurately, at the idealized image of himself in which he once believed.

Another example mentioned by Freud of the non-exhibitionistic narcissist is that of the enigmatic upper-class Victorian woman. Though attractive to her lover for the charm of her mysterious inaccessibility and apparent self-sufficiency, she is in fact totally absorbed in her own beauty and self-importance. Unlike the male homosexual described in the Leonardo essay, this type of woman does not love herself through others, but the man who will satisfy her insatiable need "of being loved" (*SE* 14 [1914]:89). Strictly speaking, such women love not the man himself but his love for them. The man who finds favor with this kind of woman is one who gives the most promise of gratifying her exaggerated self-love, though his love in the end will prove insufficient to fill her bottomless pit of need. The dissatisfactions reported by men who love such women typically center on "his doubts of the woman's love" born of her lack of empathy and "his complaints of her enigmatic nature," quickened by the absence of genuine self-revelation and mutuality of communication (ibid.).

The excessive self-valuation that characterizes those described as narcissistic in their object choice is attributed by Freud to serious disturbances in psychosexual maturation during the transition from the second developmental stage of primary narcissism to object love (*SE* 14 [1914]:87–8; 16 [1916–17]:426–7). Freud himself, however, does not use this essentially correct insight about the stage at which narcissistic disturbances arise to explore in depth the etiology of the narcissistic character type. Because he considered narcissists unanalyzable, which we now know they are not, Freud had little clinical data with which to work. It has thus remained for creative disciples like Jacobson (1964); Reich (1953, 1973), Mahler (1968), Kohut (1971, 1977, 1978), Kernberg (1975, 1976, 1984), and Rothstein (1980) to mine the origins of narcissistic disorders.[26]

There has been considerable confusion in psychoanalytic circles about the precise way of distinguishing the narcissist's object choice, with its grandiose presentation of self and needfulness, which Freud considers pathological, from its opposite, the "normal," "anaclitic," or "true" object choice (see Balint 1960).[27] The confusion stems in part from Freud's acknowledgment that narcissistic motives also play an indispensable role in the normal person.[28] For example, the idealization of the object in roman-

26. It is now generally believed that deep narcissistic pathology develops during the preoedipal period prior to the onset of the neurotic conflicts that primarily attracted Freud's attention, but there are several differing accounts of the dynamics involved. See Kohut 1971, 1977, for a discussion of narcissistic disorders from the perspective of self-psychology, Rothstein 1980 for one from the point of view of psychoanalytic structural theory, and Kernberg 1970, 1975, 1984 for that of a modified object-relations theory.

27. The term *anaclitic type* (*Anlehnungstypus,* meaning literally "leaning up against type") derives from Freud's middle period, when he was working with independent ego instincts and viewed the sexual instincts of the infant as propping themselves up against the ego's self-preservation instincts (*SE* 14 [1914]:87). The idea is that the infant arrives at its first sexual object on the basis of the valuations made by the ego instincts (*SE* 7 [1905]:222). See Laplanche and Pontalis 1973, p. 31. The ego instincts will be discussed more fully in ch. 8, but it is noteworthy here that the infant's first anaclitic object choices are "the woman who tends" and "the man who protects" (*CP* 4 [1914]:47). This may seem to imply that an essentially egoistic motivation deriving from the ego's self-preservation instincts lies behind this form of object choice; in other words, that Freud posits an alternative to the narcissistic type that is equally rooted in self-interested motivations. Fromm mentions this aspect of Freudian theory as one of his reasons for concluding that Freud is wedded to psychological egoism. But Freud himself nowhere draws this conclusion and in fact goes out of his way to highlight the nonpossessive feelings of affection and tenderness that go hand in glove with the form of object love that results from the sexual instincts leaning on the self-preservation drives. He also insists that the affection that develops in this way is based on a primordial sense of "gratitude" for parental care and affection. "When a child hears that he owes his life to his parents, that his mother gave him life, the feelings of tenderness in him mingle with the longing . . . to repay the parents for this gift and requite it by one of a like value" (*CP* 4 [1910]:200).

28. Speaking of narcissistic disorders in which "the ego has taken itself as an object and is behaving as though it were in love with itself," Freud states that this "is only an extreme exaggeration of a normal state of affairs" (*SE* 22 [1933]:102–3). Elsewhere, he observes that the "primary narcissism" of infancy "fundamentally persists" into normal adulthood, even

tic love is in part attributed to the projection of narcissistic perfections onto the beloved that the lover is unable to realize. What distinguishes "normal narcissism," as Freud calls it (*SE* 14 [1914]:74), from pathological narcissism is not whether narcissistic motives are present, but how they are present, particularly whether the value of the self or the object predominates.

In normal love, which Freud characterizes as active and outgoing, as "attached" to an object rather than to the self, one values the other as well as the self, so that if narcissistic motives are present in the form of excessive idealization of traits in the beloved that one would like to possess, the valued characteristics are recognized as belonging to another person separate from oneself.[29] If this were not so, Freud would have no reason to contrast his concept of normal object love with the narcissistic object choice. It is, in fact, one of the main features of his developmental psychology that primary narcissism, which is characterized by exclusive valuation of oneself, is normally transcended with the appearance of object love, "without the narcissism necessarily disappearing on that account" (*SE* 16 [1916–17]:416). In other words, in loving another, narcissistic motives play a not insignificant role even in the normal case, but nonnarcissists do not love the other *solely* for the ways in which the object aggrandizes or gratifies the self narcissistically (further support for this contention is provided in ch. 9 below).

In distinguishing between narcissistic and normal object choice, the issue is not which motive is exclusively present but which is the *dominant motive* governing the relationship (see Goldberg 1974, Eisnitz 1974, Wallwork 1982). Freud explicitly rejects the suggestion that "human beings are divided into two sharply differentiated groups, according as their object-choice conforms to the . . . [normal] or to the narcissistic type" (*SE* 14 [1914]:88). He assumes, rather, that most object choices combine both types—the active, outgoing love of another and the love of the self found in the other. But the normal narcissism that psychoanalysis attributes to everyone does not manifest "itself in a dominating fashion in . . . [every]

---

after object love has developed (*SE* 14 [1914]:75). "A certain amount of libido is always retained in the ego; even when object-love is highly developed, a certain degree of narcissism continues" (*CP* 4 [1917]:350).

29. As Pulver points out, the expression "'true object relationship'" in Freudian theory "is generally considered [by psychoanalysts] to mean the perception of and reaction to the object as a separate individual with his own needs, desires, and reactions. Any mode of relating to objects in which true object relationships are impaired or do not exist is called narcissistic" (1970, p. 330).

object-choice" (ibid.).[30] If this were not the case and an alternative to domination by narcissistic motives did not exist, there would be no way of distinguishing the relatively normal lover from the one who, in loving, seeks only or primarily to love him or herself. It is this critical distinction that Rieff overlooks in describing the Freudian self as always chasing its own narcissistic tail through other people. Rieff's characterization fits the narcissistic object choice but not its opposite.

NARCISSISM AS A MODE OF RELATING

A third usage of the term *narcissism* refers not to the choice of a loved object but to a mode of relating to the environment characterized by a withdrawal of interest in it. In contrast to the first two forms, the narcissistic mode of relating *presupposes successful attainment of normal interest in the external world, including other people*. Freud has this form of narcissism in mind when he states that "it come[s] into being at the expense of object-libido. The libido that has been withdrawn from the external world has been directed to the ego and thus gives rise to an attitude which may be called narcissism" (*SE* 14 [1914]:74–5). Commonly known as "secondary narcissism" to highlight the reassertion of primary narcissistic traits in someone who has shown a capacity for objective interests and love of others, the narcissistic mode of relating is usually accompanied by psychological withdrawal of interest in and love of others, increased emotional investment in oneself manifested by heightened introspection and self-regarding behavior, and regression to infantile modalities of thought and behavior, especially the overvaluation of one's needs, attributes (e.g., power or brilliance), and accomplishments. The introversion that characterizes this form of behavior is thus commonly accompanied by regression (*SE* 14 [1914]:84).

30. Eisnitz follows Freud, despite his profession to the contrary, when he writes: "I suggest . . . that narcissistic object choice be defined as that wherein the major cathexis is directed to the self representation, and attachment object choice as that wherein the major cathexis is directed to the object representation . . . Most object choices can then be seen to represent a mixture of both types, although, typically, one or the other element is predominant" (1974, p. 279). With respect to the specific issue of whether Freud recognizes the importance of intrapsychic representations in identifying narcissism, which Eisnitz denies, it is sufficient to recall what Freud told a meeting of the Vienna Psychoanalytic Society on 13 Feb. 1907: viz. that he would not consider those who masturbate with images of others autoerotic (Nunberg and Federn 1962, cited by Pulver 1970, p. 331). Object cathexis can persist in fantasies and dreams; conversely, interpersonal relations may be characterized by a predominant cathexis of the self. What is critical in delineating narcissism is whether the dominant cathexis is directed at the self-representation.

The numerous examples cited by Freud include hypochondria, psycho-somatic diseases of all sorts, sleep, even schizophrenia. Despite the apparent differences among these examples, Freud believes, naively in the case of schizophrenia,[31] that they have in common defensive withdrawal from object relations in response to exhaustion, illness or some perceived threat, frustration, or disappointment in the environment (SE 14 [1914]:82–7). The hypochondriac, for instance, withdraws both interest and love "from the objects of the external world and concentrates both of them upon the organ that is engaging his attention" (SE 14 [1914]:83).[32]

Fortunately, we need not sort through Freud's complex views on the various manifest forms of secondary narcissism, which can range from daydreaming to a schizophrenic break with reality, to appreciate that nor-mal object love is often presupposed in characterizing these deviations from it. Freud refers to the "familiar *egoism* of the sick person" and of the hypochondriac as well as to the "*egoism* of dreams" as examples of the narcissistic mode of withdrawing the interest normally invested in other persons and causes (emphasis added). Freud's assumption that secondary narcissism is usually marked by an increase of egoism (SE 14 [1914]:82–5) would seem to imply that the alternative, object love, is genuinely other-regarding, since a regression to egoism presupposes a different moti-vational starting point.

Unlike the traditional moralist's wholesale condemnation of egoism and pride, which contemporary critics of cultural narcissism like Lasch echo in their criticism of self-interested activities like jogging and aerobics, Freud has some good things to say about secondary narcissism, reasoning that it is essential to do justice to one's own needs and interests both for their own sake and in order to relate well to others. Human beings have a need periodically, after investing themselves in others or their work, he argues, to withdraw into themselves once again in sleep, in introspection and, sometimes, in self-love and egocentric conduct, much as an amoeba with-

31. Schizophrenics are by no means as narcissistic as Freud assumes in "On Narcissism." See Fromm-Reichmann 1959, pp. 161–3; Bleuler 1978; Karon and Vandenbos 1983; Boyer and Giovacchini 1980; Fine 1986, p. 48. In other formulations on schizophrenia, Freud emphasizes the ego's conflict with reality resulting in denial as a central characteristic defense. He attributes this denial to an abnormal or defective ego. See Gunderson 1979, p. 384.

32. "'Concentrated in his soul,' says Wilhelm Busch of the poet suffering from toothache, 'in his molar's narrow hole'" (SE 14 [1914]:82). Superficial contemporary examples of sec-ondary narcissism in which the motivations are more conscious than in Freud's examples are provided by Lasch (1979), who makes use of this type of narcissism in depicting the recent retreat of Americans into purely personal preoccupations like getting in touch with one's feelings, doing aerobic exercises, taking classes in belly dancing, immersion in the wisdom of the East, jogging, and so forth.

draws its protrusions, known as pseudopodia, into the original mass before sending them out again (*SE* 16 [1916–17]:416).[33]

The idea behind this zoological analogy is that human beings, after extending themselves in the surrounding environment, need to renew themselves periodically—an idea that anticipates Ernst Kris's well-known proposal regarding "regression in the service of the ego."[34] Kris (1952) vividly describes the ability of the creative person to let his or her ego go down into the unconscious and emerge again, and thus, by oscillating between absorption in the free play of primary process and cognitive distance from it, to use the id in the service of the ego's creative activity. Freud's views are seldom cited in connection with regression in the service of the ego, even by Erikson who makes so much of this phenomenon in *Young Man Luther,* perhaps because the narcissistic mode is so frequently associated in Freud's writings with pathologies like hypochondria and schizophrenia. But Freud is clear that the "withdrawal of object-libido into the ego is certainly not pathogenic" in itself (1952, p. 428). And he nicely illumines the regressive move in the service of the ego in what he says about how Leonardo da Vinci—by recovery of the maternal stimulus that guided him at the beginnings of his artistic endeavors—recovered spontaneously from the deep neurotic disturbance that bothered him before he broke through to paint the Mona Lisa (*SE* 11 [1910]:133–4). Freud further underscores his belief that narcissistic regression can facilitate the creative resolution of a problem by citing several lines of Heine's poetry:

> Disease at bottom brought about
> Creative urgence—for, creating,

33. Referring to the movement back and forth between object libido and narcissism, Freud writes: "For complete health it is essential that the libido should not lose this full mobility" (*SE* 17 [1917]:139). The point of the amoeba analogy, he says, is that the pseudopodia can be retracted at any time so that the protoplasmic mass might be *"restored."* Elsewhere, Freud speaks of "the recuperation afforded by sleep" and other measures by which "all investments of objects . . . are abandoned and withdrawn again into the ego" (1952, p. 424, compare *SE* 16 [1916–17]:417).

34. The concept of regression in the service of the ego refers to the ego's ability to initiate regression, including the flexibility to adopt more primitive modes of functioning than usual. Controlled ego regressions are essential to art, humor, play, sexual relations, psychoanalysis, and to imaginative and creative activity in general. Kris and the numerous analysts who make use of his insights place greater emphasis than Freud on the ego's initiation of regression and on the fact that such regression can be interrupted by the ego at any time and guided to some extent by it. But these points are consistent with what Freud says both about artistic creativity and the ego (see, e.g., *SE* 7 [1942]:305–10; letter dated 6 Mar. 1910, in Meng and Freud 1963, pp. 34–5).

> I soon could feel the pain abating,
> Creating, I could work it out.
>
> (*CP* 4 [1914]:42, n.1)

Kris's point that regression in the service of the ego involves an oscillation between illusion and reality is similarly illustrated by Freud's discussion of drama in "Psychopathic Characters on the Stage" (*SE* [1942]:305–10). Drama opens up sources of enjoyment that would otherwise be inaccessible, Freud argues, by allowing the spectator to identify himself, as children do in play, with a hero who feels and acts on impulses that are forbidden to most people in ordinary life. The spectator is spared the pains and sufferings that actual conduct such as that depicted would almost certainly involve, because he knows that it is someone other than himself that is acting and suffering on the stage, and "after all it is only a game, which can threaten no damage to his personal security." In these circumstances, he can allow himself the narcissistic satisfaction of "being a 'great man'" and giving "way without a qualm to such suppressed impulses as a craving for freedom in religious, political, social and sexual matters" (*SE* 7 [1942]:306).

Pathology occurs when the narcissistic regression process of reworking fails and the person can no longer redirect the interest and love withdrawn back to objects again. Then the narcissistic modality functions not as "a protection against disease" (*CP* 4 [1914]:42; *SE* 21 [1916–17]:417) but as one of its contributing causes. The "accumulation of narcissistic libido over and above a certain level becomes intolerable," and the person who fails to redirect his libido back to others falls mentally "ill of an excessive accumulation of it" (1952, p. 428).[35] Freud could scarcely be more explicit than this about the dangers of narcissism when it involves a permanent withdrawal of interest in or love of others. Yet he is realistic enough to recognize that we cannot continually pour ourselves out in love, as some Christian moralists prescribe, without deleterious psychic consequences. Temporary self-love is often necessitated by our psychic makeup and justified by its importance in preserving the integrity of the agent and, indi-

---

35. Freud's letters indicate that he realized that self-absorption during an illness could feed on itself, making the patient physically and mentally sicker. He wrote to his fiancée in 1884 (letter 39, in E. L. Freud 1960, p. 100) how he countered a bout with sciatica, which had kept him in bed for days, by finally deciding "to abandon the luxury of being ill." Having decided to do so, he found to his surprise that he could walk and work again. He comments: "Here I am in the saddle once more, have no pains despite the long day, only feelings of fatigue which is understandable, can work again and am immensely, immensely pleased that I have recovered by my own decision. I can't really explain it to myself, but it is a fact."

rectly, by its contribution to the well-being of others; but self-love is not commended as a dominant permanent behavioral modality by Freud.

The unavoidable implication of the analysis of narcissism so far is that the term gets much of its meaning from its antithesis to object love when it refers to a developmental stage, self-centered love, or withdrawal as a behavioral modality. The developmental stage of primary narcissism is identified chiefly by its contrast with the succeeding stage, when love is turned outward toward others. The narcissistic object choice, in which the aim is self-love, is set over against the outgoing love of others known as the "anaclitic object choice." The mode of relating known as "secondary narcissism" is described as a compensatory retreat from fullsome investment emotionally and cognitively in activities and persons other than oneself. Freud captures succinctly the essence of these conceptual contrasts when he writes that "a limitation of narcissism can, according to our theoretical views, only be produced by one factor, a libidinal tie with other people. Love for oneself knows only one barrier—love for others, love for objects" (*SE* 18 [1921]:102).

Thus far, however, our evidence for the existence of non-egoistic motivations is predominantly negative. This evidence needs to be supplemented, as it will be in chapter 8, by a direct study of whether object love entails other-regard. Meanwhile, Freud's fourth and final subtype of narcissism introduces very different considerations, which serve nicely as a bridge to this later discussion.

NARCISSISM AS SELF-ESTEEM

Freud's final form of narcissism refers to a positive attitude toward oneself—that is, to self-respect or self-esteem (*Selbstgefühl*). Otto Rank (1911), in the first psychoanalytic paper devoted specifically to narcissism, had extended the term's meaning from sensual love of oneself to vanity and self-admiration. Expanding on Rank's analysis, Freud, in his essay of 1914, makes narcissism synonymous with *Selbstgefühl*, meaning self-respect, self-confidence, self-esteem, and self-reliance.[36] Self-respect, he argues, involves an affirmation of oneself that has affective as well as cognitive aspects and may be unconscious as well as conscious. Self-affirmation or esteem issues from a favorable evaluative judgment that is directed at the whole, subjectively experienced person that is the locus of agency and of continu-

36. Strachey translates *Selbstgefühl* as "self-regard" in the *SE;* but "self-respect," "self-esteem," or "self-confidence" are closer to its meaning.

ous memory and identity over time.[37] Because people frequently deceive themselves, however, self-respect is not always sound. There is, therefore, a latent distinction in Freud between superficial, inauthentic "narcissistic" self-regard, which is attributed to infantile grandiosity, and a deeper, more authentic and realistic self-esteem. It is the latter attitude of self-esteem in normal persons that interests us here, since infantile grandiosity has already been discussed.

On the face of it, there is something paradoxical about Freud's viewing self-esteem as a form of narcissism at all, because the relatively mature adult, as envisioned by psychoanalysis, does not derive self-esteem from being predominantly narcissistic in the ordinary sense of the term, with its strong overtones of egoism, unwarranted grandiosity, and self-absorption. We cannot, for example, substitute infantile megalomania for a real accomplishment and still experience authentic self-esteem. Nor is regression in the form of withdrawal from others or wanton selfishness what Freud has in mind in speaking of self-esteem as a basic ego strength. The fact is that self-esteem, by contrast with the other forms of narcissism, is won initially in interpersonal relations, or at least in solitary pursuits that are believed to be valued by others. There is thus a major drawback in using the term *narcissism* for self-esteem, since a word which usually refers to a love of self that is egoistic and self-absorbed is thereby being used for behavior that does not necessarily have these characteristics at all. It is as if Narcissus had left the pool and had begun to get self-respect from meaningful work and love.

The two criteria of narcissism that justify use of the term in connection with self-esteem are, first, the notion of self-love in the specific sense of "self-affirmation," and, second, the developmental point, so important to the psychoanalytic perspective, that self-esteem arises from early sensual narcissism, as both a continuation of one important part of it and a transformation of its infantile elements.

The several ways in which self-esteem diverges from the other forms of narcissism result in its standing in a very different relationship to object love. Whereas the predominance of egoistic motives in the other forms of narcissism compete with any real concern for others, self-esteem appears to be complementary to object love. Individuals with high self-esteem are precisely those we expect to be interested in others, while those with low

37. That Freud is aware that the sense of selfhood involves awareness of continuity through time is indicated in *Group Psychology and the Analysis of the Ego*, where he speaks of the individual possessing "his own continuity, his [own] self-consciousness," as well as a sense of separateness from others (*SE* 18 [1921]:86).

self-esteem are likely to concentrate on themselves. Freud had difficulty stating the complementarity of self-esteem with object love in his 1914 paper "On Narcissism," because the energy theory led him to suppose that an investment of libido in the self (or self-representation) required its withdrawal from others (or object representations), and vice versa.[38] Applied to self-esteem in connection with Freud's amoeba analogy, the implication seemed to be that love of another lowers self-regard, whereas the withdrawal of love from others increases self-esteem by reinvesting love in the self once again. But such implications are patently absurd, since, except in some extreme cases of romantic love ("I am worthless in comparison with you, my beloved"), love tends to augment the lover's sense of self-worth.[39] Moreover, narcissistic patients tend to have chronically low self-esteem, while, conversely, successful therapy, by strengthening the sense of self-worth, commonly gives a boost to intimate relations.

However, those psychoanalysts—Schafer (1968), Pulver (1970, p. 334), Kernberg (1975), and Teicholz (1978)—who have criticized Freud's concept of an inverse relationship between object love and self-esteem have failed to observe that Freud was not entirely consistent on this point, even in his first paper on narcissism. For Freud also argues the opposite point: that the inability to love is a source of low self-esteem and that love of another augments self-regard. Thus he writes that "the realization of impotence, of one's own inability to love, in consequence of mental or physical disorder, has an exceedingly lowering effect upon self regard" (*SE* 14 [1914]:98). And again: "Everything a person . . . achieves . . . helps to increase his self-regard" (ibid.), and "part of the self-regard . . . proceeds

38. Freud's economic point of view grossly misled him vis-à-vis a hypercathexis of the self (or self-representation) being at the expense of cathexis of objects in the environment (or object representatives). As Pulver points out, "increased libidinal investment of the self is not necessarily accompanied by decreased cathexis of objects" (1970, p. 332). A seriously disturbed person with a "narcissistic personality disorder" may be very much involved with objects, upon whom he or she is profoundly dependent. Further, a person may withdraw from others and still be intensely involved with them in thought and daydreams. Fantasies, in fact, commonly involve object representations, as when "the sleeper shares his slumbers with an introjected [good] object" (Kanzer 1955, p. 261; Balint 1960, pp. 22–3). Freud helped precipitate these and other criticisms of his 1914 economic hypothesis about the hypercathexis of the self being at the expense of relating to objects. For example, in "Mourning and Melancholia" (1915) he argues that the loss of the object does not mean the loss of the fantasy of the object and a continuing intense involvement with the representation of the object that lowers rather than raises self-esteem.

39. Dare and Holder (1981, p. 324) present a more persuasive clinical interpretation of cases of romantic love in which low self-esteem is correlated with high regard for objects than does Freud.

from gratification of object-libido" (*CP* 4 [1914]:58). The main problem with Freud's early work on narcissism does not lie with any failure on his part to perceive that narcissism as self-esteem is enhanced rather than diminished by object love. It lies, rather, with the economics of the metapsychology and, consequently, with the intellectual aerobatics required to fit love of "self" and "others" into the drive-discharge theory then in its ascendancy.

In fact, it was precisely the impossibility of fitting the subtle clinical expressions of narcissism to propositions about drives that sowed the seeds of the self-psychology and object-relations theory of Freud's later writings, the full flowering of which eventually overwhelmed the drive-discharge paradigm. The essay "On Narcissism" was a watershed precisely because it launched Freud on a train of thought about *self*-love and *object* love that led directly into such major theoretical developments as the collapse of the first dual instinct theory, the discovery of the importance of identification, the formulation of the second dual instinct theory, the development of the structural theory, and the elaboration of psychoanalytic ego psychology, including the concept of the superego (B. E. Moore 1975, p. 243). As Freud's thoughts on narcissism matured through the subsequent metamorphoses of his general theory, he found a variety of ways of doing justice to the complementarity that exists between self-esteem and non-self-referential motivations. Freud succeeded so well in fact that his later writings anticipate most of the major revisions and refinements in the psychoanalytic theory of narcissism as self-esteem that have occurred subsequently.

Chapter 8
Object Love

To the Freudians . . . love is 'really' amoral
sexuality, though usually sublimated and
deflected from its coital aim . . . The
Freudian derives all ideals from attempts
to satisfy organic needs.

—Singer

Freud describes . . . sex as the 'real life drive'
and with sex are connected all the inner
tendencies toward higher development,
union and perfection. This lends to sexuality
a character of revolutionary spirituality
which Christendom was far from ascribing
to it.

—Mann

Of all the slowly developed parts of analytic
theory, the theory of the instincts is the one
that has felt its way the most painfully
forward.

—Freud

The contention that Freud's theory of narcissism is compatible with
moral conduct succeeds only if object love is in some significant sense non-
egoistic. Otherwise, despite the contrasts that can be drawn between narcissism and object love, both may be construed as merely different kinds of
self-regarding behavior.

The psychoanalytic concept of *object love* and its proximate equivalents,
object libido and *object cathexis,* refer to the attachment of the sexual drive
(libido) to some representation of an object outside the individual. Object
love involves love's turning outward, away from the self and toward other
persons. But whether this implies an authentic concern for other persons
for their own sake is by no means unambiguous from Freud's writings or
those of his followers. On the one hand, psychoanalysts differentiate object

love from narcissism in ways that suggest a degree of altruistic attachment. Phrases like "normal love," "genital sexual organization," and "mature object choice" are codes for sets of feelings and motivations that seem non-egoistic and that are judged to be developmentally superior to primary narcissism and different from secondary narcissism. But when the dynamics of such relations are discussed, the reader is left perplexed as to whether the more "mature," "normal" behavior is believed to be simply a more subtle, but fundamentally no less exploitative, way of serving self-interested ends. This is especially the case because discussions of object love are usually interlarded with professions of strict adherence to Freud's drive theory, which in its original form views all behavior as growing out of biologically based drives ultimately directed at the individual's own sensual satisfaction.[1]

It is the drive theory that underlies the common claim that, for Freud, love, even when it is seemingly other-regarding, is basically self-serving (see, e.g., Asch 1952, p. 19; Fromm 1955, p. 74; Allport 1964, pp. 148–9, 162; Hoffman 1976, p. 124). Prior to his articulation of the drive theory in the period 1900–19, Freud's own work contained little to suggest that he himself doubted the genuineness of the individual's capacity for other-regarding behavior. He appears simply to have assumed that normal people can be benevolent. In *Studies on Hysteria* (1893–5), for example, Freud, stressing that "hysteria of the severest type can exist in conjunction with gifts of the richest kind" and fine moral character, praised Frau Emmy von N for the "moral seriousness with which she viewed her duties" and "her benevolent care for the welfare of all her dependents" (*SE* 2 [1893–5]:103). No attempt is made in Emmy von N's case or, for that matter, in any of the other cases discussed in *Studies on Hysteria* to take normal benevolent conduct at other than its face value.

When Freud gets to his drive-discharge theory, however, he erects a model of human motivations that has been widely taken not only to raise suspicions about, but to radically undercut, the very possibility of genuine other-regarding behavior.[2] In the now classic schema of instinctual *source, aim,* and *object,* other persons appear to have a role only as the instrumental means through which the egoistic aim of drive satisfaction is achieved.

---

1. Freud writes that "the aim which each of . . . [the sexual instincts] strives for is the attainment of 'organ-pleasure'" (*SE* 14 [1915]:125–6; see also *SE* 7 [1905]:184).

2. The drive-discharge theory is in principle capable of undercutting commonsense perceptions of other-regarding conduct because it purports to describe the basic springs of human conduct. For Freud's own statements about the drives as "the ultimate cause[s] of all activity," see *SE* 23 (1940):148; also *SE* 7 (1905):168; 14 [1915]:122.

Here is how, in his most famous statement of the drive theory, Freud describes what underlies "love." It has its "source" (*Quelle*) in "the somatic process which occurs in an organ or part of the body and whose stimulus is represented in mental life by an instinct [*Trieb*]" (*SE* 14 [1915]:123). The "aim" (*Ziel*) of an instinct "*is in every instance satisfaction,* which can only be obtained by removing the state of stimulation at the source of the instinct" (*SE* 14 [1915]:122, emphasis added). The "object" (*Objekt*) of an instinct, which is where other people come in, "is the thing in regard to which or through which the instinct is able to achieve its aim" (*SE* 14 [1915]:122). The "object" of an instinct is selected "only in consequence of [its] being peculiarly fitted to make satisfaction possible" (*SE* 14 [1915]:122).

This is a powerful statement powerfully put. It is not surprising, then, that secondary interpreters should hold that, for Freud, love boils down to pure self-interested sexual desire and the urge toward instinctual gratification. Thus, Fromm has Freud saying, "Individuals need each other as *means* for the satisfaction of their physiologically rooted drives" (1973, p. 46, emphasis added). "Love . . . is by its very nature egotistical and antisocial" (Fromm 1955, p. 74). And Rorty concludes that in "Freudian thought . . . everything everybody does to everyone else (even those they love blindly and helplessly) can be described . . . as manipulation . . . All personal and social relations, even the tenderest and most sacred, [can be interpreted] . . . in terms of 'making use of' others" (1986, p. 16).

But the drive-discharge theory set out in "Instincts and their Vicissitudes" (1915) is not as rigid as it is often taken to be from the bare-bones outline above. Nor is it the whole of Freud's view of object relations. Those who take Freud's source—aim—object statement as the centerpiece of his thought on object love and use it to paint him as arguing for an exclusively egoistic view of human nature do so only by ignoring the complexities of the drive theory, articulated before, after, and in "Instincts and their Vicissitudes," as well as the development of his thought beyond the drive-discharge paradigm.

DRIVE THEORY

It is true that for Freud, instinctual aims are the wellsprings of human motives. Yet, there is a surprising flexibility inherent in his understanding of the "aims" that determine and define motives.[3] It is often overlooked

3. Freud stresses the flexibility of the objects of the instincts; but this flexibility is not germaine to the issue of whether there is room in the drive-discharge theory for other-regarding behavior. That issue turns on the aims of the instincts undergirding the motives, regarding which the flexibility of Freud's theory is often overlooked.

that Freud does not stop with his declaration that "the *aim* of an instinct is in every instance satisfaction" (*SE* 14 [1915]:122). He immediately goes on to explain that "although the *ultimate aim* [*Endziel*] of each instinct remains unchangeable, there may yet be *different paths* leading to the same ultimate aim; so that an instinct may be found to have *various nearer or intermediate aims* [*mannigfache nähere oder intermediäre Ziele*], which are combined or interchanged with one another" (ibid., emphasis added; *GW* 10 [1915]:215).

The invariable "ultimate aim" that Freud is talking about here is none other than pleasure. And since the long-range aspects of this ultimate aim mean that it does not logically have to preclude non-egoistic conduct (see ch. 6 above), the question then becomes whether the various intermediate aims, which Freud viewed as more closely tied to the biological instincts and which provide the *specific content* underlying most motivations, are sufficiently flexible to develop into genuine other-regard.

The first hint that this may be the case is contained in Freud's deliberate use of the German word *Trieb* rather than *Instinkt* in discussing the biologically rooted urges or drives that motivate human behavior. *Trieb* refers to a pressure (the verb *treiben* means "to push") that is relatively indeterminate and variable in its aim, especially as compared with *Instinkt,* which designates behavior that is strictly predetermined by heredity, as in the lower animals.[4] *Trieb* is much closer to the English words *urge, drive,* and *impetus* than to the narrow, fixed-aim connotations of the English word *instinct* that the *Standard Edition* uniformly employs when Freud uses *Trieb*.[5] Freud, however, very carefully distinguishes between these two terms in ways that are significant for understanding the motivational implications of his drive theory. He uses *Trieb,* not *Instinkt,* to refer to psychological urges or drives, and it is this much more open-ended term that appears in the title and throughout the object-relations discussion in "Instincts and their Vicissitudes" (*Triebe und Triebschicksale*), an essay whose very title, if it had been more accurately translated "*Drives* and their Vicissitudes" might have led to a less thoroughgoing reductionistic reading of Freud than is usually the case.

The point behind Freud's careful choice of terminology here is that human beings, unlike the lower animals, are endowed with urges toward

4. Very occasionally, Freud used the term *Instinkt,* but only to refer to preset, animal-like patterns. See *SE* 14 [1915]:195.

5. See the General Preface to the *SE* (1. : xxiv–xxv) and the Editor's Note to "Instincts and their Vicissitudes" (*SE* 14 [1915]:111–14) for the editor's reasons for choosing *instinct* over *drive* or *urge.* The *SE* does note when Freud uses the German *Instinkt,* but it uses the English word *instinct* as the translation for both *Trieb* and *Instinkt*.

aims that are plastic and capable of being altered in the course of development.[6] The mere fact that Freud saw motives as biologically based, therefore, does not mean that he denied the possibility that motives could develop in an other-regarding direction.

Freud further allowed for this possibility by the extremely broad meaning he frequently assigned to such key concepts as *libido* and *objects*. Libido, already something other than simple quantifiable sexual energy or excitation, becomes, as Freud works out the drive theory, markedly more subjective and qualitative.[7] It comes to encompass emotional and mental, as well as physiological, components—that is, "all the activities of the tender feelings which have primitive sexual impulses as their source" (*SE* 11 [1910]:222).[8]

For the libido to cathect an object can mean for Freud not the mere investment of quantities of instinctual energy but the transferral of *value* from the self to another person or thing (*SE* 14 [1914]:88). Thus, still speaking within his drive-discharge perspective, Freud is able to say that "the greatest intensity of sensual passion will bring with it the *highest mental estimation of the object*" (*CP* 4 [1912]:206, emphasis added). And, although Freud's language admittedly gives some grounds for the criticism that he views the object as mere means, it is often overlooked that when it is invested with libidinal value, the object can be lifted out of being a mere means to the lover's egoistic satisfactions and transformed into that which is valued for itself—in Kantian terms, treated as an end. Indeed, Freud (*SE* 7 [1905]:150–1; 14 [1914]:73–102; 16 [1916–17]:412–30) argues that object love commonly involves such high exaltation of the loved object that the self is actually impoverished by comparison with the beloved, and that when this happens, Freud does not hesitate to refer to the lover's motives on behalf of the beloved as 'altruistic' in the normal ethical sense: "When

6. Regarding the plasticity of the libido (*Plastizität der Libido*), see, e.g., *SE* 11 (1910):54; 16 (1916–17):345.

7. Freud argues as early as 1910 that psychoanalysis uses "the word 'sexuality' in the same comprehensive sense as that in which the German language uses the word *lieben* ['to love']" (*SE* 11 [1910]:223). See also *SE* 18 (1921):91; 23 (1940):148. For elaboration and clinical illustrations, see *SE* 14 (1914):73–102; 14 (1915):243–58; 16 (1916–17):412–30.

8. This understanding of libido allows Freud to pack into drive theory more than biological tension reduction. Thus he says that the absence of "tender feelings" in a love relation can create mental frustration and disappointment, even where full genital release is achieved. "We have long known . . . that mental absence of satisfaction with all its consequences can exist where there is no lack of normal sexual intercourse; and as therapists we always bear in mind that the unsatisfied sexual trends . . . can often find only very inadequate outlet in coitus or other sexual acts" (*SE* 11 [1910]:223).

the condition of love is developed to its fullest intensity," he writes, "altruism [*Altruismus*] coincides with the investment of an object with libido" (Freud 1952, p. 424; *GW* 11 [1916–17]:433).[9]

But Freud's more expansive views of libidinal cathexis of objects and the flexibility he allows in drive and aim merely lay the groundwork for his principal attempt to account, within the confines of the drive theory, for how libido can develop out of egoism into genuine other-regard. This he does by tracing the dynamics of aim inhibition and sublimation in such a way that these processes can accommodate a much broader range of motivations than the bare-bones drive theory suggests.

With aim inhibition and sublimation, Freud seeks to explain the redirection or transformation of direct sexual aims, which "are at bottom self-interested," into aims of a "higher" order (*SE* 16 [1916–17]:345). In *aim inhibition* external or internal obstacles block an instinct's direct mode of satisfaction in such a way that the instinctual drive is diverted and re-oriented toward a quest for attenuated satisfaction from activities or relations that approximate, to a greater or lesser extent, the original sexual aim. *Sublimation* (*Sublimierung*) involves an even more far-reaching alteration of the original (sexual) aim, in that the original goal is completely ex-

9. Freud writes that "complete object-love of the attachment type . . . displays . . . marked sexual overvaluation. . . . This sexual overvaluation is the origin of the peculiar state of being in love, a state suggestive of a neurotic compulsion, which is thus traceable to an impoverishment of the ego as regards libido in favour of the love-object" (*SE* [1914]:88). See also *SE* 14 [1914]:99–100.

10. Freud says of sublimation that "it consists in the sexual trend abandoning its aim of obtaining a component or a reproductive pleasure and taking on another which is related genetically to the abandoned one but is itself no longer sexual and must be described as social. We call this process 'sublimation,' in accordance with the general estimate that places social aims higher than the sexual ones, which are at bottom self-interested" (*SE* 16 [1916–17]:345); see also *SE* 11 (1910):53–4. Freud later proposed that the aggressive instincts may also be sublimated. See *SE* 21 (1930):80, n.1, and Freud's letter to Marie Bonaparte dated 27 May 1937, in E. Jones 1957, p. 464.

See Ricoeur 1970, pp. 483–93 for a discussion and critique of Freud's difficulties in explaining the precise processes involved in sublimation. Ricoeur's criticisms of Freud's successive efforts to understand sublimation to the contrary notwithstanding, Freud does make plausible use of the biological concept of developmental transformation to argue that sublimation provides a creative and progressive "way out, a way by which the claims of the ego [as well as the id] can be met *without* involving repression" (*SE* 14 [1914]:95). Ricoeur argues that because such creative progression cannot be "elaborate[d] with the resources of the Freudian metapsychology, . . . [it can only be] presupposed in an unthematized way by analytic practice" (1970, pp. 491–2). But this fails to take sufficiently seriously what Freud was trying to do and what he thought he had succeeded in doing, if only in a highly general way, with the concept of sublimation.

tinguished and then supplanted with a new, nonsexual aim that is valued socially.[10] Since Freud argues that sexual aims are originally self-interested, it would appear that only sublimation, which completely supplants the initiating sexual aim, and not aim inhibition, allows for genuine "transformation" (*Umbildung*) of the original sexual motive away from self-interest to genuine other-regard.[11] This is important, because Freud tends to explain interpersonal and social relations in terms of aim inhibition rather than sublimation (see e.g., *SE* 18 [1923]:258).[12] From this, most secondary interpreters have concluded that he believed that in these areas so crucial to morality, "no genuine transformation of motives [takes places]" (Allport 1964, p. 552).[13]

However, a close reading of Freud shows that he believed that aim inhibition, like sublimation, is capable of affecting a permanent transformation of motives. Thus, he noted that "instincts which are 'inhibited in their aim' . . . come to a stop on their way to satisfaction, so that a *lasting* object-cathexis comes about and a *permanent* trend [of feeling] [is established]. Such, for instance, is the relation of tenderness, which undoubtedly originates from the sources of sexual need and invariably *renounces* its satisfaction" (*SE* 22 [1933]:97, emphasis added; see also *SE* 18 [1921]:138, 258). In this account, the developmentally earlier satisfaction is clearly "abandoned" or "exchanged" for a different kind of satisfaction that is less possessive and egocentric.

Elsewhere, in discussing the transformation of the infant's selfishly erotic love into the mature adult's "affectionate emotional tie," Freud cautions against judging the aim-inhibited motive by its genetic origins (*SE* 4 [1900]:250; 18 [1921]:138). In any given case, it is possible that "a former complete sexual current," which still exists unconsciously "as a form and

11. Freud states that through sublimation the "*aim*" of a motive and not simply the *means* of satisfying an earlier aim is fundamentally changed (*SE* 11 [1910]:54; 18 [1923]:256; see also *SE* 9 [1908]:187). He writes: "The most important vicissitude which an instinct can undergo seems to be *sublimation:* here both object and *aim* are changed, so that what was originally a sexual instinct finds satisfaction in some achievement which is no longer sexual but has a higher social or ethical valuation" (*SE* [1923]:256, emphasis added in part). Through sublimation, the original "unserviceable aim" is actually "*replaced*" by one that is higher" (*SE* 11 [1910]:54, emphasis added).

12. By contrast, Freud uses sublimation primarily to account for artistic and intellectual creativity.

13. Secondary interpreters often reason that if with aim inhibition the instinct is only deflected or diverted from its original aim, objects remain mere means. But Erikson recognizes that Freud never advocated men or women treating one another as objects on which to live out their sexual idiosyncrasies (1964, p. 234).

possibility," has been affected by aim inhibition and the substitution of "affection" in such a way that it has no "operative force" as a motive "at the present moment," and thus does not render unreal or ungenuine the affection that aim inhibition has created (*SE* 18 [1921]:138; see also *SE* 4 [1900]:250; 14 [1915]:285–6). For Freud, it is as erroneous in accounting for the origins of other-regarding motives like affection to "judg[e] the normal entirely by the standards of the pathological"—that is, the sublimated motive by its genetic (or still present unconscious) origins—as it is to underestimate the importance of the repressed unconscious (*SE* 18 [1921]:138).

What this means is that Freud's use of aim inhibition rather than sublimation to describe the dynamics of interpersonal and social relations does not indicate a disbelief in true other-regard. He does this because he wishes to keep clearly in mind his discovery that hidden sensual longings persist beneath the surface of all close human relations. The point is that sexuality is not completely extinguished and replaced by nonsexual motives in interpersonal relations, as would be the case with sublimation. But aim inhibition can effect sufficient, and sufficiently lasting, deviations from the original aim that the self-interested sexual currents, although always present "as a form and possibility" and capable of being "put into activity again by means of regression," are not functioning as present motives.

With respect to the transformation of motives necessary for genuine other-regard, Freud explicitly acknowledges the kinship of aim inhibition and sublimation. He states:

> If we choose, we may recognize in [the] diversion of [an] aim a beginning of the *sublimation* of the sexual instincts, or on the other hand we may fix the limits of sublimation at some more distant point . . . The inhibited instincts are capable of any degree of admixture with the uninhibited; they can be transformed back into them, just as they arose out of them . . . *On the other hand it is also very usual for directly sexual impulsions, short-lived in themselves, to be transformed into a lasting and purely affectionate tie* [14] (*SE* 18 [1921]:139, emphasis original in part, added in part).

It is sometimes argued that the inhibition of the originally egoistic sexual aims that develop into "social feelings" and "social instincts" is a

14. Because Freud never fixed its meaning and sometimes used it to cover all the processes by which sexual drives are deflected from their original goals (see *SE* 9 [1908]:171), the term *sublimation* is sometimes used in place of *aim-inhibition* to account for other-regard. See, e.g., *SE* 12 (1911):61 and Freud's letter to Putnam dated 8 July 1915 (in Hale 1971, pp. 189–90) in which he proposes that consideration of others and kindness to them should be treated as "sublimations of instinct" (see also *SE* 18 [1921]:138).

purely arbitrary societal imposition, and hence that, for Freud, sociability is not an inherent part of human nature.[15] But Freud makes it perfectly plain that although environmental factors are important, aim inhibition is in significant part a natural developmental process wired into the organism from birth and is not solely a product of the imposition of alien societal standards.[16] In his 1915 article "Thoughts for the Times on War and Death," Freud explicitly posed to himself the question "How . . . do we imagine the process by which an individual rises to a comparatively high plane of morality?" (*SE* 14 [1915]:280–1) and responded that one factor is an inborn, hereditary "tendency (disposition) towards the transformation of egoistic into social instincts" (*SE* 14 [1915]:282).[17] Although in this 1915 piece, Freud does not elaborate on the nature of this inborn disposition, earlier he had stated his "belief" "that something *in the nature of the sexual instinct itself* is unfavourable to the realization of complete satisfaction" (*SE* 11 [1910]:188, emphasis added).[18] This "something" that inhibits satisfaction is elsewhere said to be "*organically determined, . . . fixed by heredity,* and . . . can . . . occur without any help at all from education" (*SE* 7 [1905]:177–8, emphasis added).[19]

15. See, e.g., Asch 1952, p. 19; Fromm 1955, p. 74.

16. Freud's understanding of natural instinctual development is often missed because interpreters impose upon his thought a strong presumption that an instinctual drive must be fully manifest as soon as the creature is born. Freud sometimes uses *Instinkt* in this way, but he makes it clear in what he says about the drives (*Triebe*) in *Three Essays* that he believes, like Hartmann and Erikson after him, that there are delayed manifestations of inherited dispositions (see also *SE* 19 [1924]:174), which will not occur without the appropriate environmental conditions. Nonetheless, there is a definite pattern of development that is given with the instinctual equipment with which the human organism is endowed. Thus, Freud argues that humankind's instinctual "heritage . . . comprises all the forces that are required for the subsequent cultural development of the individual, but they must be sorted out and worked over" (*CP* 5 [1919]:95). This working over requires certain societal conditions, mediated by parents.

17. It is probable that what Freud had in mind was the natural development of sexuality into affection, for he states that it is "by the admixture of *erotic* components [that] the egoistic instincts are transformed into *social* ones" (*SE* 14 [1915]:282).

18. He made the same point again, much later, in *Civilization and its Discontents* (see *SE* 21 [1930]:105). For Freud, some repression is both normal and desirable, because without it, there is complete psychic chaos, which is undesirable both for the individual and for society. He would thus be disinclined to join in either Norman O. Brown's (1959, 1966) celebration of polymorphous perversity or Herbert Marcuse's (1955) utopian speculations about the desirability of an unrepressed society and culture.

19. The "natural" instinctual origin of aim inhibition is one of several warrants that Freud gives for treating both aim inhibition and sublimation as essential aspects of normal development. As he puts it, "*Normality* is a result of . . . repression" (*SE* 7 [1906]:277, emphasis

For Freud, this naturally occurring aim inhibition works in concert with social inhibitions and culture to transform the child's egoism into genuine other-regard. But environmental factors are not by themselves sufficient for the transformation that is required; for environmental factors like rewards and punishments can produce only an enlightened egoism. The "person who is subjected . . . [only to external pressures] will choose to behave well in the cultural sense of the phrase," but "no ennoblement of instinct [*Triebveredlung*], no transformation of egoistic into altruistic inclinations . . . [will have] taken place in him" (*SE* 14 [1915]:283–4; *GW* 10:335). There is an enormous difference, Freud argues, between the person who "acts morally" only for egoistic reasons—that is, because "such cultural behaviour is advantageous for his selfish purposes"—and the person who acts morally "because his instinctual inclinations compel him to" (*SE* 14 [1915]:284). The latter individual has undergone "the transformation of instinct" [*Triebumbildung*] that differentiates the "truly civilized" from "cultural hypocrites."

And lest skeptics who have firmly fixed in their minds the purely egoistic Freud of popular thought continue to doubt that the founder of psychoanalysis entertained the possibility of a natural development out of egoism, it should be noted that as early as *The Interpretation of Dreams,* at the very beginning of the drive theory, he wrote: *"The character of even a good child is not what we should wish to find it in an adult. Children are completely egoistic; they feel their needs intensely and strive ruthlessly to satisfy them*—especially as against the rivals, other children . . . But . . . *we may expect that, before the end of the period which we count as childhood, altruistic impulses and morality will awaken in the little egoist"* (*SE* 4 [1900]:250, emphasis added).

Of course, the emergence of genuine benevolence from affection is not the whole of the psychoanalytic explanation of altruism. As Freud also explains, there is nongenuine altruism, a reaction formation against sadism, that comes in the form of excessive pity, "exaggerated kindness," and the sentimentality that some "friends of humanity and protectors of animals" display (see *SE* 14 [1915]:129, 281–2; 21 [1928]:178). But Freud is careful to distinguish sublimation from reaction formation. These are "two different processes," he writes (*SE 7* [1905]:178, n.2).[20] "Sublimation [and

---

original); "generally speaking, only a part of . . . [the sexual instincts] is made use of in sexual life; another part is deflected from sexual aims and directed towards others—a process which deserves the name of 'sublimation'" (*SE* 9 [1908]:171).

20. Freud distinguishes sublimation from reaction formation in a footnote added to the 1915 edition of *Three Essays.* In the 1905 text (*SE* 7 [1905]:178), both are ascribed to "the mental dams" of "disgust, shame and morality."

aim inhibition] can . . . take place by other and simpler mechanisms" than reaction formation and, unlike reaction formation, can support *genuine* other-regard. This is because sublimation and aim inhibition can produce a true *transformation* of the "aim" of the original motive that allows for a satisfying *expression* of the underlying drive, whereas in reaction formation, although the latent motive superficially turns into its opposite in a defense against unacceptable sadism, it leaves the aggression unconsciously present and bottled up.[21] The unacceptable motive remains unconsciously active and thus can generate outbursts or surreptitious satisfactions of the repressed (and otherwise disguised) hostility or hatred.[22] In other words, the seemingly benign motives set in place by reaction formation continue to be fueled unconsciously by the opposing hostile, aggressive motives that originally gave rise to them. The existence of these two contrasting mechanisms of sublimation and reaction formation, the one productive of genuine altruism, the other not, requires true Freudian "suspicion" of altruistic motives. But it does not subvert the distinction between genuine other-regard and the inauthentic "kindness" that ends by giving vent to aggression, however disguised.

BEYOND DRIVE THEORY

Despite what he does with aim inhibition and sublimation, the notion that libido can develop in a way that leads out of egoism into genuine other-regard troubled Freud, and he struggled with the issue throughout the period (1900–19) in which he was developing his drive theory. Even when his commitment to the drive theory was at its height, there was a side of Freud that was pulling him away from drive theory. In "Instincts and their Vicissitudes," he expressly notes that "the case of love . . . refuses to be fitted into our scheme of the instincts" (*SE* 14 [1915]:133). To "say of an instinct that it 'loves' the objects towards which it strives for purposes of

21. Freud argues that "sublimation is a way . . . by which . . . [instinctual] demands can be met *without* involving repression" of the sort utilized in defenses like reaction formation (*SE* 14 [1914]:95; see also *SE* 11 [1910]:53–4).

22. As an example of reaction formation, Freud says of Dostoevsky that his "exaggerated kindness" led him "to love and to help where he had a right to hatred and revenge, as, for example, in his relations with his first wife and her lover." But "in little things he was a sadist towards others" (*CP* 5 [1928]:223–4). See also Freud's interpretation of Emile Zola's description of a girl's self-sacrificial conduct in *La joie de vivre* (*SE* 7 [1905]:238, n.2). Needless to say, it is often impossible in ordinary interactions to determine whether kindness is due to a reaction formation, sublimation, or a compromise formation between the two.

satisfaction . . . strikes us as odd. Thus we become aware that the attitudes of love and hate cannot be made use of for the relations of *instincts* to their objects" (*SE* 14 [1915]:137).

The alternative move that Freud makes at this point to explain love (and hate) is to focus on the ego and its object relations. "Love," Freud says, is "reserved for the relations of the *total ego* [or self as a whole] to objects" (ibid., emphasis original). This move takes Freud out of the whole context of drive theory and into notions of the ego, as representative of the whole self, relating to other selves.[23] This is not to say that he does not couch some of his ego-oriented explanations of love in the language of drive theory, as, for example, when he speaks of the ego's vaguely defined (and somewhat catchall) *self-preservation instincts* as anaclitically guiding the libido[24] and attaching it to external objects.[25] But when he attempts to describe the origins and growth of love and affection, Freud clearly slips out of drive theory and concentrates on describing the dynamics of the subjective experience of the individual's real and imaginary relations with other people as central factors in the development of personality.[26] And it is in

23. Although Freud's first concerted formulation of a systematic ego theory did not come until 1923, in *The Ego and the Id,* psychoanalysis in the drive-theory period did not overlook or underrate the importance of the ego, as the discussion in the text demonstrates. See, e.g., *SE* 7 (1905):134; 11 (1910):213–5; 11 (1912):180–1; 12 (1911):218–26; 14 (1914):50; 17 (1917):138; 18 (1922):251–2.

24. As when the newborn's ego instincts direct the sexual instincts to find their first object in the form of the mother's breast, which provides both the vital nourishment necessary for survival and sensual satisfaction of libidinal desires (*SE* 11 [1912]:180; see also *SE* 7 [1905]:222; 14 [1914]:87). For further discussion of Freud's doctrine of anaclisis, see ch. 7, n. 27.

25. Freud holds that the ego instincts serve the biological function of self-preservation (*Selbsterhaltungstriebe*) (*SE* 11 [1910]:213–15), but he is not very clear about either the nature of the ego instincts or what is involved in the concept of self-preservation—whether it entails only biological survival or also maintenance of identity, i.e., *self*-preservation. Freud sometimes appears to assume that the ego instincts are egoistic unless pushed in an other-regarding direction by aim-inhibited or sublimated sexual drives; but at other times he seems to imply that they can be directed outward, as "ego interests," in a way that is not necessarily egoistic. For example, some disinterested aspects of a scientist's pursuit of truth might have "survival value" and thus serve the self-preservative instincts, without being completely egoistic.

26. This is the essential claim of "object relations theory," which in its broadest sense designates theories or aspects of theories that explore the relation between real, external people and internal images and residues of relations with them and the significance of these for psychic functioning (Greenberg and Mitchell 1983, p. 12). Of course, Freud tries to fit his increasing emphasis on object relations into drive theory, but in the process he expands it to the point of breaking with its bare-bones formulation in "Instincts and their Vicissitudes."

this object-relations work that he most clearly and convincingly makes room for the possibility of genuine other-regard, at least at this point in the development of his thought.

It is chiefly under the rubric of "affection" (*Zärtlichkeit*) that Freud smuggles an object-relational account of genuine other-regard into psycho-analytic theory. The importance of this concept is highlighted by the fact that affection is one of the two currents—the other being sensuality (*Sin-nlichkeit*)—that together constitute what we know as love. For Freud, sensuality is egoistic or possessive; it signifies the desire "to have" the object. The other aspect of love is described as "affection" (*Gefühle*) or "tenderness" (*Zärtlichkeit*), Freud's terms for the nonpossessive, nonsensual currents of love that bind people together over time in reciprocity or mutuality (*SE* 7 [1905]:200). Recognition of affection as a separate current of love does not mean, of course, that Freud comes anywhere near to embracing the bloodless, disinterested *agapē* of the Christian tradition. This is because both elements of love—sensuality and affection—are al-ways present and intertwined in varying degrees in virtually all human relations and at all stages of human development.

Surprisingly, given Freud's renowned emphasis on sexuality and the power of the sexual instincts in shaping human relations, he seems to view affection as every bit as basic as sensuality in attaching the developing child to his or her primary caretakers (*SE* 11 [1912]:180–1). While affection properly so called does not appear in the Freudian schema until the child arrives at the anal stage (between ages two and four), Freud notes that significant precursors to what will later develop into affection are to be found in the earliest stages of infancy. Concomitantly, he stresses that the original infant–mother relation is crucial to the individual's later capacity (or lack thereof) for affection. Freud recognizes that from the very begin-ning of life, the child responds as a participant in a relation with his or her primary caretaker(s) in which his or her vital needs are met and sensual satisfaction is experienced (ibid.). For Freud, the crystallizing image of this all-important initial relation is the infant at the mother's breast (*SE* 7 [1905]:222). And while he does not fully spell out the interactional dynam-ics of this "original relationship" in non-drive-theory terms, he does em-phasize that it involves a real relation (that can be either gratifying or frustrating) with a real external object, namely, the mother's breast.[27] This

27. In a blend of drive theory and nascent object-relations observations, Freud postulates that right from the outset, the infantile ego guides sensual desires in a way that binds the child to others and allows for the development of precursors of both affection and sensual love (see n. 24 above). The ego valuations that are crucial to the infant's early bonding include the

image of the infant at the breast is for Freud "the prototype of every relation of love"—whether experienced as primarily sensual or as predominantly affectionate (ibid.).[28] Thus, speaking of the later time in life in which genuine affection has emerged, Freud stresses the link with earliest infancy. He writes: "Children learn to feel for other people who help them in their helplessness and satisfy their needs *a love which is on the model of, and a continuation of, their relation as sucklings to their nursing mother*" (*SE* 7 [1905]:222–3, emphasis added). This later love combines the *"child's affection* [die zärtlichen Gefühle] *and esteem for those who look after him* with sexual love" (*SE* 7 [1905]:223, emphasis added). Significantly, the developing child's love is triggered not merely by an upsurge of instinctual impulses but also by symbolic stimuli that incite primal memories of the infant's earliest relation to the mother's breast and thereby generate wishes for the repetition of previously experienced interactional and physiological pleasure.[29]

Despite Freud's emphasis on the initial infant–mother relation as the

---

subjective sense of "appreciation" that the infant feels toward gratifying external objects—at first the breast, but at some undefined later point the mother herself (*SE* 16 [1916–17]:329).

Greenberg and Mitchell argue that this contradicts other formulations that seem to hold that the earliest state of relatedness to objects is a state of autoeroticism or narcissism (1983, p. 40). But the alleged inconsistency is resolved if, following the distinctions formulated in ch. 7 above, it is assumed that the ego instincts that relate the neonate under anaclisis to its mother at the outset of life continue to relate the growing infant to significant caretakers after sexuality has partially split off and become, first, autoerotic and, then, narcissistic before "primary object choice" takes place (see *SE* 7 [1905]:222; 11 [1912]:180–1; Laplanche and Pontalis 1973, p. 31).

28. Freud writes that even after sexual activity has become detached from the taking of nourishment, an important part of this first and most significant of all sexual relations is left over, which helps to prepare for the choice of an object and thus to restore the happiness that has been lost (*SE* 7 [1905]:222).

29. Freud's explanation of how symbolic stimuli, by triggering memories, generate *wishes* for the repetition of previous experiences with significant others considerably complicates the simple drive-theory explanation of motivation. For *wishes*, though defined by Freud as the psychic representations of drives, differ from direct drive satisfaction in their tendency to seek out symbolic stimuli that are mentally associated with gratification and to seek to re-find earlier objects or to repeat early pleasurable or unpleasurable experiences with new objects.

The significance of the symbolic triggering and direction of wishes in psychoanalytic theory is indicated by the centrality of this process in the phenomena of transference which is undoubtedly one of Freud's most original and radical discoveries (Malcolm 1982, p. 6). The concept of *transference* at once qualifies the significance of biological instincts and explains how they are to be understood; we cannot know our motives except by understanding them historically as a product of the developing self's interaction with, and fantasies about, other persons over the long course of childhood development.

template for all later affection (as well as sensuality), he clearly recognizes that affection in a true or complete sense is not found at the earliest stages of life. Affection in any meaningful sense presupposes both genuine awareness of self and other and a corresponding interest in the separate other. Freud understands that the newborn's limited cognitive capacities render him or her unable to distinguish self from other, inner from outer, and perforce, unable "to form a total idea of the person . . . [whose breast] is giving him satisfaction" (*SE* 7 [1905]:222). In addition, until the auto-erotic and narcissistic stages are traversed (see ch. 7 above), the individual experiences little genuine interest in others, even after he or she has become cognitively able to recognize them as separate.

It is at the anal stage that real affection first appears in spontaneous response to "the 'affection' shown to the child by its parents and atten-dants" (*CP* 4 [1912]:205; see *SE* 11 [1912]:181). Although at the anal stage there is a continuation of strongly autoerotic and narcissistic orienta-tions, the individual, having moved beyond the exclusive preoccupation with self that characterizes these earlier stages, is now capable for the first time of relating to another person with an appreciation of their sepa-rateness. This is part of what Freud means when he speaks of the anal child's *"primary object choice"* (*SE* 11 [1912]:180).

Gratitude plays a powerful role in generating this first true affection. Not only is the anal child grateful to his caretakers for the satisfaction of his physiological needs (which, in addition to preserving the self also "af-fords . . . an unending source of sexual excitation" (*SE* 7 [1905]:223); he is also grateful to his parents for their various expressions of affection for him. This gratitude fires in the young child a desire to reciprocate with a gift of his own—his feces. "Faeces are the child's first *gift*, the first sacrifice on behalf of his affection, a portion of his own body which he is ready to part with, but only for the sake of some one he loves" (*SE* 17 [1918]:81; see also *CP* 2 [1917]:168; *SE* 17 [1917]:130). What is going on here with the anal child is in fact benevolent action. Toilet learning presents "the first occasion on which the child must decide between a narcissistic and an object-loving attitude. He either parts obediently with his faeces, 'offers them up' to his love, or else retains them for purposes of auto-erotic grati-fication and later as a means of asserting his own will" (*CP* 2 [1917]:168). Normally, people succeed in making this move to benevolent action and give up the valued feces to please their parents.

The anal child also experiences and expresses deep affection for his parents and others outside the dynamics of toilet training, as Freud's report of a three-year-old's conversation with his aunt in a dark room makes clear:

"'Auntie, speak to me! I'm frightened because it's so dark.' His aunt answered him: 'What good would that do? You can't see me.' 'That doesn't matter,' replied the child, 'if anyone speaks, it gets light'" (*SE* 7 [1905]:224, n.1). Freud comments: "Thus what he was afraid of was not the dark, but the absence of someone he loved; and he could feel sure of being soothed as soon as he had evidence of that person's presence" (ibid.).

Moreover, affection and benevolent action often extend beyond the anal child's primary caretakers. In his study of "Little Hans," Freud explores how identification with the good parent can have this result. He notes that "in his final phantasy of bliss, . . . [Little Hans] imagined he had children, whom he took to the W.C., whom he made to widdle, whose behinds he wiped—for whom, in short, he did 'everything one can do with children'" (*SE* 10 [1909]:107). In this passage, Hans is seen as obtaining a kind of vicarious excretory pleasure from this fantasy. But he is also obtaining such pleasure from doing for someone else what "had been the source of pleasurable sensations for him" (*SE* 10 [1909]:108).

Although not normally mined for such material, Freud's discussions of some of the component instincts that go to make up the polymorphous perversity of infantile sexuality suggest ways in which various developments at the anal stage help to lay the groundwork for modes of identification and entering into the experience of others that are necessary for mature moral behavior. For example, the sadism that is particularly marked in the anal child is based upon the child's experiencing vicariously what happens to others. Freud writes:

> Our view of sadism is . . . prejudiced by the circumstance that this instinct . . . seems to strive towards the accomplishment of a quite special aim—not only to humiliate and master, but, in addition, to inflict pains. Psycho-analysis would appear to show that the infliction of pain plays no part among the original purposive actions of the [sadistic component] instinct. A sadistic child takes no account of whether or not he inflicts pains, nor does he intend to do so. (*SE* 14 [1915]:128)

It is only when sadism has been transformed into masochism and the individual has experienced sexual pleasure from sensations of pain that "the sadistic aim of *causing* pain can arise" (*SE* 14 [1915]:128). And this phenomenon, although commonly viewed negatively, involves the individual in *identifying* with others. For the post-masochistic sadistic aim in fact involves the individual "masochistically" enjoying the pain "inflicted on other people [or rather, the sexual excitement associated with the pain] . . . through his identification of himself with the suffering object"

(*SE* 14 [1915]:129). "A sadist is always at the same time a masochist" (*SE* 7 [1905]:159).

The sadistic child can even be said in his identifications to "suffer with" the victim of his aggressive actions or fantasies. This sets the stage for the transformation of subsequent sadism into "pity" (*Mitleid*) or "compassion" that occurs when sadism is turned into its opposite by the ego's reaction formation against it (*SE* 14 [1915]:129).[30] Thus compassion is based on or employs the same formal mechanisms as those underpinning the sadism that develops in the young child.

Similarly, scopophilia (pleasure in looking) provides some rudiments for what later evolves into empathy. As Freud notes in the case of "Little Hans," the young child takes "pleasure . . . in looking on while some one . . . [he] loves performs the natural [eliminatory] functions" (*SE* 10 [1909]:127) or when they appear before him naked (*SE* 10 [1909]:160–2). While this may seem very far removed from morality, as Fenichel (1953, pp. 377–9) points out, in the Freudian account of scopophilia "one looks at an object in order *to share in* its experience" (emphasis original). Such sharing is a crucial component of a sense of justice and fair play and of the ability to take the interests of others into account.

When we turn to Freud's account of the dynamics of the oedipal stage, we find that affection plays an important role in mediating the child's well-known hostility toward the parent of the same sex and passionate possessive love for the parent of the opposite sex and is crucial to the successful resolution of the oedipal crisis. Speaking of the male child, to whom he primarily confined his attention,[31] Freud notes that in the oedipal boy, profound affection, love, and respect for the father conflict with hatred of him as rival for the love of the mother (*SE* 13 [1913]:129).[32] This affection builds on and continues the feelings for the parent developed earlier and is buttressed in part by gratitude stemming from the discovery that the father

---

30. See also Freud's 1911 reference to "too strongly repressed sadism expressed in over-goodness and self-torture," in letter 41 to Putnam, in Hale 1971, p. 130.

31. In the pre-1920 period under discussion, Freud sometimes discussed the oedipal complex explicitly from the point of view of girls, but infrequently and generally only in passing (see, e.g., *SE* 15 [1916–17]:297).

32. He writes: "The hatred of his father that arises in a boy from rivalry for his mother is not able to achieve uninhibited sway over his mind; it has to contend against his old-established affection and admiration for the very same person" (*SE* 13 [1913]:129). Affection for the father in combination with narcissistic identification with him stimulate "compassion" (*Mitleid*—literally "suffering with") when the oedipal boy imagines that his father is in danger of being hurt or injured—e.g., by castration when the boy observes the penis disappear during copulation in the primal scene (*SE* 17 [1918]:88).

helped give the child life (*SE* 11 [1910]:172) and in part by the father's continuing care, support, and reciprocal affection. In the oedipal child, "feelings of tenderness unite with impulses which strive at power and independence, and . . . generate the wish to return . . . [the gift of life] to the parents and . . . repay them with one of equal value" (ibid.).

This leads the oedipal child to fantasies of rescuing both father and mother. For the son, the fantasy "of rescuing [the] father from danger and saving his life" has as its dominant meaning the defiance of setting accounts square with the rival—of owing him nothing (*SE* 11 [1910]:172–3, original emphasis omitted). Oedipal rescue fantasies as they apply to the mother, however, are more truly "tender"—but also more sensual. In the child who feels gratitude to his mother for giving him life, rescue fantasies shade into and covertly express the meaning of a desire to give the mother a child or make one for her—"one like himself" (*SE* 11 [1920]:173).[33]

At some point in the oedipal complex, "the affection [for the father] which . . . [has] been pushed under" by oedipal rivalries must become strong enough to reassert itself and lead the child to feelings of remorse and guilt for his oedipal animosities and desires—to kill, to possess (*SE* 13 [1913]:143). When this happens, the child willingly accepts the father's prohibitions against incest, and this sets the stage for the formation of conscience through acceptance of the esteemed parent's moral standards (ibid.). At this point in his work (pre-1920), Freud did not have a full concept of the superego and accordingly tended to frame the resolution of the oedipal complex in general terms, speaking of the child's repression of incestuous desires and acceptance of parental prohibitions.[34] Acceptance of the incest taboo and the development of conscience simultaneously inhibit the child's sensual love for the parent of the opposite sex and transmute passionate sensuality into filial affection. By these oedipal processes, the affectionate current comes to dominate both aggression and sensuality in the child's subsequent relations with the parents.

During latency, the affectionate currents of sexual life that have been developing throughout childhood are further reinforced and stabilized by

33. In both these examples of rescue fantasies, there are at play in the child's mind clear manifestations of elementary notions of the reciprocity upon which so much mature morality is based.

34. The specific dynamics involved in the successful resolution of the oedipal complex are initially worked out in the context of explaining the emergence of conscience in the history of the race, after the murder of the father of the primal horde (see *SE* 13 [1913]:141–46). But Freud does say that these dynamics are similar to those of the oedipal son (see, e.g., *SE* 13 [1913]:143).

the repression of the young child's sexuality that follows successful resolution of the oedipal complex.[35] The repression of sexual and aggressive tendencies make it easier for the latency child to feel spontaneous affection "for other people who help them in their helplessness and satisfy their needs" (*SE* 7 [1905]:222).

At puberty, the individual's affectionate and sensual "love" life takes on a new complexity. Affection and sensuality must coalesce for the individual to be able to engage in satisfying love. Freud writes that "to ensure a fully normal attitude in love, two currents of feeling have to unite—. . . the tender, affectionate feelings and the sensuous feelings" (*CP* 4 [1912]:204; see also *SE* 7 [1905]:227; 11 [1912]:181). Likewise, in friendship, the sensual current, largely repressed but nevertheless surely present, must support the more conscious elements of nonsensual affection.

Although Freud is famous for bringing out the aspects of narcissism that are present in romantic love (an issue that is discussed in ch. 9 below),[36] he also attends closely to the necessity of affectionate, non-self-centered other-regard in the mature romantic love relation. Indeed, Freud goes so far as to treat as psychopathology and perversion the absence of affection in romantic love.[37] This comes out clearly in his discussion of the condition that Freud terms "psychical impotence,"[38] in which the sensual current is split off from and "forced to avoid the affectionate current" so that the "whole sphere of love . . . remains divided" (*SE* 11 [1912]:182–3). People who experience this disturbance, which Freud finds not uncommon in the modern age, can express sensuality freely only with a psychically debased sexual object. The "overvaluation that normally attaches to the sexual object . . . [is] reserved for the incestuous object and its representatives" (*SE* 11 [1912]:183). Freud sees this as a severely limited and crippled form of

35. Freud writes that perverse "sexual aims . . . become mitigated and . . . now represent what may be described as the 'affectionate current' of sexual life" (*SE* 7 [1905]:200). This claim is part of Freud's thesis that most of the higher cultural achievements of humankind are fueled by perverse component instincts of infantile sexuality that have been "suppressed, restricted, transformed and directed to higher aims" (*SE* 11 [1910]:215).

36. See *SE* (1914):73–102; Rieff 1961, pp. 173–4.

37. Balint notes that the "orthodox" psychoanalytic concept of mature genital love is a fusion of genital satisfaction with pregenital tenderness. He agrees with Freud that affection must go along with a form of identification within which the "interests, wishes, feelings, sensitivity, shortcomings of the partner attain—or are supposed to attain—about the same importance as our own" (1959, p. 115).

38. *Psychical impotence* involves either a "failure to perform the act of coitus in circumstances where a desire to obtain pleasure is present" or the carrying out of the sex act "without getting any particular pleasure from it" (*SE* 11 [1912]:184).

loving. Without the presence of affection to support and guide libido, the individual cannot draw on the important infantile traces that would normally pattern and fuel his loving (compare *SE* 7 [1905]:208 and 11 [1912]:181 with 11 [1912]:182–3). As a result, sexual activity "is capricious, easily disturbed, often not properly carried out, and not accompanied by much pleasure" (*SE* 11 [1912]:182). Equally, object choice is severely limited to debased objects whose very selection in turn debases the lover's sense of self. And there is not "much refinement" in the "modes of behavior" harnessed to love (*SE* 11 [1912]:183).

Freud's observations about the emergence of affection over the course of human development obviously take him quite far from the unadorned drive theory of his original metapsychology, in which the drives impinge upon the psyche from without and are discharged through other people as instinctual "objects" or means of gratification. While Freud did attempt to account for nonpossessive affection and other-regard within his original drive-discharge scheme by means of his notions of aim inhibition, sublimation, and object cathexis, these convoluted permutations of drive theory proved inadequate to capture fully the thrust of his object-relational observations that came out in connection with the issue of love and other-regard. As a result of this and other factors, the metapsychology itself underwent a radical revision in the "great turning point of 1920," as Freud broke through to concepts that more easily accommodated affection and other-regard and that allowed him to integrate his emerging object-relations approach with his continuing adherence to the instinctual underpinnings of psychic life.[39]

THE 1920 REVISION: EROS, A NEW VISION OF LOVE

With *Beyond the Pleasure Principle* (1920), Freud began to rework his basic discharge paradigm of the instincts and came up with two grand opposing categories: the life instincts, or Eros, and the death instincts.[40]

---

39. Among the considerations that led Freud to revise his first instinct theory and posit two major classes of instincts were the need to account for repetition phenomena and regression, the importance in clinical experience of aggression, masochism, sadism, and ambivalence, and the need to account for intrapsychic conflict after the ego instincts of the first dual instinct theory turned out to be explicable in narcissistic terms (see *SE* 18 [1920]:7–64; Laplanche and Pontalis 1973, pp. 98–9).

40. Of course, the new theory of instincts never completely replaced its predecessors and continued to exist side by side with ideas rooted in drive theory, to which in some ways Freud adhered throughout his life.

The life instincts subsume both the "sexual instinct proper and the instinctual impulses of an aim-inhibited or sublimated nature derived from" them, as well as the instincts of self-preservation previously enumerated by Freud (*SE* 19 [1923]:40). They embody "the will to live" (*SE* 18 [1920]:50) and have as their goal the creation and maintenance of ever greater unities (*SE* 18 [1920]:43, 60–1, n.1; 23 [1940]:148). In seeking "to form living substance into ever greater unities," the life instincts aim at prolonging life and bringing it to a state of ever increasing complexity and "higher development" (*SE* 18 [1923]:258–9; 19 [1923]:40).

By contrast, the death instincts[41] embrace both self-destructive tendencies and, when externally directed, aggressive instincts (*SE* 22 [1933]:211) and strive "towards the dissolution of what is living" (*SE* 20 [1926]:265). They seek "to undo connections and so to destroy things" (*SE* 23 [1940]:148), to reduce tension to zero and bring living matter back to the inorganic state (*SE* 18 [1920]:38, 55–6; 22 [1933]:210–11).

Although Freud posits the life and death instincts as a great duality and describes them as "a theoretical clarification of the universally familiar opposition between Love and Hate," he cautions against "introducing ethical judgements of good and evil" that would make the life instincts entirely desirable and the death instincts completely undesirable (*SE* 22 [1933]:209). "Neither of these [classes of] instincts is any less essential than the other," he writes. "The phenomena of life arise from the concurrent or mutually opposing action of both . . . An instinct of the one sort can scarcely even operate in isolation; it is always accompanied—or . . . alloyed—with a certain quota from the other side, which modifies its aim or is, in some cases, what enables it to achieve that aim" (ibid.). Aggression, for example, is a necessary complement of the self-preservation instincts that Freud classifies under Eros, because self-preservation must have "aggressiveness at its disposal if it is to fulfill its purpose" of defending the individual. Similarly, love, "when it is directed towards an object, . . . need[s] . . . some contribution from the [aggressive] instinct for mastery if it is in any way to obtain possession of that object" (*SE* 22 [1933]:209–10).

Freud saw himself as breaking radical new ground with his new theory of the instincts, and indeed, the paradigm he proposed alters the understanding of the very notion of the psyche and instinct in ways that bring with them a significant revision at the metapsychological level of the Freudian view of object relations and other-regard. The psyche is now conceived in

41. The term *Thanatos* is now commonly used for the death instincts but does not appear in Freud's own writings, although E. Jones (1957, p. 273) states that Freud occasionally used it in conversation (see Laplanche and Pontalis 1973, p. 447).

terms more of a biological organism than a mechanical apparatus, and the instincts are now seen more broadly, not only as psychic representatives of biological stimuli,[42] but also as urges inherent in psychic life that represent dynamic forces of the mind subject to developmental transformations. As such, the instincts are no longer viewed as alien stimuli impinging on the psyche from without that disturb the organism's mechanistic efforts to remain unstimulated and that demand discharge leading to tension reduction under the pleasure principle. Tension reduction is no longer the universal goal of motivation.[43] Insofar as the life instincts help to guide psychic life, the urge to ever greater unity tends to join the individual with other people—individually, in love relations, and communally, in civilized society. Freud states not only that "Eros desires contact because it strives to make the ego and the loved object one" (*SE* 20 [1926]:122), but also that "civilization is a process in the service of Eros, whose purpose is to combine single human individuals, and after that families, then races, peoples and nations, into one great unity, the unity of mankind . . . libidinally bound to one another" (*SE* 21 [1930]:122). As Guntrip points out, Freudian Eros is "essentially cooperative . . . [in] nature [and] is especially capable of being taken up into the life of the person in relation to another person" (1973, p. 37).

What all this reflects is a profound alteration of the relation of instincts to objects at the metapsychological level. Whereas before, the objects of the instinctual drives were understood predominantly as instrumental means of tension reduction by which an individual could satisfy his instinctual needs, now the object, in the form of another person, exists as that to which

42. Freud presents the instinct as "the psychical representative of organic forces" (*SE* 12 [1911]:74). See also *SE* 7 (1905):168 (passage added in 1915); 14 (1915):122; 23 (1940):148.

43. Motivation in Freud's post-1919 metapsychology is grounded in the goals and aims of the life and death instincts and not in the pleasure principle understood as the universal tension-reducer. Since the life instincts have as their goal the creation and maintenance of ever greater unities, they may actually increase psychic tension. As Loewald points out, this new "idea of a life instinct bespeaks an orientation toward a view in which life is not altogether motivated by forces of the past but is partially motivated by an attraction coming from something ahead of us" (1980, p. 140). With these metatheoretical changes, Freud is in a position to argue that the libido can aim at "a positive fulfilment of happiness" not simply at the "avoidance of unpleasure" (*SE* 21 [1930]:82). However, Freud retains his earlier notion of tension reduction as the final goal of the life and death instincts, since in the end death triumphs over life by bringing all things back to the unstimulated condition of inorganic matter (*SE* 18 [1920]:38–40, 44–5; 23 [1940]:148–9). But this is not the motive behind every act. As long as life lasts, the motives generated by the life instincts oppose those generated by the death instincts in active and vital duality (*SE* 21 [1930]:118, n.2).

the life instincts inherently direct the individual to relate throughout the processes of development. "The sexual instincts are . . . the part of Eros which is directed towards objects," Freud writes (*SE* 18 [1920]:60, n.1). The libido or Eros is a "basic object-seeking life-drive" (Guntrip 1973, p. 95, discussing Fairbairn's developments based on Freud; see Fairbairn 1952, pp. 82–3).

Moreover, the object is now seen to play an essential part in helping to *constitute* the subject, since the object who participates with the developing individual in object relations is essential to the very organization of instincts in the subject's psychic life. For example, the mother, by responding to the infant's needs and furnishing him or her with her love, helps the infant to organize his or her instinctual responses to her and to the world.[44]

As part of his new instinct theory, Freud further develops his notion that there are both sensual and nonsensual currents of love. He continues to delineate two distinct ways in which the individual is "tied" or bound— now, by the life instincts or Eros—to other people. One remains sensual and is possessive love, the desire "to *have*" another person (*SE* 18 [1921]:106). This emphasis on sensuality as one of the currents of love represents a continuity with Freud's earlier views, except that to the notion of "possession" he significantly adds the notion of *union*. "Eros . . . [is] the instinct which strives for ever closer union," Freud writes (*SE* 20 [1926]:265), and by *union* he means to connote a kind of bonding that is more object-oriented and less need-driven than the sensuality of the drive-theory period.[45] The other, nonsensual aspect of Eros that directs the individual toward others throughout life is "identification."[46] This concept is extremely important vis-à-vis Freud's treatment of other-regard and helps to spell out the precise dynamics of the nonsensual aspects of object rela-

44. The development of the ego and superego that organize, control, and guide the instincts is explained in Freud's mature writings in terms of such interactional processes as identification, internalization, and introjection (see, e.g., Guntrip 1973; Loewald 1980, pp. 127, 135).

45. Brown has drawn attention to the importance of "union" in Freud's mature theory, but he overstates the case when he says that the "possessive" use of Eros collapses into "union" with the other in Freud's post-1919 writings (1959, pp. 40–5).

46. *Identification* was first introduced in *The Interpretation of Dreams*, where it refers to "the relation of similarity" whereby persons are linked by "a common [unconscious] element" in dreams and hysterical symptoms (*SE* 4 [1900]:320, 150). The dynamics of identification with a lost object were first explicated in detail in "Mourning and Melancholia" (*SE* 14 [1917]:240–2, 249–51, 255–6). But in Freud's post-1919 work the concept becomes much richer as he fills in the role of identification in normal development and weaves it into his instinct theory.

tions that had previously gone under the rubric of "affection." Identification is a form of nonsensual relating in which the individual values attributes of another and feels emotionally bound to the other by virtue of feeling similar in some respect to him or her. In consequence, the individual models himself or herself on the other by setting up the other as "object" inside the ego (*SE* 18 [1921]:106; 19 [1923]:29).[47] This involves both putting oneself in the *place* of another and altering or accommodating the self *to* the other—what we now know in Piagetian terms as the interrelated developmental processes of assimilation and accommodation. As such, identification plays a major part "in determining the form taken by the ego [or self] and . . . makes an essential contribution towards building up . . . its 'character'" (*SE* 19 [1923]:28).[48]

As one of the two basic ways of "erotic" bonding, identification exists in rudimentary form from the earliest time of life. Indeed, Freud came to see identification as one aspect of the primal emotional tie with the object and in fact went so far as to say—as he had previously observed about affection—that identification represents "the earliest expression of an emotional tie with another person" (*SE* 18 [1921]:105; see also *SE* 18 [1921]:107). In *The Ego and the Id* he states that, "At the very beginning, in the individual's primitive oral phase," possessive sensual love (object cathexis) and identification exist side by side and indeed "are . . . indistinguishable from each other" in binding the infant to the mother (*SE* 19 [1923]:29). Given the infant's limited cognitive capacities, the notion that "identification" takes place at this earliest stage must mean that it includes, in its earliest forms, a kind of primitive merging of the infant's nascent self

47. The notion of modeling oneself on someone else is so important to the psychoanalytic concept of *identification* that the term is sometimes defined as referring only to this process. But modeling takes place only in the context of feeling similar to or like the person one models oneself after. Hartmann and Loewenstein understand this when in their influential article on the superego, they note that "identification" may mean "to 'take the place' of the other person," as in role-playing (1964, p. 151). This is the meaning employed by Freud in *Group Psychology* when he refers to horizontal bonding among members of a group. However, identification is stronger affectively and more unconscious than our ordinary understanding of role-playing. For a good comparison of the psychoanalytic concepts of identification, introjection, imitation, and merging, see Schafer 1968, pp. 140–80.

48. It is noteworthy that identification in "building up . . . 'character'" conforms to the general goal of Eros, which is to form "ever greater unities, so that life may be . . . brought to higher development" (*SE* 18 [1923]:258). Freud lays particular stress in his account of character formation on the psychodynamics of identification with abandoned or lost "love-objects," though he also observes that alteration of a person's character by means of identification can occur without actually giving up the object (see, e.g., *SE* 19 [1923]:28–30).

with the breast and later with the mother as she is gradually differentiated from the self (see, e.g., *SE* 21 [1930]:64–73). As with the sensual links of the child to his earliest caretaker(s) and as is true of what Freud previously said about infantile precursors of affection, "the effects of the first identifications made in earliest childhood will be general and lasting" (*SE* 19 [1923]:31).

Before the onset of the oedipal crisis, identification helps to ground the child's affection for both parents insofar as the child has not yet begun to distinguish between the sexes (*SE* 19 [1923]:31, n.1). With the knowledge of sexual differences, the little boy, on whose oedipal dynamics Freud focuses, begins to develop an object cathexis toward his mother and, by means of identification, to "exhibit a special interest in his father; he would like to grow like him and be like him, and . . . takes his father as an ideal" (*SE* 18 [1921]:105). The valuing that comes from identification and the wish to be like him supplements and reinforces the affection that is derived from the child's gratitude for being taken care of by the father, as previously discussed, and from aim inhibition, which likewise continues to be a source of affection (see *SE* 18 [1921]:111–12). Freud's grasp of the process of identification enriches his understanding of the affection that the child carries into the oedipal period and that must eventually outweigh oedipal hostility to the same-sex parent. As the oedipal crisis deepens, identification takes on a more hostile coloring and "becomes identical with the wish to replace" the father with respect to the mother. Even so, identification remains profoundly ambivalent, and the simultaneous preservation of earlier affection means that "it can turn into [a feeling] . . . of tenderness as easily as into a wish for . . . [the father's] removal" (*SE* 18 [1921]:105). At the conclusion of the oedipal crisis, Freud's concept of identification allows him to specify the development of conscience and the child's acceptance of the incest taboo in terms of identification with and introjection of the rival parent's moral standards. Freud's mature understanding of the foundations of the superego, and hence of moral conscience, rests on the object-relations dynamics that are encapsulated in his description of the operation of identification.

Because Freud roots identification in Eros, the concept gives instinctual grounding to the evolving object-relational aspects of his thought (including the oedipal crisis and the structural formations evolving from it—i.e., the ego and the superego) that in his earlier writings could not be explained satisfactorily in instinctual terms. This allows him to integrate object-relations observations and explanation of affection into his metapsychology, where before the two parts of his work were markedly incongruent. It also allows him to encompass within his view of love a wide variety of emotional relations drawing on differing degrees and combinations of sensuality and affection, narcissism and selflessness, that in their complexity permit of other-regard without artificially having to separate out the egoistic aspects of love.

> The nucleus of what we mean by love naturally consists . . . in sexual love with sexual union as its aim. But we do not separate from this . . . what in any case has a share in the name 'love'—on the one hand, self-love, and on the other, love for parents and children, friendship and love for humanity in general, and also devotion to concrete objects and to abstract ideas . . . All these tendencies are an expression of the same instinctual impulses.
>
> (*SE* 18 [1921]:90)

With his enlarged conception of love rooted in the life instincts or Eros, broadly conceived, Freud is no longer so troubled by difficulties in integrating love into the metapsychology and is much more comfortable with the ordinary-language implications of the word *love* than he was before the 1920 revision of his instinct theory. He notes:

> Even in its caprices the usage of language remains true to some kind of reality. Thus it gives the name of 'love' to a great many kinds of emotional relationship which we too group together theoretically as love; but then again it feels a doubt whether the love is real, true, actual love, and so hints at a whole scale of possibilities within the range of the phenomena of love. We . . . have no difficulty in making the same discovery from our own observations. (*SE* 18 [1921]:111)[49]

In his discussions of some specific kinds of love, such as romantic love and group solidarity, Freud points very concretely to possibilities of genuine other-regard. For example, in talking about the dynamics of romantic love, which he still maintains must synthesize "unsensual, heavenly love and . . . sensual, earthly love," the relation to the loved object is characterized by the interaction of uninhibited instincts and of instincts inhibited in their aim (*SE* 18 [1921]:112). As previously noted, aim inhibition allows for other-regard, and Freud observes that "the depth to which anyone is in *love,* as contrasted with his purely sensual desire, may be measured by the . . . share taken by the aim-inhibited instincts of affection" (ibid., emphasis added).

In his post-1919 period he is able to go into much greater detail, consistent with the metapsychology, on how the lover can relate to the beloved

49. See *SE* 18 (1921):91; compare *SE* 14 (1915):137.

in non-egoistic ways.[50] This involves a valuing of the loved object in which, initially, in a process that draws on both identification and an urge to possession, "a considerable amount of narcissistic libido overflows on to the object" (ibid.). In many forms of love choice, the object may even serve as a substitute for an unattained ego ideal, so that the other is loved on account of real or imagined "perfections" which the lover has striven to reach for his own ego or self. Instead of seeking to be *like* the loved object, as would be the case in a pure form of nonsensual identification, the lover seeks union with the valued object. In some respects, this represents a "roundabout way" of satisfying the lover's narcissism.[51] But at the same time, once the libidinal investment is made, the lover's own ego becomes "more unassuming and modest" in relation to the beloved. Freud concludes that "traits of humility, of the limitation of narcissism, and of self-injury"— all supporting the capacity to act in the interests of the beloved—"occur in every case of being in love" (*SE* 18 [1921]:113). In the extreme—indeed, pathological—case, the ego becomes overly attenuated and the object over- ly idealized, to the point where the "entire self-love of the ego" is swallowed up by the object, and irrational acts of self-sacrifice follow "as a natural consequence" (ibid.). But this pathological form merely takes too far the tendency to act for the loved other that Freud sees as inherent in the romantic love relation.

When he comes to addressing the "social feelings" that arise in the context of group relations, Freud again points to benevolent acts as natural consequences of libidinal or "erotic" ties between people. He boldly de- clares that "love relationships (or . . . emotional ties) . . . constitute the essence of the group mind" (*SE* 18 [1921]:91). More specifically, he is of the opinion that a sense of group solidarity arises by operation of identifica- tion when members feel that they share "an important . . . common quali- ty" based upon "having the same ego ideal"—that is, the same leader, symbol, or ideology (*SE* 18 [1921]:93–5). What this means is that the

50. Freud anticipated the basically object-relational account of the genesis of non-egoistic love that he presents in the post-1919 period in his seminal 1914 essay "On Narcissism" (see, e.g., *SE* 14 [1914]:88) and again in ch. 26 of *Introductory Lectures on Psycho-Analysis* (*SE* 16 [1916–17]:417–18). But he could not reconcile these early object-relational observations regarding the gensis of other-regard with the original drive-discharge theory.

51. Some interpreters maintain on the basis of what Freud says about the importance of the child's relations with his or her parents in determining later choices of loved objects that he views mature love as little more than a "reprint" of earlier object relations (see *SE* 7 [1905]:228). But in fact Freud believed in the normal ego's capacity to assess love objects realistically. He explicitly stated that the aspect of "the capacity to love . . . [that] undergo[es] full psychical development . . . is directed towards reality, and can be made use of by the conscious personality" (*CP* 2 [1912]:313). See also *SE* 7 (1905):116.

libidinal ties binding the individual to the group extend in two directions: first, vertically, binding him or her to the leader or ideology, and second, based on this tie, horizontally, binding him or her to the other members of the group because of the similarities and identifications created by the first kind of tie (*SE* 18 [1921]:95). The individual's libidinal relation to the leader or ideology closely parallels the lover's relation to the beloved in that it involves narcissistic idealization in which the leader or ideology is seen to embody perfections previously (and perhaps contemporaneously) sought by the individual's own ego (see, e.g., *SE* 18 [1921]:112–6). It is also very much like the child's relation to the parents, with the leader as "substitute father" (*SE* 18 [1921]:94; see also *SE* 18 [1921]:127). With the group leader as idealized object, the individual member will act in the interests of, and sometimes sacrifice himself for, the group leader or ideology (*SE* 18 [1921]:94, 127), although such actions, to the extent that they approach "blind obedience," do not constitute genuine morality as Freud conceives it (see *SE* 14 [1915]:283–4). However, the ties to fellow members that arise because they share the same ego ideal result in the emergence of "sympathy" which does support genuine other-regarding behavior.[52] The libidinal tie forged by identification places a limitation on narcissism.[53] Because he identifies himself with fellow members of the group, he "derives from this community of . . . egos the obligations for giving mutual help and for sharing possessions which comradeship implies" (*SE* 18 [1921]:134).[54] Freud specifically states that the sympathy that leads to benevolent action with respect to other group members involves more than

52. Freud observes that "identification" always involves a degree of "displaced narcissism," but he also argues that he is "not disputing the ethical value of . . . [the] kindness" that results from "this sympathy by identification" (*SE* 21 [1928]:190).

53. In *Group Psychology*, Freud stresses the narcissistic motives that are satisfied by the relations with the group—or, to be more precise, the symbolic representations of the group—within which other-regarding acts toward members occur. This lends a degree of uncertainty to statements that imply a genuineness of other-regarding acts. But Freud's mixed-motive theory enables him to distinguish an agent's motives in a relation from the motives that primarily explain the acts that occur within such relations. For Freud, other-regarding acts occur primarily in the context of relations in which the agent enjoys narcissistic satisfaction of some sort; but these acts are genuinely other-regarding, nonetheless. For further discussion, see Wallwork 1982.

54. The differentiating moral element here is not affection or "liking" alone, but the added aspect of sharing. We may identify with someone—in friendship or love—without there being any particular moral aspects to the relation. Even if a gift is given, if it is simply because one likes the other person, it is doubtful that the gift giving is a moral action. But if the gift is at some cost to oneself and is justified by something like the thought that the other will enjoy it more than I will or that I have enough and he or she has too little, then the action involves a degree of benevolence and, possibly, a perceived unfairness, that make the action moral.

a "community of [self] interest." He holds that without the addition of libido—that is, instinctual ties to other people—"no lasting limitation of narcissism" can be effected and there will not be the requisite "considerateness" and "tolerance" of fellow group members.[55] Genuine altruism and benevolence do not, therefore, translate into mere self-interest. "In cases of collaboration libidinal ties are regularly formed between . . . fellow-workers which prolong and solidify the relation between them to a point beyond what is merely profitable . . . In the development of mankind as a whole, just as in individuals, love alone acts as the civilizing factor in the sense that it brings a change from egoism to altruism" (*SE* 18 [1921]:103).[56]

The move from narcissism to altruism and other-regard that grows out of the establishment of libidinal ties to others in various love relations grounds the psychoanalytic understanding of the motivational springs of authentic morality. Genuine morality is instinctually grounded in natural desires springing from Eros, whereas inauthentic morality consists in narcissistic and egoistic obedience to moral principles in order to avoid punishments or to gain rewards (*SE* 14 [1915]:283–4). In taking this position, Freud is presupposing that morality requires not only certain rational capacities but also other-regarding dispositions. This view is contrary to that of Kant and his followers, who hold that morality is based on the dictates of practical reason operating in *opposition* to desire.[57] It is the logical implication of Freud's position that without some benevolent senti-

55. Before the turn in his theory that began in 1920, Freud held that groups are held together by shared self-interest. But by 1921, he was able to argue on the basis of his new view of Eros that groups are held together not only by narcissistic motives but by identification, sympathy, and acts of mutual aid.

56. In addition to the argument in the text above that explains sympathy and other social feelings in terms of identification grounded instinctually in Eros, Freud also maintains that sympathetic concern and the sense of equality with other members that groups elicit are *in part* a product of reaction against envy. Writing of the young child's identification with other children, Freud argues that his or her initial jealousy cannot be maintained in the face of parental hostility without damaging consequences, and so the child is forced to identify with the other children (*SE* 18 [1921]:117–21). Lakoff (1964, p. 191) and Rawls (1971, pp. 539–40) use this additional explanation to argue that Freud undermines the social sense of equality and fairness by viewing it solely as a reaction formation against envy and jealousy. However, Freud not only nowhere claims that the argument in *Group Psychology* that Lakoff and Rawls cite is the sole explanation of the sense of social equality, he explicitly denies it, claiming that "we do not ourselves regard our analysis of identification [here] as exhaustive" (*SE* 18 [1921]:121). For further discussion, see ch. 13 below.

57. Duty, Kant announces, "rejects all kinship with the inclinations" (1956, p. 89). See also Kant 1959, pp. 14, 16, 17–18.

ments, practical reason would be bereft of the other-regarding guidance that is essential to appreciate the ultimate *raison d'être* of morality itself, which is genuine concern for and fairness to others as well as oneself. Thus, Freud replaces Kant's "pathology of desire" with "a pathology of duty" (Ricoeur, 1970, p. 448).

But if Freud is decidedly non-Kantian in his late writings, he claimed to use Eros in the same wide sense as the term love is used in Platonic and Christian ethics (*SE* 18 [1921]:91; 7 [1905]:134, preface to the 4th ed. added in 1920). Freud has been ridiculed by Rieff (1961, pp. 168–9) and Morgan (1964, pp. 159–67), among others, for suggesting that this "wider" use of Eros corresponds to its meaning in Plato's philosophy and in St. Paul's understanding of *agapē*. And there are, to be sure, important differences. But Freud's critics, in turn, overly dramatize the factors separating the psychoanalytic approach to a love-based morality from these other philosophies of love by ignoring Freud's wider definition of Eros in his mature writings in favor of his earlier concept of aim-inhibited sexual love, interpreted in narrow drive-theory terms. The fact of the matter is that the narrowly possessive and discharge-seeking connotation of the sexual instincts in Freud's earlier writings yields in the post-1919 period to a concept of Eros that encompasses sympathetic identification that in turn supports the respect and benevolent concern for others upon which genuine morality rests.

Yet Freud's continuing insistence on the ubiquity of narcissistic motivations must never be overlooked. He saw it as part of his mission of enlightenment to break through our moral complacency and hypocrisy and to confront uncomfortable truths about the seamy underside of human behavior, especially of purportedly "moral" conduct. And so he insists on the intransigence of narcissism and of aggression and on the "overdetermination" of all behavior—in his words, on "the much trampled soil from which our virtues proudly spring" (*SE* 5 [1900]:621). It is thus one of Freud's main themes that morality occurs within the limitations and constraints of the human being's biological and psychic existence. Ethics is something done not by disembodied reason, but by reason working with the other-regarding sentiments that develop naturally out of humanity's instinctual erotic equipment.

But even when our moral intentions are genuine, they are commonly joined with narcissistic (and aggressive) aims that cannot help but influence the decisions we reach and how we go about implementing them. "So . . . human beings . . . have a whole number of motives for assenting [to an action]—some noble and some base, some which are openly declared and others which are never mentioned," Freud declares (*SE* 22 [1933]:210). This does not mean that narcissistic and aggressive motives always predominate over other-regarding ones. But it does mean that we are neither as good nor as bad as we are sometimes apt to think.[58] From these insights, Freud hoped to help bring about a more rational, gentler, truer approach to ethical dilemmas as they arise in the relation of individuals to communities and to each other.

58. See *SE* 14 (1915):282, 285; 21 (1930):134 n.1. For Freud, there is a narcissistic component to all forms of love, from friendship to erotic passion, even if only in the attenuated form of vicarious identification with some attribute we lack that the other possesses. But this does not mean that we are not also motivated in part by other-regarding considerations. Because the motives that guide our interpersonal relations are usually a mixture of self-interested and other-regarding ones, it is the proportion of each that is usually important in how we act, rather than the extremes of complete egoism or complete selflessness.

PART III
Normative Implications

Chapter 9
On Modifying Normative Standards: The Case of the Love Commandment

> Anyone . . . compelled to act continually
> in accordance with precepts which are not
> the expression of his instinctual inclinations
> is living, psychologically speaking, beyond
> his [moral] means, and may objectively be
> described as a hypocrite, whether he is
> clearly aware of the incongruity or not.
>
> —Freud

The preceding chapters have shown that Freud's views of determinism, hedonism, and narcissism are not necessarily incompatible with the possibility of genuine moral conduct insofar as it pertains to other-regard in individual object relations. There remains, however, Freud's justly famous attack on what he terms, rather overbroadly, "the morality of civilized society," which is principally set forth in *Civilization and its Discontents* (*SE* 21 [1930]:64–145). In this classic work, Freud takes aim at the overly repressive moral strictures that society places on its members to control their libidinal and aggressive instincts. His focus is the so-called love commandment, the injunction to "love thy neighbor as thyself," that is central to Judeo-Christian morality (*SE* 21 [1930]:109; see, e.g., Lev. 19:18; Mark 12:31; Matt. 22:39; Rom. 13:9; Gal. 5:14; James 2:8).

It is often thought that Freud is impugning all universal moral prescriptions of other-regarding behavior, in part, perhaps, because his tone is so vehement and leveling and in part because his own description of his target is very general—civilized morality as such and that core principle of other-regard, the love commandment, that so many moral philosophers have taken as the most basic requirement.[1] Freud treats the love commandment

---

1. See, e.g., the selections in Beach and Niebuhr (1955) and Aquinas, *Summa Theologica*, I–II, 100, 3 *ad* 1 and 11 *ad* 1. For an excellent discussion of the love commandment as the first principle of common morality in Western ethics, see Donagan (1977, pp. 59ff). Donagan notes that "although the Golden Rule has always enjoyed popular esteem . . . , most tradi-

as if it were a monovalent standard, whereas in fact there are many different interpretations of what it requires.[2] Moreover, he gives it a reading so stringent that what he is attacking is very different from the moral imperatives embraced in the name of the love commandment by such diverse thinkers as Aquinas, Luther, Kant, Mill, Tillich, Niebuhr, and Donagan. What Freud has in mind is a particular version of the love commandment, rooted in Christian morality, that calls for the individual to selflessly love all persons—friend or foe—alike, in the sense of extending affection and libidinal investment equally to all, which Freud regards as psychologically unrealistic and ethically perverse.[3] Here, Freud sees himself as attacking the

---

tional moral theologians and philosophers have attached more weight to the . . . [love commandment]."

2. As Frankena observes, the love commandment is so ambiguous that everything "depends on how one interprets it" (1963, p. 42). Within the Judeo-Christian tradition, there are three major interpretations that are sufficiently important to warrant discussion here.

In one interpretation, love of neighbor is identified as the core of morality, in accordance with the modest use of it in Leviticus and those New Testament passages in which the love commandment is presented as a concise summary of the Mosaic or natural moral law. Here charitable giving to others in need is required, as long as the cost to the agent is not excessive (see Green 1982; Johnston 1962, p. 170). This interpretation is not challenged by anything Freud says, because it is close to the ethic that he finds most compatible with psychoanalysis.

A second interpretation is that of Christian theologians who insist on the purity of heart stressed in the Sermon on the Mount. Of this, Bultmann writes: "What God forbids is not simply the overt acts of murder, adultery, and perjury, with which law can deal, but their antecedents: anger and name-calling, evil desire and insincerity (Mt. 5:21f., 27f., 33–37). What counts before God is not simply the substantial, verifiable deed that is done, but how a man is disposed, what his intent is . . . . The demand for love . . . knows no boundary or limit . . . (1951, pp. 13–18). See Calvin 1962, p. 354.

But there is a third interpretation that demands considerably more charity of the religious believer than secular morality requires, but less than what is called for by the Sermon on the Mount. For example, Jewish teachings require deeds of loving kindness (*Gemillath Hassadim*) that underlie the elaborate system of charity developed in traditional Jewish communities (see Green 1982; Simon 1975). Among Christians, the neighbor love required of ordinary Christians has been interpreted since the early Roman church as considerably more demanding than secular morality but less demanding than that required of saints (see Troeltsch 1960).

Given the variety among and within these three major interpretations of the love commandment, it is scarcely surprising that philosophers like Frankena (1963, pp. 42–3) have despaired of finding an analytically correct specification of what love requires. It is partly for this reason that I have chosen in this chapter to follow Freud's own manifold assumptions about the love commandment, without attempting to impose a conceptual straitjacket on his pursuit of this topic.

3. Because it is a Christian version of the love commandment that Freud has in mind, the vehemence of his attack and his incautious use of language are to be understood in part as a product of his animus against Christianity. Freud was morally outraged by Christianity's claim

popular—and psychologically insidious—understanding of the love commandment, and thus its culturally significant reality, quite aside from how the imperative of universal love might be parsed in philosophical circles.[4] It is important to note, however, that his critique does not extend to other-regarding behavior in general, but only to the need to fit moral precepts within the parameters set by the facts of psychological existence as revealed by psychoanalytic insights. Despite the unsparing nature of his criticisms of excessive moral strictures, Freud's purpose was not to deny the need for rules of civilization but to make civilized morality more compatible with the human spirit—a task that is itself a moral endeavor (see *SE* 21 [1930]:115).

Freud's most concerted critique of the love commandment is contained in *Civilization and its Discontents,* but he had previously addressed the question of the psychological possibility of fulfilling its demands in *Group Psychology and the Analysis of the Ego.* A consideration of both works is necessary to grasp fully Freud's views on this core element of "civilized morality."

In *Civilization and its Discontents,* Freud criticizes the love commandment along five psychological and normative lines, the first of which is also the extent of his prior examination of it in *Group Psychology.* These are: first, that it cannot be kept; second, that its call for treating "neighbors" with equal love is unjust to those to whom we are tied by special relations; third, that it ignores the evidence that not all persons are equally worthy of love; fourth, that it handles aggression so poorly that it actually encourages hostility toward outsiders; and fifth, that it is a source of considerable unhappiness to those who attempt to obey its grandiose requirements (see *SE* 21 [1930]:109–45).

The first of these points uses the basic "ought implies can" argument to discuss the degree to which it is reasonable, in light of psychological capaci-

---

to cultural superiority over Judaism, in part because, as a Jew with firsthand knowledge of anti-Semitism, he had reason to be impressed not by Christian love but by Christian hatred of those outside the faith (see *SE* 18 [1921]:134–5; 21 [1930]:114–15; and letter to Rolland, dated 4 Mar. 1923, in E. L. Freud 1975, pp. 341–2. See also Wallwork 1982: p. 266).

4. Because Freud's target is the common understanding among lay Christians, it is thus not surprising that the ethical writings of at least some theological ethicists generally escape his criticisms: for example, Aquinas, recognizes that neighbor love should include the self, and that universal love of humankind is impossible if it is interpreted as requiring the same kind of affection for everyone. (*Summa Theologica,* II–II, Q. 25, art. iv. and viii.). Additionally, Aquinas maintains, as does Freud, that we ought to love our near ones more than others (*Summa Theologica,* II–II, Q. 26, art. vi).

ties, to command impersonal or "universal" love of neighbor. The remainder are primarily ethical arguments, although they rely heavily on the psychoanalytic description of depth dynamics to bring out the normative issues at stake. In making these arguments, Freud goes considerably beyond the widely accepted use of psychological science in normative ethics—that is, to ascertain whether it is possible to be moral at all—and uses descriptive psychology to criticize normative standards themselves for their unanticipated and counterproductive consequences. In particular, he shows that moral standards such as the love commandment, as he rigidly construes it, turn out to engender psychological reactions that tend to undermine the very "moral" behavior being prescribed and that may exact unconscionable costs from those trying to obey them.

"THE COMMANDMENT IS IMPOSSIBLE TO FULFILL"

Although in both *Group Psychology* and *Civilization and its Discontents*, Freud clearly accepts that intimate relations, either sexual love or friendship, "impose duties . . . for whose fulfillment" the individual properly "must be ready to make sacrifices" (*SE* 21 [1930]:109; see *SE* 18 [1921]:102–3, 134), he questions whether it is psychologically possible for the individual to meet the universal requirement of the love commandment and extend love equally to strangers, given the instinctual limitations of narcissism and aggression (*SE* 21 [1930]:109; 18 [1921]:134–5). He suggests that narcissism limits the objects to those which love can realistically be extended, because, in his mixed-motive theory, narcissism is an important element that directs object choice. Of course, there is more to object choice than narcissism (see ch. 8 above); in addition, narcissism is broadly understood to include loving not only aspects of oneself in another but also one's ideals and aspects of others, such as parents, with whom one was once identified, such that the reach of identification can be great. But it remains the case for Freud that, at least in part because of the role of narcissism in the bonding process, love is not something human beings can cast abroad indiscriminately. Object love is not infinitely plastic, and not everyone can be loved equally, as the version of the love commandment that Freud is criticizing would have it. Thus, while innate aggression can be countered fairly successfully by strong libidinal ties with intimates and comrades, narcissistic limits on identification mean that the same power of love is not available to control and counter aggression when it comes to strangers.

At the same time, the narcissistic dynamics that make it unrealistic to expect love to be extended universally and in equal intensity to all mean that the individual can extend beneficence beyond the circle of his or her intimates. Identification with others who are seen as like oneself in certain significant respects, embodied in the ego ideal, allows the individual to take the interests of strangers as like his or her own and to act on their behalf (see *SE* 18 [1921]:100–4). But for Freud, such concern for others normally ends at the boundaries of the group. Indeed, part of the cohesiveness of any group derives from its emphasis on the ways its heroes, symbols, myths—that is, the sources of its identity—differ from those of other groups. This "narcissism of minor differences" (*SE* 21 [1930]:114) tends to divide people and set them aggressively at odds with one another in defense of narcissistic investments and certainly undermines the ability of both individuals and groups to adhere to the love commandment's ideal of including all persons within the circle of love and concern. As Freud notes: "It is always possible to bind together a considerable number of people in love, so long as there are other people left over to receive the manifestations of their aggressiveness" (ibid.).

Against visions of worldwide community, then, Freud argues that there will always be outsiders whom we will not only fail to love but will actually hate (*SE* 18 [1921]:102–4; 21 [1930]:114). This is true even though the group leader embodies an ideal of "an all-embracing love of mankind," as Christ is said to do for Christians, who are exhorted by his example to love universally (*SE* 18 [1921]:134–5). Freud seems to suggest that despite the psychological support for extending love in imitation of Christ that identification with him provides,[5] the best that Christians generally end up doing

5. In the "Postscript" to *Group Psychology* (*SE* 18 [1921]:134–5), Freud highlights how identification with Christ provides Christians with a powerful psychological support for acting in accordance with its ideal of love that is absent in hierarchically organized secular groups like the army. The crucial difference between the Church and the army centers, in Freud's opinion, on the way soldiers relate to their superior compared with the way Christians relate to Christ. In the case of the soldier, the superior officer is taken as an ideal and is unquestionably obeyed. For a soldier to identify himself with the general would be ridiculous because it would involve trying to act as he does—that is, to command others. But the Christian does not make himself similarly ridiculous by identifying with Christ. The Church adds libidinal ties that differ significantly from the libidinal pattern found in the army. The Church resembles the army (and other hierarchical groups) insofar as "every Christian loves Christ as his ideal and feels himself united with all other Christians by the tie of identification" (ibid.). But the Christian not only must idealize Christ, he or she "has also to *identify* himself with Christ and *love* all other Christians as Christ loved them" (ibid., emphasis added). Freud comments, ironically, regarding "this further development in the distribution of libido in the [Christian] group" that it is probably "the factor upon which Christianity bases its claim to have reached a higher ethical level" (*SE* 18 [1921]:135). For further discussion of the psychodynamics involved in Freud's interpretation of identification with Christ, see Wallwork 1982; pp. 285–8.

is to "love all other *Christians* as Christ loved them" (*SE* 18 [1921]:134, emphasis added).[6]

Despite his emphasis on narcissism and aggression as establishing barriers to extending love beyond the boundaries of specific groups, Freud admits, if only in a backhanded way, that it may be possible to care about everyone to some small degree, but it is only a very "small modicum of . . . love [that] will fall to . . . [the] stranger" (*SE* 21 [1930]:110). This is in keeping with his observation in *Group Psychology* that Eros directs human beings to ever widening circles of humanity, even while the death instinct and aggression counter this move. Presumably, the small degree to which we can love everyone is sufficient to give everyone "equal consideration" in treating them with fundamental human decency—that is, in avoiding injuring them and in respecting their individual rights. But Freud seems to believe that the love commandment requires more than a "modicum" of universal regard. His treatment of it indicates that he understands the commandment to require universal affection, so that one is to have the *same* libidinal investment in strangers as in family, friends, and comrades.[7] And this, to Freud, is plainly impossible for the vast majority of human beings.[8]

There are, however, less stringent interpretations of the command to love thy neighbor as thyself, and it is therefore useful to examine the normative objections that Freud levels at the commandment to see if they apply to and effectively undermine all versions of it, including those that do not require the same depth of feeling to be accorded to all persons. More-

6. Freud does not think the Christian's identification with Christ's allegedly all-embracing love generally leads to universal love, because church members have to find something of themselves in others in order to love them, and non-Christians obviously do not share the same ego ideal as Christians. Moreover, "the narcissism of minor differences" leads Christians to deprecate outsiders, even when they are actually not all that different, which is why Freud suggests that the love commandment normally gets translated as embracing with Christlike love only other Christians.

7. This is a rather unusual reading. As Furnish (1982) points out in a response to my 1982 article on Freud's critique of the love commandment, neither the Hebrew Scriptures nor the New Testament emphasize deep affection. In Leviticus the principle of love of neighbor has to do with refraining from economic exploitation, not affection. Similarly, in the New Testament, it has to do not with universal affection but with "nonretaliation, refusing to show partiality, and active good will and service to those in need."

8. Freud is willing to acknowledge, however, that capacities for sublimation of aggression and libido differ, and that a small minority of exceptional, "saintly" people do succeed in "directing their love, not to single objects but to all men alike"—for example, St. Francis of Assisi (*SE* 21 [1930]:102). E. R. Wallace is thus wrong in arguing that Freud has no way of distinguishing between the behavior of Mother Teresa and that of Charles Manson (1986b, p. 94). Even so, Freud has ethical reservations on the value and legitimacy of such universal love (see *SE* 21 [1930]:102).

over, by looking at Freud's normative critique of the love commandment, it is possible to discern some of the content of his own normative views on social ethics.

THE UNFAIRNESS OF EQUAL UNIVERSAL LOVE

Freud's second major objection to the love commandment is the predominantly ethical claim that even if we could manage to love a complete stranger equally with an intimate, it would "be *wrong* to do so" (*SE* 21 [1930]:109). "My love is valued by all my own people as a sign of my preferring them, and it is an injustice to them if I put a stranger on a par with them," Freud writes (*SE* 21 [1930]:109–10). When Freud speaks of an "injustice" in treating a stranger on a par with an intimate, he has in mind the "duties" imposed by special relations that arise out of the reciprocal nature of social interactions (*SE* 21 [1930]:109). An "injustice" is done to one party when that party does not receive the preference that is due and can be reasonably expected because of the relationship.

The importance of reciprocity in normal relations that underlies Freud's concept of injustice in this second criticism is reflected in his view that the abandonment of mutuality in "normal" love constitutes a perversion. Freud is morally distressed by those highly exaggerated forms of romantic love that involve the kind of overidealization that "may be described as 'fascination' or bondage," in which there is an extreme and long-lasting impoverishment of the lover's ego (*SE* 18 [1921]:113–14). He objects because special relations built on these grounds are unfair to the lover, in that they lower his self-regard excessively and lead to an unwarranted neglect of the self's legitimate interests vis-à-vis the other, who fails to return anything equivalent to what he or she has been given.[9] The implicit ideal

---

9. One of Freud's major moral concerns was to help people stand up for their own rights and interests. Unlike the mainstream of Western moralists, who assume that human beings naturally take care of their own interests and so have to be exhorted to look out for others, Freud was impressed by the human tendency to subordinate one's own interest in favor of a loved one or the aims of a group. He objected ethically to such subordination both because the self's legitimate interests are unfairly neglected and because people who fail to take care of their own interests tend not to be very good at looking out for the interests of others.

Freud gave early expression to these views in an 1885 letter to his fiancée, Martha Bernays: "Look here, I really don't understand you at all. To be quite so good-natured as to let people get away with everything and to become incapable of taking offense really ceases to be a virtue . . . A human being must be able to pull himself together to form a judgment, otherwise he turns into what we Viennese call a *guten Potschen* [a doormat] . . . I know that with you all this springs from pity, but human beings, apart from feeling pity for others, must have consideration for themselves as well" (E. L. Freud 1975, pp. 159–60).

behind Freud's disparagement of such an arrangement is a concept of re-ciprocal exchange in which the lover is replenished by the return of love even as he is diminished by altruistic behavior (ibid.; see also *SE* 14 [1914]:87–90, 98–102). Likewise, when someone becomes nar-cissistically self-absorbed and makes a habit of withdrawing from other people with whom he or she is involved in special relations, this is unfair to those others who have reason to expect that love will be reciprocated in roughly equivalent measure.[10]

For Freud, the median position between the extremes of self-sacrifice and self-absorption is a form of reciprocity or mutuality that is the key to a healthy relationship. Here, the self both gives and receives back again. There is no narrow calculation of egoistic or narcissistic satisfactions, though these must be roughly equivalent to the agent's expenditures over time. When the other is in need, one does not normally calculate the costs and benefits of helping the other, but rather expects that the relationship will provide sufficient rewards in the long run to cover current expendi-tures. Initially, love tends to be narcissistically expensive because the be-loved is grossly "overvalued"; but this is not a problem for Freud as long as the depletion is eventually restored by the return of love. "Love in itself, in the form of longing and deprivation, lowers the self-regard; whereas to be loved, to have love returned, and to possess the beloved object, exalts it again" (*CP* 4 [1914]:57). Happiness in love involves both a transfer of libido from the self to the other and a "return of the libido from the object to the ego" (ibid.). From this vantage point on reciprocity in love, it is readily apparent why Freud thinks one party is unfairly treated and has a right to complain when the partner squanders love indiscriminately on strangers. The other is not returning what is due in terms of the implicit contract governing the relationship. The problem with the love command-ment, then, in part is that it counsels promiscuity. "A love that does not discriminate," Freud writes, "seems to me to forfeit a part of its own value, by doing an injustice to its object" (*SE* 21 [1930]:102).[11]

10. Such narcissistic withdrawal is also disastrous for the agent, because as Freud puts it, the human ego is "obliged to send forth its libido in order not to fall ill of an excessive accumulation of it" (1952, p. 428). In other words, excessive self-love may be worse than excessive altruism, even from an exclusively prudential point of view.

11. The argument that the love commandment is unfair to those to whom we are commit-ted by special relations applies as well to some act-utilitarian theories that require one *always* to act in such a way as to increase the greatest good of the greatest number. Surely such conduct tends to be unfair to intimates unless some further assumptions are made, as they are by J. S. Mill, for example, to the effect that the greatest good is realized by everyone's attending to his or her own special relations, because the fact that most people usually know the needs of their

"NOT ALL MEN ARE WORTHY OF LOVE"

Freud's third major objection is directed primarily against the familiar proposition that we are to assume a generally benevolent attitude toward whatever strangers we happen to meet (*SE* 21 [1930]:102, 110–14).[12] The norm once again is reciprocity, but here the accent is on our relations with non-intimates or strangers. His argument is that we are not obliged to love others more than they love us and that, in general, the stranger is quite likely to be hostile: "Men are not gentle creatures who want to be loved . . . ; they are, on the contrary, creatures among whose instinctual endowments is to be reckoned a powerful share of aggressiveness. As a result, their neighbour is for them not only a potential helper or sexual object, but also someone who tempts them to satisfy their aggressiveness on him" (*SE* 21 [1930]:111). Despite the ubiquity of innate aggressiveness, in most circumstances aggression awaits provocation or is sublimated, according to Freud (ibid.). Especially in intimate relations, aggression tends to be inhibited and deflected by countervailing libidinal forces. Those to whom we are tied by special relations are not readily disposed to harm us, or, if they are, the effects are usually harmless humor or mild hostilities encased in affectionate feelings. Strangers, however, have considerably less hesitation in injuring us, in taking advantage of us when the opportunity arises, and in enriching themselves at our expense. These psychological facts must be taken into account, Freud urges, in determining our reciprocal obligations to strangers.

The love commandment is unfair to those it instructs because it fails to prepare them adequately to defend themselves against the aggressiveness they are bound to encounter in life.

> In sending the young out into life with such a false psychological orientation, education is behaving as though one were to equip people starting on a Polar expedition with summer clothing and maps of the Italian Lakes . . . The strictness of those demands would not do so much harm if education were to say: 'This is how men ought to be, in order to be happy and to make others happy;

---

intimates better than those of strangers means that they generally do a better job of meeting those needs.

12. It confirms our earlier argument that Freud rules out selfless universal love, understood as equal affection for everyone, only as psychologically impossible that he here employs ethical, not psychological arguments against treating everyone initially with a generally benevolent attitude. If he could rule out equal treatment in this sense, by contrast with equal affection, as psychologically impossible, he would not need to invoke ethical considerations at all.

but you have to reckon on their not being like that.' Instead of this the young are made to believe that everyone else fulfils those ethical demands—that is, that everyone else is virtuous. It is on this that the demand is based that the young, too, shall become virtuous.

(SE 21 [1930]:134, n.1)

The moral position in social ethics is wary willingness to extend basic fairness, not blindly optimistic, open-minded embrace.

Not all strangers are equally hostile toward us. Some, for example, are inhibited by engrained moral attitudes. Freud is ready to respond in kind to nonmalevolent strangers. "If he [a stranger] behaves differently, if he shows me consideration and forbearance as a stranger, I am ready to treat him in the same way" Freud declares (<i>SE</i> 21 [1930]:110). Indeed, if the "commandment had run 'Love thy neighbour as thy neighbour loves thee,'" Freud says, he would not object to it (ibid.).

THE LOVE COMMANDMENT INTENSIFIES AGGRESSION

Freud's fourth charge against the love commandment is that its call for universalizing love paradoxically tends to intensify outgroup hostility. The focus here again is on the treatment of strangers; but the normative concern is not, as in the third criticism, with giving them more than their due, but with giving them less. The ethical principle that informs this fourth criticism is non-injury, or nonmaleficence,[13] which Freud assumes we owe to everyone, although it can be overruled in cases of self-defense or justified punishment. Freud's argument is that the love commandment heightens aggression in the name of love by encouraging denial and repression of instinctive tendencies that can only be sublimated, not eliminated. Denial and repression make aggression, like sexuality, all the more unruly and dangerous because eventually instincts always find channels of expression. Since aggression cannot be eradicated, there are only two options for handling it. Either aggression is sufficiently available to consciousness to be guided by reason, or it is left to find whatever paths happen to be available, regardless of consequences. By repudiating all 'non-loving' inclinations and requiring unalloyed love for everyone, the love commandment is ultimately unable to guide aggressive impulses. Indeed, it makes it hard to justify even indirect expressions of hostility through jokes and gibes which,

13. This principle proscribes killing, infliction of pain, or, generally, injury of others. As Ross points out, it is "a duty whether or not we have an inclination that if followed would lead to our harming them" (1930, p. 22).

Freud observes, provide "a convenient and relatively harmless satisfaction of the inclination to aggression, by means of which cohesion between the members of the community is made easier" (*SE* 21 [1930]:114).

To the contrary, the lofty standards of the love commandment actually tend to foster self-righteous deprecation of outsiders, who are condemned for not subscribing to principles of conduct as virtuous as those of true believers.[14] Because moral righteousness is preserved by projecting disavowed motives onto nonbelievers, this devaluing of others tends to be exceptionally cruel and serves as a spur to aggression against them.[15] For these reasons, the love commandment historically has had the odd consequence of promoting "extreme intolerance," resulting in the massacres of the Jews in the Middle Ages, for example (ibid.; see also *SE* 22 [1933]:210). Among Christians, awareness of intolerance and cruelty is supposed to lead to repentance, but in Freud's view this time-honored response only serves to reinforce the original principle with its overblown piety and denial of hostility, which is the root of the problem. What is needed is a lowering of moral expectations combined with less self-deception about one's own motivations.

The principle of nonmaleficence augments the role of reciprocity in Freud's ethic. Combined with what Freud says elsewhere about gratitude, justice, and truthtelling, it indicates that his ethic includes general obligations to others that require more than formal reciprocity alone. Freud believes that these substantive moral principles should govern our behavior toward other people even when there has been no prior relation at all and apart from any mutually advantageous interaction or exchange.

THE LOVE COMMANDMENT AS A SOURCE OF UNHAPPINESS

Freud's final criticism of the love commandment is that trying to live up to its unrealistic requirements is a significant source of unhappiness. Freud does not object to the love commandment simply because it is a superego

14. It follows, Freud argues, that "once the Apostle Paul had posited universal love between men as the foundation of his Christian community, extreme intolerance on the part of Christendom towards those who remained outside it became the inevitable consequence" (*SE* 21 [1930]:114).

15. Freud points out in *The Future of an Illusion* that individuals within a group or culture often find narcissistic satisfaction in the mere holding of high ideals rather than the practice of them (*SE* 21 [1927]:13). The narcissistic satisfaction provided by the cultural ideal also fosters enmity by encouraging hypocritical comparisons between the in-group's ideals and the behavior of those outside.

demand that inhibits instinctual gratification.[16] For Freud, some moral requirements are essential for any life worthy of human beings.[17] The problem lies, rather, with the commandment's overblown requirements, any departure from which is an occasion for the intensification of guilt feelings, even when the departure is merely a thought or a wish (*SE* 21 [1930]:124). The love commandment is often interpreted in a way that makes it impossible or exceedingly difficult to fulfill; yet little attention is paid to psychological difficulties and, when it is, we are admonished that "the harder it is to obey the precept the more meritorious it is to do so" (*SE* 21 [1930]:143). The mistaken assumption is that "a man's ego is psychologically capable of anything that is required of it, that his ego has unlimited mastery over his id" (ibid.). The psychic cost to the individual is "extraordinary severity of conscience," measured not only in the traditional terms of conscious guilt for disobedience, but in debilitating neurotic symptoms and in "permanent internal unhappiness" (*SE* 21 [1930]:128).[18]

One of the main themes of *Civilization and its Discontents* is the way in which civilized morality, as exemplified by the love commandment, lowers the general level of happiness in modern societies. But it is no less true that for Freud some moral principles are necessary for social existence. Freud is no opponent of culture and civilization per se, no naive admirer of man in his original state of nature. Without moral rules, Freud recognizes, we would all suffer the greater miseries of a Hobbesian state of all against all (*SE* 21 [1927]:15). "If one imagines [the] prohibitions [of civilization] lifted," Freud warns, what one would have is rampant rape, murder, and theft. For "then . . . one may take any woman one pleases as a sexual object, . . . without hesitation kill one's rival . . . or anyone else who stands in one's way, . . . [and] carry off any of the other's man's belongings without asking leave . . . [—that is, until one runs into] the first difficulty: everyone else has exactly the same wishes as I have and will treat me with no more consideration than I treat him" (ibid.). Civilization consists—and must consist—in part of "the regulations necessary . . . to adjust the relations of men to one another" (*SE* 21 [1927]:6). Freud is a critic of certain

16. Freud writes: "Everyone of discernment will understand . . . that it is not merely a question of the *existence* of a superego but of its relative strength and sphere of influence" (*SE* 21 [1930]:125, n.2, emphasis original).

17. Freud recognizes that moral rules are "in the interest of man's communal existence, which would not otherwise be practicable" (*SE* 21 [1927]:40), and that without them, we would be reduced to an unbearable state of conflict (*SE* 21 [1927]:15).

18. Freud writes in this connection: "The more virtuous a man is, the more severe and distrustful is . . . [the superego's] behaviour, so that ultimately it is precisely those people who have carried saintliness furthest who reproach themselves with the worst sinfulness" (*SE* 21 [1930]:125–6).

features of civilization's moral heritage, but not an advocate of its destruction (*SE* 21 [1930]:115–16). He appreciates the rule-utilitarian argument that the gains to everyone from moral constraints on instinctual gratification have a moral weight that goes far toward justifying the cost in internal unhappiness that each individual must pay. The inherent instinctual aggressiveness of human beings perpetually threatens society with disintegration and *requires* civilization "to use its utmost efforts in order to set limits to man's aggressive instincts and to hold the manifestations of them in check by psychical reaction-formations" (*SE* 21 [1930]:112). Freud knows that society must have its methods "to incite people into identifications and aim-inhibited relationships of love" (ibid.). His point is simply that the price of the love commandment, as he understands it to operate in the individual psyche and in culture, is simply too high, since similar (or even greater) benefits in terms of societal peace and happiness can be obtained from more reasonable moral standards. "When we justly find fault with the present state of our civilization . . . when, with unsparing criticism, we try to uncover the roots of its imperfection, we . . . are not showing ourselves enemies of civilization. We may expect gradually to carry through such alterations in our civilization [especially, in its moral code] as . . . will escape our criticisms" (*SE* 21 [1930]:115).

Indeed, Freud's critique of the love commandment furnishes the outlines of an ethic that he would find compatible with psychoanalytic insight and his goal of shaping moral prescriptions to human psychological possibilities. If the highly idealized version of the love commandment that Freud attacks is inadequate as a guide to moral conduct because its demands to cultivate thoroughgoing selflessness and to make an equally deep emotional investment in all persons are futile and ultimately self-defeating, there nevertheless remains a place for ideals and moral edicts that are intended to counter humankind's aggressiveness and narcissism (see *SE* 21 [1930]:112). Freud clearly recognizes the importance of obligations based on reciprocity, nonmaleficence, and a level of restriction of instinctual desires justified by considerations of public utility. But such an ethic would have to acknowledge both the individual's entitlement to a certain measure of happiness and satisfaction—indeed, that maximum measure of happiness consistent with the well-being of others and the functioning of society—and also the priority and distinctive nature of obligations incurred in special relations.[19] There is in this ethic no *duty* to incur great self-

19. It should be noted that leading theologians and philosophers have always found ways of underscoring the obligations incurred in special relations, without undermining charity toward strangers. However, they have not always been very clear about how to resolve con-

sacrifice on behalf of non-intimates or non-group members. The principle of nonmaleficence, not supererogation, guides Freud's moral views and suggests to him that we would all be better off trying to put into practice the moral minimum—enunciated by the maxim *primum non nocere*, "above all, or first, do no harm"—rather than trying unsuccessfully to realize the high moral aspirations frequently associated with the law of love. But though Freud is firmly opposed to acts of supererogation without regard to self-concern and our obligations in special relations, it is not inconsistent with his position to have as a general principle mutual aid—that is, the notion that one should go out of one's way to assist someone, even a stranger, when the cost to oneself is not unreasonably great.[20] Freud was not in favor of moral callousness or eschewing basic human decency.[21] He lamented the fact that "our times have unfortunately made us so shy and suspicious that we no longer dare take human sympathy in others for granted" (letter 199 [1923], to Édouard Monod-Herzen, in E. L. Freud 1975, p. 341) and presumably believed that human sympathy was something that should be extended—warily. Freud himself went considerably beyond the moral minimum and sometimes exerted himself on behalf of others at considerable personal cost. He incurred significant financial loss, for example, to treat those who could not otherwise afford his ministrations,[22]

flicting obligations so as to avoid the injustices that concern Freud. See Aquinas, *Summa Theologica*, II–II, Q. 26, art. vi.

20. Freud was somewhat leery of making principles like mutual aid into "commandments" or "duties," because he feared the destructive consequences of superego retaliation for non-compliance. He leaned toward encouraging other-regarding behavior by way of virtues rather than duties. Truly moral conduct is motivated by "good" impulses, he argues (*SE* 14 [1915]:283), even if good motives are never unalloyed with "bad" impulses. Thus, it is better to encourage cultivation of desirable dispositions that spontaneously result in care for others than to require such care as a moral "commandment."

21. Browning is thus wrong to conclude that Freud is led by his belief in the death instinct and innate aggression to the position that reciprocity does "not support loving initiatives toward the other—be it neighbor, stranger, or overt enemy" (1987, p. 138). Browning appears to base his interpretation on certain polemical passages in *Civilization* in which Freud argues that not all persons are worthy of love. But Freud's point is not to read some people out of the moral community of humankind, but rather to drive home the educational point—against naive beliefs in the innate gentleness and kindness of *Homo sapiens*—that we should be prepared for our neighbors to act egoistically and aggressively, even when we act kindly toward them (see *SE* 21 [1930]:134, n.1).

22. For ten years, Freud set aside one or two hours a day to treat indigent patients free of charge—until he discovered that patients who did not pay anything did not benefit as much from psychotherapy, in part because the work was too far removed from the real world, in part because they were deprived of a strong motive for bringing the treatment to an end (see *SE* 12 [1913]:132).

and he gave generously of his time and money to colleagues and friends.[23]

That Freud's apparent repudiation of the love commandment is actually a reinterpretation of it along more modest lines is indicated by his explicit embrace of an ethic of universal love. Four years before his harsh indictment of the love commandment in *Civilization and its Discontents,* Freud wrote to Romain Rolland, whose broad humanism he respected, that "I myself have always advocated the love of mankind not out of sentimentality or idealism but for sober, economic reasons: *because in the face of our instinctual drives and the world as it is* I was compelled to consider this *love as indispensable* for the preservation of the human species as, say, technology (letter 217 [1926], in E. L. Freud 1975, p. 364; emphasis added). In 1933, Freud returned to this theme and explicitly embraced the classic rubric of the love commandment, which he now interpreted much more broadly than in *Civilization and its Discontents,* in terms of harnessing the life instincts, or Eros, against man's propensity for cruelty and war. "If willingness to engage in war is an effect of the destructive instinct, the most obvious plan will be to bring Eros, its antagonist, into play against it. Anything that encourages the growth of emotional ties between men must operate against war . . . There is no need for psycho-analysis to be ashamed to speak of love in this connection, for religion itself uses the same words: 'Thou shalt love thy neighbour as thyself'" (*SE* 22 [1933]:212). But ever the realist, Freud adds, "This, however, is more easily said than done" (ibid.).

23. For example, he helped finance Rank's education (Gay 1988, p. 471) and provided continuing financial help for the "Wolf Man" after he returned to Vienna (Gardiner 1971, pp. 265–7). He even gave a penniless student patient a large sum of money upon completing his consultation (see Eissler 1964). Freud wrote to one lifelong friend that he had always been permitted to give something to many people in his life, whereas fate had allowed him to receive only from this friend (letter 193, in E. L. Freud 1975, p. 335). As Eissler points out, Freud's use of the word *dürfen* ("to be permitted") here implies that charity is a *privilege for the giver.* This attitude is "a rare index of the truly charitable" (1964, p. 206, n.5).

Chapter 10
Normative Aspects of Psychoanalytic Practice

> The work of psycho-analysis puts itself at the orders of precisely the highest and most valuable cultural trends.
>
> —Freud

The evidence brought forward so far that Freud recognized the genuineness of other-regarding motives and utilized norms like injustice, reciprocity, nonmaleficence, and utility in critiquing excessively high moral ideals indicates that the founder of psychoanalysis assumed the validity of some moral sentiments and was not personally opposed to making use of traditional moral principles in his "applied" psychoanalytic work. But this evidence stops short of demonstrating that psychoanalysis is inevitably bound up with certain moral propositions. The entanglement of psychoanalysis with normative standards will be explored in this chapter.

That psychoanalysis is bound up with any moral standards whatsoever has been questioned on the grounds that it is a supposedly value-free science and therapy. Hartmann, for example, contends that psychoanalysis includes within its study of the content and form of the mental life of individuals the values that are inherently part of mental life but treats them like any other facts. It observes, describes, classifies, and explains moral phenomena, studies their role or function, and assesses their degree of power or authority, of rigidity or flexibility, without passing judgment as to what is good or bad. Moral evaluations, Hartmann (1960) argues, are beyond the psychoanalyst's competence as a scientist and his task as a therapist.

The warrant in Freud for treating psychoanalysis as value-neutral is the following, often quoted passage from *New Introductory Lectures:* "Psychoanalysis . . . is incapable of creating a *Weltanschauung* of its own. It does not need one; it is a part of science and can adhere to the scientific *Weltanschauung*" (*SE* 22 [1933]:181). However, it is to be noted that Freud does not say in this passage (or anywhere else) that the scientific world view to which psychoanalysis adheres is non-evaluative. To the contrary, and in marked contrast with some of his younger followers, Freud appreciated that the scientific world view holds certain values, like the value of knowledge and its disinterested pursuit, in very high esteem. Thus, Freud is not embarrassed to write that the psychoanalyst has "a *duty* . . . to carry on . . . research without consideration of any immediate beneficial effect" (*SE* 16 [1916–17]:255, emphasis added) and that "the great *ethical element* in ψA [psychoanalytic] work is truth and again truth" (in Hale 1971, p. 171, emphasis added).[1] He would have agreed with C. P. Snow's thesis in "The Moral Un-neutrality of Science" (Snow 1962; cited by Ramzy 1983, p. 555) that the scientific world view places great weight on the intrinsic value of pursuing the truth, facing the truth, and acting on the truth—even when this involves the sacrifice of personal interests.[2] Indeed, it can be plausibly argued—as it has been by Rieff (1961), Kohut (1977), and Meissner (1983)—that the single most important value to Freud and, by implication, to psychoanalysis is unflinching devotion to the truth, no matter how unpalatable.[3] It is the intrinsic value of understanding the deep truths about human beings and their behavior that undergirds the psychoanalyst's commitment to nonjudgmental analysis, which allows hidden truths about the self to rise to consciousness.[4]

1. Regarding the intrinsic value of knowledge and truthfulness, Freud states emphatically that science emphasizes "submission to the truth and rejection of illusion" (*SE* 22 [1933]:182). Hence, in saying that psychoanalysis is committed only to the scientific *Weltanschauung,* Freud is not saying that it is value-free but that its values are those of science. Meissner has recently made much the same point (1983, pp. 587–8).

2. Freud is quoted as having said: "During my whole life I have endeavoured to uncover truths [*Wahrheiten aufzudecken*]. I had no other intention and everything else was completely a matter of indifference to me. My single motive was the love of truth" (quoted by Sterba 1978, p. 186).

3. Rieff has popularized a view of Freud, which Kohut (1977, pp. 64–6) echoes, as devoted to truth at the expense of health values. He offers as evidence several autobiographical statements in which Freud indicates that he was originally drawn to medicine not by "any craving . . . to help suffering humanity," but by "an overpowering need to understand something of the riddles of the world in which we live and perhaps even to contribute something to their solution" (*SE* 20 [1927]:253). But the dichotomy Rieff draws between truth and health values is a false one. Freud did not view the pursuit of truth as in any sense incompatible with the realization of such values as freedom and happiness. To the contrary, Freud sees psychological knowledge as not only intrinsically good—"It is well worth while trying to solve *any* psychological problem for its own sake" (*SE* 13 [1913]:22)—but as a means to the realization of the values of both freedom (autonomy) and happiness. His writings are full of references to the various benefits of psychoanalytic knowledge and therapy and to the conviction that the truth both frees and heals (see, e.g., *CP* 2 [1913]:354).

4. This commitment to truth has radically different implications when applied to the human psyche than it does when applied to the nonhuman phenomena studied by the natural

Freud also associates humanistic values with psychoanalysis's commitment to the scientific Weltanschauung that are somewhat foreign to the standard form of understanding of the sciences as value-neutral. The scientific method, in its persistent questioning of authority, settles differences not by external force or irrational persuasion but by appealing to the common rational nature of the disputants (see *SE* 21 [1927]:53; 22 [1933]:213). It thus encourages such virtues as patience (*SE* 21 [1927]:54), courage (in critiquing authority and facing reality), humility (before the evidence), mutual tolerance, and respect (*SE* 12 [1914]:152; see also Ramzy 1983).

But this is not all. Freud believed that the scientific Weltanschauung also entails devotion to the good of humankind. That is to say, the scientist is not only supposed to be disinterested in the pursuit of knowledge, he or she is to be so in the context of concern for the good of others. The scientist's altruism should be at least as strong as that of the traditionally religious person. The scientific Weltanschauung, Freud writes, is devoted to "the same [ultimate] aims as those whose realization . . . [the religious person] expect[s] from . . . God . . ., namely the love of man and the decrease of suffering" (*SE* 21 [1927]:53). But the scientist is less impatient and self-seeking than the religious person, because he or she expects these goals to be realized only imperfectly, only "very gradually, only in the unforeseeable future, and for a new generation of men" (*SE* 21 [1927]:54). The scientist is willing to suffer for humanistic goals even where no compensation is possible during his or her one and only life (ibid.).

THERAPEUTIC VALUES AND NORMS

Freud was no less aware that the value-neutral stance that the analyst adopts in therapy is also justified by moral values that are constitutive of the therapeutic relationship. That is to say, the analyst's seeming neutrality toward the patient's behavior is not strictly speaking value-neutral at all, but

---

sciences. For one thing, it implies, as the pursuit of objective knowledge of the external world does not, that self-knowledge has a special value, quite apart from personal happiness. Indeed, the audacity to know oneself in psychoanalysis has been called an "extreme fulfilment of the classical command engraved over the entrance of the temple of Apollo in Adelphi: *Gnothi seauton*—Know thyself" (Sterba 1969, p. 439). The intrinsic value of self-understanding calls for such virtues as openness and honesty with oneself, courage in facing the chaos within and the difficulty of overcoming natural tendencies to sham, evasion, self-deception, and hypocrisy, as well as tolerance of disavowed parts of oneself (*SE* 12 [1914]:152). These virtues are rather obviously not necessarily part of the scientific attitude outside clinical psychiatry.

an instrumental means in the service of the twin moral goals that govern psychotherapy: the relief of suffering and improvement of the patient's capacity for enjoyment and freedom of action.[5]

"Patients . . . are *best helped* if . . . [the analyst] carries out his task coolly," Freud counsels (*SE* 20 [1926]:254). By this he does not mean that the therapist should be as impersonally detached as a natural scientist, his famous recommendations to the contrary, that the psychoanalyst serve as a mirror and act like a surgeon, notwithstanding.[6] Freud did not believe that therapy could occur in the absence of "sympathy and respect" (*SE* 2 [1893–5]: 282–3). To the contrary, he urged analysts to meet their patients with "the most sympathetic spirit of inquiry" (*SE* 7 [1905]:16) and cautioned against too austere a therapeutic style lest the patient suffer more deprivation than any sick person can be expected to tolerate (*SE* 12 [1915]:165).[7] What Freud appears to have had in mind in recommending neutrality in the context of helping the patient is what is now called "benevolent" or "com-

5. Psychoanalysis is one of the healing arts and as such shares the age-old values of healers, ancient and modern; thus it seeks to reduce pain and suffering (see Ramzy 1983, p. 563). Freud even suggests (*SE* 20 [1926]:255–6) that "'secular pastoral worker' . . . might well serve as a general formula for describing the function which the analyst . . . has to perform in his relation to the public." Because patients come to analysis seeking not only self-knowledge but relief from their suffering, there has from the very first existed "an inseparable bond between cure and research," Freud writes (*SE* 20 [1926]:256). "Knowledge brought therapeutic success. It was impossible to treat a patient without learning something new; it was impossible to gain fresh insight without perceiving its beneficent results" (ibid.). Psychoanalysis in Freud's view is no panacea. It helps to relieve mainly neurotic suffering; the patient may continue to suffer from the common human misery (*SE* 2 [1893–5]:305). The psychoanalyst examines the patient's value structure neutrally in order to help the patient understand unconscious conflicts between what he or she desires to do and what he or she believes one should not do, between inborn needs and desires and acquired defenses (see Ramzy, 1983, p. 564).

6. Freud is famous for recommending that the analyst maintain a certain emotional distance from the patient. In this connection, he uses the analogy of the surgeon to recommend that the analyst put "aside all his feelings, even his human sympathy, and concentrate . . . his mental forces on the single aim of performing the operation as skilfully as possible" (*SE* 12 [1912]:115). But Freud was aware that a surgical strike is a temporary strategy and that it is not inconsistent with maintenance of a respectful and sympathetic relationship. Indeed, he criticized some of his early disciples for taking his "precepts [about analytic neutrality] literally or exaggerat[ing] them" (Meng and Freud 1963, p. 113). In a 1927 letter, he criticized the "listless indifference" of one of his disciples and commended, instead, "a cordial human relationship" with patients in analytic treatment (ibid.). For discussion, see Kohut 1977, pp. 255–6.

7. He also states in this connection that "some concessions must of course be made to him [the patient], greater or less, according to the nature of the case and the patient's individuality. But it is not good to let them become too great" (*SE* 17 [1919]:164).

passionate" neutrality—that is, a warmly tolerant understanding that communicates concern for the patient's well-being in a nonthreatening way that enables the patient to bear the frustrations of the analytic situation and to bring forward the unconscious beliefs, feelings, and motivations that are a primary cause of his or her suffering.[8] In this benignly supportive environment, the analyst refrains from expressing moral disapproval and from moral instruction, not because he or she is neutral about values but precisely because the therapist's commitment to the intrinsic value of beneficence dictates that in this setting the best therapeutic method is to concentrate on clarifying and interpreting nonjudgmentally.[9] The analyst inhibits the wish to heal now, adopting a stance of temporary goallessness, for the sake of the long-range goal of analysis[10]—namely, to heal as effectively as possible. This goal is not only the negative one of reducing the patient's suffering that Freud's famous line about substituting ordinary unhappiness for neurotic misery (*SE* 2 [1893–5]:305) is often taken as implying, but also the positive one of enabling the patient to enjoy life as fully as possible and to "make the best of him[self] that his inherited capacities will allow" (*SE* 18 [1923]:251; see also *SE* 17 [1919]:164).

Once the analyst's interpretive work succeeds in relieving suffering by improving the patient's access to and control over disavowed motivations,

8. See Stone 1961, pp. 27–32, for a discussion of the analyst's "benevolent neutrality." Greenson (1958) is responsible for the term *compassionate neutrality*. Kohut recommends "muted responsiveness" (1977, pp. 249–66). Such advocacy of benevolence is opposed by Brenner (1979, p. 137), among others, who claims to speak for "an unconvinced minority" of contemporary psychoanalysts who do not believe that the analyst should try to foster rapport by being tactful and humane with analytic patients, as proposed by Zetzel (1966) and Greenson (1965). But even Brenner acknowledges that "a patient should be able to count on his analyst's professional commitment to him as a 'doctor'" (1979, p. 152), which would appear to commit the physician to the Hippocratic oath's duty of beneficence. Although Greenson is misinterpreted by Brenner (1979) as stressing the analyst's humaness at the expense of his analytic work, Greenson (1965, pp. 157–8) makes it clear that the humaness of the analyst comes through in the way in which he works analytically with patients. For a good recent discussion of neutrality, see Hoffer 1985.

9. It is not, as Ernst Ticho (1970, p. 132) would have it, that the analyst holds values firmly without acting on them. The analyst is clearly guided in working with patients by such values as truth telling, beneficence, and respect for autonomy. It is precisely these values that lead the psychoanalyst to conclude that ordinarily it is not helpful for the therapist to express moral disapproval of the patient's behavior or otherwise teach or preach values to the patient.

10. Sterba's report (1978, p. 180) of the Wednesday meetings he attended at Freud's apartment between 1928 and 1932 quotes Freud as worrying that excessive therapeutic ambition gets in the way of the radical truthfulness demanded of the scientifically oriented therapist.

the analyst leaves it up to the patient to decide what he or she wants to do with the newly won self-knowledge (*SE* 20 [1926]:201). The analyst refrains from directing the analysand as to how to act, out of respect for the intrinsic worth of patient autonomy, or self-determination. This means that even if the analysand chooses to act as a scoundrel, the analyst will not intervene, in order to allow the patient the freedom to act in light of who he has come to be. The assumption is that the patient is an autonomous person with his or her own values and that he or she deserves the respect which autonomous persons are rightfully accorded. As Freud says regarding the value of autonomy: "The analyst respects the patient's individuality and does not seek to remould him in accordance with his own—that is, according to the physician's personal ideals; he is glad to avoid giving advice and instead to arouse the patient's power of initiative" (*CP* 5 [1923]:127).

Psychoanalysis differs in its high regard for autonomy from more supportive and ideologically oriented therapies that use the power of the transference to convert the patient to the therapist's personal values and world view. Freud could not be clearer that he disapproved of various therapeutic departures from orthodox techniques on the grounds that they threaten to violate the principle of respect for patient autonomy. He states in criticism of the modifications proposed by Jung and Putnam that they fail to treat the patient as a self-determining moral agent equal in dignity to the analyst:

> We refuse most emphatically to turn a patient who puts himself into our hands in search of help into our private property, to decide his fate for him, to force our own ideals upon him, and with the pride of a Creator to form him in our own image and see that it is good . . . The patient should be educated to liberate and fulfil his own nature, not to resemble ourselves . . . We cannot accept . . . [the] proposal either . . . that psycho-analysis should place itself in the service of a particular philosophical outlook on the world and should urge this upon the patient for the purpose of ennobling his mind. In my opinion, this is after all only to use violence, even though it is overlaid with the most honourable motives. (*SE* 17 [1919]:164–5)

Whenever the analyst is tempted to become a teacher, model, or ideal, Freud cautions, the work of analysis is in danger of being subverted by reimposition of precisely the kind of heteronomy (rule by other persons or conditions) from which the patient previously suffered.

> However much the analyst may be tempted to . . . create men in his own image, he should not forget that that is not his task in the analytic relationship, and indeed that he will be disloyal to his task if he allows himself to be led on by his

inclinations. If he does, he will only be repeating a mistake of the parents who crushed their child's independence by their influence, and he will only be replacing the patient's earlier dependence by a new one. In all his attempts at improving and educating the patient the analyst should respect his individuality. (*SE* 23 [1940]:175)[11]

MORAL ASPECTS OF THE RULES OF TECHNIQUE

Another way in which psychoanalytic technique is entangled with morality is by the rules that govern the analytic relation itself. The first of these rules is the analyst's "duty to tell the patient [what psychoanalytic treatment involves as a commitment] . . . before he [or she] finally decides upon the treatment" (*SE* 12 [1913]:129).[12] This duty to obtain informed consent rests partly on the principle of truth telling but is also warranted by what Freud refers to as the patient's "right," as a self-determining agent equal in dignity to the analyst, to be provided with the information necessary to make an informed choice.[13] If the patient is not provided with this information, he or she has the right, Freud acknowledges, to complain at a later date about having been "inveigled into a treatment whose extent and implications he did not realize" (ibid.). The duty to respect patient autonomy is similarly protected by acknowledgment of the patient's right "to break off

11. Freud also writes: "As the inhibitions in development are undone it inevitably happens that the physician finds himself in a position to point out new aims for the impulses which have been set free. It is but a natural ambition for him then to endeavour to make something specially excellent out of the person whose neurosis has cost so much labour, and to set up high aims for these impulses. But here again the physician should restrain himself" (*CP* 2 [1912]:331).

12. Freud also observes in this connection that "psychoanalysis is always a matter of long periods of time . . . of longer periods than the patient expects. It is therefore our duty to tell the patient this. . . . I consider it altogether more honourable, and also more expedient, to draw his attention—without trying to frighten him off, but at the very beginning—to the difficulties and sacrifices which analytic treatment involves" (*SE* 12 [1913]:129).

13. The analyst has a parallel right, Freud argues, to treat only those patients who are morally worthy of psychoanalytic attention (*SE* 2 [1893–5]:265). Today, the notion that analysts should morally appraise candidates for analysis is in wide disrepute (see, e.g., Sterba 1969, p. 440). But Freud justifies this partly on the grounds that the analyst must believe that his considerable time and effort are worth spending on a particular patient. For, "if the physician has to deal with a worthless character, he soon loses the interest which makes it possible for him to enter profoundly into the patient's mental life," Freud writes (*SE* 7 [1904]:254; see also *SE* 2 [1893–5]:265). Nowadays, analysts advise against letting such moral appraisals enter into the selection of patients for analysis (Tyson and Sandler, pp. 221ff.), yet most would refuse to take into analysis a professional criminal who sought to alleviate guilt feelings about killing or robbing.

[treatment] whenever he [or she] likes," even though the physician may believe that this will be harmful (ibid.). In this circumstance, the analyst should not hide from the patient what he or she believes to be the likely consequences of early termination (see *SE* 12 [1913]:129–30). But ultimately, whether to continue or to terminate lies in the patient's hands.

Keeping promises is another principle that the psychoanalytic relation presupposes as a condition of the possibility of analytic knowledge. The patient promises at the outset to obey "the fundamental rule" of free association, which is to practice the most complete candour and truthfulness possible (*SE* 23 [1940]:173).[14] Such truthfulness goes beyond ordinary truth telling, because the patient is obliged by the promise to seek to tell not only everything that he or she knows subjectively, but also those things that are disavowed and that one has difficulty knowing because one does not care to admit them to oneself (*SE* 20 [1926]:188; 23 [1940]:172–4).[15]

In return, as part of what Freud calls "the pact," the reciprocal agreement that grounds psychoanalytic work morally, the analyst promises several things. In the first place, the analyst promises implicitly to avoid injuring, exploiting, or otherwise harming the patient who, by virtue of the transference, is peculiarly vulnerable. In this connection, Freud singles out for special mention the analyst's duty to avoid exploitation of the transference for sexual gratification. The analyst, he writes, is "absolutely debarred"

14. Freud's patients were also asked to promise not to make any important decisions during the course of the analysis. Freud writes in this connection: "One best protects the patient from disasters brought about by carrying his impulses into action by making him promise to form no important decisions affecting his life during the course of the treatment, for instance, choice of a profession or of a permanent love-object, but to postpone all such projects until after recovery" (*CP* 2 [1914]:373). The importance of nonmaleficence in the ethic that led Freud to this position would seem to support warning third parties of serious harm in situations like the "Tarasoff" case. However, Freud had too much respect for patient autonomy to intervene in a patient's life except in extreme cases where the patient was in danger of seriously harming him or her self (ibid.).

15. Freud writes regarding the truthfulness expected from the analysand: "What we want to hear from our patient is not only what he knows and conceals from other people; he is to tell us too what he does *not* know. With this end in view we give him a more detailed definition of what we mean by candour . . . He is to tell us not only what he can say intentionally and willingly, what will give him relief like a confession, but everything else as well that his self-observation yields him, everything that comes into his head, even if it is *disagreeable* for him to say it, even if it seems to him *unimportant* or actually *nonsensical*" (*SE* 23 [1940]:174). Because "analysis is entirely founded on complete candour," the analyst has a correlative obligation to treat even the most distasteful topics openly and in detail: "This obligation to candour puts a *grave moral responsibility* on the analyst as well," Freud writes (*SE* 20 [1926]:207, emphasis added; see also *SE* 12 [1915]:164).

from forgetting the rules of technique and his sworn duty as a physician to honor the maxim *primum non nocere* "for the sake of a wonderful experience."[16] The domain of "the wonderful experience" from which the analyst is morally debarred includes the showing of affection.[17] The grounds for this latter exclusion are in part that affection can become a slippery slope leading to sexual relations, in part that explicit expressions of affection would disrupt the relationship in ways that would prevent the time together being used to the optimum to improve the patient's mental health.[18] Such affection would also pose difficulties for the therapist's (and the patient's) other intimate relations—that is, third parties would suffer.

Another rule that guides the psychoanalyst's work is the principle of confidentiality. The physician is obligated to protect the patient's privacy. Whether or not the protective privilege of medical confidentiality should yield in cases where serious harm to third parties may result, as in the "Tarasoff" case in which a therapist failed to warn a woman of his patient's intention to murder her, Freud does not say—not surprisingly, given his time and place. But he does indicate that the analyst should not yield the duty of confidentiality to simple utilitarian calculations. For example, one does not discuss successful psychotherapy cases publicly if the privacy of the patient would be violated, even though publication of this material might be beneficial to clinical science. The reason for this is primarily respect for the patient as a person whose privacy deserves to be protected. But the principle of respect for persons is not the only source of the psychoanalyst's duty of confidentiality. The importance of the principle of confidentiality is reinforced in the analytic situation by the implicit promise that the analyst makes at the outset of an analysis to practice the "strictest discretion." As Freud put his views on the nature of the reciprocal promise making that constitutes the psychoanalytic relation:

> We form a pact with each other. The sick ego promises us the most complete candour—promises, that is, to put at our disposal all the material which its self-

16. Freud frequently reiterates the moral requirement that the analyst not yield to sexual desire. For example, he writes that "to yield to the demands of the transference, to fulfil the patient's wishes for affectionate and sensual satisfaction, is . . . justly forbidden by moral considerations" (*SE* 20 [1926]:227).

17. "Real sexual relations between patients and analysts are out of the question, and even the subtler methods of satisfaction, such as the giving of preference, intimacy and so on, are only sparingly granted by the analyst" (*SE* 23 [1940]:176).

18. Freud makes it clear that part of "the justification" for requiring analytic abstinence is that it "creates the most advantageous conditions for both parties: for the doctor a desirable protection for his own emotional life and for the patient the largest amount of help that we can give him to-day" (*SE* 12 [1912]:115).

perception yields it; we assure the patient of the *strictest discretion* and place at his service our experience in interpreting material that has been influenced by the unconscious. Our knowledge is to make up for his ignorance and to give his ego back its mastery over lost provinces of his mental life. This pact constitutes the analytic situation. (*SE* 23 [1940]:173, emphasis added)[19]

However, there are limits to the analyst's preference for the values inherent in the psychoanalytic situation—that is, the quest for truth and self-knowledge, beneficence, respect for autonomy, and confidentiality. The physician also has "duties . . . toward science" and to the common good that requires that new knowledge beneficial to patients be shared with colleagues. Freud writes in the prefatory remarks to the "Dora" case history:

> In my opinion the physician has taken upon himself duties not only towards the individual patient but towards science as well; and his duties towards science mean ultimately nothing else than his duties towards the many other patients who are suffering or will some day suffer from the same disorder. Thus it becomes the physician's duty to publish what he believes he knows of the causes and structure of hysteria, and it becomes a disgraceful piece of cowardice on his part to neglect doing so, as long as he can avoid causing direct personal injury to the single patient concerned. (*SE* 7 [1905]:8)

Freud concludes that the principle of confidentiality can be safeguarded even as the duty of beneficence or utility is honored by making sure that case material is sufficiently well disguised to prevent a breach of the patient's privacy. Freud assures the reader that he has himself done this in the "Dora" case: "I have taken every precaution to prevent my patient from suffering any such injury" (ibid.).

Psychoanalysis is not value-free, then. If it were, it would be a mere technology that could be used in the service of any values whatsoever, good or bad. Rather than being neutral in the sense of "anything goes," psychoanalysis utilizes a kind of neutrality that is based on an ethical position involving such principles as respect for persons, truthfulness, keeping promises, and confidentiality. The analyst's tolerance, even of those values that are normally not in the analyst's value system, is based on the value placed on truth and patient autonomy and on the belief that a nonjudgmental approach is most apt to benefit the patient. In other words, the fact that

---

19. The analyst promises confidentiality in part in order to facilitate trust: "The complete consent and complete attention of the patients are needed, but above all their confidence, since the analysis invariably leads to the disclosure of the most intimate and secret psychical events" (*SE* 2 [1893–5]:265).

the imposition of values is contrary to analytic work does not mean that values do not pervade the whole psychoanalytic relation. Neutrality itself is justified in moral terms. As Meissner puts it: "Not only is it impossible to keep . . . values out of our analytic work, but, . . . there are times when it is not only therapeutically useful but mandatory that we include them" (1983, p. 596).

PART IV
Foundations of Ethics in Freudian Theory

Chapter 11
Toward a Psychoanalytically Informed Ethic

> Our appointed task of reconciling men to
> civilization will to a great extent be
> achieved . . . when we put forward rational
> grounds for the precepts of civilization.
> —Freud

Contemporary psychoanalysts often acknowledge that as science and therapy, psychoanalysis is unavoidably intertwined with value commitments—with ideals of truth and of patient autonomy and self-responsibility and with concepts of happiness and freedom and the good or worthwhile life (see, e.g., Ramzy 1983; Meissner 1983; Gedo 1983; Erikson 1964, pp. 73, 111–13, 219–23, 236–8; 1968 p. 25). But particularly among academic interpreters of Freud, it is widely believed that psychoanalysis has nothing to contribute to justifying the values that its practice presupposes and seeks to further. Indeed, it is widely held that psychoanalysis's relativistic implications subvert the justificatory task in ethics (Ricoeur 1970; E. R. Wallace 1986b, p. 94). Sometimes this subversive implication is derived from the psychoanalytic construct of the superego, which would seem to entail extreme ethical relativism.[1] The argument here is that if "morality" is synonymous with the superego, as Freud sometimes implied,[2] and if the superego is nothing more than a set of purely arbitrary

---

1. The ethical relativist thesis with which psychoanalysis is sometimes linked is to be distinguished from the weaker claim that psychoanalysis is committed to "cultural relativism" or "psychological relativism." Cultural and psychological relativism are factual, not ethical, doctrines. Cultural relativism claims only that as a matter of fact ethical standards vary cross culturally; psychological relativism holds that it is an empirical fact that individuals hold differing moral standards. *Ethical relativism* is the more radical thesis that ethical disputes cannot be settled, because conflicting ethical judgments are equally valid. It is a metaethical, not an empirical, theory. It is about the possibility of justifying ethical judgments. For discussion of this distinction, see R. B. Brandt 1959, pp. 83–113, 271–94. Brandt is among those who think that the psychoanalytic concept of the superego implies ethical relativism (ibid., p. 143).

2. Freud sometimes seems to equate the superego or conscience, with the whole of moral functioning (see *SE* 22 [1933]:61, 66–7). In *The Ego and the Id*, Freud states that the

standards that the individual internalizes by identifying with and introject-
ing the prohibitions and ideals of his or her parents and other authority
figures, then the ethical claims articulated as the demands of the superego
amount to nothing more than strategies for obtaining rewards and avoiding external punishments and internal guilt in particular situations.[3] There
is no principled basis, then, for choosing one set of ethical norms over
another as guides for action, no grounds for reasoning that might persuade
in the presence of conflict—either of wants or of preferred norms.

A second major source of the belief that psychoanalysis has nothing to
contribute to the philosophical task of justifying ethical standards—indeed, that it actually subverts this task—derives from the concept of the
ego as confined to a form of instrumental or means–end rationality in
which the ends of actions are nothing more than arbitrary personal preferences. In this connection, it is sometimes asserted that psychoanalysis is
one of the principal cultural sources of the collapse of the ancient concept of
substantive practical rationality.[4]

THE SUPEREGO ARGUMENT FOR ETHICAL RELATIVISM

Most psychoanalysts do not dispute the basic portrait of the epis-
temologically blind, autocratic superego.[5] This means that the response to

---

"injunctions and prohibitions" of parents and other authority figures that are introjected
into the ego at the close of the oedipal complex "remain powerful in the ego ideal and continue, in the form of conscience, to exercise the moral censorship" (*SE* 19 [1923]:37). "In
this way," Freud writes a year later: "the Oedipus complex proves to be . . . the source of our
individual ethical sense, our morality" (*SE* 19 [1924]:167–68; see also, e.g., *SE* 19
[1924]:170; 21 [1930]:136–37).

3. Some scholars try to limit the superego's relativistic implications for ethics by drawing
a sharp distinction between origins and justification and then holding that those who derive
relativistic implications from the concept of the superego are guilty of committing the genetic
fallacy by confusing an explanation of the genesis of moral standards with the quite different
issue of whether those standards are justified (see, e.g., Allport 1950, pp. 109–10). But if the
superego represents the whole of morality, the concept of the superego is more than an
explanatory account; it is a thesis about the nature of morality itself: to wit, that the criteria we
use for making moral judgments are based on nothing more than irrational respect for the
arbitrary maxims of parents and other authority figures. This in turn entails the relativist
conclusion that all conflicting ethical judgments are equally valid, since there is ultimately no
way to argue for or against differing standards.

4. This is Rieff's thesis in *Freud: The Mind of the Moralist* (1961).

5. Hartmann et al. state that one should "hesitate to ascribe to the superego anything that
could be termed 'knowledge'" or reasoning (1964, p. 160), resting their claim on Freud's

the charge that the psychoanalytic concept of the superego necessarily implies extreme ethical relativism must hinge on disentangling morality from an exclusive identification with the superego. And indeed, notwithstanding certain pronouncements by Freud that seem to equate morality pretty much in its entirety with superego functions,[6] it is the case that the technical concept of the *superego* is both broader and narrower than the ordinary concept of morality, which in some crucial respects escapes the conceptual net cast by the various uses of the technical term.

The superego is broader than morality because it includes a wide range of ideals or standards that do not relate so much to *moral* right or good as to notions of aesthetics or social convention. Standards for personal appearance, vocational prestige and social status, matters of etiquette, questions of artistic excellence and beauty, can all fall under the sway of the superego without necessarily involving issues of true morality. Conversely, the superego is narrower than the ordinary concept of morality because a number of everyday moral judgments may derive as much from empathic concern for others and from rational deliberation as from introjected prohibitions and fears of punishment. A person may drop what he or she is doing and come to the aid of another in part out of sympathetic identification with the individual in need and in part out of a more or less rational calculation that a world in which the principle of beneficence is implemented is safer and better for all, including the individual who is applying it in any particular instance, than is a world in which callous indifference to the needs of others is the accepted rule and practice.

This is not to say that superego considerations do not also enter into any given moral decision. In seeking to rescue someone from potential danger, for example, a person may also be acting out of a wish to avoid the moral condemnation that would be visited upon him were he to fail to live up to parental ideals and also out of positive identification with protective parental figures whose traces are now enshrined in the idealized images of the superego.[7] But normally, the superego is responsible only for certain aspects of morality; superego functions take over the whole of moral func-

---

comment that "analysis . . . shows that the super-ego is being influenced by processes that have remained unknown to the ego" (*SE* 19 [1923]:51).

6. See n. 2 above.

7. Before he came up with the concept of the *superego,* Freud often referred to these introjected, idealized traces of parents and other authority figures as the "ego ideal" (see, e.g., *SE* 14 [1914]:93–7, 100–2; 18 [1921]:110, 112–14), and he continued to use this term even after he introduced the term "super-ego." But despite its name, the ego ideal is by structure and origin part of the superego, not the ego.

tioning only in severe obsessional disorders.[8] In the absence of marked pathology moral judgments and actions rely not only on the internalized standards and automatic self-scrutiny of the superego, but also on such ego functions as reality testing, memory, conceptualization, thought, delibera- tion, and action. In fact, morality is normally impossible without an ego that identifies conflict situations in the real world, thinks about normative standards, evaluates which standards are applicable, and chooses the course of action believed to be right. Moreover, an ego that can do all this can also evaluate internalized ethical standards to ascertain whether, as Freud put it, ethical "precepts are justified rationally" (*SE* 23 [1939]:122). Thus, even ideals, standards, rules, and prohibitions that originated as primitive au- thoritarian introjections can be subjected to the more rational scrutiny of the mature ego.[9] Once it is clearly recognized that the superego does not hold a monopoly on all aspects of moral functioning, the way is clear to conceptualizing a kind of ethics that does not necessarily entail ethical relativism. Hartmann is often credited with first pointing to the possibility of a more adaptive, ego-based ethics, primarily in his essay *Psychoanalysis and Moral Values* (1960).[10] And Erik Erikson is well known for refining and

8. When obsessional disorders cause superego functions to take over the whole of morali- ty, the individual becomes very rigid and severe with self and others and expends a great deal of energy compulsively going over his conduct and thoughts, trying to smoke out and control "evil" tendencies. By contrast, the schizophrenic is incapable of moral functioning, in part because his premoral narcissism prevents the requisite development of object cathexis with others. Although the schizophrenic may be subject to the edicts of harsh inner voices that command his psychotic thoughts and behavior, his orientation is to avoid punishment from alien forces. Guilt is infrequent or unknown.

9. R. B. Brandt is thus wrong in asserting that psychoanalysis "contains no theory of the extinction of ethical values. It has nothing to say about changes in ethical standards during adult years, as a result of information and reflection" (1959, p. 143).

10. Other authors have also distinguished between superego moralism and ego ethics in various ways. Thus, Fromm (1947) sees ego ethics as involving realization of the humanistic virtues associated with what he calls the "productive character" and superego morality as involving blind surrender to an internalized external authority (see Fromm 1947). Likewise, existentialist psychotherapists distinguish "neurotic guilt" from "real guilt." Neurotic guilt is "stimulated by impulsivity per se within an intrapsychic context—determined by the past and therefore inappropriate in the present—associated with a blurred perception of reality . . . [,] unrealistic expectation of punitive retaliation . . . [, and] arousal of aggression which is di- rected against [the] self—[combined with an] implicit threat of physical mutilation." Real guilt is stimulated "by a deed or contemplation of a deed within an interpersonal context— determined by the immediate situation—derived from a clear perception of reality . . . [and] of one's action upon others—[combined with] repentance and atonement directed at repara- tion of relationship— . . . [and accompanied by an] implicit threat of psychological separa- tion" (Haigh 1961, p. 129). On the basis of this contrast, Haigh concludes that neurotic guilt is "a symptom of sickness," real guilt "an inevitable condition of human existence" (ibid.).

further developing the distinction between superego morality and ego ethics.[11]

What is not so widely appreciated is that Freud himself was well aware of the difference between superego moralism and a more ego-syntonic ethics. It is precisely this distinction that he had in mind when he wrote: "It may be said . . . of the ego that it strives to be moral . . . and of the super-ego that it can be supermoral and then become as cruel as only the id can be" (*SE* 19 [1923]:54). He often discussed the harshness of the primitive superego and contrasted it with the developmentally later role of the ego in moral behavior.[12]

THE EGO AND MEANS—END RATIONALITY

The distinction between superego morality and ego-based ethics that Freud, as well as other psychoanalytically oriented moral theorists make, clearly assumes a fairly prominent role in moral functioning for ego rationality. Yet those who believe that psychoanalytic theory entails an extreme ethical relativism that subverts the rational justification of ethical standards rely in part on what they take to be psychoanalysis's weak conception of the ego. In *The Ego and the Id*, for example, Freud described the ego as "a poor creature owing service to three masters"—id, superego, and external reality (*SE* 19 [1923]:56). He seemed to present the ego as possessing for an independent resource only the reality principle (*SE* 19 [1923]:25)—paltry indeed when compared with the pleasure principle—

11. For example, in *Insight and Responsibility,* Erikson forcefully declares: "I would propose that we consider *moral rules* of conduct to be based on a fear of *threats* to be forestalled. These may be outer threats of abandonment, punishment and public exposure, or a threatening inner sense of guilt, of shame or of isolation. . . . In contrast, I would consider *ethical rules* to be based on *ideals* to be striven for with a high degree of rational assent and with a ready consent to a formulated good, a definition of perfection, and some promise of self-realization. . . . The moral and the ethical sense are different in their psychological dynamics, because the moral sense develops on an earlier, more immature level" (1964, p. 222; emphasis original). He further holds that ego ethics fosters the actualization of a schedule of virtues appropriate to a person's age, stage, and condition, whereas superego morality is more punitive and repressive (ibid., pp. 111–57).

12. In *Group Psychology and the Analysis of the Ego* Freud contrasts the harshness of the ego ideal or conscience with the "real ego" (*SE* 18 [1921]:109–10). In *The Question of Lay Analysis* he discusses neurotic superego functioning as primitively punishing the ego (*SE* 20 [1926]:223). In *Civilization and its Discontents* he addresses the stages of development of conscience and contrasts the roles of the superego and ego in moral behavior (*SE* 21 [1930]:123–33). In *New introductory Lectures on Psycho-Analysis* he discusses the relationship of the superego to the ego in the formation and functioning of conscience (*SE* 22 [1933]:57–67).

and as limited in its activity mostly to mediating among the interests of the three authorities it serves (*SE* 19 [1923]:56).

Likewise, he compares the ego's dealings with the id to those of "a submissive slave who courts his master's love" and its dealings with the superego to a spineless politician "who sees the truth but wants to keep his place in popular favour" and so "only too often yields to the temptation to become sycophantic, opportunist[ic] and lying" (ibid.). The ego is like the submissive slave in that it dutifully "obey[s id] instincts" and like the politician in that it temporizes in disguising "the id's conflicts with reality and . . . with the superego" (ibid.).

If this view of its powers were definitive, the Freudian ego would function only in the truncated terms of what Max Weber called bureaucratic or means–end rationality (*Zweckrationalität*).[13] Instead of generating substantive normative standards based on its own reasoning, it would be able to do no more than determine the most practical means to achieve id-based desires (within the limitations set by the superego and reality) and then furnish the means chosen with ethical-sounding justifications—or, as Freud put it, to "clothe the id's [unconscious] . . . commands with its [own preconscious] rationalizations" (ibid.). This is the ego that Yankelovich and Barrett, among others, harp on when they write: "The Freudian ego has no purpose of its own. It is 'the servant of the id'. . . . The drives of sex and aggression define the root motives of human life. The ego is then merely a calculating and control mechanism to help ensure their fulfilment. Such is the view implied by the notion that the ego has no energies of its own and derives whatever force it has from the 'all but omnipotent pleasure principle'" (1970, pp. 82–3).

Rieff, who like Yankelovich and Barrett has argued that psychoanalysis is one of the principal cultural forces in our era responsible for the collapse of belief in substantive rationality (*Wertrationalität*), charges that the Freudian ethic is fundamentally nihilistic. In *Freud: The Mind of the Moralist* he identifies the Freudian ethic as an "ethic of honesty" (1961, pp. 350–1)[14]

13. Max Weber defines *Zweckrationalität* as a this-worldly, relativistic form of consequential reasoning. In its pure form, it treats values as "simply . . . given subjective wants" and focuses chiefly on means and consequences. It contrasts with *Wertrationalität* which is rational action oriented to absolute values (see M. Weber, 1964, pp. 116–77). For a good discussion of Weber's typology of action, see Little 1974.

14. In their recent sociological study of the beliefs that shape the way in which contemporary Americans live, Bellah et al. similarly argue that psychotherapeutic culture places great importance on honesty, as a consequence of the collapse of belief in substantive rationality. For when all values are viewed as depending on changing personal preferences, it is only through open "communication that people have a chance to resolve their differences, since there is no larger moral ideal in terms of which conflicts can be resolved . . . Solving conflicts becomes a

and declares that "for Freud, . . . honesty brings one into touch with the emotional depths, where all beliefs are equivalent. . . . To accept the equivalence of all beliefs is to dare life without them" (ibid., p. 351). He goes on to say that,

> as a purely explanatory and scientific ideal, honesty has no content. Though the Freudian training involves intellectual judgment (it is, after all, psycho*analysis*), based on a calm and neutral appraisal of all the demanding elements of a life-situation, still, the freedom to choose must end in choice. Here, at the critical moment, the Freudian ethic of honesty ceases to be helpful.
>
> Being honest, admitting one's nature, does not resolve specific issues of choice. The Freudian ethic emphasizes freedom at the expense of choice. To achieve greater balance within the psyche, to shift the relative weights of instinct and repression, installs no new substantive rules of decision. (Ibid., p. 352)

Despite the reading of Freud in which the ego sounds only in means–end rationality, however, psychoanalytic theory does not unequivocally embrace the weak ego on which the charges of extreme ethical relativism depend. Freud himself objected to making his comments about the ego in *The Ego and the Id* "a corner-stone of a psycho-analytic *Weltanschauung*" (*SE* 20 [1926]:95) and expressly repudiated a one-sided view of the ego as weak and spineless. And even in *The Ego and the Id* the metaphors of the submissive slave and the opportunistic politician are offered only as characterizations of certain postures taken by the ego toward its three referents. The ego is also said to be capable of controlling, inhibiting, and mastering alien impulses and requirements. In *Inhibitions, Symptoms and Anxiety,* in which Freud set about exploring the strengths and capabilities of the ego, he explicitly points out that "The ego . . . can exert a very extensive influence over processes in the id . . . and . . . is able to develop . . . surprising powers. . . . We are very apt to think of the ego as powerless against the id; but when it is opposed to an instinctual process in the id it has only to give a *'signal of unpleasure'* in order to attain its object with the aid of . . . the pleasure principle" (*SE* 20 [1926]:91–2).[15] To concentrate exclusively "on

---

matter of technical problem solving, not moral decision. Lying, which would interfere in a critical way with the ability to communicate accurately and resolve interpersonal conflicts, is thus wrong, but, even here, wrongness is largely a matter of practicality—it doesn't pay" (1985, p. 7).

15. In this work, Freud emphasizes that the ego "controls [both] the path to action in regard to the external world . . . [and] access to consciousness" (*SE* 20 [1926]:95). When it comes to the specific issue of how to "reconcile this acknowledgement of the might of the ego with the description of its position . . . in *The Ego and the Id,*" Freud does not completely denigrate his prior observations of the ego's dependent relation to the id and the superego, but rather calls for a balanced view of the ego in which "knowledge of the way in which repression works" keeps the analyst from focusing only on its dependencies (ibid.).

the weakness of the ego in relation to the id and of our rational elements in the face of daemonic forces within us" is, Freud warns, to adopt "an extreme and one-sided view" (*SE* 20 [1926]:95) that is not at all the position he embraced.

Those who argue that psychoanalysis exists in opposition to the possibility of substantive rationality and the basic tenets of civilized morality also overlook the fact that in his work on civilized culture, Freud expressly saw the ethical significance of his theory as a whole as supporting, not subverting, morality. The aim of the psychoanalytic investigation of morality, Freud argued, is not to overthrow morality but to find those ethical principles that are most congruent with human nature. Thus Freud characterized as "simple-minded" the "fear . . . that all the highest goods of humanity [including the] ethical and social sense . . . will lose their value or their dignity because psychoanalysis is in a position to demonstrate their origin in elementary and animal instinctual impulses" (*CP* 5 [1923]:128).

He emphasized that "it is not our intention to dispute the noble endeavours of human nature, nor have we ever done anything to detract from their value" (*SE* 15 [1916–17]:146–7) and declared that psychoanalytic "treatment should find a place among the methods whose aim is to bring about the highest ethical and intellectual development of the individual" (letter 80 dated 30 Mar. 1914, in Hale 1971, p. 176).[16]

One of the main themes of Freud's late period is that religion places ethics on such a weak foundation that the entire moral consensus that

---

16. It is in Freud's later writings that most of his positions on ethical issues are articulated. Until about 1920, Freud was content to focus psychoanalytic study on the unconscious and to leave the study of morality, religion, and other higher cultural activities to other disciplines. Only when he began to conceive of psychoanalysis as a general psychology did he also begin to tackle some of these larger cultural issues. Prior to that, he often deals with ethical questions by simply stating that he takes ethical principles for granted. He seemed to take comfort in declaring that, "'As to morals, that goes without saying,' as the hero of Vischer's novel *Auch Einer* was wont to say" (*CP* 1 [1905]:262); and when he felt compelled to go beyond this glib response, he confessed that he did not really understand the foundations of morality. Thus, in a letter to Putnam in 1915, he stated: "When I ask myself why I always have striven honestly to be considerate of others and if possible kind to them and why I did not give this up when I noticed that one is harmed by such behavior and is victimized because others are brutal and unreliable, I really have no answer. It surely was not the sensible thing to do. . . . Why I—as well as my six adult children—are compelled to be thoroughly decent human beings, is quite incomprehensible to me" (Hale 1971, p. 189–90). Although these comments are sometimes taken as implying that Freud had no ethical interests whatsoever, the fact is that in his late writings, he attempted to provide answers to these questions. In so doing, he partially fulfilled his youthful dream of contributing something to the solution of philosophical and "cultural problems" (*SE* 20 [1925]:72).

sustains social cooperation in modern societies is in danger of collapsing as secularization continues its inevitable progress.[17] In marked contrast to ethical relativists who see reason as incapable of justifying normative standards, Freud declares that the time has come to "put forward rational grounds for the precepts of civilization" (*SE* 21 [1927]:44). He does not regard the past as a golden moral age of substantive rationality but as a time of authoritarian religious ethics that need to be put on more reasonable foundations.[18] Psychoanalysis has a major contribution to make to this task by presenting clinically informed criticisms of the old ethic and by highlighting the resources in human nature on which such a rational ethic might be built. Thus Freud observes: "We still know too little about the human soul. Only when this knowledge is greater, will we learn what is practicable in the field of ethics, and what we can do in the way of education without doing harm" (letter 36 in Hale 1971, p. 122).

The idea that Freud aspired to have psychoanalysis contribute to a secular, reason-based ethic may seem odd in light of the fact that so much of Freud's career went to demythologizing the role of reason in human affairs. No one has done more to challenge the belief that dispassionate consideration of evidence and arguments are the predominant determinants of human conduct. But while Freud clearly perceived the limits of reason, he nevertheless aimed to help people to become more rational than they otherwise would be by giving them tools to begin to understand the irra-

---

17. Religion no longer has the same influence on people that it used to," Freud observed. "This is . . . because people find . . . [its promises] less credible. . . . So long as . . . [the great mass of the uneducated and oppressed] do not discover that people no longer believe in God, all is well. But they will discover it . . . Is there not a danger . . . that the hostility of these masses to civilization will throw itself against the weak spot that they have found in their task-mistress? If the sole reason why you must not kill your neighbour is because God has forbidden it and will severely punish you for it in this or the next life—then, when you learn that there is no God and that you need not fear His punishment, you will certainly kill your neighbour without hesitation, and you can only be prevented from doing so by mundane force. Thus . . . the relationship between civilization and religion must undergo a fundamental revision" (*SE* 21 [1927]:38–9).

18. Freud criticized religion not only for placing ethics on an inadequate foundation but also for encouraging hypocrisy. He writes that people "have always known how to externalize the precepts of religion and thus to nullify their intentions," and that "priests, whose duty it was to ensure obedience to religion, have met them half-way in this. . . . One sinned, and then one made a sacrifice or did penance and then one was free to sin once more . . . It is no secret that the priests could only keep the masses submissive to religion by making . . . large concessions . . . to the instinctual nature of man. . . . In every age immorality has found no less support in religion than morality has" (*SE* 21 [1927]:37–8).

tional aspects of themselves and thus to take the first steps toward bringing into the province of reason what had previously been that of passion.

THE RATIONAL FOUNDATIONS OF ETHICS

Although Freud never directly pursued the question of what he would consider to be the "rational bases" for ethics, much can be adduced from the criticism he directed at the existing foundations of morality and from what he says about such perennial ethical issues as happiness as the goal of life, love of others as a natural disposition, the good of community, and the value of shared rules.

With respect to metaethics—that is, how we establish and justify moral norms—it is clear that Freud rejected the ontological notion embraced by both religious ethics and classical Western philosophy that there is a super-sensible moral order, a transcendent nonnatural realm, that gives us objective moral values. In letters to Pfister, Freud asserts that the ontological belief in "a moral world order" is a "pious illusion" that is "in conflict with reason" and contrary to "all that we experience and have to expect in this world" (in Meng and Freud, 1963, pp. 123, 129). For Freud, such a hold-over of religious belief is incompatible with the thoroughly this-worldly or naturalistic approach to human life that is assumed by modern thought in general and by the science of psychoanalysis in particular.[19]

The ontological approach to the foundations of morals, whether religious or philosophical, was also faulted by Freud because it tends to place a halo around conventional moral standards that do not merit such respect and that can actually endanger the social structure. Freud explains:

> Through some kind of diffusion or infection, the character of sanctity and inviolability—of belonging to another world, one might say—has spread from a few major prohibitions onto every other cultural regulation, law and ordinance. But on these the halo often looks far from becoming: not only do they invalidate one another by giving contrary decisions at different times and places, but apart from this they show every sign of human inadequacy. It is easy to recognize in them things that can only be the product of shortsighted apprehensiveness or an expression of selfishly narrow interests or a conclusion based on insufficient premises. The criticism which we cannot fail to level at them also diminishes to an unwelcome extent our respect for other, more justifiable cultural demands. (*SE* 21 [1927]:41)

Likewise, Freud found unacceptable secular intuitionist claims (such as those set forth in 1903 by G. E. Moore in *Principia Ethica*) of access to a

---

19. For further discussion, see Wallwork and Wallwork, 1989.

nonnatural moral order on the grounds that this approach fails to provide good reasons for the ethical standards it commends.[20] The secular ethical intuitionist would have us intuit as self-evident various moral propositions, whereas the religious ethicist would have moral standards be handed down by divine commandment. But in either case, nothing can be said for or against said moral standards except that they were so discovered or received. Such nonnatural mysticism is contrary to the secular, this-wordly assumption that "there is no appeal to a court above that of reason" (*SE* 21 [1927]:28), which informs the entirety of Freud's work, as well as to psychoanalysis's emphasis on trying to find out precisely why we do what we do and on taking responsibility for the reasons that inform our actions. In Freud's words, what is actually "revealed" to whoever claims to have received moral insight from on high is only "primitive, instinctual impulses and attitudes . . ., valuable for an embryology of the soul when correctly interpreted, but worthless for orientation in the alien, external world" (letter of 1930 to Rolland in E. L. Freud, 1975, p. 393).[21] The "grandiose," "mysterious" *ought* of morality that intuition allegedly apprehends "in a mystical fashion" is in its origin nothing more than "the will of the father" (*SE* 23[1939]:122).

Freud's own metaethical position is that moral rules and principles are grounded ultimately in happiness, broadly conceived, and in the "two-fold foundation" of "love" and "social necessity" (*SE* 21 [1930]:101; 21 [1927]:41); thus, they can be rationally justified.[22] Moral obligations are not objective realities to be discovered in the external world or divine commands sent down by God. "It would be an undoubted advantage" over traditional religious and philosophical approaches, Freud writes

if we . . . leave God [or a supersensible moral order] out altogether and honestly admit the purely human origin of all the regulations and precepts of civilization.

20. Sterba's notes on the Wednesday meetings at Freud's apartment in 1928 indicate that Freud was just as critical of "the high esteem of the irrational" in the secular mystic *Weltanschauung* as he was of traditional religion (1978, p. 179).

21. Freud writes similarly of intuition in *Future of an Illusion:* "It is once again merely an illusion to expect anything from intuition and introspection; they can give us nothing but particulars about our own mental life, which are hard to interpret, never any information about the questions which religious [and metaphysical] doctrine finds it so easy to answer" (*SE* 21 [1927]:31–2).

22. Freud argues in *Civilization* that communal life and the moral precepts that govern it are both grounded in "the compulsion to work, which was created by external necessity, and the power of love, which made the man unwilling to be deprived of his sexual object—the woman—, and made the woman unwilling to be deprived of the part of herself which had been separated off from her—her child. Eros and Ananke [Love and Necessity] have become the parents of human civilization too" (*SE* 21 [1930]:101).

Along with their pretended sanctity, these commandments and laws would lose their rigidity and unchangeableness as well. People could understand that they are made, not so much to rule them as . . . to serve their interests; and they would adopt a more friendly attitude to them, and instead of aiming at their abolition, would aim only at their improvement. This would be an important advance along the road which leads to becoming reconciled to the burden of civilization. (*SE* 21 [1927]:41; see also *SE* 7 [1905 or 1906]:307–8)

Freud's position with respect to the *justification* of moral rules—that is, that they are to be grounded in rationality—must be distinguished from his highly dubious theory as to the *origin* of certain moral prescriptions, such as the command against murder and the incest taboo. Freud never repudiated the notion that these fundamental moral rules originated not in rational deliberation and insight into social necessity but in primordial human events—in particular, the killing of the primitive father (see, e.g., *SE* 13 [1913]:100–61; 21 [1927]:42; 23 [1939]:110, 119, 121–2). Freud believed that the reaction to this original patricide is what gave moral rules their peculiar power. But however unscientific Freud's ideas on the historical, phylogenetic origins of certain moral principles may have been, he nevertheless consistently argued that humanity has developed to a point where the historical residues on which morality was founded should be put aside and replaced "by the results of the rational operation of the intellect" (*SE* 21 [1927]:44) so that morality can be independently justified by rational deliberation.[23]

Freud's Critique of Kant's Ethics

The question then becomes, how did Freud understand reason to work in generating substantive norms that are more than mere subjective personal preferences and that have adjudicating force in situations of conflict? Did he point in a direction that might lead to a way out of the post-Kantian dilemma in which it is said that morality must be grounded in human reason alone even though our conception of the limits of reason—a conception due in no small part to Freud himself—seems to imply that reason is completely incapable of generating substantive norms?

The Kantian belief is that reason can generate principles by its purely formal ability to test them under the criterion of universalizability. It is not surprising that scattered remarks in Freud's mature corpus make clear that

23. That the human capacity for reason remains preeminent in Freud's metaethics is of course not to say that Freud ever failed to appreciate the subverting (or sometimes supporting) role of the passions in all human endeavor, including morality.

he did not accept the Kantian view of the nature of practical reason, characterized as it is by the dualism by which Kant distinguished between the
rational self that generates categorical moral imperatives and the sensuous
self that is subject to the play of impulse, habit, and desire.

For Kant, truly moral actions must be performed out of a sense of duty
and reverence for moral law alone and never for an ulterior purpose, such as
satisfaction of an inclination, even an other-regarding one. "The essential
thing in all determination of the will by the moral law," Kant writes, "is that
the will as free should not only be determined without the cooperation of
sensuous desires, but that it should even oppose such desires, and restrain
all natural inclinations that might prevent the realization of law" (*Kritik der
praktischen Vernunft* [in *Sämtliche Werke*, 5. 77]; cited and trans. by Randall
1965, 2:154). This is what Kant called the "fact of reason" (*Factum ra-
tionis*), which he saw as evidence that conscience was a law unto itself—
"self-constrained" and "absolutely inexplicable" (Kant 1956, pp. 68, 82,
89).

Although Freud would agree with Kant's depiction of conscience versus
desire as a matter of purely phenomenological description—that is, what
conscience feels like when it is operating[24]—he clearly finds the Kantian
attempt to separate practical reason from the sensuous self as an actual
requisite for the moral life both psychologically impossible and, as an
attitude toward sensuality, morally self-defeating. From the vantage point
of psychoanalytic insight into developmental vicissitudes, Freud argues
that conscience, far from being "inexplicable" and ineluctably separate from
desire, is in fact developmentally grounded in desire, for it is derived from
the "first object cathexes of the Id, from the Oedipus complex" (*SE* 19
[1923]:48; see also *SE* 19 [1923]:52). Any attempt to sever conscience
completely from desire is bound to fail. The "super-ego is always close to
the id and can act as its representative *vis-à-vis* the ego," Freud declared
(*SE* 19 [1923]:48–9). That moral conscience seems so certain of its sovereign independence is only because it rests on desires that are unconscious.

---

24. In *Totem and Taboo* Freud writes: "What is conscience [*Gewissen*]? On the evidence of
language it is related to that of which one is 'most certainly conscious' . . . Conscience is the
internal perception of the rejection of a particular wish operating within us. The stress . . . is
upon the fact that this rejection has no need to appeal to anything else for support, that it is
quite 'certain of itself' [*ihrer selbst gewiss ist*]. This is even clearer in the case of the consciousness
of guilt [*Schuldbewusstsein*]—the perception of the internal condemnation of an act by which
we have carried out a particular wish. To put forward any reason for this would seem super-
fluous: anyone who has a conscience must feel within him the justification [*Berechtigung*] for
the condemnation" (*SE* 13 [1913]:67–8; *GW* 9 [1913]:85).

Thus, even when it appears to be acting independently of desire, conscience actually "reaches down into the [instinctual] Id" (*SE* 19 [1923]:49). That which is in us of the "highest" is thus simultaneously that which is the "lowest" (see *SE* 18 [1923]:37; 19 [1923]:52; 19 [1924]:167–70).

For Freud, the moral imperative cannot be categorical, in the sense of being explained by itself. In reality, it is motivated by desire. It is only by understanding the subtle unconscious connections between conscience and desire that we can begin to find that degree of distance from desire that is optimal for practical reason.[25] Freud's clinical experience convinced him that it is psychologically impossible to act as Kant instructs—that is, out of a "holy will" motivated by nothing more than respect for duty alone, because desires are always present somewhere in the unconscious background of our conscious reasoning about what we want to do, even when we feel ourselves to be thinking relatively disinterestedly about various courses of action. Freud is in the Aristotelian-Humean philosophical tradition in assuming that in order to guide action, practical reason must be motivated by some desire, want, or interest. Freud understands that moral judgments and conduct are always inspired by a mixture of other-regarding and self-interested motives, both of which Kant contrasted with the allegedly truly moral sentiment of duty for its own sake. As Freud realized, wants are part of human nature that the moralist ignores at the risk of imperiling moral behavior. "There is a limit beyond which . . . [the human] constitution cannot comply with the demands of civilization" (*SE* 9 [1908]:191).

Moreover, from the Freudian perspective, the Kantian moralist who would act out of respect for moral law alone cannot actually do so, because this very desire for moral purity is motivated partly by the narcissistic pleasure found in identification with an ideal self. Freud explains: "A man, when he cannot be satisfied with his ego itself, may nevertheless be able to find satisfaction in the ego ideal which has been differentiated out of the ego" (*SE* 18 [1921]:110). "This ideal ego is now the target of the self-love which was enjoyed in childhood by the actual ego. The subject's narcissism makes its appearance displaced on to this new ideal ego, which, like the

25. In pointing to the connections between conscience and desire, Freud observes that the "super-ego . . . came into being through the introjection into the ego of the first objects of the id's libidinal impulses—namely, the two parents . . . Kant's Categorical Imperative is thus the direct heir of the Oedipus complex" (*SE* 19 [1924]:167; see also p. 170). Later, Freud explains that the aggressiveness of conscience that brings about instinctual renunciation expresses more the child's aggression toward parental authority than that authority's actual aggression toward the child (*SE* 21 [1930]:126–30).

infantile ego, finds itself possessed of every perfection" (*SE* 14 [1914]:94). One simply cannot be as completely disinterested as Kant presumes, and to pretend that one can be is a prescription for hypocrisy.

Similarly, Freud teaches that the contemptuous attitude toward sensuous motivations enshrined in Kant's portrayal of the moral self is usually self-defeating because the effort to isolate reason completely from its connections with the rest of the self has a tendency to boomerang.[26] Practical reason, isolated from affect, as it is in obsessional neuroses, often ends up losing the very control of the self that it sought, because the sensuous parts of the self against which conscience wars find numerous ways of rebelling that defeat the very effort to be moral through rigid conscientiousness. As Freud notes, "When saints call themselves sinners, they are not so wrong, considering the temptations to instinctual satisfaction to which they are exposed in a specially high degree—since, as is well known, temptations are merely increased by constant frustration, whereas an occasional satisfaction of them causes them to diminish, at least for the time being" (*SE* 21 [1930]:126). Temptations that are so rigidly denied may well gain strength and break through moral constraints.

In addition, insofar as the Kantian moralist succeeds in dutifully repressing natural inclinations and isolating the intellect from affect, he or she will still be vulnerable to excesses of guilt. A strong conscience monitors thoughts as well as acts, with the result that highly moral people often feel intensely guilty for fantasies that have not been carried out. Freud writes:

> The super-ego torments the sinful ego. . . . The more virtuous a man is, the more severe and distrustful is its behaviour, so that ultimately it is precisely those people who have carried saintliness[27] furthest who reproach themselves with the worst sinfulness. This means that virtue forfeits some part of its promised reward; the docile and continent ego does not enjoy the trust of its mentor, and strives in vain, it would seem, to acquire it (*SE* 21 [1930]:125–6).

Freud discovered that such guilt can lead highly moral people to actually commit immoral deeds out of a need to punish themselves for their evil thoughts. Guilt in this case is not the result of an immoral act, but its cause.[28] For, as Freud explains, "An increase in [the uncon-

26. As Freud puts it, "the sacrifices imposed upon . . . [the civilized person] . . . reach such a pitch that the 'civilized' aim and end will itself be indirectly endangered" (*CP* 2 [1908]:76).

27. Freud here uses *Heiligkeit*, literally "holiness," which was also Kant's term for the will that acts on the basis of duty alone.

28. See also "Criminals From A Sense of Guilt" (*SE* 14 [1916]:332–3).

scious] . . . sense of guilt can turn people into criminals. . . . [A] very powerful sense of guilt . . . is . . . not . . . [the crime's] result but its motive. It is as if it was a relief to be able to fasten this unconscious sense of guilt on to something real and immediate" (*SE* 19 [1923]:52).

Freud also fully appreciated what Kant did not, that a strict conscience that imagines itself free of the limitations of human nature tends to be so severe that the autonomy of the ego that Kantians view as essential to moral action is actually subverted. Instead of giving rise to "energetic and self-reliant men of action or original thinkers," an overweening superego far more often produces "well-behaved weaklings" (*SE* 9 [1908]:197). According to Freud, "All who wish to be more nobleminded than their constitution allows fall victims to neurosis; they would have been more healthy if it could have been possible for them to be less good" (*SE* 9 [1908]:191).

With these insights, Freud criticizes duty from the perspective of the very autonomy that Kant thought the will's self-legislation would insure. The very effort to become autonomous by the strict self-rule prescribed by the Kantian backfires, and the person ultimately loses the battle for self-mastery to cordoned-off unconscious desires. Alienated from conscience, inclinations become a subversive force that undermines the freedom of the self from within.

Although he certainly set himself off from the Kantian approach to practical moral reasoning, Freud did not mean to imply that a person cannot ever think in relatively disinterested terms about moral principles and problems. To the contrary, he himself stresses the importance of reason acting somewhat independently of desires. In his essay, "The Future Prospects of Psycho-Analytic Therapy," Freud writes: "Powerful though men's emotions and self-interest may be, yet intellect is a power too—a power which makes itself felt, not, it is true, immediately, but all the more certainly in the end. The harshest truths are heard and recognized at last, after the interests they have injured and the emotions they have roused have exhausted their fury" (*SE* 11 [1910]:147).[29]

PRACTICAL MORAL REASONING AND DESIRE

By contrast with Kant, for whom practical reason is supposed to behave as if it were not incarnated in a human body, Freud treats practical rationality as deliberation or reflection about ways of satisfying the desires or

29. See too Freud's well-known statement about the soft, but powerful, voice of reason in *Future of an Illusion* (*SE* 21 [1927]:53; see also *SE* 14 [1915]:187).

interests of human agents that are broadly laid down by a biological tendency. In this view, one has a reason for acting when there is something one wants or in which it is in one's interests to have. It is compatible with this account of practical rationality for a person to act against even strong present desires because an ego interest to be realized in the future may count more heavily than a present libidinous want or aggressive wish.[30] Freud's view of rationality also allows for a person to act out of non-egoistic desires, since through such mechanisms as identification and sublimation, an individual can take another person's ends as his own and derive satisfaction from their fulfillment and so desire or be interested in the well-being of another.[31] To act morally is not, as Kant thought, to act against inclination; it is to act out of those other-regarding inclinations that underlie all genuinely moral conduct.

Kant would object to grounding morality in reasoning about the satisfaction of desires and interests in the belief that this would make moral principles arbitrary and unreliable in the extreme. For Kant, any moral principle that depends on desires and interests is too contingent, because its acceptance then depends on whether those for whom it is prescribed happen to believe in a proposed end or are moved by a particular sentiment, and Kant views emotions, desires, and interests, even altruistic ones, as arbitrary, weak, and changeable in the face of conflict with convenience, self-interest, or inclination (see Blum 1980, p. 37). Kant focuses on how desires and interests vary among individuals and over time within the same individual. He has no concept of ego-syntonic interests or desires rooted in character which can therefore remain steadfast over time; nor does he trust benevolence to stand up to self-interest and the Humean "passions." Accordingly, Kant holds that we should look only to purely rational motives—the sense of duty—and not to emotions for moral motivation. He assumes that, unlike benevolence, the sense of duty can withstand the pressures of desire or self-interest that would lead a person to do something contrary to a morally good—that is, beneficent—act (see Kant 1959, p. 16; Blum 1980, pp. 36–8).

30. Freud recognizes that prudential interests and interests in the welfare of others may conflict with present desires. The contrast he draws between "ego interests" and libidinal "desires" is based on this distinction and shows that in Freud's view not all reasons for action depend on the most powerful current desires.

31. That Freud believed that reasons based on desires and interests need not be self-interested has been established in ch. 6–8 above. See Foot 1978, pp. 148–73, for a good, relatively recent defense of the claim that all reasons for action depend on an agent's interests or desires.

Freud not only rejects explicitly Kant's assumptions about the reliability of the categorical imperative as a guide to moral action, he also rejects implicitly Kant's views of the arbitrary nature—and, indeed, moral unseemliness—of interests and desires. Ego rationality—Freud's version of practical reason—is an adaptive capacity that relates and adapts the entire self—id, ego, and superego—to the external world of persons and things[32] and includes not only intelligence and cognition, but also a definite structure of relatively stable preferences, sentiments, dispositions, and attitudes—some of them other-regarding—that represent the transformations or sublimations of raw id instincts over the long course of normal human development. These relatively stable dispositions are central to the self's integrity and are continually reinforced by the individual's interest in maintaining self-esteem.[33] Practical reason takes account of the rough order of priority among normally developed human desires and interests, in that it stands back from the press of desires and evaluates them in terms of their authenticity and compatibility with the integrity of the self and reorders and coordinates them in accordance with their relative contribu-

32. In psychoanalytic literature, the concept of *adaptation* has frequently been used, following Hartmann, to depict the ego's adjustment of the self to the environment. But the term is used here to include not only autoplastic adaptation, but also alloplastic adaptation, which involves adjusting the environment to the self. That this broader concept is what Freud had in mind is indicated by the following passage in which he takes issue with the excessive passivity of the ego in the exclusively autoplastic interpretation: "The ego learns that there is yet another way of securing satisfaction beside the *adaptation* to the external world which I have described. It is also possible to intervene in the external world by *changing* it, and to establish in it intentionally the conditions which make satisfaction possible. This activity then becomes the ego's highest function; decisions as to when it is more expedient to control one's passions and bow before reality, and when it is more expedient to side with them and to take arms against the external world—such decisions make up the whole essence of worldly wisdom" (*SE* 20 [1926]:201, emphasis original). Commenting on this notion of a "higher ego-function" beyond the aim of biological survival, Guntrip observes that it suggests an entirely different evaluating function, i.e., preserving "the higher values of the true self," or the integrity of the person (1973, p. 106).

33. Freud appears to have been searching for a view of practical reason that would avoid the extremes of both the Humean subordination of reason to the passions and the Platonic-Kantian isolation of reason from the passions. In Freud's mature work, reason has a distinctive role to play in guiding conduct dispassionately, but it is not set over against natural inclinations in the arrogant, defiant manner of the Platonic-Kantian conception. Freud writes: "There is no natural opposition between ego and id; they belong together, and under healthy conditions cannot in practice be distinguished from each other" (*SE* 20 [1926]:201). Loewald points out how Freud's mature concept of "the ego . . . [as] an organization . . . continues, much more than it is in opposition to, the inherent tendencies of the drive-organization" (see 1960, p. 23).

tion, alongside competing desires, interests, settled dispositions, commitments, and loyalties, to the person we want to be.[34]

In Freud's view, these settled, ego-syntonic dispositions are not as capricious as Kant's crude view of the emotions assumes. True, when raw desires are totally repressed, they have a tendency to disrupt conscious thought and action in the way that Kant presumes—which is one reason why obsessional neurotics try to exclude all expressions of desire from morality. But not all desires intrude disruptively on the ego, certainly not those that have been consistently exposed and explored by an ego that has remained in touch with unconscious wishes and is able to channel them where they will do the least harm or the most good. In contrast to Kant, who views all inclinations, including benevolent ones, as "pathological" when they intrude into what ought to be a "pure" realm of unmotivated moral duty,[35] Freud recognizes that other-regarding sentiments from deep within the self are more reliable than cognitive decisions divorced from affect. Freud sees dispositions as providing a far more genuine basis on which to ground morality than categorical imperatives, since they express the self more authentically than disembodied cognitive judgments. Absolutist principles are often not particularly trustworthy guides in complex moral situations because, too often, they lead their duty-bound devotees to sacrifice people to principles; their rigidity leads to the neglect of important subtleties; and the unacknowledged unconscious motives they repudiate tend to erupt without warning to cancel the alleged superiority of the stability of principles over sentiments in the moral life.

Thus, Freud holds that far from being antithetical to morality, psychoanalysis's focus on the emotions and dispositions has an expressly moral

34. Freud points to the evaluative functions of practical reason when, e.g., he observes with respect to a neurotic patient's struggle with newly released unconscious desires: "The patient . . . [is required to] fit these emotions into their place in . . . his life-history, subject them to rational consideration, and appraise them at their true psychical value" (*CP* 2 [1912]:321–2).

35. Kant articulates his position that all natural inclinations toward moral behavior are "pathological" thus: "There are . . . many persons so sympathetically constituted that without any motive of vanity or selfishness they find an inner satisfaction in spreading joy, and rejoice in the contentment of others which they have made possible. But I say that, however dutiful and amiable it may be, that kind of action has no true moral worth. It is on a level with [actions arising from] other inclinations . . . But beneficence from duty, when no inclination impels it and even when it is opposed by a natural and unconquerable aversion, is practical love, not pathological love; it resides in the will and not in the propensities of feeling, in principles of action and not in tender sympathy; and it alone . . . [has moral worth]" (1959, pp. 14–16).

aim. One of the primary purposes of the psychoanalytic criticism of repressive moralities within both the self and the larger culture is to enable
persons, by resolving the neurotic conflicts generated by excessive superego moralizing, to gain the increased capacity for moral authenticity that
comes from getting in touch with genuine other-regarding sentiments.
Thus, Freud states that "The work of psycho-analysis puts itself at the
orders of precisely the highest and most valuable cultural trends, as a better
substitute for the unsuccessful repression" (*SE* 11 [1910]:53).

He elaborates on the moral service of psychoanalysis thus:

> People are afraid of doing harm by psycho-analysis; they are afraid of bringing
> the repressed sexual instincts into the patient's consciousness, as though that
> involved a danger of their overwhelming his higher ethical trends . . .
> But . . . the final outcome that is so much dreaded—the destruction of the
> patient's cultural character by the instincts which have been set free from repres-
> sion—is totally impossible. . . . Our experiences have taught us with certain-
> ty . . . that the mental and somatic power of a wishful impulse, when once its
> repression has failed, is far stronger if it is unconscious than if it is conscious; so
> that to make it conscious can only be to weaken it. An unconscious wish cannot
> be influenced and it is independent of any contrary tendencies, whereas a con-
> scious one is inhibited by whatever else is conscious and opposed to it. . . . *These
> [unconscious] wishes are destroyed by the rational mental activity of the better impulses
> that are opposed to them. Repression is replaced by a condemning judgement carried out
> along the best lines.* That is possible because what we have to get rid of is to a great
> extent only the consequences arising from earlier stages of the ego's develop-
> ment. . . . In his present-day maturity and strength, he will perhaps be able to
> master what is hostile to him with complete success. . . . It then becomes pos-
> sible for the unconscious instincts revealed by . . . [psychoanalysis] to be em-
> ployed for the useful purposes which they would have found earlier if develop-
> ment had not been interrupted . . . [i.e.,] for . . . socially valuable [goals]. (*SE*
> 11 [1910]:52–4, emphasis added in part)

Surprisingly for someone to whom a dark view of human nature is
generally attributed, Freud believes that most human beings possess a core
of genuinely other-regarding motives and mechanisms for sublimation[36]

36. Freud held that sublimation provides a "quite natural psychological explanation" of
genuine morality, as contrasted with the pseudo-morality of the narcissist and the reaction-
formation morality of the obsessional neurotic. (See letter in Hale 1971, p. 190, and Sterba
1969, p. 189). But he was also aware that sublimation is often inhibited by the tangle of
internal obstacles and defenses that constitute a neurosis. It is not only our evil and selfish
motives that commonly get repressed, but also the spontaneous, naturally good inclinations
that arise as a consequence of sublimation. Freud comments: "It really does happen that, in
contrast to the usual state of affairs, the conscience, the better, the 'nobler' impulses suffer

that, if allowed expression, can provide a basis for the formation and adoption of moral principles to guide public and private conduct.[37] According to Freud, the respect for the dignity and worth of persons that undergirds all authentic morality is an outgrowth of love,[38] but it is not something chosen as an optional value. Rather, it is a fundamental aspect of personality formation, and so basic that those who do not share it stand not only almost beyond the pale of ordinary moral discourse, but also outside what can be considered normal psychology. It is the mark of the severe sociopath or psychopath or the extreme narcissistic personality disorder to lack the other-regarding sentiments essential to morality.[39] This is because Freud views the self as irreducibly social. The self does not exist except as constituted through the long process of psychosocial development, beginning with the infant's deep attachment to the mother, during which he or she comes to understand him or her self through such processes as identification, object love, introjection, internalization, and transference.[40] These complex interactional processes require both that the self direct its affections outwardly toward the world of persons and that it recognizes that the others who respond are fundamentally very much like the self (see, e.g.,

---

repression instead of the instinctually 'wicked' and unacceptable" (letter in Meng and Freud 1963, p. 126). Freud was confident of leaving moral "synthesis" to the fully analyzed patient in part because he assumed that the moral sentiments that existed in a patient would find a natural place in the person's character structure after analysis. "In the technique of psycho-analysis there is no need of any special synthetic work; the individual does that for himself better than we can" (ibid., p. 62). See also *SE* 12 [1912]:119.

37. Freud thought that in most people, other-regarding sentiments are sufficiently strong to support moral conduct toward intimates. But he expressed conflicting opinions about the extent to which other-regarding sentiments support *social obligations* in the larger society. (Compare *SE* 14 [1915]:284 with *SE* 14 [1915]:282 and 21 [1930]:140–41.) In his late writings, especially *Future of an Illusion,* he expressed the hope that most people are or can be motivated to comply with reasonable social obligations (see *SE* 21 [1927]:8–9).

38. See ch. 7 and 8 above.

39. Freud implies that psychopaths suffer from a defect not of cognitive reasoning but of normal emotional development. One cannot bring them into the moral community by presenting them with good reasons, but only, if at all, by employing therapies designed to alleviate their serious emotional pathologies.

40. Each of these processes refers to ways of handling *inter*personal relations. For example, identification is in part a matter of empathy, of imagining oneself in another person's shoes, in part a matter of imitation or modeling oneself on others. But it also involves a degree of merging, so that the boundaries between self and other become blurred. Freud's views on identification imply that the self requires for its development and flourishing intimate engagement with others, because it is through identification with others and modeling oneself after them that the self develops over time.

SE 14 [1914]:73–102; 14 [1917]:243–258; 18 [1921]:69–143). Out of this process grows genuine other-regard. Because part of what it means to be a self is to recognize that others also possess dignity and worth, unqualified egoism is not usually an option for normal people. Our interpersonal feelings and commitments are too deeply rooted for us to completely disregard the interests of others.

Freud's belief in other-regarding sentiments as the natural emotional underpinnings of morality did not keep him from a full appreciation of the strenuousness of the truly moral life. Somewhat ironically, insofar as he posits other-regarding sentiments as the natural basis for morality, Freud is in partial agreement with the so-called humanistic psychology movement associated with Rogers, Maslow, Perls, and Fromm that arose in part in reaction to what was taken to be the threat to traditional moral values posed by psychoanalytic orthodoxy and that holds that authentic morality results from the actualization of certain natural tendencies at work in the human organism. But Freud departs significantly from humanistic psychologists in repudiating the idea that everything natural must be morally good and that everything that is morally good comes to us naturally. Freud, who on the most abstract level balances the principle of Eros with that of Thanatos, the life instincts with the death instincts, never forgets that along with benevolence, human beings also have a natural tendency to be brutal, violent, cruel, and egoistic and that, unless carefully monitored and guided, sublimated and repressed, these aspects of human nature can be as powerful as, and often more powerful than, other-regarding moral motives. Accordingly, Freud holds no truck with the sort of easy optimism of the self-realization psychologists.

"Belief in the 'goodness' of human nature is one of those evil illusions by which mankind expect their lives to be beautified and made easier while in reality they only cause damage," Freud warns (*SE* 22 [1933]:104). By helping people to hide their baser motives from themselves, the illusion of human goodness is likely to increase the power of egoistic and aggressive inclinations that always lie just below the surface of human behavior and that lead so-called virtuous people to do evil in the name of the right and the good.

Similarly, though he sometimes appreciates the inspirational functions of moral discourse,[41] Freud realizes that the sort of exhortations that

41. He wrote to Rolland that he "revered" him as an "apostle of love for mankind" and for writing so movingly about "the most precious of beautiful illusions, that of love extended to all mankind" (letters 200 and 217, in E. Freud 1975, p. 341, 364). But he saw his own contribution as that of the critic who presupposes the existence of high goals, but tries to keep people

moralists throughout history have held dear can have little effect on the repressed passions that threaten our best ethical efforts (letter to Putnam, dated 14 May 1911, in Hale 1971, p. 121, and *SE* 12 [1915]:164).[42] Instead, he saw the path to the moral life as lit by precisely the sort of brutally honest, continuous effort to discover and own up to our true desires and impulses, bad and good, that is attempted in psychoanalysis. What is base in the individual is not to be repudiated or denied, but rather to be uncovered and then guided and sublimated into morally acceptable channels. In a nutshell, Freud would have us follow this principle: "Be as moral as you can honestly be and do not strive for an ethical perfection for which you are not destined" (letter in Hale 1971, p. 122). If we do this, Freud observes, morally acceptable sublimations will tend to follow naturally as a matter of course, to the extent that individual character permits.[43] With characteristic realism, he states that after a successful analysis of inner defenses, "whoever is capable of sublimation will turn to it inevitably as soon as he is free of his neurosis. Those who are not capable of this at least will become more natural and more honest" (letter to Putnam, in Hale 1971, p. 122).

---

honest even as they aspire to realize what is possible. Thus he writes: "I have not pleased, comforted, edified . . . [my readers]. Nor was this my intention; I only wanted to explore, solve riddles, uncover a little of the truth" (letter 223, in ibid., p. 370).

42. Regarding moralistic language, Freud observes: "When levelled at the passions, lofty language achieves very little, as we all know" (*CP* 2 [1915]:382–3).

43. Freud's experience showed him that sublimation tends to follow release of repressed instinctual desires. "The patient's capacity for sublimating his instincts plays a large part [in the cure] and so does his capacity for rising above the crude life of the instincts" (*SE* 23 [1940]:181).

Chapter 12
How Is Practical Reason Guided? Happiness and the Basic Goods of Life

We . . . turn to the . . . question of what men themselves show by their behaviour to be the purpose and intention of their lives. What do they demand of life and wish to achieve in it? The answer to this can hardly be in doubt. They strive after happiness; they want to become happy and to remain so . . . Reflection shows that the accomplishment of this task can be attempted along very different paths; and all these paths have been recommended by the various schools of worldly wisdom and put into practice by men.

—Freud

Freud distinguishes two types of practical reason in the course of explicating the ego's functions (see, e.g., *SE* 21 [1930]:140–1). First, there are personal reasons for action that deal with the well-being of the agent, which Freud refers to as "egoistic" or "narcissistic" reasons, even though they may include the welfare of other persons, insofar as the agent is interested in them. Second, there are social or impersonal reasons for action that have to do very broadly with the welfare of others or the community. For Freud, ethics is concerned primarily with social reasons for action, because its chief function is to adjudicate conflicts of interest. This aspect of practical reason will be discussed in chapter 13. The focus of this chapter is Freud's normative theory of personal reasons for action—the reasons that ought to guide individuals as they go about living their individual lives. These personal reasons are important morally in part because they make up the reasons that ultimately justify distinctively moral reasons for action; but they are also important ethically, because they identify the premoral goods that occasion many of the interpersonal conflicts that it is the function of moral principles to adjudicate.[1]

In Freud's naturalistic theory, practical reason is directed toward certain values, as ends of action. Value is accounted for in terms of human desires and interests: people want certain things in order to survive or to satisfy their interests, and these are called "good." The range of possible goods that reason might embrace is not infinite, as proponents of unqualified means—end rationality assume. It is limited to objects and experiences that are capable of satisfying the desires and interests of human beings, who, despite their differences, are basically similar cross-culturally.[2]

Freud assumes that one ultimate good end guides the decisions of all rational persons, and that is happiness. In chapter 2 of *Civilization and its Discontents*,[3] he explicitly takes up the perennial philosophical questions: How should we live? What should be "the purpose and intention" of our lives? What do we "demand of life and wish to achieve in it?" (*SE* 21 [1930]:76). The "answer . . . can hardly be in doubt," he replies. Human beings "strive after happiness; they want to become happy and to remain so" (ibid.).

Freud is here in agreement with the mainstream of the Western moral tradition, which, since the ancient Greeks, has singled out happiness as the *summum bonum*. But Freud implicitly gives a peculiar twist to the Aristo-

---

1. The term *premoral good* is used here to indicate a connotation of *good* that is different from the strictly moral meaning. A premoral good is a value—like health or beauty—that is good to pursue in that it is normally good for human beings, but it is not itself either moral or immoral. In fact, the pursuit of a premoral good may actually be immoral in certain circumstances—as when scientific knowledge is pursued by means of medical experiments on uninformed human subjects. The adjective *premoral* is used to make the point that the good in question is presupposed by ethical theory, either because it is "the basic or ultimate criterion or standard of what is morally right, wrong, obligatory, etc." (Frankena 1963, p. 13) or because a primary task of ethics is to impartially resolve conflicts among people over these goods.

2. This is why psychology is indispensable to ethics. It provides knowledge of the needs, desires, and interests that ethical thinking must take into account in establishing a priority system. Psychoanalysis is especially helpful in this endeavor because, as a depth psychology, it adds enormously to our understanding of the subtle intertwining of various desires and interests and thus to our assessment of their relative weight. It was one of Freud's main contentions that, because contemporary moral precepts run roughshod over so many strong natural desires, civilized people often find it impossible to guide their conduct toward the high values they profess (see, e.g., *SE* 14 [1915]:284).

3. This chapter was discussed briefly at the end of ch. 4 above in connection with Freud's *psychological* theory of qualitative hedonism. Here our concern is with what it reveals about Freud's *evaluative* theory of the nonmoral or premoral goods that confer genuine happiness.

telian notion that the best procedure for ascertaining the way to happiness is to observe the "man of practical wisdom"—that is, the person who has great experience and judgment in acting with just the right intensity of feeling, in just the right way, at just the right time. For Freud, as for many of those who follow his lead, a deep analysis of the self is a prerequisite for anyone who would ascertain the best path to happiness in life, since it is first necessary to clear away the psychic obstacles, developmental fixations, and defenses that cause people to misconstrue their desires and to pursue them irrationally if the deepest and most authentic desires of the self are to come into focus.[4] However, analysis is clearly not a sufficient condition for happiness, since other factors such as innate endowment, normal psycho-sexual development, ego capacities, environmental opportunities, and sheer luck are also important to success in the pursuit of happiness.

In the ensuing discussion of happiness as the supreme goal of life, Freud proceeds to identify eleven different "paths," "activities," or "strategies" for achieving happiness, as recommended by various philosophical and religious schools and practiced by ordinary people (*SE* 21 [1930]:77). These are unrestricted want satisfaction; isolation, as protection against suffering at the hands of other people; participation in the human commu-nity; intoxication and other mind-altering drug dependency; asceticism (e.g., yoga); creative sublimation; illusory escape into fantasy; delusional remolding of reality; mutual love; aesthetic enjoyment; and freedom.[5]

At first glance, Freud seems to write as if these eleven paths are simply different ways of achieving the same end of happiness in life and hence value-neutral. But in fact, he makes clear evaluative judgments in discussing them, and this normative ordering is further buttressed by evaluations made elsewhere in his writings, as when he discusses criteria of successful psychotherapy or distinguishes psychopathology from mental health. In-deed, Freud speaks of "negative" and "positive" paths to happiness (*SE* 21 [1930]:76). Although he uses these terms primarily to indicate that "nega-

4. Whereas Aristotle sought to identify the basic values that are truly worth pursuing by looking at persons who appeared to possess worldly wisdom, and whereas Mill sought to identify goods by examining the considered opinions of persons who had experienced the con-trasting pleasures of alternative goods (see Mill 1962a, p. 259), Freud tried to search out the best paths to happiness by looking at what relatively mature patients find worthwhile after psychoanalysis. For Freud, happiness is to be found not by focusing abstractly on "the problem of values," but by looking at what psychologically mature persons find worthwhile after cour-ageously and honestly confronting the inner obstacles and defense mechanisms that prevent people from freely exploring the full range of activities that make life truly worth living.

5. Freedom as a source of qualitatively distinct pleasure is added in a footnote (*SE* 21 [1930]:80, n. 1).

tive" paths to happiness seek "an absence of pain and unpleasure" and "positive" paths aim at experiencing strong feelings of pleasure (ibid.), one gets the impression that he is also trading on the evaluative senses of *negative* and *positive* to distinguish relatively undesirable activities from more desirable ones. Thus, a person might subjectively seek positive satisfaction, for example, through experiences induced by mind-altering chemicals; but Freud would evaluate this "negatively" as potentially dangerous to the agent's health and destructive of his or her ability to contribute constructively to the well-being of others and the community. Freud does not address precisely why the "positive" paths are better than the defensive, or "negative," paths; but the answer that would seem to be most consistent with his thought as a whole is that activities born of compromise formations in which such defenses as repression and reaction formation play a prominent role fail to resonate with the deepest layers of the self, whereas the goods achieved by sublimation, such as love and creativity, express the deepest aspects of the self in *ego-syntonic ways*.

Freud designates six of the paths to happiness as negative: unrestricted want satisfaction, isolation, intoxication, asceticism, illusion, and delusion.[6] Heavy reliance on them is undesirable, although Freud recognizes that almost all lives will include modest use of some of these defensive strategies to cope with the difficulties of life. Unrestricted want satisfaction is self-defeating, Freud holds, because it puts enjoyment before the caution required to assure that basic needs and more highly valued desires are satisfied realistically. Isolation, as a defensive strategy against the sufferings that may come from human relations, is rejected by Freud as a major component of an acceptable life plan on the evaluative grounds that "there is . . . another and *better* path: that of becoming a member of the human community" (*SE* 21 [1930]:77–8, emphasis added). Intoxication, though admittedly a temporarily effective way of withdrawing from the difficulties presented by reality, is criticized for its potential misuses, for its "*injuriousness*." There is "danger" in the withdrawal from reality that intoxicating media offer, Freud states derogatorily. And alcoholism, for example, "wastes a large quota of energy which might have been employed for the

6. Sterba reports that Freud told a Wednesday meeting at his apartment on 20 Mar. 1930 that he felt gigantic disgrace (*eine Riesenschande*) for having omitted from *Civilization and its Discontents* another route to happiness, that of the complete narcissist, which he also evaluates negatively, as "so very sad." Sterba's notes indicate that Freud said of this endeavor: "It is [that of] the person who relies completely upon himself. A caricature of this type is Falstaff. We tolerate him as a caricature, but otherwise he is unbearable. . . . This unassailability by anything is only given to the absolute narcissist" (Sterba 1978, p. 185).

improvement of the human lot" (*SE* 21 [1930]:78, emphasis added). Asceticism is said to provide a way of reducing the pressure of desires so that
nonsatisfaction is not felt as painfully; but Freud contends that it does so at
excessive cost—namely, "diminution in the potentialities of enjoyment"
(*SE* 21 [1930]:79). Illusory satisfactions in fantasies and delusional re-
moldings of reality are both criticized for their lack of truthfulness, a fault
that Freud examined more thoroughly in *The Future of an Illusion* (1927),
which preceded the discussion of the good life in *Civilization and its Discontents*. There, Freud argued his well-known case against religion, that its
wish-fulfilling illusions and delusions may make believers subjectively happier in this world than they might be otherwise, but that such beliefs are
ethically undesirable, nonetheless, because they detach the believer from
truths about the human condition and, hence, from realistic efforts that
would be more effective than religious practices in dealing with those
problems that are amenable to practical solutions.[7]

By contrast, Freud endorses the remaining strategies: participation in
the human community,[8] sublimation (as in the pursuit of knowledge and

7. Freud writes that it is "an enormous relief to the individual psyche" when the sources
of anxiety within the self and the external world are explained by religion (*SE* 21 [1927]:30).
For "if everywhere in nature there are Beings [or a Being] around us of a kind that we know in
our own society, then we can breathe freely, can feel at home in the uncanny and can deal by
psychical means with our senseless anxiety" (*SE* 21 [1927]:17). Moreover, a way of dealing
with anxiety is proffered, since the believer can try to influence the relevant deity through
sacrificial offerings, prayers, and other ritualistic acts. Nonetheless, despite these benefits in
terms of subjective satisfaction, Freud disapproves of religion, primarily on the grounds that
its beliefs are fundamentally unrealistic. In his words, "Ignorance is ignorance" whatever its
pleasurable benefits, and that is sufficient to discredit whatever satisfaction it may offer (*SE* 21
[1927]:32). An auxiliary argument against religious illusions and delusions is that their moral
standards tend to be excessively repressive, which increases the degree of unhappiness in
society.

8. Not only is community a "*better* path" than isolation (*SE* 21 [1930]:77–8); the good
of community is also presupposed in his discussion of the value of creativity and freely chosen
productive work (*SE* 21 [1930]:79–80, 80, n. 1), both of which are valued in part for their
contribution to society. Later in *Civilization,* the value of social solidarity is again stressed
when Freud argues that even for primitive man "it cannot have been a matter of indifference to
him whether another man worked with or against him. The other man acquired the value for
him of a fellow-worker, with whom it was useful to live together" (*SE* 21 [1930]:99). Similarly, in *The Future of an Illusion* Freud indicates that there is value to be found in shared emotional
experiences and shared ideals among those who identify with one another: "[Communal
ideals and] the creations of art heighten . . . [the individual's] feelings of identification, of
which every cultural unit stands in so much need, by providing an occasion for sharing highly
valued emotional experiences" (*SE* 21 [1927]:14). These hints of the value of human solidarity bring to mind the work of Freud's great contemporary Emile Durkheim, who centered

artistic creativity), mutual love, aesthetic enjoyment, and freedom, as each embodying a qualitatively distinct enjoyment that is valuable both for itself and for the very special contribution that it makes to happiness in the individual's life as a whole and, by extension, to societal happiness. Freud describes each of these desirable activities as having the "positive" aim of "experiencing . . . strong feelings of pleasure," as contrasted with the mere "negative" aim of coping with pain and suffering that the other, disparaged strategies focus on.

As a consequence of the change in his instinctual theory introduced in *Beyond the Pleasure Principle* (see ch. 6 above), Freud came to subscribe to a form of qualitative hedonism similar to that of J. S. Mill, which holds that each qualitatively distinct enjoyment is valuable for the very special satisfaction it gives. Thus Freud asserts that each of the "positive" activities or paths to happiness yields a "special quality" of enjoyment. The "special quality" of intellectual and other creative work,[9] the "special quality" of friendship and the "fulfilment" of interpersonal love,[10] the "peculiar, mildly intoxicating quality" of aesthetic enjoyment, and "the special satisfaction" found in freely chosen work[11] make these activities intrinsically better than other pursuits (*SE* 21 [1930]:77–83) and means that they should be chosen over other paths to happiness, other things being equal.

Freud appears to presuppose that qualitatively distinct pleasures are associated with different kinds of objects, so that the satisfaction derived from love of another person differs qualitatively from that found in discovery of a new truth or creation of an aesthetically beautiful object, and all

---

his ethic on the incomparable value of human community (see Durkheim 1933, 1951, 1898, 1961; Wallwork 1972).

9. See *SE* 21 (1930):79. Freud stresses the value that he places on intellectual creativity in his own life when he writes to Pfister that "I cannot face with comfort the idea of life without work; work and the free play of the imagination are for me the same thing, I take no pleasure in anything else" (letter of 6 Mar. 1910, in Meng and Freud 1963, p. 35). But then, in another letter, dated 7 Feb. 1930, he says that "there is a special value in personal relations which shared work and interests cannot completely make good" (in ibid., p. 132).

10. See, e.g., *SE* 21 (1930):82; 12 (1915):169. Freud again underscores the inestimable value of love in its full sense when he observes that the psychotherapist is apt to have greater difficulty resisting the spiritual-emotional allure of love preferred by the patient than resisting explicitly sexual seductiveness (see *CP* 2 [1915]:389).

11. Freud (*SE* 21 [1930]:80, n. 1) argues that freely chosen professional work is "a source of special satisfaction." It seems unlikely that Freud intends to imply that freedom or autonomy is valuable *only* insofar as it is a source of "special satisfaction." However, the special subjective pleasure taken in voluntary actions is one part of freedom's value, just as pleasure is also part of the value of truthfulness, though the latter rests on other grounds as well. See below.

these different kinds of satisfaction go to make up the truly fulfilled life (see *SE* 11 [1910]:54; 11 [1912]:179–90). It is a major theme of Freud's that a life plan should include a plurality of aims rather than a single dominant end. In 'Civilized Sexual Morality and Modern Nervous Illness" (*SE* 9 [1908]:196–8), for example, he takes it for granted that the sexually liberated person will not focus exclusively on sexual gratification but will also pursue sublimated activities such as artistic creativity, the pursuit of knowledge, or other activities that will make a social contribution.

Similarly, in the "Five Lectures on Psycho-Analysis" Freud commends psychoanalytic therapy for its ability to help the patient realize a life plan in which direct sexual pleasures are enjoyed alongside sublimations that contribute to "the highest and most valuable cultural trends" (*SE* 11 [1910]:53). And in *Civilization and its Discontents* Freud looks on a plurality of aims as a prudent measure against the likelihood of dissatisfaction from the failure of a single aim:

> Any choice [of a path to happiness] that is pushed to an extreme will be penalized by exposing the individual to the dangers which arise if a technique of living that has been chosen as an exclusive one should prove inadequate. Just as a cautious businessman avoids tying up all his capital in one concern, so, perhaps, worldly wisdom will advise us not to look for the whole of our satisfaction from a single aspiration. Its success is never certain, for that depends on the convergence of many factors. (*SE* 21 [1930]:84)

Freud's letters reveal that he reached this conclusion in part by discovering in his own life that a single-minded pursuit, like scientific research, tends to become an inner tyrant that brings more misery than satisfaction, in part because no achievement is ever good enough, but also because other enjoyments are foresworn.[12]

The value of love is especially pronounced in Freud's writings. In 1915, for instance, he writes: "The love between the sexes is undoubtedly one of the first things in life, and the combination of mental and bodily satisfaction attained in the enjoyment of love is literally one of life's culminations. Apart from a few perverse fanatics, all the world knows this and conducts

---

12. Freud spelled out his personal life plan in a letter to his fiancée in 1885: "My ambition would be satisfied by a long life spent learning to understand something of the world, and my plans for the future are that we get married, love each other and work with the object of enjoying life together instead of exerting every ounce of my energy trying to pass the post first, like a race horse" (letter 86, E. L. Freud 1975, p. 185; see also letter 40, ibid., pp. 101–2). For discussion, see Eissler 1964.

life accordingly; only science is too refined to confess it"[13] (*CP* 2 [1915]:389).

Freud sometimes treats the qualitatively distinct pleasures of community, knowledge, creativity, love, beauty, and freedom as themselves *intrinsically good,* instead of as mere *means* to the overarching intrinsic good of happiness. From this perspective, the relation of these positive experiences to happiness in life is not a contingent or an instrumental one, as it is with such defensive strategies as intoxication and asceticism, but a part–whole relation. Happiness is *constituted* by experiences of the positive sort.[14] Genuine happiness cannot exist in the absence of pursuits involving some or all of these separate goods.

Freud clearly thinks that more than subjective pleasure alone is involved in the constitution of value. In *The Future of an Illusion,* for example, he makes clear that although religious people derive happiness and consolation from illusory beliefs that help them to bear "the troubles of life and the cruelties of reality" (*SE* 21 [1927]:49; see also *SE* 21 [1927]:16–17) and even goes so far as to note that "science can be no match for [religion] . . . when it soothes the fear that men feel of the dangers and vicissitudes of life, when it assures them of a happy ending and offers them comfort in unhappiness" (*SE* 22 [1933]:161), this does not make an illusory way of living "good." If happiness is a product of illusion or delusion, it would be better to be less happy but clear-eyed and truthful (*SE* 21 [1927]:16–17, 30, 49). Thus Freud urges his readers "to do without the consolation of the religious illusion" (*SE* 21 [1927]:49) and to "stand up to the hard test" of reality (*SE* 21 [1927]:50), even though one might be happier subjectively living within the soothing framework of a religious

13. Years earlier, Freud expressed much the same valuation of love when he wrote to his fiancée: "Our happiness rests irrevocably in our love" (letter dated 9 Sept. 1883, cited and trans. by Eissler 1964, p. 191). Two years later he wrote to her in like vein: "If today were to be my last on earth and someone asked me how I had fared, he would be told by me that in spite of everything—poverty, long struggle for success, little favor among men, oversensitiveness, nervousness, and worries—I have nevertheless been happy simply because of the anticipation of one day having you to myself and of the certainty that you love me" (letter dated 2 Feb. 1886, in E. L. Freud 1975, p. 201).

14. In Hardie's useful terminology, happiness is here not a single "dominant end," but an "inclusive end" (1965, pp. 277–95; 1968). To pursue a dominant goal is to pursue one specific state or object; to pursue an inclusive goal is to pursue a variety of states, each of which contributes something necessary to the overall condition sought. With respect to happiness as an inclusive end, Kenny points out that "the desire for happiness [in this sense] is the desire for the orderly and harmonious gratification of a number of independent desires" (1970, p. 48).

ideology.[15] For Freud to argue in this way, the sources of genuine happiness must have a realistic basis beyond mere subjective satisfaction.

Nozick's discussion of an "experience machine" cleverly helps to bring out why more than subjective pleasure is involved in Freud's understanding of reality in the constitution of value (see Nozick 1974, pp. 42–5). Nozick postulates a device that, by artificially stimulating the brain, could create the illusion of any and all of the experiences one desired. The individual would fully believe—think and feel, experience from the inside—that he was writing a great novel, enjoying the bounties of friendship, fulfilling a lust for power, or whatever, all the while he was really lying in a tank with electrodes attached to his brain doing nothing at all (ibid., pp. 42–3). Nozick asks: "What else can matter to us, other than how our lives feel from the inside?" And he answers, correctly, that in addition to our experiences, it matters to us that "we want to *do* certain things, and not just have the experience of doing them"; that "we want to *be* a certain way, to be a certain sort of person"—someone courageous, kind, intelligent, witty, loving, for example—and not just "an indeterminate blob"; and that we want "*actual* contact with . . . [a] deeper reality," not just the simulation of that experience (ibid., p. 43). Beyond that, he suggests that "what we desire is to live (an active verb) ourselves, in contact with reality" (ibid., p. 45). Similarly, Freud holds that it is better to live less happily in contact with reality than secure in the enveloping cocoon of a religious illusion.

Freud's psychological theory undergirds this aspect of his hypothesis regarding the basic goods worth pursuing in life by emphasizing that sublimated pleasures are made possible by the ego's actual dealings with reality. Genuine goods involve realistic commerce with the actual world; the modest satisfaction of truthfulness is to be preferred over most other values.[16] Accordingly, Freud declares that "the question is not what belief

15. Without religious illusion, Freud argues, people "will . . . have to admit to themselves the full extent of their helplessness and their insignificance in the machinery of the universe; they can no longer be the centre of creation, no longer the object of tender care on the part of a beneficent Providence. They will be in the same position as a child who has left the parental house where he was so warm and comfortable" (*SE* 21 [1927]:49). But this is more than merely acceptable to Freud. It is necessary. "Men cannot remain children for ever," he declares; "they must in the end go out into 'hostile life.' We may call this '*education to reality*'" (ibid., emphasis original). Freud hopes that humankind will learn to "stand up to the hard test" and states that "It is something, at any rate, to know that one is thrown upon one's own resources" (*SE* 21 [1927]:50).

16. None of this is meant to imply that Freud fails to appreciate the value of *artistic* illusion. Freud valued illusion as indispensable to the enjoyment of certain aesthetic forms. What he objected to was not "the play of the imagination" (Meng and Freud 1963, p. 35)—indeed, he

is more pleasing or more comfortable or more advantageous to life, but of what may approximate more closely to the puzzling reality that lies outside us" (letter dated 2 Feb. 1930, in Meng and Freud 1963, p. 133; see also *SE* 16 [1916–17]:255; 21 [1927]:53–6; 23 [1937]:248; Hale 1971, p. 171).

Part of what it means for something to be good for a human being, Freud assumes, is that it is found in activity. The subjective experience of love, for example, is not sufficient; the value is partly in the relation, in *loving* the other and *being loved* in return (*SE* 14 [1914]:99–100). Similarly, it is not just the subjective satisfaction of work that Freud values, but the fact that "no other technique for the conduct of life attaches the individual so firmly to reality" (*SE* 21 [1930]:80 n. 1).[17] This is in part because work gives the individual "a secure place in a portion of reality, in the human community" (ibid.). Happiness, as Aristotle argued, is found in action.[18]

Indeed, for Freud, truthfulness and active engagement are justified more by their contribution to well-being in the sense of functioning well than to happiness in the contemporary, exclusively subjective sense of that term.[19] To find happiness in the sense of enjoying a variety of qualitatively distinct pleasures is for Freud partly a matter of actualizing certain human capacities or tendencies, such as the ego's rationality and active commerce with the environment of persons and things. This actualization is sufficiently

---

deeply cherished it—but moving too far away from the real world. In his opinion, true art offers a deeper understanding of reality, even as it compensates for the difficulties of living realistically (*SE* 13 [1913]:187). The artist "finds the way back to reality . . . from this world of phantasy by making use of special gifts to mould his phantasies into truths of a new kind, which are valued by men as precious reflections of reality" (*SE* 12 [1911]:224). Art becomes dangerous only when reality is confused with fantasy and one cannot return to the real world after absorption in a work of art. Illusions may be valued as long as they "are recognized as such" (*SE* 21 [1930]:80)—that is, as human wish-fulfilling creations. In fact, Freud argues not just for truthfulness and liberal education but also for the prominence of art in our lives. The aesthetic and the truthful touch on each other and inform one another.

17. Freud realized in his own life that truly creative work almost invariably entails considerable discomfort. He remarked: "I have been very idle because the moderate amount of discomfort [*Mittelelend*] necessary for intensive work has not set in" (letter dated 16 Apr. 1896, cited by E. Jones 1953, p. 345). And occasionally he found his creativity obstructed when he felt extraordinarily well: "I am enjoying too much comfort here to have any ideas," he wrote in 1918 (letter 182 in E. L. Freud 1975, p. 323).

18. Freud presumably studied Aristotle with Brentano, who was something of an expert on the Greek philosopher. See Gay 1988, p. 29.

19. This is why Freud claims that the aim of psychoanalysis is not, as with some other therapies, "to make everything as pleasant as possible for the patient, so that he may feel well," but rather to make the patient "stronger for life and more capable of carrying out the actual tasks of his life" (*CP* 2 [1919]:398).

important to trump the happiness criterion on its exclusively subjective sense.

However, Freud diverges significantly from Aristotle and the recent self-realization psychologies that stem from his work (like those of Maslow, Perls, Rogers, and Fromm) in his basic approach to the question of the relation of natural human capacities to the ideal of happiness. In contrast to the classical theory of happiness represented by Aristotle, Freud's normative ideal of the relatively happy person is not that of the person who actualizes innate potentialities within a particular social environment, because the mature person who is capable of finding deep and authentic satisfaction in life is the outcome of a complex development the course of which is influenced by environmental factors and by intrapsychic vicissitudes that go far beyond the actualization of innate capacities alone. Indeed, some innate instincts need to be suppressed and transformed beyond what is innately given for the sort of development that makes happiness in life possible. In the absence of such instinctual transformation, the individual suffers from the psychic and social dissatisfactions that accompany the serious perversions.

For, despite his own reliance on qualitatively distinct pleasures, Freud did not see subjective experience as always a reliable guide to true or authentic well-being—that is to say, to the smooth and mature psychic functioning that is the source of the deep, if mild, continuous self-confidence and contentment that accompany most of a person's activities. Subjective evidence is not sufficient, in part because people who have become fixated at early developmental stages have no idea of what they are missing. Nor do people who neglect certain basic desires understand through introspection the deleterious psychic consequences of such neglect. Moreover, Freud realizes that extremely unfavorable life circumstances can be "stupefying" and can lead to "the cessation of expectations, . . . cruder or more refined methods of narcotizations," and other "mental protective devices" that grossly distort the individual's "receptivity to sensations of pleasure and unpleasure" (SE 21 [1930]:89). It is on the basis of these and other limitations of the subjective evidence for happiness that Freud and his psychoanalytic descendants argue that some people who claim to be relatively happy are missing out on valuable experiences or that they would experience more satisfaction if their desires were different in specifiable ways (see De Sousa 1982, pp. 146–7).

Freud's alternative approach to both the classical and the modern subjective criteria for happiness draws on both, but within a developmental context that looks to full psychological maturation for an ideal of human flourishing, the realization of which makes possible the deepest satisfactions (see, e.g., his 1931 essay on "Libidinal Types," *SE* 21 [1931]:217–20). As De Sousa points out in an interesting explication and defense of Freud's distinctive approach here, Freud's theory of personality development provides a systematic perspective on the variegation of human tastes, dispositions, and enjoyments that in different balances give us different "normal" personality types, from which deviations can be evaluated as more or less pathological. Freud's ideal is rooted in natural (i.e., instinctual) desires and is based on facts about individuals; but it is not fully realizable by any particular individual and does not rest on subjective feelings alone for its validation. "A [developmental] *theory*, based on facts about individuals, to be sure, but which need not reflect the subjective preferences of any particular one, determines the normal wants and pleasures of men in general," De Sousa writes (1982, p. 141). This theory of fully developed human nature identifies the various desires the satisfaction of which yields authentic happiness in the sense of both reasonably good psychic functioning and deep subjective and realistic satisfaction. The ideal itself is a theoretical fiction in that no one can realize it in actual life; but there are several normal personality types that Freud identifies as approximating it, each of which exemplifies several aspects of the ideal.[20] The character traits of these normal personality types that Freud especially stresses are love, self-reliance, creativity, and participation in the community.

It is particularly important to the discussion of the application of practical reason to morality in chapter 13 below that each of these normal personality types is presumed to be oriented toward the good of others as well as that of the community. It is thus not an arbitrary matter whether the individual takes an interest in the community and the moral regulations that make it possible.

20. Freud distinguishes three "pure" types that fall within the range of normal personality development: the *erotic*, the *obsessional*, and the *narcissistic*. The erotic type's main interest is in loving, but most of all in being loved, which tends to make such people dependent on others. The obsessional type is distinguished by the predominance of the superego and the fear of conscience. Such people "develop a high degree of self-reliance; and, from the social standpoint, they are true, pre-eminently conservative vehicles of civilization" (*SE* 21 [1931]:218). The narcissistic type is geared mainly toward self-preservation; he or she is independent and not easily intimidated. "People belonging to this type impress others as being 'personalities'; they are especially suited to act as a support for others, to take on the role of leaders and to give a fresh stimulus to cultural development or to damage the established state of affairs" (ibid.). In practice, most normal personalities are mixed types—erotic-obsessional, erotic-narcissistic, or narcissistic-obsessional. The fourth mixed type, the erotic-obsessional-narcissistic type, is said not to be a type at all but "the absolute norm, the ideal harmony" (See *SE* 21 [1931]: 219).

If one asks how Freud can *logically* pass from this purported *fact* about human development to a normative ideal—that is, from "is" to "ought"—the answer lies, though Freud nowhere explicitly provides it, in the ancient Greek notion, revived by contemporary moral philosophers, that whatever fulfills its function well is "good." From such factual premises as "This knife cuts well" and "This fisherman catches lots of fish everyday," the evaluative conclusions validly follow that "This is a good knife" and "He is a good fisherman." These arguments are valid because the concepts of a knife and a fisherman are functional concepts—that is, *knife* and *fisherman* are defined in terms of the purpose or function that knife and fisherman are normally expected to serve.

The suppressed premise in Freud's argument is the Aristotelian one, derived perhaps via Brentano, that "human being" is also a functional concept in the sense that the human being has certain essential charac-teristic functions. Hence, from the factual statement, if true, that this woman is flourishing in the sense of being a loving, self-reliant, creative contributor to society, it follows that she is a good person. Freud's twist on this is that these functions are laid down ultimately by biology: that is, it is the sexual instinct, or Eros, that establishes that to be a human being is to establish meaningful contact with other individuals and the community. This is why Freud claims, early in his work, that the sexual instinct carries the germ of altruism that normal development actualizes (*SE* 14 [1914]:78; 14 [1915]:125; 16 [1916–17]:413–14).

DIVERGENCES FROM THE MORAL TRADITION

Freud's substantive answer to the normative question "What things are worth pursuing in a life oriented toward happiness?" finally is not unlike that of J. S. Mill, who also commends knowledge, intellectual creativity, aesthetic creativity, the appreciation of beauty, intimate personal relations such as friendship, and participation in the community.[21] Freud also resem-bles Mill in his respectful attitude toward the individual's right, as an autonomous being, to choose his own life plan.[22] Because people differ

21. See Edwards 1979 for a good discussion of Mill's ethical hedonism. That Freud knew Mill's utilitarian writings well is confirmed by his letters to Silberstein, in one of which, Freud states that he is attending Brentano's course on Mill's utility principle (quoted by McGrath 1986, p. 101, n. 19).

22. Freud greatly respected Mill for putting into practice in his own life the doctrine of liberty he preached. In 1883 he wrote of Mill: "Very possibly he was the man of the century most capable of freeing himself from the domination of the usual prejudices" (letter 28, in E. L. Freud 1975, p. 75).

greatly and their situations are so diverse and complex, each individual is to be left alone to determine the combination of good-producing activities and defensive strategies that is best for him or her: "There is no golden rule which applies to everyone: every man must find out for himself in what particular fashion he can be saved" (*SE* 21 [1930]:83).[23]

But contra the moral tradition represented by Mill, Freud includes erotic sensuality as an indispensable aspect of the so-called higher pleasures of love in his list of the primary goods of life. For Freud, sexual pleasure is intrinsically desirable, as well as good for its salutary consequences. He instructs that "a certain portion of the repressed libidinal impulses has a claim to direct satisfaction and ought to find it in life. Our civilized standards make life too difficult for the majority of human organizations. . . . We ought not to exalt ourselves so high as completely to neglect what was originally animal in our nature. Nor should we forget that the satisfaction of the individual's happiness cannot be erased from among the aims of our civilization" (*SE* 11 [1910]:54).

In Freud's view, Mill is both "prudish" and "unearthly," especially in his treatment of love, shorn as it is of both sensuality and sexuality (see letter 28 in E. L. Freud 1975, pp. 75–6). Mill's shortcoming here is not idiosyncratic. The entire Western moral tradition has denigrated sexual pleasure by comparison with allegedly "higher" mental activities. Civilized culture "does not like sexuality as a source of pleasure *in its own right*," Freud dryly observes (*SE* 21 [1930]:105, emphasis added; see also Meng and Freud 1963, p. 16).[24]

Here, Freud lands smack-dab in the middle of the mind–body problem. He repudiates the dualistic conception of the self that derives from Plato and rejects its moral implication that well-being has to do only with the state of the soul independent of the body. By including sexuality in the list of intrinsic goods, Freud overturns the traditional application of the notion of qualitatively distinct pleasures, which was to denigrate sensual pleasures

---

23. If Freud's reliance here on the individual's subjective ordering of desires seems to raise the specter of subjective relativism regarding the comparative importance of values, it is nonetheless the case that this variability occurs within the context of a theory that identifies certain wants as more desirable than others. The "positive fulfilment of happiness" that all persons are presumed to seek is to be found among a limited range of basic goods, even though there are very diverse ways of enjoying these and of combining them with one another as well as with more idiosyncratic interests and talents in a satisfactory life plan. The crucial point is that the individual is not rudderless; ends are not chosen arbitrarily, human nature being constituted the way it is.

24. For a good discussion of the problem that the Western philosophical tradition has had with the animal side of human behavior and its consequence, the distorted traditional philosophical picture of human nature, see Midgley 1978.

as "brutish" or "beastly" in comparison with the elevated pleasures of the mind and spirit. Freud argues that erotic enjoyments have a "special quality" that is often more intense and powerful than the so-called "higher" pleasures—indeed, that because "sexual love . . . has given us our most intense experience of an overwhelming sensation of pleasure . . . [it] has thus furnished us with a pattern for our search for happiness" in other spheres (*SE* 21 [1930]:82).[25] Freud concludes from this that something of incommensurable value is lost when erotic pleasures are repressed in the service of more cultivated values. Erotic pleasure enters into most allegedly "higher" pursuits, adding a creative power and richness of texture and enjoyment to those activities that is needlessly sacrificed when sexuality is too heavily inhibited.[26] Thus, the repression of sexuality entails a loss of the specific intrinsic good not only of bodily enjoyment that is conjoined with a specific mental pleasure, but also of other cultural activities.

In receiving this message, however, popular culture has tended to misunderstand Freud as propounding an ethical egoism or a "culture of narcissism" that is quite the reverse of what he had in mind, which was to reform rather than to overthrow the existing moral culture. Freud actually cautions *against* the strategy of "unrestricted satisfaction of every need . . . as . . . [a] method of conducting one's life" (*SE* 21[1930]: 77). But it is nonetheless Freud's position that there are egoistic or narcissistic goals centering around sensual pleasure that are valuable in themselves and therefore worth pursuing whatever other goals a person might also have in life.

A second noteworthy way in which Freud departs from the Western moral tradition is in failing to mention "moral conscientiousness" as a path to happiness. The reason for this striking omission from the discussion of happiness in *Civilization and its Discontents* is most likely Freud's interest in steering people away from the harmful consequences of irrational guilt—that is, guilt for the violation of standards that are not reasonable or for mere wishes never carried into action. Clinical experience, as well as cultural observation, convinced Freud that conscientiousness is not good in itself,

25. Whereas the Western moral tradition holds that sensuality threatens to undermine higher aspirations, Freud insists that direct expression of sexuality acts as a template for the pursuit of higher cultural achievements. He explains: "The sexual behaviour of a human being often *lays down the pattern* for all his other modes of reacting to life. If a man is energetic in winning the object of his love, we are confident that he will pursue his other aims with an equally unswerving energy; but if . . . he refrains from satisfying his strong sexual instincts, his behaviour will be conciliatory and resigned rather than vigorous in other spheres of life as well" (*SE* 9 [1908]:198).

26. Freud speaks of the general "inner impoverishment" that accompanies severe sexual repression.

Kant's comparison of conscience to the starry heavens notwithstanding (*SE* 22 [1933]:61).[27] In fact, as noted previously, moral conscientiousness often actually encourages positively immoral deeds by concealing egoistic or aggressive behavior under the guise of self-righteousness.

But if Freud does not follow Kant in giving pride of place to conscientiousness as a "moral virtue," he nevertheless does recognize that the ego enjoys a very special pleasure when it acts in conformity with its own standards. "There is always a feeling of triumph when something in the ego coincides with the ego ideal," he notes (*SE* 18 [1921]:131).[28] Freud even praises conscientiousness of the right kind—namely, that which obeys reasonable principles.[29] For example, in instructing psychoanalysts, Freud counsels that they should proceed with as much "*conscientiousness* as a chemist" (*SE* 12 [1915]:170, emphasis added).[30]

In order to appreciate what Freud had in mind regarding the right kind of "conscientiousness," however, we need to know what the moral principles are that the conscientious person respects and how they are to be put into practice. This raises the question that is addressed in the next chapter, that of what psychoanalysis implies about the justification of moral principles. As noted at the outset of this chapter, Freud approaches the issue from the perspective of social reasons for action, as contrasted with the personal reasons that we have been examining in this chapter. Yet it is noteworthy that Freud's list of personal reasons includes social reasons insofar as it includes the goods of love and community.

27. Freud comments dryly on Kant's comparison: "The stars are indeed magnificent, but as regards conscience God has done an uneven and careless piece of work" (*SE* 22 [1933]:61).

28. Freud makes much the same point in *An Outline of Psycho-Analysis:* "If the ego has successfully resisted a temptation to do something which would be objectionable to the superego, it feels raised in its self-esteem and strengthened in its pride, as though it had made some precious acquisition" (*SE* 23 [1940]:206).

29. See *SE* 12 (1915):163–71.

30. Freud likewise instructs psychoanalysts that their "own conduct [must] be irreproachable" (*SE* 7 [1905]:267).

Chapter 13
Normative Principles and Social Theory

> Going back to ethics, we may say . . . that a
> part of its precepts are justified rationally by
> the necessity for delimiting the rights of
> society as against the individual, the rights
> of the individual as against society and those
> of individuals as against one another.
>
> —Freud

Freud is usually viewed as having little appreciation of the importance of the
moral principles in guiding an individual's conduct. He is, after all, severely
critical of superego morality and of certain traditional moral precepts, such
as the love commandment, and his normative concerns seem to focus on the
individual in close interpersonal relation in which friendly dispositions and
virtues like honesty usually suffice. Likewise, he emphasizes the inherent
conflict between moral requirements and the press of the instincts and the
resulting unconscious guilt. Some of Freud's most memorable statements
stress the extent to which unreasonable moral demands for instinctual
renunciation make the individual a virtual "enemy of civilization" (*SE* 21
[1927]:6).[1] After Freud, the view of the lofty moral demands of civilization
is forever shadowed by the specter of our relentless discontent.

Yet, when Freud does turn to the importance of moral principles in
guiding the self or ego in its interpersonal relations, he makes it plain that

---

1. In his later, speculative writings, Freud made extensive, forceful pronouncements on
the conflict between the individual and civilization or culture. In *The Future of an Illusion*
(1927), for instance, he comments: "It is remarkable that, little as men are able to exist in
isolation, they should nevertheless feel as a heavy burden the sacrifices which civilization
expects of them in order to make a communal life possible. . . . The decisive question is
whether and to what extent it is possible to lessen the burden of the instinctual sacrifices
imposed on men, to reconcile men to those which must necessarily remain and to provide a
compensation for them" (*SE* 21 [1927]:6, 7). Similarly, the predominant thrust of *Civilization
and its Discontents* (1930) is the conflict between the "claim of the individual and the cultural
claims of the group" and whether "an accommodation" between the two "can be reached by
means of some particular form of civilization or whether this conflict is irreconcilable" (*SE* 21
[1930]:96). See also, e.g., *SE* 21 (1930):97, 111–12, 115, 141, 143; 22 (1933):204–12.

he believes that some moral rules or principles are absolutely "indispensable to human society" (*SE* 22 [1933]:168). Conflicting interests and claims inevitably arise among individuals in social interactions (*SE* 21 [1927]:6) and as a "kind of highway code" (Meng and Freud 1963, p. 123), moral rules determine "the manner in which the relationships of men to one another, their social relationships, are regulated—relationships which affect a person as a neighbour, as a source of help, as another person's sexual object, as a member of a family and of a State" (*SE* 21 [1930]:94–5). Accordingly, moral rules are to be assessed in terms of how well they are able to accommodate the interests of the individual with the competing interests of other individuals and of the social aggregate (see, e.g., *SE* 21 [1927]:44; 21 [1930]:115–16).[2]

SOCIAL REASONS FOR ACTION

Freud is often taken to be purely Hobbesian with respect to his views on the nature and origin of moral and sociopolitical obligations. His well-known view of civilization and its moral constraints as entailing an evolutionary process that emerges out of a primal state in which, in pursuit of instinctual satisfaction, the strongest dominate and exploit weaker individuals until the weaker individuals band together to resist seems to make him one with the Hobbesian position that social bonds are based on enlightened self-interest as individuals prudently seek ways of protecting themselves against other, equally rapacious and possibly stronger individuals in what would otherwise be a war of all against all.

According to Freud, in the beginning, social relations are determined by the arbitrary will of the strongest individual, who dominates others and seeks to use them for the gratification "of his own interests and instinctual impulses" (*SE* 21 [1930]:95; see also *SE* 22 [1933]:204–5). A majority then comes together "which is stronger than any separate individual and which remains united against all separate individuals" (*SE* 21 [1930]:95). The power or "right" (*Recht*) of the community is set up against the power of the individual. "What prevails is no longer the violence of an individual but that of a community" (*SE* 22 [1933]:205). It is at this point that the primitive rule of law and morals emerges as a "decisive step" in civilization, for the members of the community must bind themselves together in a way

2. Freud recognizes that ethics deals principally with social relations. In *Civilization* he notes that "the cultural super-ego has developed its ideas and set up its demands. Among the latter, those which deal with the relations of human beings to one another are comprised under the heading of ethics" (*SE* 21 [1930]:142).

that is stable and lasting. Law and shared moral rules regulate the interactions of disparate individuals and offer a return, in terms of self-interest and social protection, for the restriction of the pursuit of instinctual gratification (*SE* 22 [1933]:95).

Freud is often quite explicit in his references to Hobbes. No more powerful description of Hobbesian man has been given than that of Freud when he writes in *Civilization and its Discontents* that

> Men are not gentle creatures who . . . at the most . . . defend themselves if they are attacked; they are, on the contrary, creatures . . .[with] a powerful share of [instinctual] aggressiveness. As a result, their neighbour . . . tempts them to satisfy their aggression on him, to exploit his capacity for work without compensation, to use him sexually without his consent, to seize his possessions, to humiliate him, to cause him pain, to torture and to kill him. *Homo homini lupus.* (*SE* 21 [1930]:111)

Similarly, Freud often makes the argument on behalf of shared moral principles that they are "necessary" to avoid the chaos that would exist if unrepressed and unsublimated instinctual impulses were allowed free reign. Thus, in *The Future of an Illusion* he writes: "How . . . short-sighted to strive for the abolition of civilization! What would then remain would be a state of nature, and that would be far harder to bear [than the pressure that civilization exercises, the renunciations of instinct which it demands] . . . Civilization . . . is . . . intended to make our communal life possible. . . . The principal task of civilization, its actual *raison d'être,* is to defend us against nature" (*SE* 21 [1927]:15).

Shared moral rules and legal regulations are "in the interest of man's communal existence" (*SE* 21 [1927]:40), Freud declares, because "everyone else has exactly the same [unconscious] wishes as I have and will treat me with no more consideration than I treat him" (*SE* 21 [1927]:15).[3] Unless individuals and their passions are constrained, communal life with all its advantages in the struggle for existence would be impossible (ibid.). Even so, "civilization has to use its utmost efforts in order to set limits to man's aggressive [and sexual] instincts and to hold the manifestations of them in check" (*SE* 21 [1930]:112).

But despite his obvious affinity with Hobbes, Freud parts company with the liberal tradition of moral philosophy (represented by Hobbes, Locke,

---

3. In *Civilization* he remarks that while primitive man knew "no restrictions of instinct . . ., his prospects of enjoying this happiness for any length of time were very slender. Civilized man has exchanged a portion of his possibilities of happiness for a portion of security" (*SE* 21 [1930]:115).

and, contemporaneously, Nozick[4]) in several important respects. He explicitly rejects the social-contract notion that enlightened self-interest provides a sufficient foundation for the social solidarity required for a common life together. As Freud remarks in *Civilization and its Discontents:* "In consequence of . . . [the] primary mutual hostility of human beings, civilized society is perpetually threatened with disintegration. The [bonds of common work and common interests] would not hold it together; instinctual passions are stronger than reasonable interests" (ibid.).

Accordingly, he roots the process of civilization not only in necessity (*Ananke*), but also in Eros, or love.[5] "Civilization," Freud reports, "aims at binding the members of the community together in a libidinal way" as well as by means of common interest and the threat of violence (*SE* 21 [1930]:108). Indeed, he defines civilization as a "process in the service of Eros, whose purpose is to combine single . . . individuals, and after that . . . peoples and nations, into one great unity . . . These collections of men are to be libidinally bound to one another. Necessity alone, the advantages of work in common, will not hold them together" (*SE* 21 [1930]:122). Eros is to fan out and include ever more people in the human community (*SE* 21 [1930]:101, 103). To this end, civilization "favours every path by which strong identifications can be established between" individuals, "summons up aim-inhibited libido . . . to strengthen the communal bond by relations of friendship," and restricts sexual life and fosters its sublimation (*SE* 21 [1930]:109; see also *SE* 21 [1930]:112; *SE* 22 [1933]:208). By means of libidinous ties to the community, the individual feels concern for the welfare of others and can be motivated to "conform to the standards of morality and refrain from brutal and arbitrary conduct" (*SE* 14 [1915]:280) even when it is "disadvantageous" in terms of pure short-range self-interest to do so.[6] "Social feelings rest on identification with other people," Freud writes (*SE* 19 [1923]:37).

4. See Nozick 1974.

5. "The communal life of human beings," Freud declares, has "a two-fold foundation: the compulsion to work, which was created by external necessity, and the power of love. . . . Eros and Ananke [Love and Necessity] have become the parents of human civilization" (*SE* 21 [1930]:101). In his open letter to Einstein, "Why War?", he again states that "a community is held together by two things," but this time they are "the compelling force of violence and the emotional ties between its members" (*SE* 22 [1933]:208).

6. In "Why War?" Freud explicitly looks to the power of Eros as a means of combatting the human tendency to ever more destructive warfare. Thus, he writes: "Our . . . theory of instincts makes it easy for us to find a formula for *indirect* methods of combating war. If willingness to engage in war is an effect of the destructive instinct, the most obvious plan will be to bring Eros, its antagonist, into play against it. Anything that encourages the growth of

Of course, Freud never forgets that "man's natural aggressive instinct, the hostility of each against all and of all against each, opposes this programme of civilization" (*SE* 21 [1930]:122). The "meaning of the evolution of civilization" for Freud is thus a "struggle between Eros and Death, between the instinct of life and the instinct of destruction, as it works itself out in the human species" (ibid.).[7]

The predominant thrust of *Civilization and its Discontents* is the conflict between the "claim of the individual and the cultural claims of the group" and whether "an accommodation" between the two, including modifications of the psychodynamics of guilt, "can be reached by means of some particular form of civilization or whether this conflict is irreconcilable" (*SE* 21 [1930]:96; see also *SE* 21 [1927]:6–7). "If civilization imposes such great sacrifices not only on man's sexuality but on his aggressivity, we can understand . . . why it is hard for him to be happy in that civilization," Freud comments (*SE* 21 [1930]:115). "The price we pay for our advance in civilization is a loss of happiness through the heightening of the sense of guilt" (*SE* 21 [1930]:192, 134; see also, e.g., *SE* 21 [1927]:10; 21 [1930]:97, 111–12, 115, 141, 143; 22 [1933]:204–12).

Many interpreters have understood Freud as regarding the conflict between the individual and the requirements of civilization as absolutely irreconcilable and as seeing repression, coercion, and culturally induced unhappiness as the permanent human lot. And Freud often suggests that the difficulties of civilization are inherent in human nature and are not something that stems from the "imperfections of the cultural forms which have so far been developed" (*SE* 21 [1927]:6).

For example, in *The Future of an Illusion* Freud observes:

> One would think that a re-ordering of human relations should be possible, which
> would remove the sources of dissatisfaction with civilization by renouncing

---

emotional ties between men must operate against war. These ties may be of two kinds. . . . They may be relations resembling those towards a loved object, though without having a sexual aim. . . . The second kind of emotional tie is by means of identification. Whatever leads men to share important interests produces this community of feeling, these identifications. And the structure of human society is to a large extent based on them" (*SE* 22 [1933]:212).

7. As he poses it at the end of *Civilization*, "The fateful question for the human species seems . . . to be whether and to what extent their cultural development will succeed in mastering the disturbance of their communal life by the human instinct of aggression and self-destruction. . . . Men have gained control over the forces of nature to such an extent that with their help they would have no difficulty in exterminating one another to the last man" (*SE* 21 [1930]:145).

coercion and the suppression of the instincts . . . [But] it is questionable if such a state of affairs can be realized. It seems rather that every civilization must be built up on coercion and renunciation of instinct . . . One has . . . to reckon with the fact that there are present in all men destructive, and therefore anti-social and anti-cultural, trends and that in a great number of people these are strong enough to determine their behavior in human society. (*SE* 21 [1927]:7)

Freud also questions

whether, and in what degree, it would be possible for a different cultural environment to do away with the . . . characteristics of human masses which make the guidance of human affairs so difficult. . . . Probably a certain percentage of mankind . . . will always remain asocial; but if it were feasible merely to reduce the majority that is hostile towards civilization to-day into a minority, a great deal would have been accomplished—perhaps all that *can* be accomplished.[8] (*SE* 21 [1927]:9)

Clearly, Freud keeps in mind the contradictions that exist between individual and society, the ineluctability of instinctual aggression,[9] and the necessity of some level of social coercion. Certainly, he could never be accused of an easy optimism. But though he believes that some of the problems of civilization will always remain with us, he also regards civilization as an evolutionary process and from time to time holds out hope that a more reasonable accommodation might eventually be worked out that will afford humankind a greater degree of happiness in society. This in fact is the point of the psychoanalytic criticism of society, as Freud makes clear when, in *Civilization and its Discontents,* he declares:

When we justly find fault with the present state of our civilization for so inadequately fulfilling our demands for a plan of life that shall make us happy, and for allowing the existence of so much suffering which could probably be avoided—

---

8. In like vein, Freud states: "We cannot see why the regulations made by ourselves should not . . . be a protection and a benefit for every one of us. And yet, when we consider how unsuccessful we have been in precisely this field of prevention of suffering, a suspicion dawns on us that here, too, a piece of unconquerable nature may lie behind—this time a piece of our own psychical constitution" (*SE* 21 [1930]:86). Elsewhere in the same work, he declares that "in the course of [cultural] development, . . . love comes into opposition to the interests of civilization . . . [and] civilization threatens love with substantial restrictions. This rift between them seems unavoidable" (*SE* 21 [1930]:103). He suggests that "perhaps we may . . . familiarize ourselves with the idea that there are difficulties attaching to the nature of civilization which will not yield to any attempt at reform" (*SE* 21 [1930]:115).

9. "What a potent obstacle to civilization aggressiveness must be, if the defence against it can cause as much unhappiness as aggressiveness itself!" Freud exclaims (*SE* 21 [1930]:143).

when, with unsparing criticism, we try to uncover the roots of its imperfection, we are undoubtedly exercising a proper right and are not showing ourselves enemies of civilization. We may expect gradually to carry through such alterations in our civilization as will better satisfy our needs and will escape our criticisms.[10] (*SE* 21 [1930]:115)

Freud's moral psychology allows for significant amelioration of humankind's social unhappiness because the opposition of individual and society, though in certain respects incurable, is not complete—at least not in the same way that it is for those liberal philosophers who, because they view the human being as an isolated, atomistic, egoistic individual, conclude that social obligations are normally contrary to the individual's self-interests. Amelioration is possible for Freud because psychoanalysis regards the individual as by nature strongly possessed of both an "urge towards happiness, which we usually call 'egoistic', and the urge toward union with others in the community, which we call 'altruistic'" (*SE* 21 [1930]:140). "The development of the individual" is "a product of the interaction between [these] two urges" (ibid.). In fact, communitarian motives are partly grounded in "egoistic" (or personal) reasons for action, inasmuch as "integration in, or adaptation to, a human community appears as a scarcely avoidable condition which must be fulfilled before . . . [the individual's] aim of happiness can be achieved" (ibid.). Thus, although Freud recognizes that "the two urges, the one towards personal happiness and the other towards union with other human beings, must struggle with each other in every individual; and so, also, the two processes of individual and of cultural development must stand in hostile opposition to each other and mutually dispute the ground" (*SE* 21 [1930]:141) he also holds that "this struggle between the individual and society is not a derivative of the contradiction—probably an irreconcilable one—between the primal instincts of Eros and death. It is a dispute within the economics of the libido, comparable to the contest concerning the distribution of libido between ego and objects; and it does admit of an eventual accommodation in the individual, as, it may be hoped,

10. Along this same line, Freud states in *Future of an Illusion,* that "We may now argue that the time has probably come . . . for replacing the effects of repression by the results of the rational operation of the intellect. We may foresee, but hardly regret, that such a process of remoulding will not stop at renouncing the solemn transfiguration of cultural precepts, but that a general revision of them will result in many of them being done away with. In this way our appointed task of reconciling men to civilization will to a great extent be achieved" (*SE* 21 [1927]:44). Indeed, one of the aims of psychoanalysis as therapy is to foster the ability of the individual to become "a civilized and useful member of society with the least possible sacrifice of his own activity" (*SE* 10 [1909]:146).

it will also do in the future of civilization, however much that civilization may oppress the life of the individual to-day (ibid.)[11]

NORMATIVE PRINCIPLES

Although Freud nowhere works out how this accommodation might be accomplished on the level of civilization, by contrast with the psychological level on which psychoanalysis works to improve the individual's accommodation to often unreasonable cultural introjects,[12] he does make it plain that a revised ethic is needed.[13] This revised ethic is to eschew both unnecessary instinctual renunciation and excessive idealism and to focus instead on what it is "reasonable" to expect of individuals in their interaction with one another, given that persons are normally concerned about others and the community as well as themselves. Thus, normative principles are reasonable if they are "a protection and a benefit for every one" (*SE* 21 [1930]:86) in "adjust[ing] the relations of men to one another" (*SE* 21 [1927]:6).

Freud did not feel it was his task as a psychoanalyst to formulate a normative theory that would specify what the most basic normative principles of such a "reasonable" ethic would be. Indeed, it is questionable

11. Contrary to the assertions of some contemporary interpreters of Freud, it is not the case that he urges an isolated, privatistic approach to the conduct of life. Rieff would thus appear to be wrong when he states that "to emancipate man's 'I' from the communal 'we' is 'spiritual guidance' in the best sense Freud could give to the words" (1961, p. 362). Freud's concern is with ameliorating cultural repression, not emancipating the individual from his cultural and communal home. Thus, he explicitly rejects "keeping oneself aloof from other people" (*SE* 21 [1927]:77). He even declares that "it is difficult to practice psychoanalysis in isolation; it is an exquisitely sociable enterprise" (letter 212, in E. L. Freud 1975, p. 355; see also *SE* 21 [1927]:77–8).

Jacobs has recently tried to correct the privatistic implications of the traditional practice of psychoanalysis. He writes: "A neurotic who has, through the analysis of oedipal and other conflicts, freed himself or herself to love and work better, but who has few concerns beyond career and family, can no longer be considered 'cured.' For such persons still suffer from a particular maladaptive form of narcissism which isolates them from their environment and threatens not only their survival, but that of the world" (1988, p. 177).

12. Most interpreters of Freud's ethics focus, as Rieff does, on the individual's accommodation to culture, rather than on the accommodation to the happiness of individuals that Freud recommends on the cultural level—that is, the level of ethical principles. One of my aims here is to explicate this other side of Freud's thought.

13. Freud does not go as far as to call for a "new ethic." Rather, he envisions a "general revision" of the received "cultural precepts" (*SE* 21 [1927]:44; see also *SE* 21 [1930]:115). Only in the area of sexual ethics does Freud think that a thoroughgoing overhaul of the traditional ethical code is required. See, e.g., *CP* 2 (1908):76–99; *SE* 9 (1908):179–204.

whether he felt that it was even necessary to spell these principles out, since he appears to have assumed that once reason is directed by Eros toward the welfare of everyone in the community, it will become apparent that certain time-honored moral principles are in the interest of everyone[14]—as long as they are not held rigidly or applied inflexibly. Like his younger contemporary, the British moral philosopher David Ross to whom we owe the notion of *prima facie* moral obligations, Freud realized that moral principles are not absolutes that apply at all times and under all circumstances, but guidelines that need to be balanced against each other in actual situations of moral decision-making where several principles are apt to be in competition or conflict.[15] Instead of looking to a single normative principle, like Kant's categorical imperative or Bentham's principle of utility, for a determinative way of always and everywhere resolving moral conflicts, Freud relies instead on the individual to do the best he can, stressing, in place of a single principle, the multiple considerations the moral agent must take into account, including his own defensive proclivities, which inhibit so many people from perceiving and judging moral conflicts aright.[16]

14. It is perhaps in this context that we should understand Freud's fondness for quoting the novelist F. T. Vischer to the effect that "what is moral is self-evident."

15. As we have seen, Freud frequently opposed the absoluteness and inflexibility of moral rules conceived as categorical imperatives (see, e.g., *SE* 13 [1913]:xiv). He hoped that the accumulating scientific evidence that moral rules are human constructs would help to diminish their sacred aura and make it easier for people to realize that all such rules should serve the mundane interests of ordinary people (see *SE* 21 [1927]:41).

What Freud says in the following passage about the "rules" of psychoanalytic technique would seem to apply equally to how he would have us think about moral principles and rules: "He who hopes to learn the fine art of the game of chess from books will soon discover that . . . the endless variety of the moves which develop . . . defies description; the gap left in the instructions can only be filled in by the zealous study of games fought out by master-hands. The rules which can be laid down for the practical application of psychoanalysis in treatment are subject to similar limitations. The . . . justification [of presenting rules for treatment here] . . . is that they are simply rules of the game, acquiring their importance by their connection with the whole plan of the game. I do well, however, to bring them forward as 'recommendations' without claiming any unconditional acceptance for them. The . . . great number of the determining factors involved prevent the formulation of a stereotyped technique, and also bring it about that a course of action, ordinarily legitimate, may be at times ineffective, while one which is usually erroneous may occasionally lead to the desired end. These circumstances do not prevent us from [formulating rules] . . . which will be found most generally efficient" (*CP* 2 [1913]:342–3).

16. Freud enunciates an ideal of "normal" practical rationality that sounds a lot like that embodied in Aristotle's man of practical wisdom. An evaluative judgment is "completely rational," he writes, when it is "derived from the actual situation, proportionate to the real circumstances and under the complete control of the conscious ego" (*SE* 18 [1922]:223).

Presumably, a normative theory would count as reasonable to Freud if it consisted of the principles that the preceding chapters have identified as those he treats throughout his writings as virtually self-evident. The most important of these is unquestionably the duty to avoid injuring others (the duty of nonmaleficence), since it is clearly one of Freud's primary concerns throughout his writings to reduce the harm that people are already doing to one another, often in the name of morality.[17] A second central normative principle that Freud takes as obviously in the interests of everyone is truth telling, it being one of psychoanalysis's principal findings that deceit in human relations has corrosive consequences far beyond those usually appreciated.[18] Promise keeping is the third norm that Freud assumes to be rather obviously reasonable, since it is essential to the success of cooperative ventures like the psychoanalytic relation, in which individuals need to be able to rely on the future actions of others.[19] Respect for the autonomy of others also ranks high in Freud's implicit normative theory, since,

17. The importance of nonmaleficence to Freud is evident in his papers on psychoanalytic technique and social criticism (see *SE* 12 [1915]:159–71; 9 [1908]:181–204). The priority of nonmaleficence over other weighty moral obligations, such as respect for a patient's autonomy, is indicated by Freud's recommendation that analysis be conducted within parameters that protect the patient from serious "injuries," while permitting the patient "as much . . . personal freedom as is compatible with these restrictions" (*SE* 12 [1914]:153).

18. Truth telling is not only crucial to the conduct of psychoanalysis, where the analysand is instructed "to make a *duty* of the most complete honesty" (*SE* 18 [1923]:238, emphasis added; see also ch. 10 above); it also guides the recommendations Freud makes about public conduct. "The compulsion to speak the truth must indeed be solidified by ethics," he writes (Freud and Bullitt, 1967, p. xii). Freud takes it as axiomatic that "a frank revelation," though difficult, is virtually always preferable to the multiplication of harms that accompanies concealment of painful truths (see, e.g., *SE* 14 [1914]:49). He recommends that the psychoanalytic community be more forthright in exposing its own disputes than conventional morality dictates, even though such publicity may harm the public image of psychoanalysis (ibid.).

Freud clearly expected complete honesty from his family, friends, and associates and was thus indignant when, years later, he learned that there had been some doubt among his followers in 1923 about whether he should be told he was suffering from a malignancy (see Jones, 1957, p. 93). When he was close to death in 1939, Freud wrote to Princess Marie Bonaparte that he disliked his doctors' mendacious reassurances that his cancer was actually receding. "I don't believe it and don't like being deceived," he wrote (letter 313, in E. L. Freud 1975, p. 458).

19. It is because promise keeping is an ethical duty that the analyst can instruct the analysand about the "fundamental rule" of psychoanalysis: "'Finally, never forget that you have *promised* to be absolutely honest, and never leave anything out because, for some reason or other, it is unpleasant to tell it'" (*SE* 12 [1913]:135, emphasis added). For other aspects of psychoanalysis that presuppose the duty of promise keeping, see ch. 10 above and *SE* 23 (1940):173.

clinically, such respect guides the analyst's behavior toward the analysand, even as it directs the analyst's attention to increased patient autonomy as the goal of the treatment.[20] But respect for each individual's autonomy is also central to Freud's social criticism, in which opposition to heteronomy (or rule by another) is a predominant theme. The duty of beneficence is limited by Freud, because it has been used so often to demand too much self-sacrifice or to justify unwarranted paternalistic interference in the autonomous affairs of others.[21] But beneficence remains an important moral guideline in interpersonal relations like friendship and the doctor–patient relation, as well as in society, where some concern for utility and the common good is expected.[22] For Freud, as for Kant, beneficence is an "imperfect obligation"; we are usually free to practice it as we see fit, except in cases where the good that we could do for others involves so little cost to ourselves that we are obliged to help.[23] Still, Freud considers it a good thing to help others, as an act of supererogation, as long as we can do so spontaneously, without debilitating guilt and resentment—that is, as a form of sublimation.

The last major principle in Freud's implicit normative theory is that of justice, which, as "reciprocity," has been shown to figure prominently in his critique of the love commandment in *Civilization and its Discontents* (see

20. Freud assumes that respect for autonomy guides the analyst at the outset of treatment when the patient's consent is sought (see *SE* 12 [1913]:129 and ch. 10 above), during treatment when interventions aim at freeing the patient from internalized authorities by siding with the patient's capacities for "self-knowledge" and "self-control" (see *CP* 2 [1912]:329; *SE* 23 [1940]:175), and at the conclusion of treatment, insofar as "the eventual independence of the patient is our ultimate goal" (*CP* 2 [1912]:319).

21. Freud warns that the therapist who seeks to be helpful to a patient by assisting too much may actually harm the patient by keeping him or her from assuming responsibility for him or her self. He writes: "Any analyst who out of the fullness of his heart, perhaps, and his readiness to help, extends to the patient all that one human being may hope to receive from another, commits the same . . . error as that of which our non-analytic institutions for nervous patients are guilty. Their one aim is to make everything as pleasant as possible for the patient, so that he may feel well there and be glad to take refuge there again from the trials of life. In so doing they make no attempt to give him more strength for facing life and more capacity for carrying out his actual tasks in it" (*SE* 17 [1919]:164).

22. In *Civilization*, Freud writes of the duty of beneficence that goes hand in glove with intimate relations: "My love is something valuable . . . It imposes duties on me for whose fulfilment I must be ready to make sacrifices" (*SE* 21 [1930]:109). Regarding the psychoanalyst's obligation to consider the patient's best interests, Freud directs psychoanalysts to follow procedures that have been shown to provide the patient with "the largest amount of help that we can give him to-day" (*SE* 12 [1912]:115).

23. Thus Freud writes: "If by a stroke of the pen one can really do something for a worthy person in need, then one has no reason to hesitate" (letter 247, in E. L. Freud 1975, p. 393–4).

ch. 9 above). However, justice as reciprocity applies primarily to interpersonal relations rather than to institutional life. Regarding the latter, it is widely thought today that Freud had little to say about the ethics of public life, except in criticism of its excessive constraints, in large part, it is said, because he failed to retain a lively interest in external reality after he turned his attention primarily to intrapsychic fantasies and conflicts in the aftermath of the collapse of the seduction hypothesis. Thus, Rorty contends that "Freud, in particular, has no contribution to make to social theory. His domain is . . . the private life, . . . the attempt of individuals to be reconciled with themselves" (Rorty, 1986:11). However, Freud not only was not blind to the importance of justice in adjudicating conflicts of interest among individuals, he viewed social justice as part of the cement that holds civilized societies together.[24] As he states in *Civilization and its Discontents:*

> The element of civilization enters on the scene with the first attempt to regulate . . . social relationships. If the attempt were not made, the relationships would be subject to the arbitrary will of the individual: that is to say, the physically stronger man would decide them in the sense of his own interests and instinctual impulses. . . . Human life in common is only made possible when . . . [t]he power of . . . [the] community is . . . set up . . . in opposition to the power of the individual. (*SE* 21 [1930]:95)

For Freud, "the essence" of this "decisive step of civilization" lies in the formation of principles of justice that henceforth regulate the distribution of the benefits and burdens of social life. *"The first requisite of civilization, therefore, is that of justice,* he declares (*SE* 21 [1930]:95, emphasis added).

It is to Freud's brief, but important, elaboration of a social ethic on the basis of this insight in his late writings that I now turn.

FREUD'S SOCIAL ETHIC

The passages on social justice in Freud's work that are best known to contemporary social philosophers are those that sound reductionist themes

24. Part of the subtext of *Future of an Illusion* is that religions have induced the masses to accept exploitative arrangements as just and that the injustices contained therein are bound to come to light with increasing secularization of modern societies (see, e.g., *SE* 21 [1927]:13). It follows as a corollary that the "rational . . . precepts of civilization" that Freud proposes as a replacement for religious ethics will have to find more equitable principles on which to distribute the benefits and burdens of cooperative existence. As he put it in a paper written in 1905 or 1906, "the less belief there comes to be in divinity, the more important becomes the *human* regulation of affairs; and it is this which, with increasing insight, comes to be held responsible for suffering" (*SE* 7 [1942]:307–8).

rather than constructive proposals. This is in large part, it would seem, because philosophers have found it difficult to penetrate beyond the popular portrait of Freud as a psychological egoist. Rawls (1971, pp. 539–40) and Lakoff (1964, pp. 183–93), for example, both take Freud to task for holding that justice is nothing more than "a mask for envy" grounded ultimately in self-interest (Rawls 1971, p. 540). They base this interpretation on several paragraphs in *Group Psychology and the Analysis of the Ego* (*SE* 18 [1921]:120–1) in which Freud argues that children develop a sense of justice, in the nursery, and in many other social situations, as a reaction to jealousy of younger rivals who are also the recipients of parental love and attention. As the child realizes the impossibility of maintaining this hostility without punishment, Freud argues, he or she is forced to identify with other children. So there grows up "a communal or group feeling," out of which arises "the first demand . . . for justice, for equal treatment for all" (*SE* 18 [1921]:120). The child reasons in effect that if I cannot be the favorite, nobody else shall be the favorite. Freud comments: "Social justice means that we deny ourselves many things so that others may have to do without them as well, or, what is the same thing, may not be able to ask for them" (*SE* 18 [1921]:121).

There are several problems with the assumption of Rawls and Lakoff that this line of reasoning threatens the integrity of the normal adult's sense of justice.[25] First, as Rawls's own counterargument makes clear, Freud's explanation of justice as a reaction formation against envy may be viewed as itself presupposing a primitive sense of justice that is a factor in the child's resentment; that is, the child's envy arises partly out of the sense that the children are not being fairly treated. Rawls does not think that Freud realized this, but there is some internal evidence that he did. For example, Freud assumes a rudimentary concept of equity in the three- or four-year-old who out of gratitude seeks to repay his parent's beneficence with a gift "of like value" (*CP* 4 [1910]:200). Secondly, for Freud to call justice a "reaction formation" is not to view it as a mere mask that is fully reducible to the original motive, as Rawls and Lakoff suppose. A reaction formation can involve a genuine transformation of a motive,[26] so that the child who

25. Lakoff writes that this argument implies that "the demand for equality is not to be taken at face value, but rather as an outgrowth of frustrated egoism, as an expression of grudging selfishness making a virtue out of failure. From the nursery to the factory, all demands for equality represent a process that starts with individual failures to find gratification and ends in unconscious efforts to enforce similar deprivations upon others" (1964, p. 191).

26. Although Freud usually holds that the repression involved in reaction formation precludes sublimation, he points out in *Three Essays on the Theory of Sexuality* that reaction

starts out disliking his or her rival for primarily egoistic reasons may, by identifying with the other child in the context of jealousy, come to perceive other points of similarity out of which genuine empathy and sympathy can arise. This would seem to be especially the case if the child is also pushed instinctively, as Freud's mature theory of Eros implies, toward concern for the other. Finally, of course, Freud was aware that origins are not to be confused with justifications in morals any more than in other areas of life (see *SE* 13 [1913]:179).

Another reason why Freud's constructive social ethic is commonly over-looked by social philosophers is because some of his offhand remarks about the unworthiness of human beings, taken out of context, appear to portray an insensitivity to issues of social justice, even a disturbing elitism that views human beings as inescapably unequal and thus deserving of differential treatment. The fact that Freud's letters occasionally refer to other human beings as "trash"[27] or "a wretched lot" (in E. L. Freud 1974, p. 3) is not necessarily significant ethically, however, if, as Freud implies, these modes of expression are really little more than relatively harmless verbal outlets for keenly felt emotions of disappointment and anger. As the following passage from a letter to Arnold Zweig in 1927 indicates, Freud was aware that he used such derogatory expressions when he was troubled by the cruelty of his fellow human beings: "With regard to anti-semitism I don't really want to search for explanations; I feel a strong inclination to surrender to my affects in this matter and find myself confirmed in my wholly non-scientific belief that mankind on the average and taken by and large are a wretched lot. Naturally I am not reproaching you with having managed not to surrender to this irrational affect" (ibid.).

---

formation may be one of the pathways of sublimation. This implies two kinds of reaction formation, as Sterba (1978, p. 188) suggested to Freud in 1931: "one form identical to the countercathexis against strong unconscious drive impulses, and another form in which the drive energy is absorbed through the establishment of the reaction formation itself." An example of the difference is that between the cleanliness of the anal compulsive as a reaction against a strong unconscious drive toward anal messiness and normal cleanliness which lacks the backlog of pressing needs (ibid.), pp. 188–9). As the discussion of sublimation in ch. 8 brought out, the concept is sufficiently broad to encompass the second type of reaction formation.

27. Freud responded with obvious irritation to Pfister's advocacy of a high-minded "love of humanity" and his criticism of Freud's ethics and sexual theory in *Was bietet die Psychoanalyse dem Erzieher?* (*Psycho-Analysis in the Service of Education*) (Leipzig, 1917) by declaring, with the clear intention of shocking his ministerial colleague into acknowledging baser unconscious feelings: "I have found little that is 'good' about human beings on the whole. In my experience most of them are trash, no matter whether they publicly subscribe to this or that ethical doctrine or to none at all" (letter dated 9 Oct. 1918, in Meng and Freud 1963, pp. 61–2). See also letter 243, in E. L. Freud 1975, 390.

It is potentially more significant ethically that Freud thought that people were unequally endowed. He even declares soberly at one point that "nature, by endowing individuals with extremely unequal physical attributes and mental capacities, has introduced injustices against which there is no remedy" (*SE* 21 [1930]:113, n. 1).[28] But the ethical implications that Freud would have us draw from the diversity of human abilities are scarcely self-evident apart from the social ethic within which he considered them. That ethic, as Freud formulates it here and there in his mature writings, gives evidence of a sophistication that apparently derives from his careful study of social and political philosophy as a youth, when he was looking forward to a career in law.[29] Though briefly sketched, Freud's mature social ethic covers such central issues as the rule of law and equal treatment, liberty, distributive justice, and just war theory.

The Rule of Law

One of the most important features of civilization for Freud is the rule of law—namely, precepts backed by communal authority (and, if need be, violence) that replace "the power of the individual . . . [with] the power of a community" (*SE* 21 [1930]:95). The rule of law is essential for civilization because humanity's instinctual predisposition to violence and selfishness requires a mechanism for making it in everyone's self-interest to "restrict themselves in their possibilities of satisfaction" (ibid.) and to band together to resist domination and exploitation by those possessing superior strength. "Human life in common is only made possible when a majority comes together which is stronger than any separate individual and which remains united against all separate individuals," Freud writes (ibid.; see also *SE* 22 [1933]:205). In order for this to happen, "the community must be maintained permanently, must be organized, must draw up regulations to anticipate the risk of rebellion and must institute authorities to see that those regulations—the laws—are respected and to superintend the execution of legal acts of violence" (ibid.).

28. Freud lamented to Putnam that "so many of the patients we really want to help are incapable of it [sublimation]. For the most part, these patients have inferior endowments and disproportionately strong drives. They would like to be better than they can be, yet this convulsive desire benefits neither themselves nor society" (letter 36, dated 14 May 1911, in Hale 1971, p. 122).

29. In a 1935 "Postscript" to his *Autobiographical Study,* Freud stated: "My interest, after making a life long *détour* through the natural sciences, medicine and psychotherapy, returned to the cultural problems which had fascinated me long before, when I was a youth scarcely old enough for thinking" (*SE* 20 [1925]:72). We now know, thanks to recent historical research and especially to Freud's letters to Silberstein, that this earlier fascination with cultural problems included political philosophy. See McGrath 1986, pp. 94–5.

Like Hobbes, Freud believes that "recognition of a community of interests" is one source of commitment to a system of law. He contends that, historically, "insecurity of life, which is an equal danger for everyone, . . . unites men into a society which prohibits the individual from killing and reserves to itself the right to communal killing of anyone who violates the prohibition" (*SE* 21 [1927]:40). But once the recognition of common interests has given rise to a system of law, the social fabric is further reinforced by the existence of a legal system. Social bonds are themselves in part legal bonds. "The recognition of a community of interests" maintained by laws "leads to a growth of emotional ties between the members of a united group of people—communal feelings which are the true source of its strength," Freud explains (*SE* 22 [1933]:205).

Freud builds several normative constraints into his view of the rule of law. First is the formal requirement that like cases be treated alike: the "assurance that a law once made will not be broken in favour of an individual" (*SE* 21 [1930]:95). But it is also important that the law be fair substantively, which means that it should not be "an expression of the will of a small community—a caste or a stratum of the population or a racial group—which, in its turn, behaves like a violent individual towards other, and perhaps more numerous, collections of people" (ibid.). A just community should be governed by "a rule of law to which all—except those who are not capable of entering a community—have contributed . . . and which leaves no one—again with the same exception—at the mercy of brute force" (ibid.). The direction of culture is from "violence to right or law" and "from unequal justice to equal justice for all" (*SE* 22 [1933]:206).[30] By equal justice for all, Freud meant equal civil liberties and fair distribution of the benefits and burdens of social cooperation.

Liberty

As a concomitant of the importance accorded respect for patient autonomy in clinical psychoanalytic practice, Freud's social ethic strongly endorses J. S. Mill's ideal of the most extensive individual liberty compatible with the liberty of others. No person is to be treated as a mere instrument of an-

---

30. Freud objected to the Germanic *furor prohibendi* (passion for prohibitions), the "tendency to keep people under tutelage, to interfere and to forbid," on the grounds that "a superabundance of regulations and prohibitions injures the authority of law." In this connection, he says: "It can be observed that where only a few prohibitions exist they are carefully observed, but where one is accompanied by prohibitions at every step, one feels definitely tempted to disregard them. . . . Furthermore, if one desires to maintain respect for laws and regulations it is advisable not to enact any where a watch cannot easily be kept on whether they are obeyed or transgressed" (*SE* 20 [1926]:235).

other's plans; no one should be interfered with unless there are clear, valid reasons for intervening. Freud is in the classical liberal tradition with which he strongly identified[31] when he demands with respect to religious freedom: "Are the authorities so certain of the right path to salvation that they venture to prevent each man from trying 'to be saved after his own fashion?'" (*SE* 20 [1926]:236). In Freud's view, "each person should judge the issue[s] on the basis of his own experience and the merit of the arguments" (letter 63, in Hale 1971, p. 153).

Sounding themes of Mill's opposition to paternalism, Freud reasons that one is seldom justified in interfering in the autonomous choices of another person except to protect third parties or to provide crucial information where serious risks are involved. But he departs slightly from Mill's categorical opposition to all forms of paternalism in countenancing modest restrictions on liberty to prevent self-inflicted harms. Thus, he observes: "Granted that many people if they are left to themselves run into danger and come to grief, would not the authorities do better carefully to mark the limits of the regions which are to be regarded as not to be trespassed upon, and for the rest, so far as possible, to allow human beings to be educated by experience and mutual influence?" (*SE* 20 [1926]:236).

In espousing liberty as the first substantive principle of a just society, Freud took issue with the then developing sociological view that liberty is a by-product of social evolution.[32] For him, it is of the essence of persons that they are autonomous beings. "The liberty of the individual is no gift of civilization," Freud states in *Civilization and its Discontents* (*SE* 21 [1930]:95). "It was greatest before there was any civilization, though then . . . it had for the most part no value, since the individual was scarcely in a position to defend it." The "urge for freedom" springs in part from the "original [human] personality" that is still untamed by civilization and its constraints and "is directed against particular forms and demands of civilization or against civilization altogether." Freud expects that the individual "will always defend his claim to individual liberty against the will of the group" (*SE* 21 [1930]:96). This defense of liberty is good for society as well as for the individual, because "what makes itself felt in a human community as a desire for freedom may be their revolt against some existing injustice, and so may prove favourable to a further development of civilization" (ibid.).

31. As McGrath (1986) brings out, Freud identified closely with German-Jewish liberalism (pp. 30–1, 184, 224, 264, 271–3). Freud wrote to Arnold Zweig in 1930: "I remain a liberal of the old school" (in E. L. Freud 1974, p. 21).

32. See, e.g., Durkheim 1933.

Freud understood his own work in psychoanalysis as in part aimed at enhancing individual liberty by increasing social tolerance for characterological differences, such as sexual deviance, through psychological education. Thus, he boldly asserted that the "disposition to perversions of every kind is a general and fundamental human characteristic" (*SE* 7 [1905]:191) and that there is "some trace of homosexual object-choice in everyone" (*SE* 20 [1925]:38). Although the established psychoanalytic movement became known for its hostility to same-sex orientation, Freud's own writings contain some surprising pleas for the fair treatment of homosexuals. In a justly famous, sympathetic letter to a despairing American mother who wrote to him for advice, Freud declares:

> I gather from your letter that your son is a homosexual. I am most impressed by the fact that you do not mention this term yourself. . . . Homosexuality is assuredly no advantage, but it is nothing to be ashamed of, no vice, no degradation, it cannot be classified as an illness; we consider it to be a variation of the sexual function produced by a certain arrest of sexual development. Many highly respectable individuals of ancient and modern times have been homosexuals, several of the greatest men among them (Plato, Michelangelo, Leonardo da Vinci, etc.). It is a great injustice to persecute homosexuality as a crime, and cruelty too.[33] (E. Jones 1957, pp. 195–6)

Similarly, in *Civilization and its Discontents,* Freud observes that a cultural community generally restricts the object of choice of the sexually mature individual "to the opposite sex, and most extra-genital satisfactions are forbidden as perversions" (*SE* 21 [1930]:104). He then goes on to say that "the requirement, demonstrated in these prohibitions, that there shall be a single kind of sexual life for everyone, disregards the dissimilarities, whether innate or acquired, in the sexual constitution of human beings; it cuts off a fair number of them from sexual enjoyment, and so *becomes the source of serious injustice*" (ibid., emphasis added).[34]

33. E. R. Wallace would have us believe that this letter is an example of Freud attempting to remove perversions entirely from "the moral domain" (1986b, pp. 88–9); but this seems unlikely given what Freud says about the "injustice" and "cruelty" of treating homosexuality as a crime. Gay cites this letter as illustrating "the defiant cast of mind" that was part of Freud's Jewish identity (1988, p. 610). But however subversive he may have been of traditional culture, Freud was also a strong advocate of established liberal moral sentiments of toleration, which he wished to extend to sexual matters. His subversive stance toward respectable sexual mores was part and parcel of his liberal ethical mind-set.

34. Freud elsewhere argues that "it is one of the obvious social injustices that the standard of civilization should demand from everyone the same conduct of sexual life—conduct which can be followed without any difficulty by some people, thanks to their organization, but which imposes the heaviest psychical sacrifices on others" (*SE* 9 [1908]:192).

Freud felt the same way about moral ideals: namely, that it is an "injustice" to expect exactly the same behavior from everyone. Not everyone is capable of sublimation or at least of sublimation to the same degree (*SE* 9 [1908]:187–8; letter 36, in Hale 1971, p. 122). Hence, ideals of the good life, such as those discussed in the preceding chapter, must be adjusted to the psychological capacities of different agents.

Distributive Justice

Surprisingly, given his reputation as a proponent of privatism, Freud expresses significant sensitivity to issues of distributive justice. In *The Future of an Illusion,* he notes that social rules and institutions "aim . . . at effecting a certain distribution of wealth . . . [and] maintaining that distribution" (*SE* 21 [1927]:6) and finds that serious problems for individuals and society as a whole reside in inequitable distributions of resources. The underprivileged classes reasonably envy the favored groups and will attempt to free themselves of "their own surplus of privation," Freud warns (*SE* 21 [1927]:12). Failing this emancipation from inequity, "a permanent measure of discontent will persist within the culture" and "can lead to dangerous revolts" (ibid.).[35] But Freud is not only speaking pragmatically when he observes the dangers of unfair distributions of social goods. He is sympathetic to protest against inequality on normative terms as well. Thus he declares, referring to "the justifiable hostility of the . . . masses," that

> if . . . a culture has not got beyond a point at which the satisfaction of one portion of its participants depends upon the suppression of another . . . portion—and this is the case in all present-day cultures—it is understandable that the suppressed people should develop an intense hostility towards a culture whose existence they make possible by their work, but in whose wealth they have too small a share. . . . It goes without saying that a civilization which leaves so large a number of its participants unsatisfied and drives them into revolt neither has nor deserves the prospect of a lasting existence. (*SE* 21 [1927]:12)

35. Freud adds that the hostility to culture engendered in the underprivileged from their "surplus of privation" is partly counteracted by narcissistic satisfaction derived from identification with the culture's ideals: "No doubt one is a wretched plebeian, harassed by debts and military service; but, to make up for it, one is a Roman citizen, one has one's share in the task of ruling other nations and dictating their laws" (*SE* 21 [1927]:13). Beyond identification, "the suppressed classes can be emotionally attached to their masters" by affection generated by the dispossessed seeing their ideals embodied in them (*SE* 21 [1927]:12–13). "Unless such relations of a fundamentally satisfying kind subsisted," Freud says, "it would be impossible to understand how a number of civilizations have survived so long in spite of the *justifiable* hostility of large human masses" (*SE* 21 [1927]:13, emphasis added).

According to Freud, the violence born of envy that one would expect to arise from economic inequity has been pretty much kept in check by religious ideologies that convince the suppressed masses that they deserve their lot, that they will receive better in an afterlife, and that God has forbidden violence and will severely punish them for it in this life or the next. But as secularization continues to erode religion's authority, Freud predicts that the suppressed classes will be increasingly inclined to revolution (*SE* 21 [1927]:39).[36] It is primarily "the oppressed," he argues, who press for "equal justice for all" (*SE* 22 [1933]:206).

In *Civilization and its Discontents*, Freud also addresses issues of distributive justice. For example, he states that "a real change in the relations of human beings to possessions would be of more help" in lessening human beings' tendency to aggression "than any ethical commands" (*SE* 21 [1930]:143). In the course of discussing communism, which Freud faults for its inaccurate psychological assumption that economic redistribution can cure aggression and all other social woes,[37] Freud proclaims that "anyone who has tasted the miseries of poverty in his own youth and has experienced the indifference and arrogance of the well-to-do, should be safe from the suspicion of having no understanding or good will towards endeavours to fight against the inequality of wealth among men and all that it leads to" (*SE* 21 [1930]:113, n. 1).

36. As a young man, Freud greatly admired Feuerbach (see McGrath 1986, pp. 104–7); his heroes—Hannibal, Marcus Brutus, and Karl Moor, the protagonist of Schiller's *The Robbers*—passionately defended freedom in the face of tyranny. This may account for the evidence in *Future of an Illusion* that he appreciated Marx's argument that religions obscure and rationalize social injustices and that it is from the oppressed that one can expect pressure for radical social change, once they have become conscious of their former alienation by illusory beliefs. Freud objects to communism primarily because it tries to cure religious illusions with equally dangerous secular illusions about the goodness of human nature and a socialist utopia (see *SE* 21 [1930]:112–13; 22 [1933]:211–12). The Soviet experience led him to discern a practical affinity between communism and despotism (see his letter to Zweig dated 26 Nov. 1930, in E. L. Freud 1974, p. 21). Yet Freud also laments the loss of the egalitarian ideal for which the Soviet experiment is responsible: "We have been deprived by it of a hope—and an illusion—and we have received nothing in exchange. We are moving towards dark times" (letter to Zweig dated 7 Dec. 1930, ibid., p. 25).

37. Freud holds that the recognition of the salutary possibilities of changing basic property relation by socialists and communists "has been obscured and made useless for practical purposes by a fresh idealistic misconception of human nature" (*SE* 21 [1930]:143). He points out that the "psychological premises on which the system is based are an untenable illusion" because aggression is inherent in humankind (*SE* 21 [1930]:113). "Aggressiveness was not created by property," he notes (*SE* 21 [1930]:113), and if we do away with personal property, other inequalities, like those created by power, remain and become the sources of new hostilities, such as despotism (see letter to Zweig, dated 16 Nov. 1930, in E. L. Freud 1974, p. 21).

Similarly, although psychoanalysis has often been castigated as a therapy for the elite only, in his address to the Fifth International Psychoanalytic Congress held in Budapest at the conclusion of World War I, Freud articulated a hope that "the conscience of society will awake and remind it that the poor man should have just as much right to assistance for his mind as he now has to the life-saving help offered by surgery" (SE 17 [1919]:167). He articulated a vision of state-supported clinics offering free psychoanalytically oriented treatment[38] to the masses "so that men who would otherwise give way to drink, women who have nearly succumbed under their burden of privations, children for whom there is no choice but between running wild or neurosis, may be made capable, by analysis, of resistance and of efficient work" (ibid.). Freud's proposal seems to have rested in part on the utilitarian notion that "the neuroses threaten public health no less than tuberculosis" (ibid.) and in part on the equitable grounds that need is the proper distributive criterion for health benefits.[39] Freud was a realist when it came to how the actual external conditions of life affect the well-being of persons[40] and argued that such "mental assistance"

38. Freud recognized that analytic technique would have to be adapted to "the new conditions" of treating the poor, uneducated masses: "It is very probable . . . that the large-scale application of our therapy will compel us to alloy the pure gold of analysis freely with the copper of direct suggestion; and hypnotic influence, too, might find a place in it again, as it has in the treatment of war neuroses. But, whatever form this psychotherapy for the people may take, . . . its most effective and most important ingredients will assuredly remain those borrowed from strict and untendentious psycho-analysis" (SE 17 [1919]:167–8).

39. Possibly thinking of the plans of Anton von Freund to establish a psychoanalytic clinic in Budapest that would make treatment accessible to the people, Freud suggests that, pending state assistance for mental health, voluntary associations should start clinics funded by private philanthropic foundations. In his obituary for von Freund, Freud praises him for sharpening "in all directions the sense of social justice" (SE 18 [1920]:267–8). Von Freund did not live long enough to set up an outpatient psychoanalytic clinic for the people of Budapest, but his example was followed, and a clinic established in Berlin by Dr Max Eitingon.

Anna Freud's biographer, Elisabeth Young-Bruehl, notes that Freud's followers responded favorably to the ethical challenge of the 1918 Budapest address. "Many analysts . . . took Freud's advice and extended psychoanalysis through clinics and institutes into 'the wider social strata,'" she reports (Young-Breuhl 1988, p. 81), and "Freud's social vision became a credo . . . [for] his daughter" (ibid.).

40. A good illustration of this is contained in a letter of 1909 to Putnam, in which he says: "I believe that your complaint that we are not able to compensate our neurotic patients for giving up their illness is quite justified. But it seems to me that this is not the fault of therapy but rather of social institutions. What would you have us do when a woman complains about her thwarted life, when, with youth gone, she notices that she has been deprived of the joy of loving for merely conventional reasons? She is quite right, and we stand helpless before her, for we cannot make her young again. But the recognition of our therapeutic limitations reinforces our determination to change other social factors so that men and women shall no longer be forced into hopeless situations" (Hale 1971, pp. 90–1).

for the poor would need to be combined "with some material support" if the lot of the least well-off were to be genuinely improved (*SE* 17 [1919]:167).

Ever mindful of the realities of human nature, Freud appreciated that, in order to have a sufficient economic base for distribution, a further condition—namely, efficiency—would be needed and that efficiency is promoted, whether we like it or not, by policies that draw on self-interest—which implies criticism of socialists for failing to understand this, as well as an implicit acceptance of rewards for effort and social contribution in distributing the goods and benefits of social cooperation.

Freud also realized, despite his emphasis on the equality of persons before the law and equal liberties, that the effort to make people equal in the respects in which they are not equal—in strength, intelligence, talent, capacity for sublimation—requires force and, ultimately, leveling under tyranny. So, in the course of enunciating his commitment to the fight against inequalities of wealth, he insists that people are not equal in some respects and that it is an injustice to assume that they are. It is in this context, triggered by discussion of the communist ideal of an equality of sameness, that Freud makes the statement about ineluctable inequality cited earlier: "To be sure, if an attempt is made to base . . . [the] fight [against the inequality of wealth] upon an abstract demand, in the name of justice, for equality for all men, there is a very obvious objection to be made—that nature, by endowing individuals with extremely unequal physical attributes and mental capacities, has introduced injustices against which there is no remedy" (*SE* 21 [1930]:113, n. 1). This passage is sometimes read, incorrectly, as implying a fundamental inequality of persons as moral agents. But Freud is not here addressing what is owed people as moral persons irrespective of their social position, but the quite different issue of what is owed them in connection with the distribution of certain goods.[41] His position is that it is both efficient and fair for some, who are more favored in the natural lottery, to receive more than others, presumably on grounds of contribution and effort, and that there are limits to how far society can go in making up for natural differences.

Freud is also inegalitarian when it comes to the distribution of political power. One of his criticisms of the communist abolition of private property is that it will not do away with the distribution problem; for power will

41. For discussion of the distinction between the equality of persons as moral agents and the inequality of persons as the recipients of different shares in the distribution of certain goods like social status and prestige, see Rawls 1971, p. 511. Darwall (1977) makes a similar distinction between "recognition respect" and "appraisal respect." See also Wallwork 1979, p. 132.

remain to be distributed. "In abolishing private property we deprive the human love of aggression of one of its instruments . . . but we have in no way altered the differences in power and influence which are misused by aggressiveness" (SE 21 [1930]:113).

Freud's view of society as a horde, a mass of equal members headed by a superior leader, has troubling implications for his view of democratic politics. In *Why War?* he states:

> One instance of the innate and ineradicable inequality of men is their tendency to fall into the two classes of leaders and followers. The latter constitute the vast majority; they stand in need of an authority which will make decisions for them and to which they for the most part offer an unqualified submission. This suggests that more care should be taken than hitherto to educate an upper stratum of men with independent minds, not open to intimidation and eager in the pursuit of truth, whose business it would be to give direction to the dependent masses. . . . The encroachments made by the executive power of the State and the prohibition laid by the Church upon freedom of thought are far from propitious for the production of a class of this kind. The ideal condition of things would of course be a community of men who had subordinated their instinctual life to the dictatorship of reason. Nothing else could unite men so completely and so tenaciously, even if there were no emotional ties between them. But in all probability that is a Utopian expectation. (SE 22 [1933]:212)

Here, Freud follows Plato in supposing that talented individuals should be educated to take a clear view of the universal interest for the benefit of the whole society. He seems to envision that talented individuals, educated for rational leadership, will make their way into positions of power, and thus he seems to hold to the principle of equal opportunity, defined as positions open to all.[42] But there is certainly a counter-egalitarian theme built into Freud's denigration of the masses in favor of leaders that is in tension with what he maintains in this same work about the equality of persons before the law and the importance of oppressed groups pushing the law in the direction of "equal justice for all" (see, e.g., SE 22 [1933]:206). Nonetheless, it is clear from Freud's criticism of leaders who "set themselves above the prohibitions which apply to everyone" that, ethically, he would expect leaders to uphold the law, including, presumably, its guarantees regarding the most basic liberties (SE 22 [1933]:206).[43]

42. Freud does not follow Burke and Hegel in envisioning a hereditary ruling stratum (see Burke 1910, p. 49; Plamenatz 1963, 1:346–51; Hegel 1942, p. 199; Rawls 1971, p. 300).

43. It is because Freud assumes justice to require that principles apply equally to everyone that he insists on laws not being broken in favor of an individual (see SE 21 [1930]:95). This

In Freud's view, it appears, free public education is important primarily for the production of the wisest political leaders, who will in turn guide the citizenry as a whole. This view contrasts with the more democratic presuppositions underlying the American system of education, in which public education is provided so as to allow an informed citizenry to choose directly among competing representatives of different political ideas.

Freud acknowledges that even a just social order will require the individual to make certain renunciations. In *Civilization and its Discontents,* he observes that inasmuch as a civilized society requires certain restrictions, "justice demands that no one shall escape those restrictions" (*SE* 21 [1930]:95–6; see also *SE* 18 [1921]:67). But he believes that in a society in which just principles prevail and in which moral precepts are recognized to be constructs of the community for the benefit of everyone in the community, these renunciations will seem less burdensome and citizens will be willing to work for the improvement of social regulations rather than their abolition. He writes: "People [sh]ould understand that they [laws] are made . . . to serve their interests; and . . . instead of aiming at their abolition, . . . aim only at their improvement. This would be an important advance along the road which leads to becoming reconciled to the burden of civilization" (*SE* 21 [1927]:41). In like vein, Freud argues that, "by withdrawing their expectations from the other world and concentrating all their liberated energies into their life on earth, they will probably succeed in achieving a state of things in which life will become tolerable for everyone and civilization no longer oppressive to anyone" (*SE* 21 [1927]:50). This may not seem like an especially inspiring vision. But it is precisely Freud's point that millenarian faith in earthly salvation is as dangerous and destructive of the relatively more tangible achievements of human progress as traditional religion. To advance social equality, what we need is not more overly ambitious formulas for social salvation, which in turn become part of the problem for which they were the intended solution, but a more honest—even skeptical—look at the real nature of human needs and possibilities, combined with modest confidence in the ability of reason to prevail in the long run.

---

leads him to observe that when leaders attempt to set themselves above the laws that "apply to everyone," they seek "to go back from a dominion of law [and justice] to a dominion of violence" (*SE* 22 [1933]:206). Even if they manage to set up new laws that legalize their special status, the new laws are not just but the outcome of "unequal degrees of power . . . ; the laws are made by and for the ruling members and find little room for the *rights* of those in subjection" (ibid., emphasis added).

International Law: The Justice of War

Given Freud's emphasis on the ethical value of the rule of law and the importance of justice in human affairs, it comes as no surprise that he objected vigorously to the behavior of the European states during World War I. In his 1915 essay "The Disillusionment of the War,"[44] Freud charges the warring states with two "misdeeds": first, violating international law, which the states had bound themselves to observe in peace time; second, undermining respect for the moral consensus of civilized peoples by arbitrary and ruthless state actions (see *SE* 14 [1915]:275–88; *CP* 4 [1915]:288–304).

Freud prefaces his criticism with an eloquent description of the values of international peace, pluralism, and cross-cultural fertilization—that is, the value of what he calls the "fellowship in civilization" and "union among the civilized races" that permitted citizens of different countries before World War I to view the whole civilized world as "a new, a wider fatherland" (*CP* 4 [1915]:290–1). This international community is compared with "a museum," wherein individuals moved unhindered, enjoying the diversities of national cultures and "all the treasures which the artists [and scholars] among civilized communities had in the successive centuries created and left behind" (*CP* 4 [1915]:291). Here, one could "appreciate impartially the varied types of perfection that miscegenation, the course of historical events, and the special characteristics of their mother-earth had produced among . . . remote compatriots" (ibid.). To such cosmopolitanism, reminiscent of Stoicism before its embrace by the Roman emperors, warfare between members of the human family is an affront.

Central to the international community in Freud's view is the consensually shaped moral tradition with regard to restraining the violence of war that is known as "just war theory."[45] War is difficult to justify in Freud's view, in part because it violates the individual's "right to his own life," but also because it destroys both the trust among peoples on which civilization rests, as well as innumerable "precious material objects which have been

44. This essay was written six months after the outbreak of World War I. Freud's personal reactions to the war are discussed in E. Jones 1955, pp. 168–206; see also ibid., pp. 367–71). According to Jones, Freud was enthusiastic about the war initially, but his enthusiasm waned as the war continued. He wrote to Abraham: "The long duration of the war crushes one" (cited in ibid., p. 180).

45. Classic just war theory is made up of two component parts: a *jus ad bellum* component that justifies the use of force and a *jus in bello* component that addresses the limits or restraints on how force may be used. See Johnson 1984, pp. 18–29.

produced by the labours of humanity" (*SE* 22 [1933]:213).[46] Nevertheless, when the aggressiveness of one state does lead to war, the attacked
state is justified in countering with force by considerations of self-defense.
However, Freud argues that in the resulting encounter the constraints of
the just war tradition should prevail. Each of the warring states should

> limit itself to establishing the superiority of one side in the contest, with the least
> possible infliction of dire sufferings that could contribute nothing to the deci-
> sion, and with complete immunity for the wounded who must of necessity
> withdraw from the contest, as well as for the physicians and nurses who devoted
> themselves to the task of healing. And of course with the utmost precautions for
> the non-combatant classes of the population—for women who are debarred
> from war-work, and for the children who, grown older, should be enemies no
> longer but friends and co-operators. And again, with preservation of all the
> international undertakings and institutions in which the mutual civilization of
> peace-time had been embodied. (*CP* 4 [1915]:292)[47]

Even warfare conducted within these moral constraints produces horrors
and sufferings enough, Freud continues, "but it . . . [need] not . . . inter-
rupt . . . the development of ethical relations between the greater units of
mankind, between the peoples and the states" (ibid.).

From the perspective these moral restraints, the conduct of the warring
states during World War I was unconscionable for the following reasons,
which Freud set out in the midst of the conflict:

> It sets at naught all those restrictions known as International Law, which in
> peace-time the states had bound themselves to observe; it ignores the pre-
> rogatives of the wounded and the medical service, the distinction between civil
> and military sections of the population, the claims of private property. It tram-

46. Freud summarizes his objections to the destruction wrought by World War I thus:
"The war . . . destroyed not only the beauty of the countrysides through which it passed and
the works of art which it met with on its path but it also shattered our pride in the achievements
of our civilization, our admiration for many philosophers and artists and our hopes of a final
triumph over the differences between nations and races. It tarnished the lofty impartiality of
our science, it revealed our instincts in all their nakedness and let loose the evil spirits within us
which we thought had been tamed for ever by centuries of continuous education by the
noblest minds" (*SE* 14 [1916]:307).

47. The first sentence of this passage employs the just war principle of proportionality,
which attempts to limit the overall damage to human values that results from war by protecting other values; the sentences that follow, the just war principle of noncombatant immunity,
also called the principle of discrimination (Johnson 1984, p. 27); the final sentence the just war
issue of just cause, Freud here implying that the cause is not just, because international
obligations were broken.

ples in blind fury on all that comes in its way, as though there were to be no future and no goodwill among men after it has passed. It rends all bonds of fellowship between the contending peoples, and threatens to leave such a legacy of embitterment as will make any renewal of such bonds impossible for a long time to come. (*CP* 4 [1915]:292–3)

It is noteworthy that Freud is here appealing to such traditional criteria of the just war as that there be a due proportion between the good to be accomplished and the evil that is done and that the conduct of the war be confined to just means, particularly with regard to protection of innocent noncombatants. He makes a point of the fact that "the enormously increased perfection of weapons" in our era makes it increasingly difficult to fight a just war today, even though, prior to the war, he had hoped, like so many of his contemporaries, that the war would be limited by shared moral considerations buttressed by "the progress of mankind in communal feelings since the era when the Greek Amphictyones had proclaimed that no city of the league might be demolished, nor its olive-groves hewn down, nor its water cut off" (*CP* 4 [1915]:292). It was partly his disillusion about the possibility of restraining the mass destruction made possible by modern means of war that prompted him to describe himself as a "pacifist" in a 1932 letter to Einstein, despite his appreciation of the argument that violence is sometimes justified by self-defense.

It is ironic that Freud, who has so often been accused of undermining public morals, worried during World War I that the arbitrary, ruthless behavior of the warring states was fostering general disrespect for law and morals among the citizens of these same states. He wrote:

The warring state permits itself every such misdeed, every such act of violence, as would disgrace the individual man. It practices not only the accepted stratagems, but also deliberate lying and deception against the enemy; and this, too, in a measure which appears to surpass the usage of former wars. The state . . . absolves itself from the guarantees and contracts it had formed with other sates, and makes unabashed confession of its rapacity and lust for power. (*CP* 4 [1915]:293–4)

For Freud, this relaxation of the moral ties among nation-states has a seductive effect on the morality of individuals, because, contrary to an influential reading of Freud's views on the stability of the superego, our moral behavior is affected by the moral quality of the societies in which we live. "Our conscience is not the inflexible judge that ethical teachers are wont to declare it, but in its origin is 'dread of community'," he writes (*CP* 4 [1915]:294). Hence, when the state or another respected community violates the moral rules that it expects its members to obey, especially if it sanctions such violations in the name of patriotism, baser passions are released, "and men perpetrate deeds of cruelty, fraud, treachery and barbarity so incompatible with their civilization that one would have held them to be impossible" (ibid.). For Freud, however, the antidote to this kind of dehumanization is not to wallow in the rhetoric of complaint of high-minded moral discourse, but rather to investigate the psychosocial origins of the problem and then, in light of the realization that humans are neither as good nor as bad as we are apt to think, to practice "a little more truthfulness and upright dealing on all sides, both in the personal relations of men to one another and between them and those who govern them" (*CP* 4 [1915]:304).

Just as a strong ego or an external communal authority is required to restrain the sexual perversity and aggressiveness of the individual, so too, Freud argues, the modern problem of nationalistic warfare requires a central international authority.[48] Like Rousseau in *A Project for a Perpetual Peace,* Freud insists that unless the proposed central authority is powerful enough to overrule its constituent states, efforts to maintain peace will fail. For "wars will only be prevented with certainty if mankind unites in setting up a central authority to which the right of giving judgement upon all conflicts of interest shall be handed over" (*SE* 22 [1933]:207). For the supreme international authority to be endowed with the necessary power, however, some unifying ideals are necessary, such as those that united the Panhellenic city-states and medieval Christendom. Unhappily, the attraction of nationalist ideals appears to doom such international ideological unity to failure for the foreseeable future (*SE* 22 [1933]:208–9). Insofar as there are grounds for modest hope, they lie with the aim of Eros, which is to unite individuals and small groups into one great unity, the unity of humankind. As Freud writes in the concluding lines of *Civilization and its Discontents:* "And now it is to be expected that the other of the two 'Heavenly Powers,' eternal Eros will make an effort to assert himself in the struggle with his equally immortal adversary. But who can foresee with what success and with what result?" (*SE* 21 [1930]:145).[49]

48. Freud's support for an international authority is consistent with his argument in *Civilization* that "civilization has to use its utmost efforts in order to set limits to man's aggressive instincts and to hold the manifestations of them in check" (*SE* 21 [1930]:112).

49. The editor of the *SE* notes that this final sentence was added in 1931, when the menace of Hitler was already beginning to be felt (*SE* 21 [1930]:145).

Chapter 14
Conclusion

To set forth the interrelated themes of Freud's moral psychology and his ethics is not to claim that the psychoanalytic view of human nature is particularly sanguine. One of Freud's primary contributions to morality is his straightforward acknowledgment of the pervasiveness of unconscious determinants of human behavior and the depth and ubiquity of aggressive instincts and narcissism in human beings. But as we have seen, there are also strands in his thought, which have been overlooked in the prevailing egoistic and deterministic interpretation of his views, that point to the genuine possibility of other-regarding behavior and authentic morality. Erotic instincts and the capacities evoked in the human being by normal development in interaction with nurturing caretakers stimulate the capacity to feel concern for the needs and interests of others even as aggression, narcissism, and the workings of the superego oppose more altruistic functions. What this requires always is a mixed-motive perspective, which gives rise to a "hermeneutics of suspicion," in which the motivations for adopting and applying moral standards must always be scrutinized carefully, lest we end up surreptitiously rationalizing harmful action. But suspicion is carried too far and requires a counterveiling suspicion of the unmasking enterprise itself if the latter ends up monolithically subverting all reasonable motives and standards.

I have argued that, despite internal tensions in Freud's view of human nature (some, but not all, of which are resolved by the evolution of his work over time), a more or less coherent ethical vision can be teased out of a nuanced reading of Freud's moral psychology. This understanding of Freud contrasts with that of post-modern moralists like Richard Rorty, who use Freud to support ethical relativism by emphasizing exclusively the decentering aspects of the unconscious at the expense of character structure that can support authentic moral judgment and action. As a kind of first order of business, Freud's complex handling of the freedom versus determinism paradox acknowledges the possibility of sufficient freedom of choice for moral agency. For Freud, augmenting individual autonomy is both among the aims of psychotherapy and, within the limits imposed by communal living and its necessary discontents, among the principal goals of liberal public policy.

Freud's understanding of what aims are worthwhile and constitute the good life is shaped by his mature views on the workings of the pleasure principle. Taking happiness as the general aim of life, both as a normative and as a dynamic psychological principle, Freud embraces a form of qualitative hedonism that takes account of his clinical appreciation of optimal psychological development, normal defenses, pathological deviations, and external sources of discontent. To achieve the modest degree of happiness open to human beings, the self must engage in an ongoing dialectical process in which direct instinctual gratification finds its limits in the self-condemnation (shame, disgust, guilt) that may be generated by instinctually satisfying acts, while pursuit of more highly sublimated, acceptable, and socially useful ends, such as the acquisition of knowledge, creativity, beauty, love, freely chosen work resulting in a contribution to the real world, finds its limitations in the bedrock of the individual's instinctual nature. Because of the conflictual nature of the individual, happiness is to be found, if at all, through the pursuit of a combination of goods that provide either direct or sublimated gratification. For Freud, sensuality is no less worthwhile than aesthetic pleasure as one of these goods. But happiness is understood to reside not simply in a series of isolated subjective satisfactions, but in the way goods contribute to the realization of the individual's human and social capacities and harmonize, to the extent that this is possible, the instinctual substratum with the rest of the personality. Self-examination, candor, and self-acceptance of one's instinctual nature is for Freud a necessary and primary ethical act.

Freud's ethic is grounded in a concept of human flourishing that includes other-regarding love and commitment to the community. People are always narcissistic to a certain extent, but most of us are not completely egoistic, or, to put it another way, the goal of personal happiness cannot be fully realized without considering the good of others. Given normally developed drives that orient us toward the good of others as well as ourselves, we will be less happy if we ignore the claims that others make on us. At the same time, we must attend to our own interests, because ignoring them undermines the feelings of self-worth out of which genuine morality springs.

There is a passivity in this conception of the foundations of ethics, in that the springs of morality act on the conscious self from a deeper realm, beyond the conscious ego. But Freud's assumption is that a person's genuine convictions come from deeper within the self than a mere conscious decision to adopt a set of values or norms. Where these deeper springs are absent, morality lacks a certain authenticity, though what is done may be sufficient for people to relate socially on a superficial basis. However, the continuity of authentic morality with the unconscious coexists with discontinuity stemming from the fact that all high motivations have their roots in morally dubious instincts and wishes that continue to press for behavioral expression against the aims of sublimated moral sentiments.

Freud's ethic reaches beyond other-regarding sentiments to concern with ethical rules and judgments. Such principles as nonmaleficence, truth telling, respect for autonomy, promise keeping, reciprocity, and justice that adjudicate interpersonal conflict and regulate interpersonal relations, both intimate and social, are grounded in the partial transcendence of egoistic hedonism and narcissism that Freud sees as occurring in the normal developmental process, even though aggression and narcissism are ubiquitous according to Freud's mixed-motive theory and serve as constant challenges to virtuous action.

Here again, Freud's understanding of human functioning in the moral domain holds onto irresolvable tensions. The very attempt to apply impersonal, impartial principles, however benign in original intent and however necessary for social cooperation, can trigger perfectionist strivings or superego repression that alienate the individual from his emotions and block the effective consideration of the interests and needs of others that is essential for full-bodied moral perception and judgment. Unlike contemporary ethical theorists rooted in Kant, Freud implicitly appreciates that attending too exclusively to the so-called "moral point of view," with its emphasis on reason and impersonal moral judgment, can result in the impoverishment of the self and a tendency to come up with the kind of rigid and truncated morality that Gilligan (1982), Baier (1987), and other feminist philosophers have recently taken on in advocating a more care-oriented approach to ethics (see, e.g., the essays in Kittay and Meyers 1987). From this more psychologically oriented point of view, the deductive application of general principles to particular situations needs to be augmented by the cultivation of a general attitude of other-regard, by empathic consideration of the needs, desires, and interests of the various individuals and groups affected by a particular moral decision, and by an acknowledgment that values may be incommensurable and conflict irresolvable.

Freud is often criticized for unduly privileging the sphere of the private self over against the claims of the community. But even in his most cogent and focused critique of social existence, *Civilization and its Discontents,* Freud acknowledges the value of the social regulations that make cooperation possible. His moral psychology suggests a social ethic in which the individual is committed to social life, first by an extended egoism in which reasonable social rules are viewed as a long-run practical benefit to the self, and second by an understanding that participation in the community is, through the workings of Eros, experienced as a good and a pleasure in and of itself. Freud's adherence to classical liberal views of personal liberty is augmented by a deep concern for the common good. This is not to say that he ever attempts to resolve the tension between the good of the individual and the good of society. To live in society is, for Freud, to be more or less unavoidably discontent. The desires, goods, and personal relations of the individual necessarily conflict with the needs and principles governing social existence. Freud's point is that the private sphere, so often condemned today as narcissistic, not only has its own validity but also imposes real limits on what can properly be demanded of the individual by public life.

In light of the dominant cultural understanding of Freud, the claim that psychoanalysis offers an essentially cogent ethical theory may continue to strike some readers as implausible even after the extensive efforts at excavation and exegesis reported here. Beyond that, the particular substantive moral views that I have attributed to Freud represent such a radical reinterpretation of specific parts of his work and its ethical import that the overall argument may seem almost counterintuitive. Certainly, many leading psychoanalysts and distinguished philosophers have put forward—or at least accepted—the notion that psychoanalysis implies a form of hard determinism and a view of human nature that undermines the very possibility of morality. The subtleties, complexities, ambiguities, tensions, and, indeed, outright confusions inherent in Freud's work have lent themselves to widely different readings. But I would argue that by pulling out and organizing the various elements of Freud's moral psychology and ethics, one can reach an understanding of his work that not only coheres but also accounts for details and nuances of psychoanalytic theory and of Freud's own ethical conclusions that are either ignored or remain anomalies in other interpretations. However surprising the view of Freud that has emerged from considering this material, I hope that the reader has been at least partially persuaded and that, whatever his or her preconceptions, he or she may even have felt somewhat like the rider astride the horse that knew where it wanted to go.

Appendix A
Why Take Psychoanalytic Findings Seriously? The Credibility of Freudian Theory

Why have I chosen to make psychoanalysis rather than some other psychological theory the dialogue partner with ethics? Two important reasons were touched in chapter 1: first, Freud's concepts have so penetrated our culture that for many people what they take to be the Freudian view of morality plays an important role in their thinking on ethical issues (see Rieff 1961; Bellah et al., 1985); second, psychoanalysis is inherently a psychology of morals (see Post 1972). The issues with which it is preoccupied, such as egoism, pleasure, object love, empathy, defensiveness, and moral conscientiousness, are pivotally important to moral conduct and to thinking about such conduct. No other contemporary school of psychology—certainly none associated with academic psychology—such as behaviorism, cognitive psychology, or even the developmental psychology of morals formulated by Piaget (1965) and substantially revised by Kohlberg (1981, 1984) and Gilligan (1982) is as preoccupied with the whole set of motivations that underlie moral behavior. Kohlberg's theory, for instance, though it focuses insightfully on how we reason about some moral dilemmas, excludes from its purview motives other than the conscious reasons for action that arise in debating hypothetical dilemmas involving issues of justice. Kohlberg's concept of the self, like Piaget's, is too superficial to capture the complex range and subtle blendings of motivations, unconscious as well as conscious, that affect how we actually behave in endeavoring to be moral.

A third reason is that psychoanalysis's unique methodology for studying the human personality in depth—utilizing free association, the couch, and transference reactions in a comparatively neutral interpersonal environment—is designed to get at what is *really* going on in moral decision making and conduct. Things are not always what they seem, in terms of either motivations or effects. What is often going on is that under the guise of doing right we are actually doing some kind of wrong, if only in the grudging spirit or self-defeating way in which we attempt to do as we ought. And sometimes what is going on is that under the guise of doing righteous right we are in fact doing cruel wrong.

In seeking to explain incongruous human behavior, psychoanalysis has forged a unique set of investigative techniques that are highly effective in probing unconscious motivations. For example, the technique of free association, by enjoining the patient to say *whatever* comes to mind, has the power to uncover the most deeply buried or cleverly disguised emotions and motivations, however unpalatable to and at variance with the subject's conscious moral beliefs and explanations for his or her behavior. Likewise, analytic technique expressly attends to and works at getting around the typical defensive strategies by which individuals hide their real motivations from themselves. The transference relation in which the patient unconsciously reenacts with the analyst the feelings, attitudes, motivations, and patterns of behavior that characterize his or her interactions with people in everyday life furnishes a lablike opportunity to examine precisely the actual dynamics of morally significant behavior. In analysis the patient is both actor and observer of self—the morally conscious being.

Admittedly, the intellectual credibility of psychoanalysis has been persistently challenged on several fronts, sometimes to the point where cultural morticians have proclaimed it (prematurely) moribund. Empiricists and positivists, such as H. J. Eysenck (1953, 1965), Ernest Nagel (1960, pp. 38–56), Karl Popper (1962, 1974), and Adolf Grünbaum (1977, 1979, 1980, 1981, 1984), taking their clues from the so-called hard sciences, charge that its method is unscientific and its theory speculative, unsubstantiated nonsense. Those critics, like Allport (1961), Yankelovich and Barrett (1970), and Sartre (1953), who pitch their tents in the humanistic camp contend that psychoanalytic theory is too scientistic, in that it inappropriately attempts to impose on that marvelously subtle and protean creature, the human being, a mechanistic model that is incapable of capturing the true nature of the human person.

A partial response to these criticisms, sufficient for present purposes, is suggested by recent assessments of psychoanalysis from three different perspectives: continental hermeneutics, Anglo-American philosophy of science, and empirical research. Because each of these approaches focuses on only limited aspects of Freud's work, none of them taken individually succeeds in being completely persuasive. But each has something of value to contribute to the ongoing debate about the validity and usefulness of psychoanalysis as a body of knowledge.

The hermeneutic defense of psychoanalysis, which overlaps to some extent with philosophy of science defenses of single-subject research (see Sherwood 1969 and Edelson 1984, 1988), is principally concerned with defending the clinical enterprise as an in-depth *interpretive* process that centers on the richly symbolic narratives that human beings employ to communicate the complex meanings and motivations that account for their behavior. Indeed, that hermeneuticists have been attracted to psychoanalysis is precisely because it shares a number of central insights and concerns, such as appreciation of the role of subjective perception and intentionality in shaping human behavior; the phenomenon of false consciousness and the need for the interpreter to go beyond subjectively intended meanings; the historical dimension of human existence and the role of narrative in understanding human behavior; the inevitability of the interpreter's preconceptions and prejudgments influencing what he or she understands and the need, in light of this, for continuing self-scrutiny on the part of the interpreter during the interpretive process; and the interpreter's status as a dialogue partner in conversation with another human subject, as contrasted with the role of the neutral observer of objective natural facts.

Although hermeneuticists are often seen as not sufficiently concerned with validating the accuracy of clinical interpretations (Edelson 1984, pp. 49–50), some, like Habermas and Ricoeur, take very seriously the issue of the proof and validity of psychoanalytic claims, which they differentiate (too sharply, as I see it) from verification in the empirical sciences. Starting from the premise that there are many different kinds of truth claims that, in order to account for human behavior, require moving beyond the limited kind of verifiability found in the empirical sciences, hermeneuticists refer to the cumulative persuasiveness of multiple, extremely complex criteria of validation. One of the most important criteria with respect to the case history is *narrative coherence,* including especially the ability of the revised narrative constructed in the clinical setting to incorporate previously anomalous details of a person's life history. The patient's assent to a clinically revised narrative is an important element of the coherence criterion because the patient is the only one with direct access to all the relevant details of the history being interpreted, including memories of internal moods and motivations. But the narrative must also be plausible to the analyst and satisfy the criterion of *intelligibility* (logic, credibility, narrative flow, and persuasive weight of reality) demanded of any historical account. In addition, the case history narrative must verify itself by presenting individual instances of behavior that *fit the generalizations of psychoanalytic theory,* which in turn are drawn from numerous case histories.

In addition to the three-pronged test of narrative coherence (patient assent, intelligibility, fit of individual instances to general theory), hermeneuticists present a second major criterion for validating psychoanalytic reconstruction in case histories: that of *praxis.* An interpretation must facilitate continuation of the self-reflective process and liberate the patient from repetitive debilitating symptoms. One of the convincing features of this criterion is that it involves the effective manipulation of unconscious psychic processes such that the analyst's application of psychoanalytic propositions in the context of the transference to a particular patient through ongoing interpretations leads to the patient's recovery and understanding of unconscious material and his or her liberation from the influence of unconscious beliefs and desires in a way that allows greater control over his or her life. One aspect of the praxis criterion is the analysand's growing ability to practice self-analysis when new problems arise outside the therapeutic setting and after termination. The augmented self-mastery experienced by the successful patient tends to confirm the accuracy of therapeutic interpretations, since it is unlikely that inaccurate interpretations would give him or her the kind of access to and control over unconscious motives that such mastery requires.

Hermeneuticists validate the broad propositions of general psychoanalytic theory, as opposed to individual-oriented interpretations, by their fit with the facts of numerous, diverse individual case histories, including those of children at each stage of development. They also claim that points of theory prove themselves in practice to the extent that hypothetical predictions derived from them by analysts for application to particular patients turn out to be true.

Hermeneuticists are acutely aware that in psychoanalysis, as elsewhere, factual explanation is significantly limited by the conceptual framework imposed by theory (Ricoeur 1981, p. 271). But they correctly see that this kind of limiting connection exists in *every* field of inquiry, as contemporary philosophers of science also emphasize (see Kuhn 1970; R. Bernstein 1983). Like any theory, at the point where the correlation between fact and theory breaks down, psychoanalysis must be subject to revision.

Although hermeneuticists tend to disparage empirical testing as unsuited to depth-psychological work (see Habermas 1971, pp. 252–73; Ricoeur 1981), their own principle of strength through cumulativeness points to the desirability of pursuing rigorously empirical methods for verifying clinically based general hypotheses whenever this is possible and appropriate—for example, in regard to the alleged etiology of paranoia in repressed homosexuality and the genesis of authority problems in unresolved oedipal conflicts.

Philosophers of science of the vintage of Nagel (1960) and Popper (1962, pp. 33–9) used to argue that Freud's general explanatory propositions were too vague and too operationally unspecific to be tested empirically (e.g., falsified). More recently, however, Grünbaum and M. Moore have argued persuasively that while some Freudian propositions are more difficult to test than others, a large number are *in principle* capable of being verified by empirical means, and even that some hypotheses were actually falsified by Freud himself (Glymour 1974, 1980; Grünbaum 1977, 1978, 1979). Grünbaum has gone on to attack the scientific credibility of psychoanalysis on the new grounds that its hypotheses, though falsifiable, have not been shown to be scientifically credible, in part because the data are irretrievably contaminated by the psychoanalytic situation. But Edelson (1984, 1988) has responded to Grünbaum by drawing on new conceptions in the philosophy of science about scientific theory, probability, and hypothesis testing to show, first, that the data are better than philosophers of science tend to think on the basis of widespread misunderstandings of psychoanalytic practice and, second, that hypotheses *can* be tested in single-subject research. Grünbaum and other philosophy of science critics of psychoanalysis's scientific credibility tend to ignore the empirical research that has been done, but Luborsky and his colleagues have developed a number of innovative ways of obtaining quantitative probative data in the psychoanalytic situation with which to test psychoanalytic hypotheses. Their work casts strong doubt on Grünbaum's negative conclusions about the credibility of psychoanalytic hypotheses (see, e.g., Luborsky, 1967, 1970, 1976, 1986; Luborsky and Mintz 1975; Luborsky et al. 1988; Luborsky and Crits-Christoph 1990; Miller et al. 1992).

Although inconclusive by itself, extraclinical or experimental testing of psychoanalytic hypotheses weighs in with yet another support of psychoanalysis's credibility, at least insofar as its concern is with the view of human personality relevant to moral psychology. Contrary to the stereotyped view of psychoanalysis as empirically untested, the quantity of empirical research data pertinent to psychoanalysis is considerable. Thus Fisher (1972, p. 350) concludes from his study of fifteen major Freudian hypotheses that much that is distinctively Freudian has been verified. Similarly, Fisher and Greenberg (1985, p. 393) state on the basis of their much larger and more sophisticated survey that "we are impressed by how often the results [of empirical research] have borne out his [Freud's] expectations." In fact, the quantity of empirical research on psychoanalysis exceeds that available for most other personality and developmental theories, such as those of Jung, Adler, Eysenck, and Allport (Fisher and Greenberg 1985, p. 396; Farrell 1981, p. 171). The existing scientific documentation leaves little doubt as to the existence of unconscious motivations (Solley and Murphy 1960; Stewart 1962; Bevan 1964, Stross and Shevrin 1969). Moreover, a surprising number of the specific unconscious dynamics depicted by Freud have received strong empirical support, including, most significantly for moral behavior, the defense mechanisms of repression, denial, sublimation, and displacement (Kline 1972:151–203; Fisher and Greenberg 1985, pp. 255–70; Farrell 1981, pp. 162–4), as well as important aspects of the developmentally based oral and anal personality typologies, the developmental etiology of male and female homosexuality in terms of parent–child dynamics, the expressive and tension-releasing function of dreams; and many aspects of the oedipal complex as applied to males, such as rivalry with the father and fantasies of sexual closeness with the mother (Fisher and Greenberg 1985; Friedman 1988). Some of these research results do not make sense in any current theoretical schema except that of psychoanalysis (Fisher and Greenberg 1985, p. 163).

Additionally, a number of researchers have found agreement between analytic reconstructions and the results of naturalistic child observation (see, e.g., Greenspan 1981, 1988, 1989; Lichtenberg 1983; Stern 1985). Recently, Barglow et al. (1989) have shown how findings from the clinical reconstructions from an analysis of a mother developed through transference interpretations converged with empirical observations originating in the analytic patient's daughter's psychotherapy and the results of empirical infant research on the same larger causative understanding of the daughter's psychopathology. Barglow et al. argue convincingly that "such a confluence of different sources of evidence, each identified by a different method of investigation, provides one kind of validation for psychoanalytic reconstructions, making it possible to provide that 'satisfactory degree of certainty' which Freud called for in the attempt to integrate the patient's 'psychic truth' with 'actual' or historical truth" (Barglow et al. 1989, p. 401).

Of course, as would be expected with any scientific theory, some Freudian formulations have been disconfirmed. Among these are several of Freud's ideas about women, such as his assumption that psychosexual maturity is marked by a shift of erotogenicity from the clitoris to the vagina and the notion that women have a significantly less severe superego and hence less need to sublimate their drives into work and creativity than do men (Fisher and Greenberg 1985, pp. 170–230, 395). As to the metapsychology, Morse's (1982) methodologically careful review of the enormous literature regarding various metapsychological propositions concludes that "empirical investigations have produced, at best, only equivocal and pallid confirmation of [this part] of Freudian theory" (cited in M. Moore 1984, p. 279). The general views of personality development and of the role of conflicting motivations in moral behavior, however, are not part of this body of work to which the empirical verdict remains "not proven." In general the basic shape of the theory and those tenets that are most important to moral psychology remain plausible.

Psychoanalysis cannot be excluded from serious consideration as a plausible theory of human nature, then, on the grounds that it fails to conform to some narrow set of "scientific" methodological criteria or because most of its data refer to meanings and motivations observed initially in a clinical setting. Psychoanalysis is constituted by a complex set of "data" and methods that straddle the usual lines of demarcation between the sciences and the humanities, because it endeavors to approach the study of subjective experience with scientific objectivity. Farrell may go too far when he claims on the basis of his book-length exploration of the experiential supports for and against Freudian theory that "the sceptic's arguments against Freud today may turn out to be just as ridiculous as the argument against Newton in the eighteenth century." But he is not wrong in claiming that Freud's ideas are at least "pointers to the truth—signposting the avenues to pursue if we wish to get at a reasonably definitive account of human nature" (Farrell 1981, p. 191). This, at least, is my assumption here.

Bibliography

Abraham, Karl. 1968. *Selected Papers of Karl Abraham*. London: Hogarth Press.

Abramson, Jeffrey B. 1984. *Liberation and Its Limits: The Moral and Political Thought of Freud*. New York: Free Press.

Ahren, Yizhak. 1980. Remarks on Freud's Determinism. *Journal of Psychology and Judaism* 4:222–7.

Alexander, F., and H. Staub. 1956. *The Criminal, the Judge and the Public*. Rev. ed. Glencoe, Ill.: Free Press.

Allison, George H. 1987. Review of *The Assault on Truth. Freud's Suppression of the Seduction Theory*, by Jeffrey Masson. *PQ* 56:364–8.

Allport, Gordon. 1950. *The Individual and His Religion*. New York: Macmillan.

————. 1964. *Pattern and Growth in Personality*. New York: Holt, Rinehart, and Winston.

Amacher, Peter. 1965. *Freud's Neurological Education and Its Influence on Psychoanalytic Theory*. Psychological Issues, monograph 16, vol. 4, no. 4. New York: International Universities Press.

Anscombe, G. E. M. 1958. Modern Moral Philosophy. *Philosophy* 33:1–19.

Apel, Karl-Otto. 1967. *Analytic Philosophy of Language and the Geisteswissenschaften*. Dordrecht: D. Reidel.

Apfelbaum, Bernard. 1965. Ego Psychology, Psychic Energy, and the Hazards of Quantitative Explanation in Psycho-Analytic Theory. *IJP* 46:168–82.

Applegarth, Adrienne. 1971. Comments on Aspects of the Theory of Psychic Energy. *JAPA* 19:379–415.

Aquinas, Thomas. 1915. *Summa Theologica of Saint Thomas Aquinas*. Trans. by the Fathers of the English Dominican Province. London: R. and T. Washbourne.

Arlow, J., and C. Brenner. 1964. *Psychoanalytic Concepts and the Structural Theory*. New York: International Universities Press.

Asch, S. E. 1952. *Social Psychology*. Englewood Cliffs, N.J.: Prentice-Hall.

Ayer, A. J. [1946] 1952. *Language, Truth and Logic*. 2d ed. New York: Dover.

Badcock, C. R. 1986. *The Problem of Altruism*. Oxford: Basil Blackwell.

Baier, Annette. 1987. Hume, the Women's Moral Theorist? In *Women and Moral Theory*, ed. Eva Kittay and Diana Meyers, 37–55. Totowa, N.J.: Roman and Littlefield.

Balint, Michael. 1939. Love for the Mother and Mother Love. *IJP* 24:33–48.

————. [1948] 1959. On Genital Love. In M. Balint, *Primary Love and Psychoanalytic Technique*, 109–20. London: Tavistock.

————. 1960. Primary Narcissism and Primary Love. *PQ* 29:6–47.

Barclay, James R. 1964. Franz Brentano and Sigmund Freud. *Journal of Existentialism* 64:1–36.

Barglow, Peter, Charles Jaffe, and Brian Vaughn. 1989. Psychoanalytic Reconstructions and Empirical Data: Reciprocal Contributions. *JAPA* 37:401–35.

Basch, Michael Franz. 1978. Psychic Determinism and Freedom of Will. *IRP* 5:257–64.

Beach, Waldo, and H. R. Niebuhr. 1955. *Christian Ethics: Sources of the Living Tradition.* New York: Ronald Press.

Beauchamp, Tom, and James Childress. 1989. *Principles of Biomedical Ethics,* 3d ed. New York: Oxford University Press.

Bellah, Robert N., et al. 1985. *Habits of the Heart.* Berkeley and Los Angeles: University of California Press.

Bennett, Jonathan. 1966. *Kant's Dialectic.* Cambridge: Cambridge University Press.

———. 1980. Accountability. In *Philosophical Subjects: Essays Presented to P. F. Strawson,* ed. Zak Van Straaten, 14–47. Oxford: Clarendon Press.

Bentham, Jeremy. 1834. *Deontology.* 2 vols. London: Longmans.

Berlin, I. 1958. *Two Concepts of Liberty.* Oxford: Clarendon Press.

Bernfeld, S. 1944. Freud's Earliest Theories and the School of Helmholtz. *PQ* 13:341–62.

———. 1949. Freud's Scientific Beginnings. *American Imago,* 6:163–96.

———. 1951. Sigmund Freud, M.D., 1882–1885. *IJP* 32:204–17.

Bernstein, Isidor. 1957. The Role of Narcissism in Moral Masochism. *PQ* 26:358–77.

Bernstein, Richard. 1983. *Beyond Objectivism and Relativism.* Philadelphia: University of Pennsylvania Press. Oxford: Basil Blackwell.

Bettelheim, Bruno. 1983. *Freud and Man's Soul.* New York: Knopf.

Bevan, W. 1964. Subliminal Stimulation: A Pervasive Problem for Psychology. *Psychological Bulletin* 61:81–99.

Bibring, E. [1936] 1941. The Development and Problems of the Theory of Instincts. *IJP* 22:102–31.

Bieber, Irving. 1972. Morality and Freud's Concept of the Superego. In *Moral Values and the Superego Concept in Psychoanalysis,* ed. Seymour C. Post, 126–43. New York: International Universities Press.

Bing, J., F. McLaughlin, and R. Marburg. 1959. The Metapsychology of Narcissism. *PSC* 14:9–18.

Binswanger, Ludwig. 1975. Freud's Conception of Man in the Light of Anthropology. In *Being-in-the-World: Selected Papers of Ludwig Binswanger,* ed. Jacob Needleman, 149–81. London: Souvenir Press.

———. 1975. Freud and the Magna Charta of Clinical Psychiatry. In *Being-in-the-World: Selected Papers of Ludwig Binswanger,* ed. Jacob Needleman, 182–205. London: Souvenir Press.

Blanshard, Brand. 1961. The Case for Determinism. In *Determinism and Freedom in the Age of Modern Science,* ed. Sidney Hook, 19–30. New York: Collier Books.

Bleuler, M. 1978. *The Schizophrenic Disorders.* New Haven, Conn.: Yale University Press.

Blum, Lawrence. 1980. *Friendship, Altruism, and Morality.* London: Routledge and Kegan Paul.

Blumenfield, David. 1972. Free Action and Unconscious Motivation. *Monist* 56:426–43.

Borger, Robert, and Frank Cioffi, eds. 1970. *Explanation in the Behavioural Sciences.* Cambridge: Cambridge University Press.

Bowlby, J. 1958. The Nature of the Child's Tie to His Mother. *IJP* 39:350–73.

————. 1969. *Attachment.* Attachment and Loss, vol. 1. New York: Basic Books.

————. 1973. *Separation: Anxiety and Anger.* Attachment and Loss, vol. 2. New York: Basic Books.

————. 1980. *Loss: Sadness and Depression.* Attachment and Loss, vol. 3. New York: Basic Books.

Boyer, L. B., and P. L. Giovacchini. 1980. *Psychoanalytic Treatment of Characterological and Schizophrenic Disorders.* New York: Jason Aronson.

Brandt, Lewis. 1961. Some Notes on English Freudian Terminology. *JAPA* 9: 331–9.

Brandt, Richard B. 1959. *Ethical Theory.* Englewood Cliffs, N.J.: Prentice-Hall.

————, ed. 1961. *Value and Obligation.* New York: Harcourt, Brace, and World.

————. 1967. Hedonism. In *The Encyclopedia of Philosophy,* ed. Paul Edwards, 3:432–5. New York: Macmillan and Free Press.

————. 1979. *A Theory of the Good and the Right.* Oxford: Oxford University Press.

Brenner, Charles. 1957. *An Elementary Textbook of Psychoanalysis.* Garden City, N.Y.: Doubleday, Anchor Books.

————. 1976. *Psychoanalytic Technique and Psychic Conflict.* New York: International Universities Press.

————. 1979. Working Alliance, Therapeutic Alliance, and Transference. *JAPA* 27, supplement:137–57.

————. 1982. *The Mind in Conflict.* New York: International Universities Press.

Brentano, F. 1973. *The Foundation and Construction of Ethics.* Ed. and trans. Elizabeth Schneewind. London: Routledge and Kegan Paul.

Brown, Norman O. 1959. *Life Against Death.* Middletown, Conn.: Wesleyan University Press. New York: Random House.

————. 1966. *Love's Body.* New York: Random House.

————. 1967. A Reply to Herbert Marcuse. *Commentary* 43:83–4.

Browning, Don. 1973. *Generative Man: Psychoanalytic Perspectives.* Philadelphia: Westminster Press.

————. 1987. *Religious Thought and Modern Psychologies.* Philadelphia: Fortress Press.

Bruner, Jerome. 1957. Freud and the Image of Man. In *Freud and the 20th Century*, ed. Benjamin Nelson, 277–85. New York: Meridian Books.

Bultmann, Rudolf. 1951. *Theology of the New Testament*. 2 vols. Trans. Kendrick Grobel. New York: Charles Scribner's Sons.

Burke, Edmund. 1910. *Reflections on the Revolution in France*. London: J. M. Dent and Sons.

Butler, Joseph. [1729] 1964. Sermons. In *British Moralists*, ed. Selby-Bigge, 1:181–244. Indianapolis, Ind.: Bobbs-Merrill.

Calvin, John. [1559] 1962. *Institutes of the Christian Religion*. 2 vols. Trans. Henry Beveridge. Grand Rapids, Mich.: William B. Eerdmans Publishing Co.

Castañeda, Hector-Neri, and George Nakhnikian, eds. 1963. *Morality and the Language of Conduct*. Detroit, Mich.: Wayne State University Press.

Chisholm, Roderick. 1967. Brentano, Franz. In *The Encyclopedia of Philosophy*, ed. Paul Edwards, 1:365–8. New York: Macmillan and Free Press.

Coen, Stanley. 1989. Intolerance of Responsibility for Internal Conflict. *JAPA* 37:943–64.

Compton, Allan. 1972. A Study of the Psychoanalytic Theory of Anxiety. I. The Development of Freud's Theory of Anxiety. *JAPA* 20:3–43.

———. 1983. The Current Status of the Psychoanalytic Theory of Instinctual Drives, I and II. *PQ* 52: 365–401, 402–26.

Cranefield, Paul. 1957. The Organic Physics of 1847 and the Biophysics of Today. *Journal of the History of Medicine and Allied Sciences* 12:407–23.

———. 1966. Freud and the "School of Helmholtz." *Gesnerus* 23:35–9.

Daley, James. 1971. Freud and Determinism. *Southern Journal of Philosophy* 9: 179–88.

Dare, Christopher, and Alex Holder. 1981. Developmental Aspects of the Interaction between Narcissism, Self-Esteem and Object Relations. *IJP* 62:323–37.

Darwall, Stephen L. 1977. Two Kinds of Respect. *Ethics* 88:36–49.

Decarie, Govin. 1965. *Intelligence and Affectivity in Early Childhood: An Experimental Study of Jean Piaget's Object Concept and Object Relations*. New York: International Universities Press.

Derrida, Jacques. 1978. *Writing and Difference*. Chicago: University of Chicago Press.

———. 1984. My Chances/*Mes Chances:* A Rendezvous with some Epicurean Stereophonies. In *Taking Chances: Derrida, Psychoanalysis, and Literature*, ed. William Kerrigan and Joseph H. Smith, 1–32. Baltimore: The Johns Hopkins University Press.

De Sousa, Ronald. 1982. Norms and the Normal. In *Philosophical Essays on Freud*, ed. Richard Wollheim and James Hopkins, 139–62. Cambridge: Cambridge University Press.

Dilman, Ilham. 1983. *Freud and Human Nature*. Oxford: Basil Blackwell.

———. 1984. *Freud and the Mind*. Oxford: Basil Blackwell.

Domas, Leanne, and Lawrence Balter. 1979. Restitution and Revenge: Antisocial

Trends in Narcissism. *Journal of the American Academy of Psychoanalysis* 7: 375–84.

Donagan, Alan. 1977. *The Theory of Morality*. Chicago: University of Chicago Press.

Doppelt, Gerald. 1989. Is Rawls's Kantian Liberalism Coherent and Defensible? *Ethics* 99:815–51.

Downie, R. S., and Elizabeth Telfer. 1970. *Respect for Persons*. New York: Schocken Books.

Durkheim, Emile. [1893] 1933. *The Division of Labor in Society*. New York: Macmillan.

———. [1897] 1951. *Suicide*. Glencoe, Ill.: Free Press.

———. 1898. L'individualisme et les intellectuels. *Revue bleue,* ser. 4, 10:7–13.

———. [1912] 1961. *The Elementary Forms of the Religious Life*. New York: Collier Books.

Eagle, Morris N. 1980. Critical Examination of Motivational Explanation in Psychoanalysis. *Psychoanalysis and Contemporary Thought* 3:329–80.

Eckstein, Friedrich. 1936. *Alte unnennbare Tage! Erinnerungen aus siebzig Lehr und Wanderjahren*. Vienna: H. Reichner.

Edelson, Marshall. 1984. *Hypothesis and Evidence in Psychoanalysis*. Chicago: University of Chicago Press.

———. 1988. *Psychoanalysis: A Theory in Crisis*. Chicago: University of Chicago Press.

Edwards, Rem B. 1979. *Pleasures and Pains*. Ithaca, N.Y.: Cornell University Press.

———, ed. 1982. *Psychiatry and Ethics*. Buffalo, N.Y.: Prometheus Books.

Eisnitz, Alan J. 1974. On the Metapsychology of Narcissistic Pathology. *JAPA* 22:279–91.

Eissler, K. R. 1964. Mankind at its Best. *JAPA* 12:187–222.

Ellenberger, Henri F. 1970. *The Discovery of the Unconscious*. New York: Basic Books.

Ellis, Havelock. 1898. Autoerotism: A Psychological Study. *The Alienist and Neurologist* 19:260–99.

Ericsson, K. Anders, and Herbert Simon. 1980. Verbal Reports as Data. *PR* 87:215–51.

Erikson, Erik H. 1963. *Childhood and Society*. 2d ed. New York: W. W. Norton.

———. 1964. *Insight and Responsibility*. New York: W. W. Norton.

———. 1968. *Identity: Youth and Crisis*. New York: W. W. Norton.

Evans, C. Stephen. 1984. Must Psychoanalysis Embrace Determinism? Or, Can a Psychoanalyst be a Libertarian? *Psychoanalysis and Contemporary Thought* 7: 339–65.

Eysenck, H. J. 1953. *Uses and Abuses of Psychology*. Baltimore, Md.: Penguin Books.

———. 1965. *Fact and Fiction in Psychology*. Baltimore, Md.: Penguin Books.

Fairbairn, W. Ronald D. 1952. *Psychoanalytic Studies of the Personality*. London: Routledge and Kegan Paul.

Falk, W. D. 1965. Morality, Self, and Others. In *Morality and the Language of*

Conduct, ed. Hector-Neri Castañeda and George Nakhnikian, 25–69. Detroit, Mich.: Wayne State University Press.

Farrell, B. A. 1981. *The Standing of Psychoanalysis.* Oxford: Oxford University Press.

Feffer, Melvin. 1982. *The Structure of Freudian Thought.* New York: International Universities Press.

Feinberg, Joel. 1965. *Reason and Responsibility.* Belmont, Calif.: Dickenson Publishing Company.

———. 1970. *Doing and Deserving: Essays in the Theory of Responsibility.* Princeton: Princeton University Press.

Feinberg, Joel, and Hyman Gross. 1975. *Philosophy of Law.* Encino and Belmont, Calif.: Dickenson Publishing Company.

Fenichel, Otto. 1945. *The Psychoanalytic Theory of Neurosis.* New York: W. W. Norton.

———. 1949. *Problems of Psychoanalytic Technique.* Albany, N.Y.: The Psychoanalytic Quarterly, Inc.

———. [1935] 1953. *The Collected Papers of Otto Fenichel,* 1st ser. Ed. Hanna Fenichel and David Rapaport. New York: W. W. Norton.

Findlay, J. N. 1968. *Values and Intentions.* New York: Humanities Press.

Fine, Reuben. 1986. *Narcissism, The Self, and Society.* New York: Columbia University Press.

Fingarette, Herbert. 1963. *The Self in Transformation.* New York: Harper and Row, Harper Torchbooks.

———. 1972. *The Meaning of Criminal Insanity.* Berkeley: University of California Press.

Fisher, Seymour, and Roger P. Greenberg, eds. 1978. *The Scientific Evaluation of Freud's Theories and Therapy.* New York: Basic Books.

———. 1985. *The Scientific Credibility of Freud's Theories and Therapy.* New York: Columbia University Press.

Flew, Antony. 1954. Psychoanalytic Explanation. In *Philosophy and Analysis,* ed. Margaret MacDonald, 139–48. Oxford: Basil Blackwell.

———. 1972. "Splitting Hairs before Starting Hares." *Personalist* 53:84–93.

Fliess, Robert. 1970. *Ego and Body Ego.* Psychoanalytic Series, vol. 2. New York: International Universities Press.

Foot, Philippa. 1978. *Virtues and Vices.* Berkeley: University of California Press.

Frankena, William. 1963. *Ethics.* Englewood Cliffs, N.J.: Prentice-Hall.

Frankena, William, and John T. Granrose. 1974. *Introductory Readings in Ethics.* Englewood Cliffs, N.J.: Prentice-Hall.

Frankfurt, Harry. 1971. Freedom of the Will and the Concept of a Person. *JP* 68: 5–20.

Freud, Anna. 1969. *The Writings of Anna Freud,* vol. 7. New York: International Universities Press.

Freud, Ernst L., ed. 1974. *The Letters of Sigmund Freud and Arnold Zweig.* New York: Harcourt Brace Jovanovich, Harvest Books.

_____, ed. 1975. *Letters of Sigmund Freud*. New York: Basic Books.

Freud, Sigmund. [1886–1938] 1953–1974. *The Standard Edition of the Complete Psychological Works of Sigmund Freud (SE)*, vols 1–24. London: Hogarth Press. *Collected Papers (CP)*, vols 1–5. New York: Basic Books. *Gesammelte Werke (GW)*, vols 1–18. Frankfurt am Main: S. Fischer Verlag.

_____. 1893. Some Points for a Comparative Study of Organic and Hysterical Motor Paralyses. *SE* 1:160–72.

_____. 1894. The Neuro-psychoses of Defence. *SE* 3:45–61.

_____. [1895] 1950. Project for a Scientific Psychology. *SE* 1:295–387.

_____. 1895. On the Grounds for Detaching a Particular Syndrome from Neurasthenia under the Description "Anxiety Neurosis." *SE* 3:90–115.

_____. 1896. Further Remarks on the Neuro-Psychoses of Defence. *SE* 3:162–85.

_____. 1896. The Aetiology of Hysteria. *SE* 3:191–221.

_____. 1898. Sexuality in the Aetiology of the Neuroses. *SE* 3:263–85.

_____. 1900. *The Interpretation of Dreams*. *SE* 4:1–338 and 5:339–621.

_____. 1901. *The Psychopathology of Everyday Life*. *SE* 6; *GW* 4.

_____. 1904. Freud's Psycho-Analytic Procedure. *SE* 7:249–54.

_____. 1905. Fragment of an Analysis of a Case of Hysteria. *SE* 7:7–122.

_____. 1905. On Psychotherapy. *SE* 7:257–68; *CP* 1:249–63.

_____. 1905. Psychical (or Mental) Treatment. *SE* 7:283–302.

_____. 1905. *Three Essays on the Theory of Sexuality*. *SE* 7:130–243.

_____. [1905 or 1906]. 1942. Psychopathic Characters on the Stage. *SE* 7:305–10.

_____. 1905. *Jokes and their Relation to the Unconscious*. *SE* 8.

_____. 1906. My Views on the Part Played by Sexuality in the Aetiology of the Neuroses. *SE* 7:271–9.

_____. 1906. Psycho-Analysis and the Establishment of the Facts in Legal Proceedings. *SE* 9:103–14; *CP* 2:13–24.

_____. 1908. Character and Anal Erotism. *SE* 9:169–75.

_____. 1908. Civilized Sexual Morality and Modern Nervous Illness. *SE* 9:181–204; *CP* 2:76–99.

_____. 1909. Analysis of a Phobia in a Five-Year-Old Boy. *SE* 10:5–149.

_____. 1909. Notes Upon a Case of Obsessional Neurosis. *SE* 10:155–318; *CP* 3:293–383.

_____. 1910. A Special Type of Choice of Object Made by Men. *SE* 11:165–75; *CP* 4:192–202.

_____. 1910. *Five Lectures on Psycho-Analysis*. *SE* 11:9–55.

_____. 1910. *Leonardo Da Vinci and a Memory of His Childhood*. *SE* 11:63–137.

_____. 1910. The Future Prospects of Psycho-Analytic Therapy. *SE* 11:141–51.

_____. 1910. The Psycho-Analytic View of Psychogenic Disturbance of Vision. *SE* 11:211–18.

_____. 1910. "Wild" Psycho-Analysis. *SE* 11:221–7.

————. 1911. Formulations on the Two Principles of Mental Functioning. *SE* 12:218–26; *CP* 4:13–21.

————. 1911. Psycho-Analytic Notes on an Autobiographical Account of a Case of Paranoia (Dementia Paranoides). *SE* 12:9–82.

————. 1912. The Disposition to Obsessional Neurosis. *SE* 12:317–26.

————. 1912. The Dynamics of Transference. *SE* 12:99–108; *CP* 2:312–22; *GW* 8:364–74.

————. 1912. On the Universal Tendency to Debasement in the Sphere of Love. *SE* 11:179–90; *CP* 4:203–16.

————. 1912. Recommendations to Physicians Practising Psycho-Analysis. *SE* 12:111–20; *CP* 2:323–33; *GW* 8:376–87.

————. 1913. On Beginning the Treatment. *SE* 12:123–44; *CP* 2:342–65.

————. 1913. On Psycho-Analysis. *SE* 12:207–11.

————. 1913. The Claims of Psycho-Analysis to Scientific Interest. *SE* 13:165–90.

————. 1913. *Totem and Taboo*. *SE* 13:1–161.

————. 1914. On Narcissism: An Introduction. *SE* 14:73–102; *CP* 4:30–59; *GW* 10:138–70.

————. 1914. On the History of the Psycho-Analytic Movement. *SE* 14:7–66; *CP* 1:287–359; *GW* 10:44–113.

————. 1914. Remembering, Repeating and Working-Through. *SE* 12:147–56; *CP* 2:366–76; *GW* 10:126–36.

————. 1914. Some Reflections on Schoolboy Psychology. *SE* 13:241–4.

————. 1915. A Case of Paranoia Running Counter to the Psycho-Analytic Theory of the Disease. *SE* 14:263–72.

————. 1915. Instincts and their Vicissitudes. *SE* 14:117–40; *CP* 4:60–83; *GW* 10:210–32.

————. 1915. Observations on Transference-Love. *SE* 12:159–71; *CP* 2:377–91; *GW* 10:306–21.

————. 1915. Repression. *SE* 14:146–58.

————. 1915. Thoughts for the Times on War and Death. *SE* 14:275–300; *CP* 4:288–317.

————. 1915. The Unconscious. *SE* 14:166–204; *CP* 4:98–136; *GW* 10:264–303.

————. 1916. On Transcience. *SE* 14:305–7.

————. 1916. Some Character-Types Met with in Psycho-Analytic Work. *SE* 14:311–33.

————. 1916–17. *Introductory Lectures on Psycho-Analysis*. *SE* 15 and 16; *GW* 11.

————. 1917. A Difficulty in the Path of Psycho-Analysis. *SE* 17:137–44; *CP* 4:347–56.

————. 1917. A Metapsychological Supplement to the Theory of Dreams. *SE* 14:222–35; *GW* 10:412–26.

————. 1917. Mourning and Melancholia. *SE* 14:243–58; *CP* 4:152–70; *GW* 10:428–46.

_____. 1917. On Transformations of Instinct as Exemplified in Anal Eroticism. *SE* 17:127–33; *CP* 2:164–71.

_____. 1918. Lines of Advance in Psycho-Analytic Therapy. *SE* 17:159–68; *CP* 2:392–402.

_____. 1919. Preface to Reik's *Ritual: Psycho-Analytic Studies*. *SE* 17:259–63; *CP* 5:92–7.

_____. 1919. The "Uncanny." *SE* 17:219–52.

_____. 1920. *Beyond the Pleasure Principle*. *SE* 18:7–64; *GW* 13:3–69.

_____. 1920. Dr. Anton von Freund. *SE* 18:267–8.

_____. 1920. The Psychogenesis of a Case of Homosexuality in a Woman. *SE* 18:147–72; *CP* 2:202–31.

_____. 1921. *Group Psychology and the Analysis of the Ego*. *SE* 18:69–143; *GW* 13:73–161.

_____. 1922. Some Neurotic Mechanisms in Jealousy, Paranoia and Homosexuality. *SE* 18:223–32.

_____. 1923. Two Encyclopaedia Articles. *SE* 18:235–59; *CP* 5:107–35; *GW* 13:211–33.

_____. 1923. *The Ego and the Id*. *SE* 19:10–59; *GW* 13:237–89.

_____. 1924. Neurosis and Psychosis. *SE* 19:149–53; *CP* 2:250–4.

_____. 1924. The Dissolution of the Oedipus Complex. *SE* 19:173–9; *CP* 2:269–76.

_____. 1924. The Economic Problem of Masochism. *SE* 19:159–70; *CP* 2:255–68.

_____. 1924. The Loss of Reality in Neurosis and Psychosis. *SE* 19:183–7.

_____. 1925. *An Autobiographical Study*. *SE* 20:7–74.

_____. 1925. Negation. *SE* 19:235–9; *GW* 14:11–15.

_____. 1925. Some Additional Notes on Dream-Interpretation as a Whole. *SE* 19:127–38; *GW* 1:559–73.

_____. 1925. Some Psychical Consequences of the Anatomical Distinction between the Sexes. *SE* 19:248–58.

_____. 1925. The Resistances to Psycho-Analysis. *SE* 19:213–22.

_____. 1926. *Inhibitions, Symptoms and Anxiety*. *SE* 20:77–172.

_____. 1926. Psycho-Analysis. *SE* 20:263–70.

_____. 1926. *The Question of Lay Analysis*. *SE* 20:183–258.

_____. 1926. To Romain Rolland. *SE* 20:279.

_____. 1927. *The Future of an Illusion*. *SE* 21:5–56.

_____. 1928. Dostoevsky and Parricide. *SE* 21:177–94; *CP* 5:222–42.

_____. 1930. *Civilization and its Discontents*. *SE* 21:64–145.

_____. 1931. Libidinal Types. *SE* 21:217–20.

_____. 1932. My Contact with Josef Popper-Lynkeus. *SE* 22:219–24.

_____. 1933. *New Introductory Lectures on Psycho-Analysis*. *SE* 22:5–182; *GW* 15.

_____. 1933. Why War? *SE* 22:199–215.

_____. 1936. A Disturbance of Memory on the Acropolis. *SE* 22:239–48.

———. 1937. Analysis Terminable and Interminable. *SE* 23:216–53.

———. 1939. *Moses and Monotheism. SE* 23:7–137.

———. [1938] 1940. *An Outline of Psycho-Analysis. SE* 23:144–207.

———. [1926] 1941. Address to the Society of *B'nai B'rith. SE* 20:273–4.

———. [1916–17] 1952. *A General Introduction to Psychoanalysis.* Trans. Joan Rivière. New York: Simon and Schuster, Pocket Book Edition.

———. 1954. *The Origins of Psycho-Analysis, Letters to Wilhelm Fliess, Drafts and Notes: 1887–1902.* Ed. Marie Bonaparte, Anna Freud, Ernest Kris. New York: Basic Books.

———. 1962. *Three Contributions to the Theory of Sex.* Trans. A. A. Brill. New York: E. P. Dutton and Co.

———. 1980. *The Concordance to the Standard Edition of the Complete Psychological Works of Sigmund Freud.* 2 vols. Ed. Samuel A. Guttman, Randall L. Jones, and Stephen M. Parrish. Boston: G. K. Hall.

Freud, Sigmund, and Josef Breuer. 1893–1895. *Studies on Hysteria. SE* 2.

Freud, Sigmund, and William C. Bullitt. 1967. *Thomas Woodrow Wilson: A Psychological Study.* Boston: Houghton Mifflin.

Friedman, Richard. 1988. *Male Homosexuality.* New Haven, Conn.: Yale University Press.

Fromm, Erich. 1941. *Escape from Freedom.* New York: Holt, Rinehart, and Winston.

———. 1947. *Man for Himself.* New York: Holt, Rinehart, and Winston.

———. 1950. *Psychoanalysis and Religion.* New Haven, Conn.: Yale University Press.

———. 1955. *The Sane Society.* New York: Rinehart and Company.

———. 1956. *The Art of Loving.* New York: Harper and Row.

———. 1959. *Sigmund Freud's Mission.* New York: Harper and Brothers.

———. 1973. Freud's Model of Man and Its Social Determinants. In *Sigmund Freud,* ed. Paul Roazen, 45–8. Englewood Cliffs, N.J.: Prentice-Hall.

Fromm-Reichmann, Frieda. 1959. *Psychoanalysis and Psychotherapy.* Chicago: University of Chicago Press.

Furer, Manuel. 1971. The History of the Superego Concept in Psychoanalysis: A Review of the Literature. In *Moral Values and the Superego Concept in Psychoanalysis,* ed. Seymour C. Post, 11–62. New York: International Universities Press.

Furnish, Victor. 1982. Love of Neighbor in the New Testament. *Journal of Religious Ethics* 10:327–34.

Gadamer, Hans-Georg. 1975. *Truth and Method.* New York: Seabury Press.

Gardiner, Muriel, ed. 1971. *The Wolf Man.* New York: Basic Books.

Gay, Peter. 1979. Freud and Freedom. In *The Idea of Freedom,* ed. Alan Ryan, 41–59. Oxford: Oxford University Press.

———. 1988. *Freud: A Life for Our Time.* New York: W. W. Norton.

Geatch, P. T. 1977. *The Virtues.* Cambridge: Cambridge University Press.

Gedo, John. 1979. *Beyond Interpretation*. New York: International Universities Press.

————. 1984. *Psychoanalysis and its Discontents*. New York: Guilford Press.

————. 1986. On the Origins of the Theban Plague: Assessments of Sigmund Freud's Character. In *Freud: Appraisals and Reappraisals*. Contributions to Freud Studies, vol. 1, ed. Paul E. Stepansky, 241–59. Hillsdale, N.J.: Analytic Press.

Gerber, Richard. 1990. Psychic Determinism and Moral Responsibility. Unpublished response to my paper on Psychic Determinism and Moral Responsibility in Freudian Theory and Practice. Paper read at the Scientific Meeting of the Washington Psychoanalytic Association, 9 March 1990.

Ghosal, Hironmoy. 1982. Psychic Determinism and Free Will. *Samiksa* 36:88–98.

Gill, Merton M. 1976. Metapsychology Is Not Psychology. In *Psychology versus Metapsychology: Psychoanalytic Essays in Memory of George S. Klein. Psychological Issues,* monograph 36, vol. 9, no. 4. New York: International Universities Press.

Gilligan, Carol. 1982. *In a Different Voice*. Cambridge, Mass.: Harvard University Press.

Glasgow, W. D. 1976. Psychological Egoism. *APQ* 13:75–9.

Glymour, C. 1974. Freud, Kepler and the Clinical Evidence. In *Freud,* ed. R. Wollheim, 285–304. New York: Anchor Books.

————. 1980. *Theory and Evidence*. Princeton, N.J.: Princeton University Press.

Goldberg, Arnold. 1974. On the Prognosis and Treatment of Narcissism. *JAPA* 22:243–54.

Gombrich, E. H. 1984. *Tributes: Interpreters of our Cultural Tradition*. Ithaca, N.Y.: Cornell University Press.

Graff, Harold, and Lester Luborsky. 1977. Long-Term Trends in Transference and Resistance: A Report on a Quantitative-Analytic Method Applied to Four Psychoanalyses. *JAPA* 25:471–90.

Gray, Paul. 1982. "Developmental Lag" in the Evolution of Technique for Psychoanalysis of Neurotic Conflict. *JAPA* 30:621–55.

Green, Ronald. 1982. Jewish Ethics and Beneficence. In *Beneficence and Health Care,* ed. Earl E. Shelp, 109–25. Dordrecht: D. Reidel.

Greenberg, Jay R., and Stephen A. Mitchell. 1983. *Object Relations in Psychoanalytic Theory*. Cambridge, Mass.: Harvard University Press.

Greenson, Ralph R. 1958. Variations in Classical Psychoanalytic Technique: Introduction. *IJP* 39:200–1.

————. 1965. The Working Alliance and the Transference Neurosis. *PQ* 34: 155–81.

————. 1967. *The Technique and Practice of Psychoanalysis,* vol. 1. New York: International Universities Press.

Greenspan, Stanley I. 1981. *Psychopathology and Adaptation in Infancy and Early Childhood: Principles of Clinical Diagnosis and Prevention Intervention*. New York: International Universities Press.

————. 1988. The Development of the Ego: Insights from Clinical Work with Infants and Young Children. *JAPA* 36, supplement:3–55.

————. 1989. The Development of the Ego: Biological and Environmental Specificity in the Psychopathological Developmental Process and the Selection and Construction of Ego Defenses. *JAPA* 37:605–38.

Gregory, Ian. 1975. Psycho-Analysis, Human Nature and Human Conduct. In *Nature and Conduct,* ed. R. S. Peters, 99–120. New York: St Martin's Press.

Grünbaum, Adolf. 1977. How Scientific is Psychoanalysis? In *Science and Psychotherapy,* ed. R. Stern, L. Horowitz, and J. Lynes, 219–54. New York: Haven Press.

————. 1979. Is Freudian Psychoanalytic Theory Pseudo-Scientific by Karl Popper's Criterion of Demarcation? *APQ* 16:131–41.

————. 1980. Epistemological Liabilities of the Clinical Appraisal of Psychoanalytic Theory. *Nous* 14:307–85.

————. 1984. *The Foundations of Psychoanalysis.* Berkeley: University of California Press.

————. 1986. Précis of *The Foundations of Psychoanalysis:* A Philosophical Critique, with commentary. *Behavioral and Brain Sciences* 9:217–84.

Grünberger, Béla. 1979. *Narcissism.* New York: International Universities Press.

Gunderson, John. 1979. Individual Psychotherapy. In *Disorders of the Schizophrenic Syndrome,* ed. Leopold Bellak, 364–98. New York: Basic Books.

Guntrip, Harry. 1964. *Personality Structure and Human Interaction.* New York: International Universities Press.

————. 1973. *Psychoanalytic Theory, Therapy, and the Self.* New York: Basic Books.

Habermas, Jürgen. [1968] 1971. *Knowledge and Human Interests.* Boston: Beacon Press.

Haigh, Gerard. 1961. Existential Guilt: Neurotic and Real. *Review of Existential Psychology and Psychiatry* 1:120–31.

Hale, Nathan G., ed. 1971. *James Jackson Putnam and Psychoanalysis: Letters between Putnam and Sigmund Freud, Ernest Jones, William James, Sandor Ferenczi, and Morton Prince, 1877–1917.* Cambridge, Mass.: Harvard University Press.

Hampshire, Stuart. 1975. *Freedom of the Individual.* Princeton: Princeton University Press.

————. [1959] 1983a. *Thought and Action.* Notre Dame, Ind.: University of Notre Dame Press.

————. 1983b. *Morality and Conflict.* Cambridge, Mass.: Harvard University Press.

Hancock, Roger N. 1974. *Twentieth Century Ethics.* New York: Columbia University Press.

Hardie, W. F. R. 1965. The Final Good in Aristotle's *Ethics. Philosophy* 40:277–95.

————. 1968. *Aristotle's Ethical Theory.* Oxford: Oxford University Press.

Hare, R. M. 1952. *The Language of Morals.* Oxford: Clarendon Press.

————. 1963. *Freedom and Reason.* New York: Oxford University Press.

Harman, Gilbert. 1977. *The Nature of Morality*. New York: Oxford University Press.

Hartmann, Heinz. 1958. *Ego Psychology and the Problem of Adaptation*. New York: International Universities Press.

———. 1960. *Psychoanalysis and Moral Values*. New York: International Universities Press.

———. 1964. *Essays on Ego Psychology*. New York: International Universities Press.

Hartmann, Heinz, and E. Kris. 1945. The Genetic Approach in Psychoanalysis. *PSC* 1:11–30.

Hartmann, Heinz, E. Kris, and R. Loewenstein. 1964. *Papers on Psychoanalytic Psychology*. *Psychological Issues,* monograph 14, vol. 4, no. 2. New York: International Universities Press.

Hartmann, Heinz, and R. Loewenstein. 1964. Notes on the Superego. In *Papers on Psychoanalytic Psychology*. *Psychological Issues,* monograph 14, vol. 4, no. 2, ed. Heinz Hartmann, Ernst Kris, and Rudolph Loewenstein, 144–81. New York: International Universities Press.

Hauerwas, Stanley. 1981. *Vision and Virtue*. Notre Dame, Ind.: University of Notre Dame Press.

Hauerwas, Stanley, and Alasdair MacIntyre. 1983. *Revisions: Changing Perspectives in Moral Philosophy*. Notre Dame, Ind.: University of Notre Dame Press.

Hegel, G. W. F. [1833] 1942. *Philosophy of Right*. Oxford: Clarendon Press.

Hobart, R. E. 1934. Free Will as Involving Determination and Inconceivable Without It. *Mind* 43:1–27.

Hobbes, T. [1651] 1947. *Leviathan,* ed. M. Oakeshott. Oxford: Basil Blackwell.

Hoffer, Axel. 1985. Toward a Definition of Psychoanalytic Neutrality. *JAPA* 33:771–96.

Hoffman, Martin L. 1976. Empathy, Role Taking, Guilt, and Development of Altruistic Motives. In *Moral Development and Behavior,* ed. Thomas Lickona, 124–43. New York: Holt, Rinehart, and Winston.

Holt, Robert R. 1965. A Review of Some of Freud's Biological Assumptions and their Influence on his Theories. In *Psychoanalysis and Current Biological Thought,* ed. N. S. Greenfield and W. C. Lewis, 93–124. Madison and Milwaukee: University of Wisconsin Press.

———. 1967. Beyond Vitalism and Mechanism: Freud's Concept of Psychic Energy. In *The Ego,* ed. J. H. Masserman, *Science and Psychoanalysis* 11:1–41. New York: Grune and Stratton.

———. 1972. Freud's Mechanistic and Humanistic Images of Man. In *Psychoanalysis and Contemporary Science,* ed. Robert R. Holt and Emanuel Peterfreud, 3–24. New York: Macmillan.

———. 1973. On Reading Freud. In *Abstracts of the Standard Edition of the Complete Psychological Works of Sigmund Freud,* ed. Carrie Lee Rothgeb, 2–79. New York: Jason Aronson.

———. 1976. Drive or Wish? A Reconsideration of the Psychoanalytic Theory of

Motivation. In *Psychology versus Metapsychology: Psychoanalytic Essays in Memory of George S. Klein,* ed. M. Gill and P. Holzman, *Psychological Issues,* monograph 36, vol. 9, no. 4. New York: International Universities Press.

————. 1981. The Death and Transfiguration of Metapsychology. *IRP* 8:129–43.

Homans, Peter. 1982. Understand thy Neighbor as Thyself: Freud's Criticism of the Love Commandment. *Journal of Religious Ethics* 10:320–6.

Home, H. J. 1966. The Concept of Mind. *IJP* 47:42–9.

Hook, Sidney. 1960. *Psychoanalysis, Scientific Method and Philosophy.* London: Evergreen Books.

————., ed. 1961. *Determinism and Freedom in the Age of Modern Science.* New York: Collier Books.

Hospers, John. 1950. Meaning and Free Will. *Philosophy and Phenomenological Research* 10:313–30.

————. 1952. Free-Will and Psychoanalysis. Abridged version of Hospers 1950. In *Readings in Ethical Theory,* ed. W. Sellars and J. Hospers, 560–75. New York: Appleton-Century-Crofts. Repr. in *Reason and Responsibility,* ed. Joel Feinberg, 272–82. Belmont, Calif.: Dickenson Publishing Company.

————. 1961a. *Human Conduct.* New York: Harcourt, Brace, and World.

————. 1961b. What Means this Freedom? In *Determinism and Freedom in the Age of Modern Science,* ed. Sidney Hook, 126–42. New York: Collier Books.

Howard, Roy J. 1982. *Three Faces of Hermeneutics.* Berkeley: University of California Press.

Hudson, W. D. 1970. *Modern Moral Philosophy.* Garden City, N.Y.: Doubleday, Anchor Books.

Hume, David. [1739] 1948. *A Treatise of Human Nature.* In *Hume's Moral and Political Philosophy,* ed. Henry D. Aiken, 3–169. New York: Hafner Publishing.

Iturrate, Miguel. 1977. Man's Freedom: Freud's Therapeutic Goal. *Review of Existential Psychology and Psychiatry* 15:32–45.

Jacobs, Daniel. 1988. Love, Work, and Survival: Psychoanalysis in the Nuclear Age. In *Psychoanalysis and the Nuclear Threat: Clinical and Theoretical Studies,* ed. Howard Levine, Daniel Jacobs, and Lowell Rubin, 173–87. Hillsdale, N.J.: Analytic Press.

Jacobson, Edith. 1964. *The Self and the Object World.* New York: International Universities Press.

Jahoda, Marie. 1977. *Freud and the Dilemmas of Psychology.* New York: Basic Books.

James, William. [1884] 1969. The Dilemma of Determinism. In *The Moral Philosophy of William James,* ed. John Roth, 103–31. New York: Thomas Y. Crowell Company.

Joffe, W. G., and J. Sandler. 1967. Some Conceptual Problems Involved in the Consideration of Disorders of Narcissism. *Journal of Child Psychotherapy* 2: 56–66.

Johann, Robert. 1955. *The Meaning of Love.* Westminster, Md.: Newman Press.

Johnson, James Turner. 1984. *Can Modern War Be Just?* New Haven, Conn.: Yale University Press.

Johnston, J. 1962. Love in the N.T. In *The Interpreter's Dictionary of the Bible,* ed. George Buttrick, vol. K–Q:168–78. New York: Abingdon Press.

Jones, David. 1973. Freud's Theory of Moral Conscience. In *Conscience,* ed. John Donnelly and Leonard Lyons, 85–114. Staten Island, N.Y.: Alba House.

Jones, Ernest. 1945. The Concept of the Normal Mind. In *The Yearbook of Psychoanalysis* 1:49–62. New York: International Universities Press.

———. 1953. *The Life and Work of Sigmund Freud,* vol. 1. New York: Basic Books.

———. 1955. *The Life and Work of Sigmund Freud,* vol. 2. New York: Basic Books.

———. 1957. *The Life and Work of Sigmund Freud,* vol. 3. New York: Basic Books.

Kalin, Jesse. 1969. On Ethical Egoism. *APQ,* Monograph No. 1:26–41.

———. 1970. In Defense of Egoism. In *Morality and Rational Self-Interest,* ed. David P. Gauthier, 64–87. Englewood Cliffs, N.J.: Prentice-Hall.

———. 1975. Two Kinds of Moral Reasoning: Ethical Egoism as a Moral Theory. *Canadian Journal of Philosophy* 5:323–56.

Kandel, Eric R. 1983. From Metapsychology to Molecular Biology: Explorations into the Nature of Anxiety. *American Journal of Psychiatry* 140:1277–92.

Kant, Immanuel. [1785] 1959. *Foundations of the Metaphysics of Morals.* Trans. Lewis White Beck. Indianapolis, Ind.: Bobbs-Merrill, Liberal Arts Press.

———. [1788] 1956. *Critique of Practical Reason.* Trans. Lewis White Beck. Indianapolis, Ind.: Bobbs-Merrill, Liberal Arts Press.

Kanzer, Mark. 1952a. The Communicative Function of the Dream. *IJP* 36:260–6.

———. 1952b. Transference neurosis of the Rat Man. *PQ* 21:181–9.

———. 1964. Freud's Uses of the Term "Autoerotism" and "Narcissism." *JAPA* 12:529–39.

———. 1968. Psychic Determinism: Freud's Specific Propositions. *PQ* 37:485–6.

Kaplan, Abraham. 1957. Freud and Modern Philosophy. In *Freud and the 20th Century,* ed. Benjamin Nelson, 209–29. New York: Meridian Books.

Karon, B., and G. Vandenbos. 1983. *Psychotherapy of Schizophrenia: The Treatment of Choice.* New York: Jason Aronson.

Katz, Jay. 1984. *The Silent World of Doctor and Patient.* New York: Free Press.

Kegan, Robert. 1982. *The Evolving Self.* Cambridge, Mass.: Harvard University Press.

Kenny, Anthony. 1970. Happiness. In *Moral Concepts,* ed. Joel Feinberg, 41–52. Oxford: Oxford University Press.

Kernberg, Otto. 1970. Factors in the Psychoanalytic Treatment of Narcissistic Personalities. *JAPA* 18:51–85.

———. 1974. Regarding the Nature of Psychoanalytic Treatment of Narcissistic Personalities: A Preliminary Communication. *JAPA* 22:255–67.

———. 1975. *Borderline Conditions and Pathological Narcissism.* New York: Jason Aronson.

———. 1976. *Object Relations Theory and Clinical Psychoanalysis*. New York: Jason Aronson.

———. 1984. Contemporary Psychoanalytic Approaches to Narcissism. In *Severe Personality Disorders,* ed. Otto Kernberg, 179–96. New Haven, Conn.: Yale University Press.

Kittay, Eva Feder, and Diana T. Meyers, eds. 1987. *Women and Moral Theory*. Totowa, N.J.: Roman and Littlefield.

Klein, George. 1976. *Psychoanalytic Theory: An Exploration of Essentials*. New York: International Universities Press.

Kline, Paul. 1972. *Fact and Fantasy in Freudian Theory*. London: Methuen.

Knight, R. P. 1946. Determinism, "freedom," and psychotherapy. *Psychiatry* 9:251–62.

Kohlberg, Lawrence. 1981. *The Philosophy of Moral Development. Essays on Moral Development,* vol. 1. San Francisco: Harper and Row.

———. 1984. *The Psychology of Moral Development. Essays on Moral Development,* vol. 2. San Francisco: Harper and Row.

Kohut, Heinz. 1971. *The Analysis of the Self.* The Psychoanalytic Study of the Child, monograph 4. New York: International Universities Press.

———. 1972. Thoughts on Narcissism and Narcissistic Rage. *PSC* 27:360–400.

———. 1977. *The Restoration of the Self.* New York: International Universities Press.

———. 1978. *The Search for the Self: Selected Writings of Heinz Kohut: 1950–1978.* 2 vols. New York: International Universities Press.

———. 1984. *How Does Analysis Cure?* Ed. Arnold Goldberg. Chicago: University of Chicago Press.

Krige, John. 1980. *Science, Revolution and Discontinuity*. Atlantic Highlands, N.J.: Humanities Press.

Kris, Ernst. 1951. Ego Psychology and Interpretation in Psychoanalytic Therapy. *PQ* 20:15–30.

———. 1952. *Psychoanalytic Explorations in Art*. New York: International Universities Press.

———. 1975. *The Selected Papers of Ernst Kris*. New Haven, Conn.: Yale University Press.

Kubie, L. S. 1947. The Fallacious Use of Quantitative Concepts in Dynamic Psychology. *PQ* 16:507–18.

Kuhn, Thomas S. 1970. *The Structure of Scientific Revolutions*. 2d ed. Chicago: University of Chicago Press.

———. 1977. *The Essential Tension: Selected Studies in Scientific Tradition and Change*. Chicago: University of Chicago Press.

Lacan, Jacques. 1977. *Écrits: A Selection*. New York: W. W. Norton.

———. 1981. *The Four Fundamental Concepts of Psycho-Analysis*. Ed. Jacques-Alain Miller. Trans. Alan Sheridan. New York: W. W. Norton.

Lakoff, Sanford. 1964. *Equality in Political Philosophy*. Cambridge, Mass.: Harvard University Press.

Laplanche, J., and J.-B. Pontalis. 1973. *The Language of Psycho-analysis*. Trans. Donald Nicholson-Smith. New York: W. W. Norton.

Lasch, Christopher. 1979. *The Culture of Narcissism*. New York: W. W. Norton.

Lerner, B. 1961. Auditory and Visual Thresholds for the Perception of Words of Anal Connotation: An Evaluation of the "Sublimation Hypothesis" on Philatelists. Unpublished doctoral dissertation, Yeshiva University.

Lichtenberg, J. D. 1983. *Psychoanalysis and Infant Research*. Hillsdale, N.J.: Analytic Press.

Lipton, S. 1977. The Advantages of Freud's Technique as Shown in his Analysis of the Rat Man. *IJP* 58:255–73.

_____. 1979. An Addendum to "The Advantages of Freud's Technique as Shown in his Analysis of the Rat Man. *IJP* 60:215–6.

Little, David. 1974. Max Weber and the Comparative Study of Religious Ethics. *Journal of Religious Ethics* 2:5–40.

Loevinger, Jane. 1976. *Ego Development*. San Francisco: Jossey-Bass.

Loewald, Hans W. 1959. The Waning of the Oedipus Complex. *JAPA* 27:751–75.

_____. 1960. On the Therapeutic Action of Psychoanalysis. *IJP* 41:16–33.

_____. 1978. *Psychoanalysis and the History of the Individual*. New Haven, Conn.: Yale University Press.

_____. 1980. *Papers on Psychoanalysis*. New Haven, Conn.: Yale University Press.

Luborsky, Lester. 1967. Momentary Forgetting during Psychotherapy and Psychoanalysis. In *Motives and Thought: Psychoanalytic Essays in Honor of David Rapaport*, ed. R. R. Holt, *Psychological Issues,* monograph 18/19, vol. 5, nos. 2–3. 177–217. New York: International Universities Press.

_____. 1970. New Directions in Research on Neurotic and Psychosomatic Symptoms. *American Scientist* 58:661–8.

_____. 1976. Helping Alliances in Psychotherapy: The Groundwork for a Study of their Relationship to its Outcome. In *Successful Psychotherapy,* ed. J. L. Claghorn, 92–116. New York: Brunner/Mazel.

_____. 1986. Evidence to Lessen Professor Grünbaum's Concern about Freud's Clinical Inference Method. *Behavioral and Brain Sciences* 9:247–9.

Luborsky, Lester, and Paul Crits-Christoph. 1990. *Understanding Transference: The CCRT Method*. New York: Basic Books.

Luborsky, Lester, P. Crits-Christoph, J. Mintz, and A. Auerbach. 1988. *Who Will Benefit from Psychotherapy? Predicting Therapeutic Outcomes*. New York: Basic Books.

Luborsky, Lester, and Jim Mintz. 1975. What Sets Off Momentary Forgetting During a Psychoanalysis? Investigations of Symptom-Onset Conditions. In *Psychoanalysis and Contemporary Science,* ed. Leo Goldberger and Victor H. Rosen, 3:233–68. New York: International Universities Press.

Machan, Tibor R. 1979. Recent Work in Ethical Egoism. *APQ* 16:1–13.

MacIntyre, Alasdair. 1958. *The Unconscious: A Conceptual Analysis*. Atlantic Highlands, N.J.: Humanities Press.

_____. 1966. *A Short History of Ethics*. New York: Macmillan.

_____. 1967. Egoism and Altruism. In *The Encyclopedia of Philosophy*, ed. Paul Edwards, 2:462–6. New York: Macmillan and Free Press.

_____. 1978. *Against the Self-Images of the Age*. Notre Dame, Ind.: University of Notre Dame Press.

_____. 1981. *After Virtue: A Study in Moral Theory*. Notre Dame, Ind.: University of Notre Dame Press.

_____. 1988. *Whose Justice? Which Rationality?* Notre Dame, Ind.: University of Notre Dame Press.

Mackie, J. L. 1977. *Ethics: Inventing Right and Wrong*. New York: Penguin Books.

_____. 1980. *Hume's Moral Theory*. London: Routledge and Kegan Paul.

Macklin, Ruth. 1976. A Psychoanalytic Model for Human Freedom and Rationality. *PQ* 45:430–54.

MacLagan, W. C. 1960. Respect for Persons as a Moral Principle. *Philosophy* 35:193–217, 289–305.

Mahler, Margaret S. 1968. *On Human Symbiosis and the Vicissitudes of Individuation*. New York: International Universities Press.

Mahler, Margaret S., Fred Pine, and Anni Bergman. 1975. *The Psychological Birth of the Human Infant*. New York: Basic Books.

Malcolm, Janet. 1982. *Psychoanalysis: The Impossible Profession*. New York: Vintage Books.

_____. 1984. *In the Freud Archives*. New York: Knopf.

Mann, Thomas. [1929] 1973. Freud's Position in the History of Modern Culture. In *Freud As We Knew Him*, ed. Hendrik M. Ruitenbeek, 65–89. Detroit, Mich.: Wayne State University Press.

Mannoni, O. 1971. *Freud*. New York: Pantheon Books.

Marcuse, Herbert. 1955. *Eros and Civilization*. Boston: Beacon Press.

_____. 1967. Love Mystified: A Critique of Normal O. Brown. *Commentary* 43: 71–5.

Masson, Jeffrey, M. 1984. *The Assault on Truth: Freud's Suppression of the Seduction Theory*. New York: Farrar, Strauss and Giroux.

May, Rollo. 1969. *Love and Will*. New York: W. W. Norton.

Mazer, M. 1960. The Therapeutic Function of the Belief in Will. *Psychiatry* 23: 45–52.

McAllister, Joseph B. 1956. Psychoanalysis and Morality. *New Scholasticism* 30: 310–29.

McGrath, William J. 1986. *Freud's Discovery of Psychoanalysis*. Ithaca, N.Y.: Cornell University Press.

Meissner, William W. 1983. Values in the Psychoanalytic Situation. *Psychoanalytic Inquiry* 3:577–98.

_____. 1984. *Psychoanalysis and Religious Experience*. New Haven, Conn.: Yale University Press.

Meng, Heinrich, and Ernest L. Freud, eds. 1963. *Psychoanalysis and Faith: The Letters of Sigmund Freud and Oskar Pfister.* Trans. Eric Mosbacher. New York: Basic Books.

Menninger, Karl. 1942. *The Human Mind.* New York: Knopf.

Menninger, Karl, with Martin Mayman and Paul Pruyser. 1967. *The Vital Balance: The Life Process in Mental Health and Illness.* New York: Viking Press, Compass Edition.

Midgley, Mary. 1978. *Beast and Man: The Roots of Human Nature.* Ithaca, N.Y.: Cornell University Press.

Mill, John Stuart. [1859] 1962a. *On Liberty.* In *Utilitarianism, On Liberty, Essay on Bentham,* ed. Mary Warnock, 126–250. Cleveland: World Publishing Co., Meridian Books.

———. [1861] 1962b. *Utilitarianism.* In *Utilitarianism, On Liberty, Essay on Bentham,* ed. Mary Warnock, 251–321. Cleveland: World Publishing Co., Meridian Books.

Miller, Cecil. 1971. Therapy, Determinism, and Science. *Southern Journal of Philosophy* 9:189–200.

Miller, Nancy, L. Luborsky, J. Barber, and John Docherty, eds. 1992. *Handbook of Psychodynamic Treatment Research.* New York: Basic Books.

Money-Kyrle, R. E. 1952. Psycho-Analysis and Ethics. *IJP* 33:225–34.

Moore, Burness E. 1975. Towards a Clarification of the Concept of Narcissism. *PSC* 30:243–76.

Moore, G. E. [1903] 1966. *Principia Ethica.* Cambridge: Cambridge University Press.

Moore, Michael. 1984. *Law and Psychiatry: Rethinking the Relationship.* Cambridge: Cambridge University Press.

Morgan, Douglas. 1964. *Love: Plato, the Bible and Freud.* Englewood Cliffs, N.J.: Prentice-Hall.

Morse, Stephen. 1982. Failed Explanations and Criminal Responsibility: Experts and the Unconscious. *Virginia Law Review* 68:971–1084.

Munsey, Brenda, ed. 1980. *Moral Development, Moral Education, and Kohlberg: Basic Issues in Philosophy, Psychology, Religion, and Education.* Birmingham, Ala.: Religious Education Press.

Murdoch, Iris. 1971. *The Sovereignty of Good.* New York: Schocken Books.

Nagel, Ernest. 1960. Methodological Issues in Psychoanalytic Theory. In *Psychoanalysis, Scientific Method and Philosophy,* ed. Sidney Hook, 38–56. New York: Grove Press.

Neu, Jerome. 1977. *Emotion, Thought and Therapy.* Berkeley: University of California Press.

Niebuhr, Reinhold. 1960. In *Reinhold Niebuhr on Politics,* ed. Harry Davis and Robert Good. New York: Charles Scribner's Sons.

Nielsen, Nils. 1960. Value Judgments in Psychoanalysis. *IJP* 41:425–9.

Nisbett, Richard E., and Timothy Wilson. 1977. Telling More Than We Can Know: Verbal Reports on Mental Processes. *Psychological Review* 84:231–59.

Nozick, Robert. 1974. *Anarchy, State and Utopia.* New York: Basic Books.

_____. 1981. *Philosophical Explanations.* Cambridge, Mass.: Harvard University Press.

Nunberg, H., and E. Federn, eds. 1962, 1967. *Minutes of the Vienna Psycho-Analytic Society,* 1 and 2. New York: International Universities Press.

Nygren, Anders. 1969. *Agape and Eros.* New York: Harper and Row.

Outka, Gene. 1972. *Agape: An Ethical Analysis.* New Haven, Conn.: Yale University Press.

Parsons, Talcott. 1964. *Social Structure and Personality.* New York: Free Press.

Parsons, Talcott, and Edward A. Shils, eds. 1951. *Toward a General Theory of Action.* New York: Harper and Row.

Pascal, B. *Pensées.* 1958. New York: E. P. Dutton and Company.

Peters, R. S. 1960. *The Concept of Motivation.* New York: Humanities Press.

Piaget, J. 1964. Relations Between Affectivity and Intelligence in the Mental Development of the Child. In *Sorbonne Courses.* Paris: University Documentation Center.

_____. 1965. *The Moral Judgment of the Child.* Trans. Marjorie Gabain. New York: Free Press.

Plamenatz, John. 1963. *Man and Society.* London: Longmans, Green.

Popper, K. R. 1962. *Conjectures and Refutations.* New York: Basic Books.

_____. 1974. Replies to My Critics. In *The Philosophy of Karl Popper,* ed. P. A. Schilpp, bk 2. LaSalle, Ill.: Open Court.

Post, Seymour C., ed. 1972. *Moral Values and the Superego Concept in Psychoanalysis.* New York: International Universities Press.

Pruyser, Paul. 1980. Work: Curse or Blessing? *Bulletin of the Menninger Clinic* 44:59–73.

Pulver, Sydney. 1970. Narcissism: The Term and the Concept. *JAPA* 18:319–41.

Putnam, Hilary. 1978. *Meaning and the Moral Sciences.* London: Routledge and Kegan Paul.

Ramzy, Ishak. 1972. The Place of Values in Psychoanalytic Theory, Practice and Training. In *Moral Values and the Superego Concept in Psychoanalysis,* ed. Seymour C. Post, 205–25. New York: International Universities Press.

_____. 1983. The Place of Values in Psycho-Analysis. *Psychoanalytic Inquiry* 3:547–72.

Randall, John Herman, Jr. 1962. *The Career of Philosophy,* vol. 1. New York: Columbia University Press.

_____. 1965. *The Career of Philosophy,* vol. 2. New York: Columbia University Press.

Rangell, L. 1969. Choice-Conflict and the Decision-Making Function of the Ego. *IJP* 50:599–602.

_____. 1971. Decision-Making Process. *PSC* 26:425–52.

_____. 1981. From Insight to Change. *JAPA* 29:119–41.

———. 1986. The Executive Functions of the Ego: An Extension of the Concept of Ego Autonomy. *PSC* 41:1–37.

Rank, Otto. 1911. Ein Beitrag zum Narzissismus. *Jahrbuch für psychoanalytische und psychopathologische Forschungen* 3:401–26.

Rapaport, David. 1950. On the Psychoanalytic Theory of Thinking. *IJP* 31:161–70.

———. 1951. The Autonomy of the Ego. *Bulletin of the Menninger Clinic* 15:113–23. Repr. in *The Collected Papers of David Rapaport,* ed. M. Gill, 357–67. New York: Basic Books, 1967.

———. 1953. On the Psychoanalytic Theory of Affects. *IJP* 34:177–98. Repr. in Repr. in *The Collected Papers of David Rapaport,* ed. M. Gill, 476–512. New York: Basic Books, 1967.

———. 1957. Psychoanalysis as a Developmental Psychology. In *The Collected Papers of David Rapaport,* ed. M. Gill, 820–53. New York: Basic Books, 1967.

———. 1957–9. Seminars on elementary metapsychology. In mimeographed copies of seminars held at Austin Riggs Center, ed. S. Miller.

———. 1958. The Theory of Ego Autonomy. *Bulletin of the Menninger Clinic* 22:13–35. Repr. in *The Collected Papers of David Rapaport,* ed. M. Gill, 722–44. New York: Basic Books, 1967.

———. 1959. A Historical Survey of Psychoanalytic Ego Psychology. *Psychological Issues,* monograph 1. Repr. in *The Collected Papers of David Rapaport,* ed. M. Gill, 745–57. New York: Basic Books, 1967.

———. 1960. *The Structure of Psychoanalytic Theory. Psychological Issues,* monograph 6, vol. 2. New York: International Universities Press.

Rapaport, David, and Merton Gill. 1959. The Points of View and Assumptions of Metapsychology. *IJP* 40:153–62.

Rashdall, Hastings. 1924. *The Theory of Good and Evil,* 2d ed. Oxford: Clarendon Press.

Rawls, John. 1971. *A Theory of Justice.* Cambridge, Mass.: Harvard University Press.

———. 1980. Kantian Constructivism in Moral Theory. *JP* 77:515–72.

———. 1982. The Basic Liberties and Their Priority. In *The Tanner Lectures on Human Values,* vol. 3, ed. Sterling M. McMurrin, 3–135. Salt Lake City: University of Utah Press.

———. 1985. Justice as Fairness: Political not Metaphysical. *Philosophy and Public Affairs* 14:223–51.

Reich, Annie. 1953. Narcissistic Object Choice in Women. *JAPA* 1:22–44.

———. 1973. *Annie Reich: Psychoanalytic Contributions.* New York: International Universities Press.

Richards, David A. J. 1971. *A Theory of Reasons for Action.* Oxford: Oxford University Press.

Ricoeur, Paul. 1965. *Fallible Man: Philosophy of the Will.* Trans. Charles Kelbley. Chicago: Henry Regnery Company.

————. 1966. *Freedom and Nature: The Voluntary and the Involuntary*. Trans. Erazim Kohák. Evanston, Ill.: Northwestern University Press.

————. 1967. *The Symbolism of Evil*. Trans. Emerson Buchanan. Boston: Beacon Press.

————. 1970. *Freud and Philosophy: An Essay on Interpretation*. Trans. Denis Savage. New Haven, Conn.: Yale University Press.

————. 1981. *Hermeneutics and the Human Sciences*. Ed. and trans. John B. Thompson. Cambridge: Cambridge University Press.

Rieff, Philip. 1961. *Freud: The Mind of the Moralist*. Garden City, N.Y.: Doubleday, Anchor Books.

————. 1968. *The Triumph of the Therapeutic*. New York: Harper and Row, Harper Torchbooks.

Roazen, Paul. 1973. *Sigmund Freud*. Englewood Cliffs, N.J.: Prentice-Hall.

Rorty, Richard. 1972. The World Well Lost. *JP* 69:649–65.

————. 1979. *Philosophy and the Mirror of Nature*. Princeton, N.J.: Princeton University Press.

————. 1980. Freud, Morality, and Hermeneutics. *New Literary History* 12: 177–85.

————. 1986. Freud and Moral Reflection. In *Pragmatism's Freud: The Moral Disposition of Psychoanalysis,* ed. Joseph H. Smith and William Kerrigan, 1–27. Baltimore: The Johns Hopkins University Press.

Rosenwald, G. C. 1972. Effectiveness of Defenses against Anal Impulse Arousal. *Journal of Consulting and Clinical Psychology* 36:292–8.

Ross, Sir W. David. 1930. *The Right and the Good*. Oxford: Clarendon Press.

————. 1939. *Foundation of Ethics*. Oxford: Clarendon Press.

Rothstein, Arnold. 1980. *The Narcissistic Pursuit of Perfection*. New York: International Universities Press.

Rubinstein, Benjamin B. 1965. Psychoanalytic Theory and the Mind–Body Problem. In *Psychoanalysis and Current Biological Thought,* ed. Norman S. Greenfield and William C. Lewis, 35–56. Madison and Milwaukee: University of Wisconsin Press.

Rychlak, Joseph. 1979. *Discovering Free Will and Personal Responsibility*. New York: Oxford University Press.

Sabine, George H. 1961. *A History of Political Theory*. New York: Holt, Rinehart, and Winston.

Sandel, Michael J. 1982. *Liberalism and the Limits of Justice*. Cambridge: Cambridge University Press.

Sartre, Jean-Paul. 1953. *Existential Psychoanalysis*. New York: Philosophical Library.

Schafer, Roy. 1968. *Aspects of Internalization*. New York: International Universities Press.

————. 1976. *A New Language for Psychoanalysis*. New Haven, Conn.: Yale University Press.

————. 1983. *The Analytic Attitude*. New York: Basic Books.

Schur, Max. 1966. *The Id and the Regulatory Principles of Mental Functioning.* New York: International Universities Press.

———. 1972. *Freud: Living and Dying.* New York: International Universities Press.

Schwartz, Wynn. 1984. The Two Concepts of Action and Responsibility in Psychoanalysis. *JAPA* 32:557–72.

Selby-Bigge, L. A. 1964. *British Moralists.* 2 vols. Indianapolis, Ind.: Bobbs-Merrill.

Sellars, Wilfrid, and John Hospers, eds. 1952. *Readings in Ethical Theory.* New York: Appleton-Century-Crofts.

Shakow, David, and David Rapaport. 1964. *The Influence of Freud on American Psychology. Psychological Issues,* monograph 13, vol. 4, no. 1. New York: International Universities Press.

Shapiro, Theodore, and Daniel Stern. 1980. Psychoanalytic Perspectives on the First Year of Life—The Establishment of the Object in an Affective Field. In *The Course of Life: Psychoanalytic Contributions Toward Understanding Personality Development,* I: *Infancy and Early Childhood,* ed. S. I. Greenspan and G. H. Pollock, 113–28. Washington, D.C.: Government Printing Office.

Sherwood, Michael. 1969. *The Logic of Explanation in Psychoanalysis.* New York: Academic Press.

Sidgwick, Henry. [1907] 1962. *The Methods of Ethics,* 7th ed. Chicago: University of Chicago Press.

Simon, Ernst. 1957. Sigmund Freud, the Jew. *Leo Baeck Institute Year Book* 2:270–305.

———. 1975. The Neighbor (*Re'a*) Whom We Shall Love. In *Modern Jewish Ethics,* ed. Marvin Fox, 29–56. Columbus, Ohio: Ohio State University Press.

Simon, Robert L., ed. 1982. Special Issue on Moral Development. *Ethics* 92:407–532.

Singer, Irving. 1984. *The Nature of Love,* 2d ed. 2 vols. Chicago: University of Chicago Press.

Slap, Joseph William, and Frederic J. Levine. 1978. On Hybrid Concepts in Psychoanalysis. *PQ* 47:499–523.

Smith, Adam. [1790] 1964. *The Theory of Moral Sentiments,* 6th ed. In *British Moralists,* ed. L. A. Selby-Bigge, 257–336. Indianapolis, Ind.: Bobbs-Merrill.

Smith, Eliot R., and Frederick D. Miller. 1978. Limits on Perception of Cognitive Processes: A Reply to Nisbett and Wilson. *PR* 85:355–62.

Smith, Joseph H. 1977. The Pleasure Principle. *IJP* 58:1–10.

———. 1978. The Psychoanalytic Understanding of Human Freedom: Freedom From and Freedom For. *JAPA* 26:87–107.

Snow, C. P. 1962. The Moral Un-neutrality of Science. In *The New Scientist: Essays on the Methods and Values of Modern Science,* ed. Paul C. Obler and Herman A. Estrind, 127–40. New York: Doubleday, Anchor Books.

Solly, C. M., and G. Murphy. 1960. *Development of the Perceptual World.* New York: Basic Books.

Spero, Moshe Halevi. 1978. Psychological Determinism and the Judaic Concept of Free Will. *Journal of Psychology and Judaism* 2:5–18.

Spruiell, Vann. 1974. Theories of the Treatment of Narcissistic Personalities. *JAPA* 22:268–78.

Sterba, Richard F. 1969. The Psychoanalyst in a World of Change. *PQ* 38:432–54.

———. 1978. Discussions of Sigmund Freud. *PQ* 47:173–91.

Stern, Daniel. 1985. *The Interpersonal World of the Infant.* New York: Basic Books.

Stevenson, Charles L. 1944. *Ethics and Language.* New Haven, Conn.: Yale University Press.

Stewart, H. F., Jr. 1962. Repression: Experimental Studies Since 1943. *Psychoanalysis and the Psychoanalytic Review* 49:93–9.

Stewart, W. 1967. *Psychoanalysis: The First Ten Years, 1888–1898.* New York: Macmillan.

Stocker, Michael. 1970. Morally Good Intentions. *Monist* 54:124–41.

———. 1976. The Schizophrenia of Modern Ethical Theories. *JP* 73:453–66.

———. 1979a. Desiring the Bad: An Essay in Moral Psychology. *JP* 76:738–53.

———. 1979b. Good Intentions in Greek and Modern Moral Virtue. *Australasian Journal of Philosophy* 57:220–4.

———. 1981. Values and Purposes: The Limits of Teleology and the Ends of Friendship. *JP* 78:747–65.

———. 1987. Duty and Friendship: Toward a Synthesis of Gilligan's Contrastive Moral Concepts. In *Women and Moral Theory,* ed. Eva Kittay and Diana Meyers, 56–68. Totowa, N.J.: Roman and Littlefield.

Stone, Leo. 1961. *The Psychoanalytic Situation.* New York: International Universities Press.

Strachey, J. 1966. Notes on Some Technical Terms whose Translation Calls for Comment. In *The Standard Edition of the Complete Psychological Works of Sigmund Freud,* vol. 1, xxiii–xxvi. London: Hogarth Press.

Strawson, P. F. 1974. *Freedom and Resentment and Other Essays.* London: Methuen.

———. 1980. P. F. Strawson Replies. Reply to Ayer and Bennett. In *Philosophical Subjects: Essays Presented to P. F. Strawson,* ed. Zak Van Straaten, 260–6. Oxford: Clarendon Press.

Stross, L., and H. Shevrin. 1969. Hypnosis as a Method for Investigating Unconscious Thought Processes: A Review of Research. *JAPA* 17:100–35.

Sulloway, Frank. 1979. *Freud: Biologist of the Mind.* New York: Basic Books.

Taylor, Charles. 1971. Interpretation and the Sciences of Man. *Review of Metaphysics* 25:3–51.

———. 1980. Understanding in Human Science. *Review of Metaphysics* 34:3–23.

Taylor, Paul W., ed. 1967. *Problems of Moral Philosophy.* Belmont, Calif.: Dickenson Publishing Company.

Taylor, Richard. 1967. Determinism. *The Encyclopedia of Philosophy,* ed. Paul Edwards, 2:359–73. New York: Macmillan and Free Press.

Teicholz, Judith Guss. 1978. A Selective Review of the Psychoanalytic Literature on Theoretical Conceptualizations of Narcissism. *JAPA* 26:831–61.

Telfer, Elizabeth. 1980. *Happiness*. New York: St Martin's Press.

Thomas, Laurence. 1989. *Living Morally: A Psychology of Moral Character*. Philadelphia: Temple University Press.

Ticho, Ernst. 1970. Differences between Psychoanalysis and Psychotherapy. *Bulletin of the Menninger Clinic* 34:128–38.

Toulmin, Stephen. 1954. The Logical Status of Psycho-Analysis. In *Philosophy and Analysis,* ed. Margaret MacDonald, 132–9. Oxford: Basil Blackwell.

Trilling, Lionel. 1955. *Freud and the Crisis of Our Culture*. Boston: Beacon Press.

———. 1965. *Beyond Culture*. New York: Harcourt, Brace.

Troeltsch, Ernst. 1960. *The Social Teaching of the Christian Churches*. 2 vols. New York: Harper and Brothers.

Tyson, R., and J. Sandler. 1971. Problems in the Assessment of Patients for Psychoanalysis: Comments on the Applications of the Concepts of "Indications," "Suitability," and "Analyzability." *British Journal of Medical Psychology* 44: 211–28.

Urmson, J. O. 1968. *The Emotive Theory of Ethics*. New York: Oxford University Press.

Van der Waals, H. G. 1965. Problems of Narcissism. *Bulletin of the Menninger Clinic* 29:293–311.

Vastos, Gregory. 1962. Justice and Equality. In *Social Justice,* ed. Richard Brandt, 221–42. Englewood Cliffs, N.J.: Prentice-Hall.

Vergote, Antoine. 1958. Philosophy's Interest in Psychoanalysis. *Philosophy Today* 2:253–73.

Waelder, Robert. 1936. Principle of Multiple Function: Observation on Overdetermination. *PQ* 5:45–62.

———. 1963. Psychic Determinism and the Possibility of Prediction. *PQ* 32: 15–41.

———. 1964. *Basic Theory of Psychoanalysis*. New York: Schocken Books.

———. 1967. Inhibitions, Symptoms and Anxiety: Forty Years Later. *PQ* 36: 1–36.

Wallace, Edwin, R. IV. 1986a. Determinism, Possibility, and Ethics. *JAPA* 34: 933–74.

———. 1986b. Freud as Ethicist. In *Freud: Appraisals and Reappraisals,* Contributions to Freud Studies, vol. 1, ed. Paul E. Stepansky, 83–114. New York: Analytic Press.

Wallace, James D. 1978. *Virtues and Vices*. Ithaca, N.Y.: Cornell University Press.

Wallerstein, Robert S. 1976. Psychoanalysis as a Science: Its Present Status and its Future Tasks. In *Psychology versus Metapsychology,* ed. Merton M. Gill and Philip S. Holzman. *Psychological Issues,* monograph 36, vol. 9, no. 4. New York: International Universities Press.

Wallwork, Ernest. 1972. *Durkheim: Morality and Milieu.* Cambridge, Mass.: Harvard University Press.

———. 1973a. Sigmund Freud: The Psychoanalytic Diagnosis—Infantile Illusion. In *Critical Issues in Modern Religion,* ed. Roger Johnson, Ernest Wallwork, et al., 251–93. Englewood Cliffs, N.J.: Prentice-Hall.

———. 1973b. Erik H. Erikson: Psychosocial Resources for Faith. In *Critical Issues in Modern Religion,* ed. Roger Johnson, Ernest Wallwork, et al., 322–61. Englewood Cliffs, N.J.: Prentice-Hall.

———. 1975a. Ethical Issues in Research Involving Human Subjects. In *Human Rights and Psychological Research,* ed. Eugene Kennedy, 69–81. New York: Thomas W. Crowell.

———. 1975b. In Defense of Substantive Rights. In *Human Rights and Psychological Research,* ed. Eugene Kennedy, 103–25. New York: Thomas W. Crowell.

———. 1979. Attitudes in Medical Ethics. In *Nourishing the Humanistic in Medicine: Interactions with the Social Sciences,* ed. William R. Rogers and David Barnard, 125–51. Pittsburgh, Penn.: University of Pittsburgh Press.

———. 1980. Morality, Religion, and Kohlberg's Theory. In *Moral Development, Moral Education and Kohlberg: Basic Issues in Philosophy, Psychology, Religion and Education,* ed. Brenda Munsey, 269–97. Birmingham, Ala.: Religious Education Press.

———. 1982. Thou Shalt Love Thy Neighbor as Thyself: The Freudian Critique. *Journal of Religious Ethics* 10:264–319.

———. 1985a. Durkheim's Early Sociology of Religion. *Sociological Analysis* 46:201–18.

———. 1985b. Sentiment and Structure: A Durkheimian Critique of Kohlberg's Moral Theory: *Journal of Moral Education* 14:87–101.

———. 1986. A Constructive Freudian Alternative to Psychotherapeutic Egoism. *Soundings* 69:145–64. Repr. in *Community in America: The Challenge of "Habits of the Heart,"* ed. Charles Reynolds and Ralph Norman, 202–14. Berkeley: University of California Press, 1988.

———. 1989. Review of Don S. Browning, *Religious Thought and the Modern Psychologies. Journal of Religion* 69:127–9.

Wallwork, Ernest, and Anne Wallwork. 1989. A Psychoanalytic Perspective on Religion. In *Religion and Psychoanalysis,* ed. Joseph H. Smith, 160–73. Psychoanalysis and the Humanities Series. Baltimore: The Johns Hopkins University Press.

Warnock, G. J. 1971. *The Object of Morality.* London: Methuen.

———. 1983. *Morality and Language.* Totowa, N.J.: Barnes and Noble Books.

Weber, Max. 1964. *The Theory of Social and Economic Organization.* New York: Free Press.

Weber, Samuel. 1982. *The Legend of Freud.* Minneapolis: University of Minnesota Press.

Weinstein, Fred, and Gerald M. Platt. 1973. *Psychoanalytic Sociology*. Baltimore: The Johns Hopkins University Press.

Weiss, Frederick A. 1968. Determinism and Freedom in Psychoanalysis: Awareness and Responsibility. *American Journal of Psychoanalysis* 28:59–68.

Weston, Michael. 1975. *Morality and the Self*. Oxford: Basil Blackwell.

White, Peter. 1980. Limitations on Verbal Reports of Internal Events: A Refutation of Nisbett and Wilson and of Bem. *Psychological Review* 87:105–12.

White, Robert. 1959. Motivation Reconsidered: The Concept of Competence. *Psychological Review* 66:297–333.

———. 1960. Competence and the Psychosexual Stages of Development. In *Nebraska Symposium on Motivation*, ed. M. Jones, 97–141. Lincoln: University of Nebraska Press.

———. 1963. *Ego and Reality in Psychoanalytic Theory. Psychological Issues*, monograph 11, vol. 3, no. 3.

Williams, Bernard. 1985. *Ethics and the Limits of Philosophy*. Cambridge, Mass.: Harvard University Press.

Winch, Peter. 1958. *The Idea of a Social Science*. London: Routledge and Kegan Paul.

Wolf, Ernest S. 1977. "Irrationality" in a Psychoanalytic Psychology of the Self. In *The Self: Psychological and Philosophical Issues*, ed. Theodore Mischel, 203–23. Oxford: Basil Blackwell.

Wollheim, Richard. 1971. *Sigmund Freud*. Cambridge: Cambridge University Press.

———. 1984. *The Thread of Life*. Cambridge, Mass.: Harvard University Press.

Wollheim, Richard, and James Hopkins, eds. 1982. *Philosophical Essays on Freud*. Cambridge: Cambridge University Press.

Yankelovich, Daniel, and William Barrett. 1970. *Ego and Instinct*. New York: Random House.

Young-Bruehl, Elisabeth. 1988. *Anna Freud*. New York: Summit Books.

Zetzel, E. 1966. Additional Notes Upon a Case of Obsessional Neurosis: Freud 1909. *IJP* 47:123–9.

———. 1970. *The Capacity for Emotional Growth*. New York: International Universities Press.

Index

Abraham, Karl, 141
Abreaction, 40, 110
Action: meaning of, 4; multiple motivation of, 10; determination of, 49, 56, 61, 62, 64, 70, 71, 78; moral, 51, 63, 72, 73; causes of, 76, 78; judgment and, 87–88; responsibility for, 95; disinterested, 122; Weber's typology of, 226; ego control of, 227. *See also* Motives; Reasons for action; Responsibility, moral; Self-determination
Adaptation, 238
Aesthetic enjoyment, 132, 133; value of, 249, 251, 252, 256
Affect: and thought, 114, 239; transformation of, 116; irrational, 273
Affection: anaclitic, 150, 173; as permanent trend, 166; and aim-inhibition, 166–67; and other-regard, 172; development of, 172–79; and identification, 182–84; universal, 194–95, 198; analyst's, 216
Afterlife, 121, 279
Agapē, 172, 189
Agency: therapeutic, 81; of transcendental subject, 100; and self-esteem, 156
Agent, 53, 72, 75–100 *passim*; in mechanistic theory, 45; moral, 136, 281, 294
Aggression: in reaction formation, 170; in sadism, 176; and death instinct, 180; and morality, 189; outgroup, 195, 197, 202–03; instinctual, 196, 201, 262, 264, 279;

of conscience, 234; and inequality, 282. *See also* Death instinct
Aim-inhibition, 104; and other-regard, 165–70, 185, 263
Allport, Gordon, 11, 50, 51, 108, 161, 166, 222, 294
Altruism, 104, 106, 139; scientist's, 134, 210; hedonism and, 136; parental, 141; excessive, 155, 169–70; in love, 164–65; transformation of egoism into, 169, 188; and reciprocity, 200; instinctual roots of, 256, 266. *See also* Benevolence; Self-sacrifice
Amoeba analogy, 153–54, 158
Anaclitic object-choice, 150, 156, 171, 173
Analogy. *See* Metaphors
Anal sadism, 175–76
Anal stage, 172, 174–76
Analysis. See Psychoanalysis
Ananke, 231, 263
Anscombe, G. E. M. (Elizabeth), 7
Anti-Semitism, 195, 273
Anxiety: signal of, 47; changes in theory of, 47, 129, 130
Aquinas, Thomas, 104, 193, 194, 195
Arbitrary: mental events as, 53, 59, 62, 77–78, 79, 82–83, 97; preferences, 222
Aristotle, 256; on virtues, 8; on responsibility, 85; on happiness, 104, 245–46, 253, 254; on practical reason, 234, 268
Art, illusion of, 252–53
Asceticism, 121, 247, 248

Asch, Solomon, 103, 161, 168
Authority figures, 222, 223
Autoerotism, 143–44, 173, 174. *See also* Narcissism
Autonomy, 6; as therapeutic goal, 52, 74; of the ego, 73; value of, 209, 236, 249, 269; analytic respect for, 212, 213, 217, 269–70, 275. *See also* Freedom

Baier, Annette, 290
Balint, Michael, 144, 150, 178
Barrett, William, 20, 50, 51, 53, 54, 67, 116, 226, 294
Behaviorism, 80
Bellah, Robert N., 1, 137, 226
Beneficence: v. benevolence, 239; limited duty of, 270
Benevolence: genuine, 105, 106, 136; and narcissism, 138, 147, 174; normal, 161; in groups, 186–88; as basic attitude, 201; analytic, 211–12; v. duty, 237, 239
Bentham, Jeremy, 89, 104, 132, 268
Bernfeld, S., 21, 39, 53
Bettleheim, Bruno, 63
Beyond the Pleasure Principle, 21, 22, 110, 116, 122–26, 179- 82, 249
Bible, 56
Bibring, E., 125
Binswanger, Ludwig, 103
Blame, 66, 85, 86, 91, 95
Blanshard, Brand, 50
Brandt, Richard: on psychological hedonism, 109; on relativism, 221; on psychoanalysis, 224
Breast: and object relating, 171, 172–73. *See also* Mother; Object love
Brenner, Charles, 9, 50, 74, 212
Brentano, Franz, 15, 32, 40, 55–56, 89, 253, 256
Breuer, Joseph, 55, 110

Brown, Norman O., 135, 168, 182
Browning, Don, 12, 50, 51, 206
Brücke, Ernst von, 54
Bultmann, Rudolf, 194
Butler, Joseph, 109, 135

Capricious. *See* Arbitrary
Caring. *See* Love
Case histories, 25, 86, 295, 296
Castration, 176
Categorical imperative, 122, 233–34, 237–39, 268
Catharsis, 110
Cathexis, 55; libidinal, of ego, 139, 140–41; and valuation, 141; of representations, 152, 158; object, 158, 160, 165, 233
Causal explanation, 19
Causal law, 67
Causation, 70, 71, 72; universality of, 50, 66, 80; of action, 56, 64; intersectional and transeunt concepts of, 65; uniformity of, 80
Cause(s): 69; motives as, 28, 31; kinds of, 50–51, 75–78, 81; drives as, 161
Cervantes, 26
Chains, 52, 69
Chance, 59, 78
Character: formation of, 12, 183; Freud on judging, 85, 214; responsibility for, 93; maturity of, 133; moral, 161, 237, 240, 241; of children, 169
Character traits, 61, 238
Choice: freedom of, 60, 67–74 *passim*, 82, 83, 131, 134, 227; limitations on, 62, 88; mature ego, 63; arbitrary, 82- 83; preconscious, 77, 85, 87; power of, 88; noninterference with, 276. *See also* Autonomy; Decision making; Freedom; Free will

Christ, Jesus, 197, 198

Christian ethics, 155, 189, 194- 95

Christianity: love commandment of, 193–207; claims to superiority of, 197

Civilization: repressiveness of, 89, 193, 257; and individual happiness, 135–36, 204, 264–67; and Eros, 181, 263; hostility of masses to, 229; justice in, 271; liberty in, 276; intolerance of, 277; inequalities in, 278

Civilization and Its Discontents, 12, 62; and psychological egoism, 103–04; on qualitative hedonism, 130–36; on love commandment, 193–207; on basic goods, 245–54, 258; on conflict between individual and group, 260–67, 271, 277; on justice, 271, 276, 279, 283; on limiting aggression, 287

Civilized morality, 193, 204, 228

"Civilized Sexual Morality and Modern Nervous Illness," 250

Clinical theory, 19–39 *passim*

Cogito, 29

Common interests, 263

Communism, 279, 281

Community: of egos, 187; universal, 197; moral, 206, 241; value of, 230, 246–56 *passim*, 266, 290–91; devotion to, 255; power of, 261; international, 284. *See also* Civilization; Society

Community of interest, 188, 263

Compassion, 141, 176

Compromise formation, 9, 66, 73, 85, 91, 170

Compulsion, 63–72 *passim*, 85, 165; hand washing, 61

Compulsion to repeat, 123

Condensation, 45

Confidentiality, 216, 217

Conflict, intrapsychic, 37, 77

Conscience: and guilt, 95–96; oedipal origins of, 177, 184, 233; severity of, 204; flexibility of, 286. *See also* Kant; Morality; Superego

Conscientiousness, 135, 258–59

Conscious mental activity, 69

Consciousness: false, 1, 293–94; data of, 10, 24, 55, 72, 80; trustworthiness of, 10, 29, 37–38, 46–47, 90; and will power, 68, 82

Courage, 210

Cranefield, Paul, 54

Creativity: enjoyment of, 131–35 *passim*; regression and, 154; sublimation and, 165, 166, 297–98; value of, 249; difficulty of, 250

Compton, Allan, 55

Cultural relativism, 221

Daley, James, 51

Death instinct: defined, 123; and hedonism, 123–24; and Eros, 125, 179–80. *See also* Aggression; Nirvana principle; Eros; Thanatos

Decision making, 155; moral, 5, 268, 293; determined, 51, 65; rational, 52, 61–64, 77, 238- 39; ego's, 85, 88, 223–24. *See also* Choice; Practical reason; Volition; Will

Deconstruction, 30

Defense mechanisms, 28, 297

Defenses: and reasons, 64; responsibility for, 91; ego's, 96, 119, 129; analysis of, 211, 294; in morality, 268

Deliberation, 60–81 *passim*

Delusion, 247

Democracy, 282

Denial, 96, 202, 297

Derrida, Jacques, 4, 59

Desire: plasticity of, 87; pathology of, 189. *See also* Drive; Eros; Love

De Sousa, Ronald, 254, 255

Determinism: psychic, 3, 53, 69, 73, 75–100 *passim*, 288; and ethics, 5; metapsychological argument for, 20, 67–69; metaphysical, 30, 49–60 *passim*, 73, 74, 78; scientific, 49, 53, 58; universal, 49–54 *passim*, 66, 70, 78, 82; proving, 50; types of, 50–51; soft, 51, 70, 71; hard, 51–69 *passim*, 74, 82, 83, 97; materialistic, 53; scientific postulate argument for, 58–60; genetic argument for, 60–67; complete psychic, 79, 83

Development, 63, 298; normal, 64, 254–55, 288–90 *passim*; out of narcissism, 142–47 *passim*

Discharge, 110, 112; and foreplay, 129

Disgust, 118

Disinterestedness, 122, 134, 135, 171, 209, 234, 235, 236

Displacement, 45, 118, 297

Dogma, 23

Donagan, Alan, 193

"Dora" case, 93, 120, 217

Dostoevsky, Fyodor, 26, 170

Drama, 155

Dreams: and psychic determinism, 75, 83; moral responsibility for, 92; and primary process, 113; and repetition compulsion, 123; egoism of, 153

Dream work, 45

Drive-discharge theory, 22, 28, 30, 112–22; Freud's dissatisfaction with, 129; and narcissism, 139, 159; and object love, 161–70, 179; v. Eros, 189

Drive: concept of, 32–33; aims of, 33, 44, 47, 162–64; original defi-

nition of, 44, 47; post–1919 theory of, 47; as ultimate cause, 161; v. instinct, 163; and wish, 173. *See also* Instinct

Dual instinct theory, 179

Duty, moral, 122, 124, 161; pathology of, 189; in special relations, 199; reasonable, 205–07; 269–71; of psychoanalyst, 209, 214–18; for own sake, 234, 239; v. desire, 237; *prima facie*, 268. *See also* Obligation

Du Bois-Reymond, Emil, 40, 54

Economic point of view, 140, 158–59

"Economic Problem of Masochism," 128

Edelson, Marshall, 294–95

Education, 229, 285; to reality, 201, 252; free public, 283

Ego: in "Project," 41; constituted by ideas, 42; structural, 47, 69, 99, 119, 127–28, 140; freedom of, 52, 57, 61, 64, 68, 81, 84, 236; self-guidance of, 52, 72, 100; as teleological concept, 55; normal, 62–63, 186, 238; neurotic, 63; mature, 64, 73, 85–100 *passim*; as cause, 72; power of, 72, 99–100, 227–28; capacity for choice of, 81, 84, 87, 88, 98, 100; functions of, 81, 87, 140, 182, 224; metaphors for, 85, 99–100, 226; and id, 87, 99, 100, 204, 226, 238; and superego, 99, 224–25, 226; and egoism, 105, 115; in Freud's early theory, 110; development of, 113; reality principle of, 114–15; and pleasure principle, 115–22, 127–36; organization of, 118, 119, 238; developmental stages of, 119, 120; cathexis of, 139–141; as self, 140, 144, 171; strength, 141; instincts, 150; impoverishment of, 165, 199; mastery, 204, 217, 236, 240; sick, 216; rationality, 222, 225, 238, 253; and morality, 223–25; weakness of, 225–26; and adaptation, 238. *See also* I; Self

Ego and the Id, 67, 99, 119, 127, 225, 227

Ego ideal, 136, 259; group, 186–87; and superego, 223; and narcissism, 234–35. *See also* Superego

Ego instincts, 44, 46, 117, 126, 150; and egoism, 117, 171; in anaclisis, 173

Ego interests, 141, 171, 237

Egoism, 1; psychological, 3, 5, 20, 101–90 *passim*; of drive theory, 30, 165; psychological, defined, 103, 105; normative, 105; of the ego, 105, 171; and the pleasure principle, 108–36; and happiness, 134, 266; and narcissism, 137–59 *passim*; and object love, 160–90; and altruism, 139; of infants, 145, 166; normal adult, 147; in children, 169. *See also* Self-interest

Ego psychology, 14, 58

Ego syntonic behavior, 66, 100, 237, 239, 247

Einstein, Albert, 286

Eissler, Kurt, 207

Ellis, Havelock, 129

"Emmy von N" case, 161

Empathy: in analysis, 139; narcissistic lack of, 149; scopophilia and, 176

Energy, psychic, 21, 28, 55; neutral, 87; principle of conservation of, 110; binding of, 114; libidinal, 140, 164; in cathexis, 140–41, 158

Envy, 188, 272, 278

Equality, 272–83 *passim*. *See also* Justice

Equal love, 195

Equilibrium, psychic, 112, 115, 125

Erikson, Erik, 14, 15, 20, 145, 221; on psychoanalysis and ethics, 1–2, 8; on ego regression, 154; on object love, 166; on child's environment, 168; on ego ethics, 225

Eros: and the pleasure principle, 125–26; concept of, 179–80, 189; objects and aims of, 181–89; and Thanatos, 242, 266; and society, 263, 266, 291

Ethical relativism, x, 221–22; 225, 227, 229, 288

Ethical theory, x, 2–8; 221–43; 244–45; 260–87; 288–91

Ethics: relevance of psychoanalysis to, 1–8 *passim*, 16, 221, 229, 245; of psychoanalysis, 208–18, 289; ego, 224–25; rational bases of, 229–43; ontological approach to, 230; intuitionist, 230–231; Freud on, 261; revision of, 267. *See also* Ethical theory; Metaethics

Evil, 106, 242

Evil impulses, 92, 106

Evolution, 276

Excuses, moral, 85, 86, 91, 92

Exhibitionism, 146

Experience machine, 252

Explanation, 19, 22; mental-state, 41–42, 76; causal, 75–76

Eysenck, H. J., 294

Fairbairn, W. Ronald D., 182

Fairness. *See* Injustice; Justice

Fantasy: importance of, 40; and reality, 43–44, 248, 253; enjoyment of, 131, 136, 175; and object representations, 158; Oedipal rescue, 177; guilt for, 235

Farrell, B. A., 298
Fatalism, 65
Fate, 56
Feces, 174
Fechner, Gustav Theodor, 110
Female psychology, 297–98
Fenichel, Otto, 176
Feuerbach, Ludwig, 279
Fiction, 59; theoretical, 111, 112
Fisher, Seymour, 297
"Five Lectures on Psycho-Analysis,"
    250
Fliess, Wilhelm, 32, 40, 41, 57, 116,
    120
Flourishing, human, x, 241, 255,
    289
Foot, Philippa, 7, 8, 237
Forces, psychic, 21, 22, 28, 29, 45,
    69, 75, 77, 82, 146
Foreplay, 129
"Formulations on the Two Principles
    of Mental Functioning," 45, 111,
    135
Frankena, William, 194
Free association, 215, 293, 294
Freedom, 3, 49–100 *passim*, 288;
    thin theory of, 70–72; value of,
    209; v. rational choice, 227; urge
    for, 276. *See also* Autonomy; Free
    will
Free will, 49–83 *passim*; illusion of,
    83; in Kant, 233. *See also* Autono-
    my; Freedom
Freud, Anna, 14, 280
Freud, Sigmund: on reductionism,
    11; humanism, 11, 15, 20, 25–26,
    56, 207, 287; disciples, 14, 15, 53,
    209; clinical perspicacity, 14–15;
    contributions, 14–16, 293; use of
    classical literature, 15, 26; philo-
    sophical background, 15–16, 32,
    274; interest in philosophy, 16,
    26, 228; moral convictions, 16,
106, 228, 269; problem of inter-
    preting, 19–48; medical school
    teachers, 21, 39, 53–54; theoreti-
    cal development, 21, 39–48, 110,
    122–23, 159, 179–80; on limita-
    tions of theory, 22–24, 34–36,
    106; diverse influences on, 26, 31,
    32; consistency, 30, 56–57, 69–74
    passim, 107; method of writing,
    30–31; Brentano's influence on,
    32, 40, 55–56, 253, 256;
    coherence of thought, 38, 39, 47–
    48, 291; on a narcissistic friend,
    148; ethic of honesty, 189, 209,
    226–27, 243; animus against
    Christianity, 194–95; generosity,
    206–07; on evaluating patients
    morally, 214; on postponing deci-
    sions in analysis, 215; and liberal-
    ism, 276, 277; Jewish identity,
    276, 277; on war, 284–87; view
    of women criticized, 297–98. *See
    also* Drive; Instinct; Metapsycholo-
    gy; Metatheory
Freudianism, vulgar, 16
Friendship, 132, 148, 178; duties of,
    196, 199, 270; value of, 249, 256
Fromm, Erich, 1, 2, 8, 20, 103, 104,
    161, 168, 224, 242, 254
Frustration, 113
Functional concept, 256
Fundamental rule, 215, 269
Furnish, Victor, 198
Future of an Illusion, 103, 134, 248,
    260, 264–65, 271, 278, 279

Gay, Peter, 32, 58, 73, 277
Gedo, John, 20, 221
Genetic fallacy, 222
Gift, 150, 174, 177, 187, 272
Gilligan, Carol, 290, 293
God, 121, 210, 229, 231, 252, 259,
    279

Goethe, Johann Wolfgang von, 22, 56
Good(s): common, x, 291; highest, 228, 245; premoral, 245; intrinsic, 251, 257; genuine, 252; and activity, 253; basic, 246–51; sensual, 257–58. *See also* Happiness
Grandiosity, 145–49 *passim*, 157
Gratification. *See* Satisfaction
Gratitude, 150, 174, 176, 184; principle of, 203
Greek dramatists, 26, 56
Greenberg, Jay, 171, 173
Greenson, Ralph, 212
Greenspan, Stanley, 143, 297
Gregory, Ian, 105, 108
Group leader: identification with, 186–87, 197–98; and the law, 282–83
Group Psychology and Analysis of the Ego, 183, 187, 195, 196, 225, 272
Groups: narcissism of, 187; altruism in, 186–87
Grünbaum, Adolf, 20, 294, 296
Guilt: attribution of, 95; and conscience, 95–96; and responsibility, 97; Oedipal, 177; avoidance of, 222; neurotic v. realistic, 224; excessive, 235; and crime, 235–36; harm of, 258–59
Guntrip, Harry, 181, 238

Habermas, Jürgen, x, 2, 20, 27, 28, 31, 33, 55, 67, 70, 295
Hallucination, 113
Happiness: and psychological hedonism, 109; as ultimate goal, 121, 126, 133, 245, 289; Kantians on, 121–22; and morality, 124; in life, 130; as inclusive end, 133, 250–51, 253; paths to, 133–36, 246–53, 289; and Eros, 181; and truth, 209; and rational ethics, 230, 231, 289; subjective, 251–54; in so-

ciety, 265. *See also* Good(s); Hedonism; Pleasure; Society, v. the individual
Hardie, W. F. R., 251
Hartmann, Heinz, 14, 20, 23; on ethics, 2; on sublimation, 120; on structuralization, 128; on narcissism, 141; on adaptation, 168, 238; on identification, 183; on value-freedom, 208; on superego, 222
Hate, 171, 176
Health values, 209
Hedonism, 106; psychological, 20, 104, 108–36, 163; classical, 104, 109, 110; qualitative, 115, 122, 127–36; quantitative, 127–33 *passim*; normative, 132, 245–59
Hegel, Georg Wilhelm Friedrich, 56, 282
Helmholtz, Hermann, 40, 54, 70
Helmholtzian school, 21, 22, 25, 32, 39, 53, 54, 56
Hermeneutic compulsion, 59
Hermeneuticists, 28, 55, 70, 294–95
Hermeneutics, 19, 294; of suspicion, 1, 33, 170, 288
Heteronomy, 213, 229, 270
Hobbes, Thomas, 70, 89, 103, 261, 262, 275
Hoffman, Martin, 104, 161
Holt, Robert, 39, 55, 56
Homeostasis, 20. *See also* Equilibrium; Tension, reduction of
Homosexuality: as choice, 68; and narcissism, 140, 149; in everyone, 277; and paranoia, 296
Honesty: with oneself, 96; ethic of, 226–27, 243; duty of analysand of, 269
Hospers, John, 50, 51, 53, 60–66 *passim*

Human beings: as puppets, 61; v. animals, 163–64; functional concept
of, 256; as trash, 273; inequality
of, 274
Humanities, 19, 22
Human nature: and ethical theory,
6–8, 228, 289–91; psychoanalytic
view of, 11–13, 137, 168, 288–
89, 294, 297, 298; as passive, 56,
58, 72; aggressiveness of, 201,
262, 264–65; goodness of, 242;
ideal of, 255; idealistic misconception of, 279
Hume, David, 70, 71, 234
Humility: in love, 186; and truthfulness, 210
Husserl, Edmund, 55
Hypochondriasis, 141, 153
Hypocrisy, 6, 7, 169, 189, 193, 210,
229, 235, 293
Hypothesis, 21, 22, 24, 56, 59, 67,
296–97

I, 41, 47, 85, 122, 147. See also Ego
Id. See Drive; Ego, and id; Eros;
Libido; Metapsychology; Unconscious
Idealization, 151, 197; narcissistic,
186–87
Identification: with parents, 175,
222; in sadism, 175–76; in normal
development, 182–84; in groups,
187, 263, 264, 278; with siblings,
273. See also Affection
Ignorance, 85
Illness: gains of, 93, 155; and narcissism, 153, 155
Illusion: freedom as, 60, 81–83; in
creativity, 155; and science, 209;
religious, 230, 242, 279; of intuition, 231; and happiness, 247,
248, 251, 252; secular, 279
Impotence, psychical, 178

Indeterminism, 74
Inequality, 273–74, 275, 281, 282
Infant: –mother relation, 172–74,
183; research, 297
Informed consent, 9, 214–15
Inhibition, 113, 114
Inhibitions, Symptoms and Anxiety, 99,
116, 227
Initiative, 52
Injustice, 85, 276, 277, 278
Instinct(s), 22; source of, 32, 117,
124–25, 161–62; aim of, 33, 47,
117–18, 125, 161–63; object of,
117–18, 144, 161–62, 181–82;
qualitative view of, 125; organization of, 127–28, 182; and love,
144, 170; sublimation of, 165–66;
aim-inhibition of, 165–69; transformation of, 169–70, 178; component, 175, 178; renunciation of,
262, 264–65. See also Drive; Eros
"Instincts and their Vicissitudes,"
162, 163, 170
Intelligibility, 24, 44, 59, 60, 295
Intentionality, 55, 57, 81, 294; irreducibility of, 47; ordinary, 79, 80;
moral, 121
Interdisciplinary study, 12
Internalization, 182; and morality,
221–22
International law, 284–87
Interpretation, 19, 25, 29, 31, 33,
217, 294–95
Interpretation of Dreams, 15, 21, 22,
25, 31, 57, 67; ch. 7 of, 44–45;
on moral responsibility, 95; on
psychological hedonism, 111, 115,
116; on ego displeasure, 118; on
identification, 182
Intolerance, 203
Intoxication, 247
*Introductory Lectures on Psycho-
Analysis*, 129

Introjection, 182; and formation of superego, 184, 222
Intuition, 231
Involuntary thoughts, 64, 65
Isolation, 247
Is-ought issue, 5, 256

Jacobson, Edith, 135, 142, 150
James, William, 51
Jewish ethics, 194
Jews, 203
Jokes, 202
Jones, Ernest, 9, 15, 50, 53, 54, 132, 133, 180
Judgment, 87
Jung, Carl, 84, 213
Justice, 106; origins of sense of, 176, 177, 272–73; as reciprocity, 270–71; social, 271–87. *See also* Equality; Liberty; Reciprocity
Just war, 284–86

Kandel, Eric, 37
Kant, Immanuel, 56, 268, 290; Freud's criticism of, x, 90, 232–36, 238–40, 258–59; on the moral subject, 6; Freud's knowledge of, 15, 16; on freedom, 89–90; on reverence for moral law, 121–22, 188–89, 233, 239; on the emotions, 237
Katz, Jay, 9
Kernberg, Otto, 150, 158
Kindness: excessive, 169, 170; ethical value of, 187; deeds of, 194. *See also* Beneficence; Benevolence
Klein, George, 20, 22, 27, 28, 30, 33, 129–30
Kleptomania, 70
Knowledge: enjoyment of pursuit of, 131, 133, 134; value of, 209, 249
Kohlberg, Lawrence, 7, 293

Kohut, Heinz, 14, 142, 145, 150, 209, 212
Kris, Ernst, 40, 58, 154, 155

Lacan, Jacques, 30, 142, 145
Lakoff, Sanford, 188, 272
Lamarck, Jean-Baptiste P. A. de Monet de, 56
Lanzer, Ernst, 65
Laplanche and Pontalis, 21, 142
Lasch, Christopher, 1, 137, 153
Latency, 177–78
Laws: natural, 21, 49, 50, 53, 54, 59, 60, 67, 75, 80; civil, 261–62, 274–75
Leonardo da Vinci, 149, 154, 277
Liberalism, German, 276. *See also* Philosophy, liberal
Libertarians, 88
Liberty, 256, 275–78, 291
"Libidinal Types," 255
Libido: theory, 139; narcissistic, 139–41, 155; concept of, 140, 164; object, 152, 154, 160, 165. *See also* Drive; Eros; Id; Instinct(s); Metapsychology
Life Instincts. *See* Eros.
Life plan, 121, 122, 130, 133, 250, 256
"Little Hans" case, 35, 175
Locke, John, 70, 89
Loewald, Hans, 47, 69, 75, 91, 96–97, 126, 181, 238
Love: and egoism, 20, 137; of others for their sake, 105, 139, 160, 164; pleasure of, 131, 133, 134, 257; chasing itself, 137–38; parental, 138, 141; and drive theory, 144, 161, 170–71, 257; romantic, 150–51, 158, 178, 185–86, 199; normal, 151–52, 161, 164, 178, 230; mature genital, 161, 178; two currents of, 172, 178, 182–

Love (*continued*)
83, 185; prototype of, 173; as civilizing factor, 188; of strangers, 197–98, 201; reciprocal, 200–01; and ethics, 231, 239, 289–90; value of mutual, 249, 250–51, 253. *See also* Eros; Libido; Object, choice; Object love; Object-relations
Love commandment, 106, 193–207
Luborsky, Lester, 296

McGrath, William, 32, 40, 54, 55, 276
MacIntyre, Alasdair, 6, 7, 8, 53, 70
Magic, 145
Mahler, Margaret, 142, 145, 150
Malevolence, 94
Malingerers, 85, 86
Mann, Thomas, 160
Marcuse, Herbert, 1, 2, 8, 122, 135, 168
Marx, Karl, 279
Masochism, 175
Masochistic personality, 61
Masson, Jeffrey, 40
Masturbation, 5, 152
Materialism, 26, 32, 53, 54, 70; of Freud's teachers, 39–40, 41; Freud on, 40–42; v. mechanistic metatheory, 44
May, Rollo, 51
Meaning(s), 25, 29, 80
Megalomania, 145
Meissner, William, 209, 218, 221
Memory, 113, 157, 173
Mental apparatus, 21, 22, 23, 67, 110, 111, 120
Mental illness, 62
Mental states, 36, 41, 51
Metaethics, 3, 6–7; psychoanalysis and, 221, 230–43, 261–67, 289–90

Metaphors, 61; physicalistic, 22, 28–29, 35, 36, 67; variety of in Freud, 35–36; biological, 47; of the ego, 85, 99–100, 226, 227; equestrian, 99–100, 291
Metaphysics, 54
Metapsychological Papers, 21, 45–46, 55, 67, 119
Metapsychology, 19–48 *passim*; revision of, 21, 110, 122–29, 170–71, 180–86; Freud's disclaimers regarding, 22–24, 36, 46; and determinism, 52, 67–69, 72; criticisms of, 165, 298. *See also* Metatheory
Metatheory: basic postulates of, 21, 23; dialectical reading of, 34–39, 47–48; and clinical experience, 36, 47; mechanistic, 41, 44–46, 91, 110; in *Interpretation of Dreams*, 44–45; organic, 45–47, 69, 110, 123, 124–25, 179–82; non-mechanistic, 47. *See also* Drive; Eros; Metapsychology
Meynert, Theodor, 53, 54
Mill, John Stuart, 55; on freedom, 89; on pleasure, 104; on psychological hedonism, 109, 132; on special relations, 200; on normative hedonism, 249, 256; Freud's criticisms of, 257; on liberty, 275, 276
Mind, and body, 12, 24, 32, 33, 37, 40–43, 44, 257
Mirroring, 145–46
"Miss Lucy" case, 42, 57
Model of the mind, 20–21, 28, 29, 57, 69, 71–72, 112; as thinglike, 30, 45; at each stage of Freud's development, 39–48, 110; as passive reflex apparatus, 40, 45, 87; wish, 44; organic, 46–47, 110, 124–28, 179–82. *See also* Metaphors; Metapsychology; Metatheory; Paradigm

Moore, Burness, 139, 142
Moore, G. E., 230
Moore, Michael, 86, 91, 94, 296
Moral conduct, costs of, 1, 196, 205
Moral cowardice, 57
Moral education, 229
Moralists, psychoanalytic, 2
Morality: impact of psychoanalysis on, 1; human capacity for, 13, 51, 68, 103–07; 135–36, 139, 188, 228; of the egoist, 105; civilized, 105, 286; and the death instinct, 124; origins of, 168–69, 232, 233, 234, 261; authentic, 169, 188, 206, 239–41, 288, 289–90; and superego, 221–25, 260; foundations of, 228, 230–32, 237, 290; ought of, 231; of narcissist, 240; of obsessional neurotic, 240; and normal psychology, 241
Moral minimum, 206
Moral obligation. *See* Duty; Obligation, moral
Moral person, 63, 85, 281
Moral point of view, 290
Moral psychology, 6–8, 71, 288, 293, 297
Moral responsibility. *See* Responsibility, moral
Moral rules. *See* Rules, moral
Mother, primary relation with, 117, 143–46 *passim*, 150, 171–74, 183–84. *See also* Anaclitic object-choice
Motives, 33; multiple, 9, 10, 85; conflicting, 9–10, 22; mixed, 10, 133, 187, 189–90, 196, 288; as causes, 75–81 *passim*; in drive theory, 162–65; transformation of, 165–70, 272–73. *See also* Overdetermination
"Mourning and Melancholia," 46, 182

Mutual aid, 206
Mutuality, 172, 187
Myth, 22

Nagel, Ernest, 294, 296
Narcissism, 3, 13, 106, 136; culture of, 1, 258, 291; and the illusion of freedom, 83; and egoism, 104, 105, 137–59; and disinterestedness, 134; and other regard, 137–59; concept of, 138, 139–41; ubiquity of, 138, 141, 146–47, 189–90, 288, 289; as developmental stage, 141–47, 173, 174; as type of object choice, 147–52; as mode of relating, 152–56; secondary, 152, 156, 161; as self-esteem, 156–59; and neighbor love, 196; of minor differences, 197, 198; of moralist, 234–35; and happiness, 247; and group ideals, 278
Narcissus, Greek myth of, 138, 143, 148
Narrative coherence, 24, 25, 295
Narrative history, 25, 294
Natural science, 19, 20, 21, 31, 40, 56, 58, 75, 209–10
Neighbor love, 193–207 *passim*
Neurophysiology, 11, 22, 40–41, 42, 57, 110
Neurosis, 148, 280
Neurotic conflict, 61, 240
Neutralization, 141
New Introductory Lectures on Psycho-Analysis, 100, 108, 125, 208
Nirvana principle, 112, 125. *See also* Death instinct
Nonmaleficence, 5; obligation of, 202, 269; analyst's duty of, 215–16
Nonmalevolence, 202, 206, 229
Nozick, Robert, 252, 263

Object: as means, 148, 161, 166, 181; choice, 148, 173, 174; representation, 158; instinctual, 160–90 *passim*; as end in itself, 164

Object libido. *See* Object love

Object love: mature, 30; and narcissism, 146, 152–53, 156, 160, 174; and self-esteem, 157–59; primary, 183. *See also* Love

Object-relations, 46, 145; internal, 55, 183; withdrawal from, 152–54; ego and, 171; Eros and, 182–83; in Freud's late theory, 184–86

Object relations theory, 14, 150, 159, 178; defined, 171

Obligation: moral, 203, 205; reciprocal, 224; social, 241. *See also* Duty

Obsession, 61, 64, 65

Obsessional neuroses, 63, 64, 90, 235

Obsessional wishes, 62

Oedipal complex, 176–77, 184; as source of morality, 222, 233; research on, 297

Oedipal stage, 176–77, 184

"On Narcissism," 139

Ontology, 230–31

Oral Stage, 183

Ordinary language, 63, 106–07, 185

Orgasm, 131, 132

Other-regard: genuine, 124, 139, 166, 166–72 *passim*, 185, 187, 237–42 *passim*, 273, 288. *See also* Benevolence; Love, of others for their sake

Ought: implies can, 5, 124, 195. *See also* Duty; Morality

Outline of Psycho-Analysis, 47

Overdetermination, 9, 10, 85, 189

Overvaluation, 145, 148–49, 165, 200

"Papers on Metapsychology," 21

Paradigm, 11, 13, 14, 22; change in Freud, 31, 39, 179, 180; inclusive, 34; mechanistic, 46; organic, 47, 123, 125, 180–81. *See also* Metaphors; Metapsychology; Model of the mind

Paradox, 67, 69, 73, 74, 88

Parapraxes, 58, 61, 62, 77, 78

Pascal, Blaise, 121

Passions, 99, 237, 243

Paternalism, 276

Personality: as destiny, 60, 61; normal, 62, 255; narcissistic disorder, 148–50, 158, 241; development of, 171; ideal of, 255. *See also* Character

Perversion, 139, 141, 178, 254; tolerance of, 277

Peters, R. S., 9

Pfister, Oskar, 131, 132, 249, 273

Phenomenology, 29, 55

Philosophy: analysis of ordinary language in, 4; traditional moral, 7, 193–94, 257, 258, 284–87; Freud on, 11, 15–16, 56, 59; of life, 13; English, 16, 55, 89; Greek, 104, 245, 254, 256; liberal, 262–63, 266, 291; feminist, 290; of science, 294, 296

Piaget, Jean, 7, 143, 183, 293

Pity, 169, 176

Plato, 95, 99, 100, 104, 189, 257, 277, 282

Pleasure: v. truthfulness, 30; qualitatively unique, 124–36, 249–59 *passim*; positive, 126, 129, 133; broad concept of, 131; in drives theory, 163; of benevolence, 104–05, 135–36; of conscientiousness, 135, 259; of freedom, 246. *See also* Satisfaction

Pleasure principle, 22, 30, 106, 108–36 *passim*; and egoism, 104, 105; pure, 114; and the reality principle, 114–22 *passim*; and asceticism, 121; speculative nature of, 129

Popper, Karl, 294, 296

Post-modernism, x, 2, 288

Power, social distribution of, 281–82

Practical reason, 10, 188–89, 222–43, 268; and happiness, 134, 255; two types of, 244–45, 259

Practical wisdom, 246

Praise, 66, 86, 91, 92

Praxis, psychoanalytic, 29, 31, 295

Predestination, 65

Prediction, 82–83, 296

Primal horde, 177, 232

Primal scene, 176

Primary Process, 28, 57; in primitive psychic system, 112–13

Primitive Psychic Apparatus, 110, 111

Principles, ethical, 7, 290; and human nature, 228; rigid, 239, 268; and conscientiousness, 259; function of, 261; reasonable, 267; traditional, 268. *See also* Autonomy; Confidentiality; Promise-keeping; Truth telling

"Project for a Scientific Psychology," 21, 32, 40, 44, 57, 67, 110, 112; goal of, 40–41; on ego defenses, 119; on pleasure and pain, 129

Promise-keeping, duty of, 215, 216–17, 269, 285

Psyche, as text to be interpreted, 29; as thinglike, 30

Psychic apparatus. *See* Mental apparatus

Psychoanalysis: and popular morals, 1, 2, 293; limited domain, 10–11; inclusive vision of human nature, 11, 37; scientific credibility, 13, 22, 293–98; evaluative aspects, 13, 209; applied, 19, 208; Freud's definition of, 36; freedom as goal, 52, 64–65, 213, 270; as a science, 56, 208, 230, 294, 296–98; and moral improvement, 106, 228, 240; and truth, 209, 269; value-free, 208, 217; and self-realization, 212, 213; as social enterprise, 267; rules of, 214–18. *See also* Freud; Metapsychology; Psychoanalytic theory; Therapy

Psychoanalyst: value neutrality, 210–12; as mirror, 211; as surgeon, 211; as teacher, 213; self-restraint, 214; abstinence, 216; duties to science, 217; conscientiousness, 259; truthfulness, 269

Psychoanalytic theory: interpretation of, 4, 19–48 *passim*; advantages of, 12, 293; as open system, 23; understandable to patients, 27; scientific credibility of, 294–98; hermeneutic defense of, 294–96. *See also* Metapsychology; Metatheory

Psychological egoism. *See* Egoism.

"Psychological man" (Rieff), 137

Psychology, scientific, 21, 40, 293

Psychopath, 241

"Psychopathic Characters on the Stage," 155

Psychopathology of Everyday Life, 30, 51, 52, 78

Psychosis, 113, 148

Puberty, 178

Punishment, 85, 86, 92, 169, 235

Putnam, James Jackson, 213

Rangell, Leo, 73, 77
Rank, Otto, 156, 207
Rapaport, David, 33, 55, 56, 73, 128
"Rat Man" case, 62–65, 79, 86
Rationality, means-end, 222, 225–30. *See also* Practical reason
Rationalization, 1, 226
Rawls, John, 6, 7, 188, 272, 281
Reaction formation: and altruism, 104, 169; v. sublimation, 169–70; and compassion, 176; and sense of justice, 188, 272; in civilized society, 205
Reality: psychic, 43–44; withdrawal from, 152–56 *passim*, 247; in constitution of value, 251–54
Reality principle: and pleasure, 105, 114–22 *passim*, 125, 128; and sublimation, 120, 252–53; and disinterestedness, 134
Reality testing, 55, 186
Reason: power of, 100, 236; dictatorship of, 282; confidence in, 283
Reasons for action, 22, 27, 31, 65, 68; as causes, 76; and freedom, 77; and desire, 237; personal v. impersonal, 244, 259; conscious, 293
Reciprocity, 131, 172, 174, 177, 199–203 *passim*, 215, 270–71
Reductionism, 22, 26, 40–43, 147, 163
Reflective equilibrium, 39
Reflex arc, 111, 112
Regression: inhibition of, 113; in service of the ego, 115, 154; and narcissism, 146, 152; and egoism, 167
Relativism: cultural, 221; subjective, 257. *See also* Ethical relativism

Religion, 207; criticisms of, 192–95, 248, 251–52; as foundation of ethics, 228–29; and injustice, 271, 279
Religious believer, 121, 134–35, 210
Remorse: realistic, 95; v. neurotic guilt, 96; oedipal, 177
Repentance, 203
Repetition compulsion, 123
Representations, psychic, 33, 55, 173, 181
Repression, 9, 63, 64, 69, 118, 240, 258, 297; ego, 44, 118; in response to guilt, 96; lifting of, 106, 240; v. sublimation, 165; normal, 168; oedipal, 177–78; of aggression, 202; of better impulses, 240–41
Reproach, 86
Research, psychoanalytic, 296–98
Respect: for analysand, 211–14, 216, 275; for persons, 216–17; 281
Responsibility, moral, 20, 49–100 *passim*; patient's, 30; legal, 85–86; in Freud's case histories, 86, 93–94; reduction of moral, 91; expansion of moral, 91, 93, 95; for dreams, 92, 95; different forms of moral, 92–95
Ricoeur, Paul, x, 1, 2, 4, 11, 55, 189, 221; on reading Freud, 20, 28–33 *passim*; on Freud's determinism, 67, 70, 81; on narcissism, 146; on sublimation, 165; on credibility of psychoanalysis, 295–96
Rieff, Philip, x, 1, 2, 8, 20, 267; on pleasure principle, 126–27, 129; on self-love, 137–38, 152; on Eros, 189; on ethic of honesty, 209, 226–27; on means-end rationality, 222

Rogers, Carl, 242, 254
Role-playing, 183
Rolland, Romain, 207, 242
Romanticism, 56
Rorty, Richard, 2, 4, 30, 162, 271, 288
Ross, David, 202, 268
Rousseau, Jean-Jacques, 287
Rule of law, 261, 274–75
Rules, moral, 7, 278; motivation to obey, 121; indispensability of, 195, 204, 260–61, 274; in Erikson, 225; justification of, 231–32, 289–90; functions of, 261–62; as social constructs, 283

Sadism, 169, 175
Sadomasochism, 123
St. Francis of Assisi, 198
St. Paul, 189, 203
Sandel, Michael, 6
Sartre, Jean-Paul, 294
Satisfaction: from nonegoistic pursuits, 109; hallucinatory, 113; mnemic image of, 113, 173; actual, 113–15; ego, 120; with life, 121, 130; want, 130, 246, 247, 258; intellectual, 131; from moral conduct, 104, 135–36, 237; of infant, 142, 171, 173; drive, 161–62, 257, 258; mental absence of, 164; renunciation of, 166; conditions of, 238; subjective, 250–51; authentic, 254; limitations on, 289. *See also* Drive; Happiness; Instincts; Love; Pleasure
Schafer, Roy, 20, 28, 158, 183
Schelling, 56
Schizophrenia, 153, 224
Schopenhauer, 54
"Schreber" case, 144

Science, 21, 23, 251; empirical, 12, 22, 294–98; value-neutrality of, 13, 208, 210; Helmholtzian view of, 21, 22; Freud's view of determinism of, 59, 60; worldview of, 208; evaluative aspects of, 209, 210. *See also* Natural science
Scientific validity, 23, 27, 294, 296, 298
Scopophilia, 176
Secondary process, 57, 113
Secularization, 229, 271, 279
Seduction hypothesis, 40, 43–44, 271
Self, 63, 72, 73, 238; radically pluralistic, x, 30; in conflict, 9–10, 44; as a whole, 88, 100, 156, 170, 238; as transcendental subject, 100; and concept of ego, 120; long-term interests of, 121–22; differentiation of, 143–45, 174, 183–84; legitimate interests of, 199; social, 241–42. *See also* Ego; I
Self-absorption, 138, 142, 143, 149, 155, 156, 200
Self-affirmation, 138, 140, 157, 289
Self-consciousness, 46, 47, 147
Self-continuity, 157
Self-control, 52, 57, 64, 68–69, 294
Self-deception, 7, 203, 210
Self-defeating behavior, 5, 96, 233, 235, 247, 293
Self-defense, 96, 285
Self-determination, 73, 94–97
Self-esteem: injury of, 5; role in choice, 76; and narcissism, 156–59; and the superego, 259; and integrity, 238. *See also* Narcissism
Self-interest, 86, 103, 134–35, 158, 161; in society, 263, 281. *See also* Egoism

Self-knowledge, 74, 77, 210, 289
Self-love, 137–38, 143–47, 148;
temporary, 155–56; and self-
esteem, 157; excessive, 200. *See
also* Narcissism
Self-presevation instincts: of ego, 44;
and egoism, 103; and Eros, 125;
in anaclisis, 150, 170; and aggres-
sion, 180. *See also* Ego instincts
Self-psychology, 14, 145, 150, 159.
See also Kohut, Heinz
Self-punishment, 94, 95–96
Self-realization, 212, 213, 225, 242,
253, 254
Self-representation, 138, 145, 158
Self-righteousness, 203, 293
Self-sacrifice, 121, 135, 136, 170,
174, 186, 187, 200, 205–06, 210
Self-understanding, 38, 295
Sexual act, pleasure of, 129, 136,
178
Sexual instincts, 117; aim of, 161;
self-interested, 162, 165–66. *See
also* Drive; Eros; Libido
Sexuality: Freud's reinterpretation of,
28; repressed, 69; broad concept
of, 131, 164; and affection, 172;
anal, 175–76; intrinsic value of,
257; tolerance of perverse, 277.
See also Eros; Homosexuality; Li-
bido; Love; Object love
Shakespeare, William, 26, 56, 137
Sidgwick, Henry, 104, 109
Silberstein, Eduard, 15–16, 26, 32,
40, 256, 274
Smith, Adam, 109
Smith, Joseph H., 128, 129
Snow, C. P., 209
Social classes, 282
Social contract, 263
Social contribution, 250, 281
Social environment, 12, 168, 278–
80, 286–87

Social ethics, 271–87
Social feelings, 167, 186, 263, 275,
286
Social instincts, 167–68
Social justice, 271–87
Social regulations, 183, 204, 241. *See
also* Civilization; Civilized morali-
ty; Morality; Rule of law; Rules,
moral
Society, v. the individual, 135–36,
204–05, 260, 261, 264–67, 276,
291. *See also* Civilization; Civilized
morality; Community; Morality
Sociology, 11
Standard Edition, 52, 53; English
translations in, 53, 82, 140, 163
State of nature, 204, 261, 262
Sterba, Richard, 56
Stewart, H. F., 118, 128
Structures, psychic, 118, 127
Studies on Hysteria, 25, 55; on volition, 57; on ego defenses, 119; on
benevolence, 161
Sublimation, 130; ego's role in, 87,
274; as therapeutic goal, 106; in
Freud's early theory, 118; Freud's
use of the term, 120; homosexual,
149; in drive theory, 165; of aggression, 165; and aim-inhibition,
166–70; differing capacities for,
198, 243, 274, 278; and other-
regard, 237, 238; and morality,
240, 270; happiness, 248–50; v.
repression, 272; and reaction formation, 272–73
Suffering, relief of, 209, 210, 211
Sulloway, Frank, 50, 51
Superego, 61; cultural, 1, 261; morality, 90, 124, 225, 240; origins
of, 95–96, 177; necessity of, 204;
and ethical relativism, 221–25;
concept of, 223; and id, 233–34;
aggressiveness of, 234, 235–36;

and society, 286–87; of women, 297

Surplus of privation, 278

Sympathy, 187, 188, 206, 211, 273

Symptoms: hysterical, 61; and psychic determinism, 75; relief of, 295

"Tarasoff" case, 215, 216

Teleology, 29, 33, 34, 44, 55, 81, 110, 122; of instincts, 32, 125–26; and pleasure principle, 110

Tenderness, 164, 166, 172. *See* Affection

Tension: reduction of, 28, 47, 110–29 *passim*, 180, 181; in passive reflex model, 40, 110; in the primitive mental apparatus, 111–13; ego, 118; increase of, 126, 129, 181

Thanatos, 180, 242. *See also* Death instinct

Therapy, psychoanalytic: abreaction in, 40; freedom as goal of, 52–87 *passim*, 211, 213; and patient responsibility, 86, 93–94, 97; acknowledgement of unconscious motives in, 88, 90–91, 93–94; moral improvement goal of, 106, 243; and qualitative hedonism, 133; and strengthened self-worth, 158; analytic neutrality in, 210–12; improved functioning goal of, 253, 266; for the poor, 280; self-mastery goal of, 295

"Thoughts for the Times on War and Death," 12, 168

Three Essays on the Theory of Sexuality, 30, 45, 120, 129

Tolerance, 188, 210, 211, 217, 277

Totem and Taboo, 233

Toulmin, Stephen, 77

Transference, 173; in analysis, 215, 216, 293, 294, 295; in nonanalytic therapy, 213

Trauma, theory of, 40, 44, 110

Trilling, Lionel, 16

Truth, 134, 171, 236, 295, 297

Truthfulness, 203, 212, 215, 217, 251–52, 253, 287

Truth telling, 214, 269

"Unconscious, The," 33, 42

Unconscious, 20, 22, 24, 61–70 *passim*; motives, 1, 27, 28, 37, 76, 79, 92–95, 240, 293–94; wishes, 22, 60, 62, 68; fantasies, 22, 66; unknown aspects of, 24, 36; processes, 29, 37, 62, 72, 295; forces, 60, 72; dynamics, 61, 297; meanings, 64, 65; and freedom, 82; evil impulses of, 92; quantitative hedonism of, 133; psychoanalytic focus on, 228

Unfairness, 187, 195, 199, 200, 201. *See also* Injustice; Justice

Unhappiness: due to superego, 96; due to love commandment, 195, 203–05

Universalizability criterion, 89, 232

Universal love, 195, 197, 198, 201, 207

Unpleasure, 181, 227

Unpleasure principle, 110, 114

Unpredictability, 83–84

Utilitarianism, 104, 256; act-, 200; rule-, 205

Utility, 216, 217, 268, 270

Valuation, 141, 166, 172, 183, 184, 186; subjective, 251, 252; reality in, 252–53

Values, 13, 238; and libidinal cathexis, 141, 164; in psychoanalysis, 208, 209, 212, 217; in-

Values (*continued*)
    trinsic, 209, 251; and desire, 245;
    naturalistic theory of, 245; of co-
    operation, 248; and hedonism,
    249, 257
Vergote, Antoine, 50
Virgil, 15
Virtues, 6, 8, 12, 189, 204, 206,
    210, 224, 225, 235, 242, 260
Vischer, F. T., 228, 268
Volition, 57, 60

Waelder, Robert, 10, 23, 55, 75, 84
Wallace, Edwin, 65–67, 198
Wallwork, Ernest, 1, 137, 151, 187,
    195, 197, 230, 249
War, 263–64, 284
War neuroses, 85, 123, 140
Weber, Max, 226
Weber, Samuel, 55
Weltanschauungen. *See* World view

Will, 64, 68, 72; -power, 68; holi-
    ness of, 121–22, 234, 235; to live,
    180; of the father, 231
Wish, 113, 173
Wish fulfillment, 22
Wissenschaft, 59
"Why War?" 263, 282
"Wolf Man" case, 207
Work, 131, 133–34, 231, 249, 253
Worldly wisdom, 238, 246, 250;
    schools of, 244
World view, 2, 73; of science, 49, 58,
    208, 230; psychoanalytic, 208,
    227; therapist's, 213; mystical,
    231

Yankelovich, 20, 50, 51, 53, 54, 67,
    116, 226, 294

Zola, Emile, 170
Zweig, Arnold, 273, 276, 279